C000175244

MACQUEEN'S LEGACY

A HISTORY OF
THE ROYAL MAIL LINE

Volume One

MACQUEEN'S LEGACY

A HISTORY OF
THE ROYAL MAIL LINE
VOLUME ONE

Stuart Nicol

TEMPUS

First published 2001

PUBLISHED IN THE UNITED KINGDOM BY:

Tempus Publishing Ltd
The Mill, Brimscombe Port
Stroud, Gloucestershire GL5 2QG
www.tempus-publishing.com

PUBLISHED IN THE UNITED STATES OF AMERICA BY:

Tempus Publishing Inc.
2 Cumberland Street
Charleston, SC 29401
(Tel: 1-888-313-2665)

www.arcadiapublishing.com

Tempus books are available in France and Germany
from the following addresses:

Tempus Publishing Group	Tempus Publishing Group
21 Avenue de la République	Gustav-Adolf-Straße 3
37300 Joué-lès-Tours	99084 Erfurt
FRANCE	GERMANY

British Library Cataloguing in Publication Data.
A catalogue record for this book is available from the British Library.

ISBN 0 7524 2118 2

Typesetting and origination by Tempus Publishing.
PRINTED AND BOUND IN GREAT BRITAIN.

Contents

Conventions of Style

The title of the Royal Mail company had two forms: Royal Mail Steam Packet Company until the 1930s and Royal Mail Lines Limited thereafter. At times in this book their initials are used for simplicity – RMSP and RML. The sub-title of the book – *A History of the Royal Mail Line* – encompasses both titles, for the phrase 'the Royal Mail Line' was commonly used by both regimes. A firm with which Royal Mail had long and close associations, The Pacific Steam Navigation Co, is also sometimes referred to by its initials – PSN.

The titles 'Commodore' and 'Senior Captain' (both carrying the same status) are used where appropriate. 'Commodore' was not officially adopted until the twentieth century but was used earlier as a courtesy title.

Measurements and monetary systems used are those existing at the time. Dimensions are generally in feet and inches; tonnages are imperial gross measurement unless stated otherwise (a unit of cubic capacity, 1 gross ton = 100 cu. ft). Monetary values are mostly in pounds sterling (£); where dollar values ($) are quoted they are United States unless specified otherwise.

There are many instances of ship names being used for more than one vessel. The relevant numbers (I, II, III and IV) are not given in the main body of text – that detail can be identified from the index.

Place names use the version in use at the time (e.g. Ceylon, not Sri Lanka).

Preface

Macqueen's Legacy was conceived during 1968, originally as the story of Royal Mail's South America services and prompted by the announcement that mail services would end early the following year. In a memorandum that I wrote at the time (not only because of the impending service closure, but also the recent acquisition of Royal Mail Lines by Furness, Withy & Co.), I pointed out that

> this is a job which should, in the interests of maritime history, be done before it is too late...Only a few weeks ago, a large quantity of Royal Mail log books and similar records were destroyed because of a lack of storage space. A similar fate overtook technical records when the Superintendent's Dept moved up to Furness House.

I spent several years trying to prevent the destruction of as much material as possible. Following the Furness, Withy takeover, most Royal Mail head office staff moved to Furness House; there followed the inevitable clearances which accompany such upheavals after almost forty years in one home. The campaign to preserve was at least partially successful – one way and another, sufficient of the Company's history survived to become the core research material. We can only lament that so much more succumbed.

The spur to produce *Macqueen's Legacy* came, as I said, with the closure of the South America mail service. The Company approved the concept of the book and through 1969 and 1970 I was able to devote considerable time to the project, perusing the directors' minute books, movement records, captains record sheets and the like. There was also a wealth of correspondence, both with companies and individuals. That, too, was priceless, for much of what I learned would not be available today. Among them were memories from former captains – Treweeks, Purcell-Buret, Berry and Fletcher among them.

I spent time at the National Library of Scotland in Edinburgh, reading the private letters and published works of the Company's founder, James Macqueen. He is an enigma; the knowledge of his life and career are skeletal and it needed this contact with his thoughts, ideas and feelings to build substance to the man behind the name.

In such ways did the book start to come together. By 1971, however, there was a cooling of interest. That was indicative of Royal Mail's rapid decline – already there was a chasm between the still-proud fleet of 1968 and the declining meaningfulness of a firm which lay half buried in the Furness Withy Group in 1971. So the book was not published.

Resurrection

Its resurrection came early in 1999. My discovery that hundreds of former staff around the world were reunited through the Royal Mail Association provided the incentive to bring the work to fruition. After so many years the South America services, notwithstanding their paramount importance, should no longer be the sole focus, and so the work has become something more. Certain areas of the story have been expanded – the first few years of the Company, for instance, with biographical material on James Macqueen, chapters dealing with the Kylsant years and their aftermath, and another with Royal Mail's history of cruising.

Thus *Macqueen's Legacy*, while not purporting to deal with all facets of this very wide-ranging Company, provides a broad canvas within which South America services – for many decades Royal Mail's major sphere of operations – are examined in context.

I was anxious to provide, for the ships themselves, greater detail than often appears in a broad-based story. For that reason, in its final form, *Macqueen's Legacy* has been divided into two volumes, with the stories of around 150 ships occupying Volume 2. Each volume stands on its own, but they belong with each other as surely as ships belong with the sea.

The manner in which *Macqueen's Legacy* came to be published is briefly referred to below. It is a happy coincidence that this should have happened in 2001 – the 150th anniversary of the year in which the Royal Mail flag was first seen in South American waters.

Acknowledgements

Firstly I must roll back the clock more than thirty years, to the then management of Royal Mail Lines who sanctioned research work which provided me with so much valuable data; and to a range of individuals and companies, too numerous to list, who willingly responded to my requests for information.

More recently there has been unstinting support from members of the Royal Mail Association (RMA). In particular, Bob Forrester and Geoff and Clive Penny have been in regular touch with me on the other side of the world, and we have engaged in a stimulating exchange of ideas and material. The following members have permitted me to quote from stories they have written for the RMA Newsletter (from which I also gleaned further information); Geoff Penny, Philip Smith, Captains Douglas Brookfield and Michael Mortimer. Capt. Sir Miles Wingate did likewise for a story in Royal Mail's house magazine in the 1960s, to which he has now added extra information. Pat and June Bushell gave their blessing to items quoted from those invaluable Company history books *Royal Mail 1839-1939* and *Eight Bells*, written by their father T.A. Bushell. I thank the National Library of Scotland for providing photocopies of some of James Macqueen's letters.

Another RMA member requires special mention. Terry Lilley was on board the Master Mariners' Headquarters Ship *Wellington,* carrying out some Royal Mail Lines research, when he perused a copy of *The Seafarer* magazine and spotted an item in which Tempus Publishing expressed an interest in histories of liner companies. Terry not only rang me in Australia that night but also talked to the publishers. That was the genesis of the publication of *Macqueen's Legacy*, and I am grateful to Terry for following up his chance sighting of a brief paragraph, and for providing more late information for the book. Thanks also go to Campbell McCutcheon at Tempus Publishing, for so promptly following up Terry's phone call and for being so supportive throughout the book's gestation.

The following have also provided permission for quotes: Oxford University Press, for extracts from *Dictionary of National Biography 1931-1940*, edited by L.G. Wickham Legg (the entry for Owen Philipps); A.P. Watt & Co. on behalf of The National Trust for Places of Historic Interest or Natural Beauty, for an extract from *Just So Stories* by Rudyard Kipling; Footprint Handbooks (formerly Trade & Travel Publications) for an extract from *Caribbean Islands Handbook*, 2001 edition; Sampson, Low Ltd, for extracts from Capt. W.H. Parker's autobiography *Leaves from an Unwritten Log-book*.

A number of other quotes have been used from material still in copyright, some from publications and publishers either unknown or no longer existing, for which I have been unable to track down copyright holders. I apologise for not being able to acknowledge them but I hope that the value of those references will see them taken in the spirit of an attempt to provide the best possible coverage of the Royal Mail story.

Stuart Nicol
Adelaide, South Australia
June 2001

Introduction

There is a fine line between the history and traditions of a long-standing company and one's own memories of a few decades ago. As I write these words in the year 2000, that 'fine line' has all but vanished.

The work that I did with Royal Mail from 1959 to 1971 – and the memories I took from it – are now part of the history of a firm whose undignified slide into oblivion began while I was still there, for the takeover by Furness, Withy during the 1960s proved to be the springboard for a proud company's decimation, compounded by later changes of ownership in more distant parts of the world.

To all intents and purposes, Royal Mail ceased to be a true shipowning and operating company at about the time I left. We can now view the Royal Mail story from such a distance that it is a closed archive; a finite period in history. That sense of distance is enhanced by the dramatic changes to our way of life in general, and to the world of shipping in particular, which have been wrought in the intervening years.

There is, for instance, the change in our manner of written communication. During my couple of years in the Outward Freight Department that was achieved with a fountain pen; no self-respecting desk was without its blotter, no desk drawer lacked its bottle of Quink. For the typists it was still the era of manual machines and carbon copies. There were no photocopiers – my special charge each day was the Daily Position List, typed on stencils and churned out by the hundred on a slightly temperamental Gestetner duplicator.

An equivalent office today, of course, would be equipped with computer workstations, laser printers, postscript software, website access, e-mail facilities, CD-ROM storage and all the other paraphernalia of the electronic age. One of the pictures which I took in the 1960s in my role as Company photographer was of RML's first computer. This monstrous being comprised an arc of steel cabinets, and whirring tapes spitting out endless punched tick-a-tape. The whole was encased in its own room; temperature and humidity were minutely controlled, and the least speck of dust threatened disaster.

I don't know what capacity and power that computer possessed but it is safe to assume it had the tiniest fraction of the capability of the desktop machine on which I am keying in these words (notice that even the terminology changes – we don't type any more). A totally different world has come about in little more than three decades; we can understand it from an aspect of the office environment without even looking at ships.

So the history and the memories mingle, and that is the manner in which this book has come together – historical facts are blended with the memories of many people. There are, for instance, my 1969 memories of the final mail voyage arrival at Southampton; the 1968 memories of barman Harold Isaacs on board *Andes* at Belfast, harking back to the same

Two commodores who spanned the entire history of Royal Mail – Capt. J.H. Jellicoe (right) (1825-1914) and Capt. G.S. Grant RD, RNR (1903-2000), a Worcester cadet who joined Royal Mail in 1921 and gained his first command in 1949. He was Commodore from April 1963 to his retirement in November 1964. Capt. Jellicoe's career is detailed elsewhere.

ship in the same yard in 1939; the memories of Capt. Geoffrey Fletcher of his years in command of *Andes* during her metamorphosis from mail ship to cruise liner and the memories of Capt. Robert Woolward of the first through voyage to the River Plate, when he commanded *Douro* during 1869.

The ultimate in that balance of history and memory was brought home to me recently with the discovery that one Royal Mail commodore had known another; they could hardly be called contemporaries, though.

One was Capt. Gilbert Grant, who still had his memories to share until his death at the age of ninety-seven, late in the year 2000 – long after the company had faded away. The other was Capt. John Henry Jellicoe, whose career with Royal Mail, spanning almost seventy-three years, began in the paddle steamer *Clyde* just twenty-four hours after RMSP's first steamer left Southampton.

Capt. Jellicoe was still a director when a young Gilbert Grant came in contact with him on the Isle of Wight; thus the brief coming together of those two people spanned the Company's entire history and beyond.

The Memory

My first, rather distant, contact with Royal Mail ships was in the early 1950s. At something like the age of ten I lived at Westcliff, a moderate walk from the shores of the Thames estuary. Once I discovered that distant shapes drifting across the horizon were ships of commerce entering and leaving the Port of London, the germ of a hobby was born. The hobby, I have to say, became an obsession, and soon extended beyond the simple pleasure of gazing at ships and identifying them, to matters like their cargoes and routes – obeche logs from West Africa, coffee from Brazil, sugar from the Caribbean, tomatoes from the Canary Islands.

There were days when I would station myself on the end of Southend Pier from sun-up to sun-down, logging every passing ship. The record for a single day exceeded 200! That mirrored the status that the Port of London had enjoyed for centuries, and if someone had told me then that such a rich tapestry of maritime history would decline so dramatically within twenty or thirty years they would have got no credence from me.

My lists were peppered with names like *Loch Ryan* and *Loch Avon*; the 'P' and 'D' and 'Y' ships and the *Highlands*. No doubt the new-generation 'E' ships, too, like *Eden* and *Escalante*. Royal Mail ships mingled with those of countless other companies, a litany indicative of London's halcyon years. Grimy concrete quays in the Royals, the India and Millwall, London, Regent's Canal and St Katherine, Surrey and Tilbury docks were so consistently full that an empty berth was almost a curiosity; there might be a dozen ships anchored, awaiting their turn, between Southend and the Nore where convoys had assembled a decade before. I periodically had close encounters with those ships when I was taken on dock cruises, travelling by launch through the King George V and Royal Albert docks. How I relished being so close to the ships which were mere friezes across the horizon at Southend.

Not content with 'off-street parking' in the dock systems, there was also 'kerbside parking' at river wharves – New Fresh, Hay's, Mark Brown, Butler's, Morocco, Bellamy's, Free Trade and so many more, spread through the reaches of Lower Pool and Limehouse, Greenwich and Blackwall, Woolwich and Gallions.

That, then, was the world of my childhood years, and when the end of schooldays loomed, there was never any doubt that I would join the workforce with a shipping company. Considering my passion for ships and shipping it was perhaps strange that I never contemplated a career at sea. I think I preferred (and later achieved) the prospect of voyaging without having to work my passage.

So it was that I found myself daily walking through the entrance vestibule of Royal Mail House in Leadenhall Street; into the rotunda with the war memorial and *Almanzora* bell on the left, and on the right a pair of double-gate lifts whose tricky hand-and-palm operation was best left to their red-coated operators (not that that stopped us driving them rather erratically at times).

That impressive war memorial always seemed to belong so perfectly in its location that it must have been designed for the spot. It wasn't, though. Originally there was a bronze plaque in RMSP's old office in Moorgate, commemorating staff who lost their lives in the First World War. On the move to the new Royal Mail House in the late 1920s the plaque was transplanted to the outer vestibule of the main entrance. After the Second World War it was moved to the rotunda, where it was joined by an oak memorial to those lost in that conflict. The bell of *Almanzora* became the centrepiece; such an appropriate relic from a ship which had sailed through both conflicts and survived.

The hub of Royal Mail's operations for decades, the ground floor of Royal Mail House – Passenger Department to the left and freight departments to the right, c.1959.

On 11 November 1947, following a service at St Andrew Undershaft, a procession led into Royal Mail House. The Rt Rev A.C. Montgomery Campbell, Bishop of Kensington and later Bishop of London, dedicated the memorials, and the event was perpetuated, with two minutes silence, on 11 November each year thereafter. History and memory merge once more, for I joined those solemn moments in later years.

The moment I began walking through those imposing marble portals I became a little cog in the great wheel of the Royal Mail story. Beyond the rotunda, heavy revolving doors led into the centrepiece of Head Office, a vast, impressive and high-ceilinged hall with freight departments to the left and Passenger and Refrigeration departments to the right. The freight areas comprised Outward, Inward and Freight Forwarding, with the Cash Dept at the far end; and adjacent to that, right next to my Gestetner duplicator, was an office for one of the Conferences.

Staff on the mezzanine floor (which some nautical type apparently christened the 'tweendecks) gazed down on us from on high – they were General Stores, Provedore, Accounts, Marine Superintendent, Marine and Publicity departments.

My first two years were spent in Outward Freight (Operations). One Outward Freight area – the Manifest Section – remains indelibly in my memory. I suspect that is because of the quite Dickensian nature of its environment – sloping desks of dark wood deeply ingrained with age, high stools and horrific purple manifests instilling a sense of timelessness which seemed to hark back to Lord Kylsant's day and beyond.

One small matter which I simply accepted at the time 'because it was there' was that most of us used as paper weights sawn-off rivet heads stamped 'RMS ANDES'. When I left the Company my rivet head sort of went with me. I am looking at it as I write – now much more interested in the fact that I possess a little piece (albeit an extraneous one) of the great ship.

The main purpose of our Operations Section was to schedule ships for the various services, which afterwards led me to wonder why I was constantly bombarded with vast quantities of Bills of Lading. I haven't the foggiest idea now what I was meant to do with them, and I don't think I had much more idea then. There are vague recollections of stuffing them in cupboards and drawers in the name of filing. One of our first daily tasks was to phone Dock Office for data on cargo loading and discharge, ship arrivals and the like. That evolved into the Daily Position List, whose production was my premier task.

By about 10.30 we were ready for morning tea. There was a mass exodus as half of the ground floor staff meandered up Lime Street to a coffee shop named Bowlers. I'm not sure how we all fitted in, but it became a coffee and doughnut ritual. Then the DPLs were ready – a rapid round of the office delivering to all staff, whipping out the pages in expert fashion and slamming them on desks while attempting each day to achieve a time-busting Personal Best. The directors had theirs neatly stapled – one day the copy which ended up with our chairman Mr Bowes (not yet knighted) had page two stapled upside down. From what filtered through to me, he didn't see the funny side of it.

Time for lunch in the fifth floor Alcantara Room; one report suggested this was once Lloyd's Captains' Room, though another gave that honour to the adjacent Andes Room, a smaller dining area for senior staff. No matter, we were in the vicinity of a special piece of maritime history, for traditionally the Captains' Room at Lloyd's was for skippers (particularly owner/skippers) who came to insure their ships and cargoes and had a room set aside for refreshments and yarning. By the time this building was used, the world of shipping had changed – the dining room's name was unaltered, but it was used by underwriters and brokers, and once-a-week lunches for members of the Honourable Company of Master Mariners.

Apparently Royal Mail took over this area for its dining facility in 1956, after what was then termed 'Lloyd's new building' went up across Lime Street. So it had only been ours for three years when I first made use of it – tucking into a three-course meal for, I think, ninepence, paid for with a pre-purchased ticket firmly impaled on a spike. I don't remember anyone not joining the repast, though the Half Moon, with its sawdust-scattered floor, seemed to support sundry Royal Mail staff afterwards.

Three o'clock. *Picardy* had berthed during the morning and now her captain had arrived at Head Office to enter the ship at the Customs House – that was another of our section's tasks. As I became familiar with the work I took on that job on occasion. It was interesting to walk the skippers down to Lower Thames Street, for they differed somewhat in their response to being under the wing of a teenager. I have to say that most were friendly and all, in my recollection, were courteous. After all, we were all 'family'.

London's King George V Dock in one of its most typical moods – a damp, cold, misty autumn after-noon. It is a scene which encapsulates the character of a port which dominated British shipping for centuries. (Author's photograph)

Upstairs

After a couple of years in Outward Freight I engineered a transfer, during 1961, upstairs to the Publicity Department. Part of the deal was that I would set up a photographic department – which I was fully qualified to do, for I had owned a camera for some months. Perhaps for the first time, but not for the last, I discovered, at the age of 18, that immaculate self-belief, coupled with determination, could take you a long way.

In a decade of varied photographic assignments there was surprising variety. Photograph the Lord Mayor arriving for lunch at head office and deliver the prints before the liqueur glasses were empty. Provide colour prints of *Andes'* cabins for use by sales staff in Passenger Department. Photograph *Pardo's* bow after a collision in the Thames which provided the daddy of all headaches for the stowaway in the chain locker.

Photographing the Queen's Rolls-Royce being loaded on a freighter for a Caribbean Royal tour provided a different sort of headache. By the time the car was loaded it was practically dark and the film speed had to be upgraded by procedures which made me cringe – stewing in developer for an extended period in vastly boosted temperatures. On occasion my lens was trained on holiday fashions for travel magazines. One involved fashion wear for cruising, and the models were Keith Potger (at the top of his musical career as a member of The Seekers) and Iris Styles, who had recently won the Ocean Princess title. Not the easiest of jobs, simulating the relaxing warmth of the Mediterranean on an *'A'* ship in 'port mode' on a cold London afternoon.

(Left): *Keith Potger pictured on* Amazon *(III) in 1965, modelling fashion wear for* Fabulous *magazine, together with the first Ocean Princess, Iris Styles.* (Author's photograph)
(Right): *Charles Chaplin on* Aragon *(II), February 1966. He was researching for shipboard scenes in* The Countess from Hong Kong. (Author's photograph)

Those were a handful of photographic forays woven into my years with Royal Mail (or Furness, Withy, as it was in later years). Photography wasn't the whole job, though. Dealing with the media was a major part, not least writing and distributing Press releases. Non-urgent matters were mailed, but many were taken by bus to the top of Fleet Street and delivered by hand. The most urgent were phoned, typed in the newspaper office under dictation.

There was no shortage of stories: '*Loch Avon* put into Falmouth yesterday with four injured seamen after 100mph gales in the Channel...' Then an editor's dream-story: '"I hate the sea", claims Captain Fletcher' (from *Andes* at San Francisco). Only occasionally were there true elements of drama. In October 1969 a fire occurred among the machinery on board *Loch Loyal* and caused the sealing of the engine room, closing of bulkheads and the evacuation of passengers and crew except for a handful of volunteers. There was significant damage, but in the event the fire was contained and the vessel safely towed to the Azores.

Another fire probably didn't reach the national Press, though it was at least as disastrous. In April 1961 *Pampas* was reported on fire, with fishmeal in holds one to five. I can hear no end of former sea staff responding that *their* fishmeal cargo once caught fire – because of countless maggots which infested this smelly, trouble-prone cargo, fishmeal was notorious for fires caused by spontaneous combustion from the friction of the moving maggots. *Pampas* suffered more than most. All holds, it seems, caught fire. The ship berthed at San Juan, and with the fire brigade in attendance began to unload the cargo. That merely transferred the problem from the ship to the wharf, for the fishmeal set fire to the pier and offices, totally destroying the offices and ship's manifests.

Before venturing outdoors in this journey of memory, I want to mention another task which was handled in the Publicity Department – production of the annually-revised *South American Handbook*. Known for many years as the 'Bible of South American travel', its origins seem to be lost in the mists of time. Royal Mail published it from 1924 through its subsidiary company Trade and Travel Publications (which also published the Company's centenary and Second World War histories). The only possible clue to the book's origins is a note in the directors' minutes in June 1903 from Philip, Son & Nephew of Liverpool, seeking advertising support for 'Mr Alcock's book *Trade and Travel in South America*'.

Royal Mail continued its publication into the early 1970s, at which point Trade and Travel was sold to Dawson and Goodall Ltd, a 200-year-old company in Bath whose printing arm, The Mendip Press, had printed the book for forty years. There are two reasons for mentioning this book. Firstly, there was probably no company better placed to produce an authoritative book than Royal Mail during its years of trading to South America, and I have referred to it often during research for *Macqueen's Legacy*. Secondly, it is one mirror of Royal Mail which is still very much alive and well. Not only does Footprint Handbooks (formerly Trade and Travel) still produce the *South American Handbook*, this single title has now become one of more than fifty popular travel guides – Royal Mail's legacy has long outlasted the Company.

Dockland

During the 1960s I really got to know the ships and London Docks. The Royals became my second home. Snippets from those days are scattered among the pages of *Macqueen's Legacy*. Ships, wharves, cranes, sheds; rare days of baking heat and more common ones of cold and murk and rain, gazing down Gallions Reach, huddled, waiting for *Drina* inward bound from the River Plate or *Pilcomayo* from the Spanish Main. Sipping stewed tea with condensed milk from a half-pint mug in a Sun tug as we hauled *Amazon* through reaches and around bends, homeward from Buenos Aires, passing Stephenson Clark colliers, Everard coasters and the ubiquitous lighters which so characterised London's River.

Arlanza, gleaming white and toweringly dominant alongside Tilbury Landing Stage while wide-bellied ferries shuttled across the river to Gravesend; the confused mêlée in C Deck Square with passengers and baggage reluctant to move further afield. The contrasting vision of a 1940s freighter, gawky, perched on the water in high ballast, derricks askew in readiness for loading, her crew already detailed to remove the tarpaulins and laboriously haul off the wood-slat hatch covers.

The relief and sheer pleasure of being handed an ice-cold beer by the chief officer of a freighter one Saturday afternoon, following hours of tramping around the Royals on a rare day when the thermometer reached 93°. Sitting in a crane operator's cab as 6,000 tons of sugar was transferred by grab from an 'E' ship to Tate & Lyle lighters (and watching the

Ebro (IV) being brought to her berth in London's Royal Docks during the 1960s to load for the West Indies. The picture typifies the image etched in the memories of people familiar with London Docks during the final days when breakbulk freighters like Ebro were still king. (Author's photograph)

spilled residue being carefully swept up, together with the grime and oil and general gunk on deck, and tipped back into the hold). Days spent on board *Loch Gowan* after thirty particularly valuable horses had been denied landing rights because of an outbreak of swamp fever in France. A Saturday afternoon on board *Aragon* showing Charles Chaplin (not yet knighted) around the ship and hosting afternoon tea.

During the infamous era of Jack Dash, when relations between dockers and employers were not at their best, and with a reduction in the requirement for dock workers, all the gangs would sign on, but since only some were actually required to work, the remainder found quiet corners in which to while away the day. One day I had to photograph some cargo or other being loaded, in the course of which I climbed down to the 'tweendecks. As I wandered between cases and boxes of cargo I suddenly stumbled on a group of these dockers, sitting around a couple of tea chests and engrossed in a game of cards. They looked up as I appeared on the scene. One gazed pointedly at my camera, and without a word motioned me to keep moving. I did.

There were occasions when my visits extended well into the evening. And there were times when magnificent food, flowing alcohol and boxes of Havana cigars were on offer. One event which combined the two occurred in September 1964 – the Company's 125th anniversary dinner on board *Aragon*. I was not, of course, an invited guest, but I was required at the start to take photographs.

My task ended when the dinner gong rang. By then I was ensconced in the stewards' pantry in the first class lounge – and there I stayed until 11 o'clock. As I yarned with the crew, drinks of indeterminate contents appeared. The contents became more indeterminate and less important as the evening progressed. By eleven I bade farewell and headed off towards C Deck Square. I understood then why the stairways in the 'A' ships had been made so wide – I needed every inch. There was a minor hiccup at C Deck Square. Whichever way I turned I kept bumping into people. The dinner had ended and our illustrious guests were milling about on the verge of departing. Coming face to face with the Lord Mayor of London, in full regalia, was perhaps the ultimate way to discover that it's not a good idea to mix your drinks.

While the docks, and ships in docks, were an integral part of my life in the 1960s, I was occasionally able to make short-sea and coasting voyages. Two rank as the most memorable, and they were only a day or two apart. The first was from London to Vigo in *Aragon*, a passage made in idyllic weather with calm blue seas and bright sun throughout – all of which engendered such a sense of wellbeing that I was sorely tempted to stow away for the remainder of the passage to Buenos Aires. A couple of days later I was on board *Arlanza* for a return voyage which, in its entirety, took place through a Force 11 storm. To be honest, while I would have loved the languid days of a South Atlantic voyage, I wouldn't have missed *Arlanza's* wild passage for anything.

Among voyages which I made in later years, one was a winter crossing of the North Atlantic in the Chandris liner *Australis*. That gale-torn passage provided an interesting comparison with *Arlanza's* Biscay crossing. The only significant difference was with the ships. *Australis* had been built many years earlier as the United States Lines flagship *America*, designed specifically to cope with the North Atlantic in winter and the brainchild of America's most gifted twentieth century naval architect, William Francis Gibbs. At more than thirty years of age she swept through the Atlantic storm like a swallow; truly in her element, savouring the challenge and rising to it splendidly.

As for *Arlanza*, her Biscay buffeting was far less comfortable. There is no suggestion of criticising her design – her 'Belfast bottom', high freeboard and shallow draft were aimed at minimising problems in the shallows of the River Plate, and they acknowledged that most of her sea miles were made in more benign conditions than those I was experiencing. The contrast between the two voyages served to highlight the individualism of ships to cater for specific trades.

Late in Royal Mail's life I joined one of its 'new' refrigerated cargo ships which maintained the meat trade after withdrawal of the 'A' ships. She was *Derwent*, formerly Shaw Savill's *Persic*, and my passage was to Lisbon, in the spring of 1970, where cars taking part in the World Cup Rally would be loaded. Starting in London, the cars which survived would end up at Mexico City where the soccer World Cup was to be held. When we reached the Tagus we soon spotted our cargo – neatly parked cars covered with numbers, names and sponsors' logos. They all looked the worse for wear after a gruelling run across Europe, and at least one was literally held together with sticky tape.

Among the competitors was Prince Michael, who was on the wharf. Apparently some cases were loaded with the car before he decided he didn't want them aboard. The cases were duly landed, but then he changed his mind and wanted them back on board. Too

Three of the judges at the inaugural Ocean Princess competition, held on Amazon (III) in January 1965. Left to right: pop singer Brian Poole, actor Ian Hendry and actress Janet Munro. (Author's photograph)

Harry Secombe (not yet knighted) hamming it up at Charing Cross station during the 1960s. He was presenting an Andes *(II) cruise ticket to the winner of an Ocean Travel Development competition.* (Author's photograph)

late – the order to cast off had already been given. The angry Prince produced my second favourite quote of the trip: *'What bloody shipping line is carrying these cars?'* Since I was standing beside him at the time I presume the question was aimed at me. I played dumb, but perhaps, in retrospect, I should have answered 'Furness, Withy'. Such an indiscretion would never have occurred when Royal Mail was independent!

The best quote, though, had come a little earlier. The media presence at Lisbon (the reason for my being there) led to *Derwent's* master, Capt. Ray Phillips, giving an impromptu press conference. One reporter was concerned about whether the cars would reach Rio de Janeiro in time for the start of the South American leg. Capt. Phillips assured him that *Derwent* would arrive on time. How could he be sure of that, the reporter wanted to know? All the reporters religiously wrote down his answer. I can't guarantee that it appeared in print, but I think it did: *'Of course we'll arrive on time – it's downhill all the way'*.

One of those rally cars was being driven by an Australian duo who had virtually become folk heroes through their exploits in rallies across the infamous outback of Australia. The suave and urbane Evan Green was teamed with a man named Jack Murray – 'Gelignite' Jack Murray, a nick-name gained from his habit of carrying sticks of the stuff to blast a path around obstructions on rally routes.

They apparently had a horrendous time on the World Cup Rally, a fact I only discovered years later when I spent a few days with them charging around the Australian inland – an occasion when the irrepressible 'Gelignite' Jack 'lost' a stick of gelignite and discovered it next day, stuffed behind the driver's seat of a car I had been driving for hours along some of the country's roughest, bumpiest roads.

Flight Of The Cherokee

By May 1968 the decision to end the South America mail service had, one suspects, already been made. That would leave only *Andes* to carry the Company's passenger flag – she had just completed her final refit, and at practically thirty years of age was clearly beginning her final lap.

Having taken the gamble of that last refit, Royal Mail anticipated at least three years of further service from her...what then? That was the crossroads we had reached. The Company faced much more competition in the strong cruise market than it had done a decade before, and the growth of interest was generally not in the exclusive first-class-only bracket in which *Andes* specialised. Thus what happened in the remaining years of *Andes'* life would influence Royal Mail's choice: find a replacement or bow out of the passenger market. The odds against her replacement were stronger because the decision would now be made not from Royal Mail Lines' perspective, but from the broader canvas of the Furness, Withy Group.

Passenger services had been fundamental since 1841. That there was a serious attempt from 1968 to increase the popularity of Royal Mail cruises is borne out by the brochure to which a photographic charter flight to Sicily contributed. It was a brochure like no other the Company had produced – a fresh and imaginative concept which drew its inspiration from the ship and her exotic stamping grounds, and relied largely on an image-building technique through photographs. Its physical size was unprecedented – 347mm by 247mm – which gave the pictures and design the space to succeed. This, then, was a commitment to the future – an acknowledgement that the days of Royal Mail's ability to largely fill its cruise ships through reputation were past.

It was only in hindsight that I viewed that brochure in such a way. At the time we tended to accept what was happening – slightly wide-eyed – simply as a 'sixties trend' with just a slight hint of doubt as to whether this was 'the Royal Mail way'. The cost was enormous in comparison with the past. An advertising agency handled the whole thing, and while that wasn't new, the free rein they were now given went beyond design and production to include a freelance photographer on board for a cruise, hiring a plane for a weekend, supporting posters and point-of-sale displays, a specialist aerial photographer and so on – that was the commitment.

Thus what I have dubbed 'the Flight of the Cherokee' encapsulated the attempts to point Royal Mail in the right direction at this crossroads of its passenger operations. There was a spare seat on the plane and I was given the chance to take part – 3,200 miles in a single-engined Piper Cherokee Six. While the rest of the Company viewed the exercise as 'we chartered a plane to take pictures from the air', the reality was infinitely greater, a logistical nightmare culminating in two incident-packed days. Ultimately, however effective that and other strategies of the time may have been in giving *Andes* a further year or two of useful life, the longer term prospects were beyond the control of such measures, for the traditional formula developed by Royal Mail for its cruising was no longer in step with the changing ideals of cruise passengers.

Photographing freight handling occa-sionally had its lighter moments. When a shipment of Galloway bulls, bound for Patagonia, was loaded on Darro *(II), one docker preferred a precarious perch outside the rails, above the murky waters of the Royal Docks, to the prospect of being within charging range of a fearsome-looking animal.*
(Author's photograph)

In the mid-1960s Cliff Richard and The Shadows were rarely out of the limelight. Here, the most identifiable of The Shadows, Hank Marvin, with wife and son Dean, are seen on Aragon *(II) in 1965 heading for a quiet holiday in Portugal.*
(Author's photograph)

The outward flight was dogged with detours because of a French air traffic controllers' strike and then bad weather – it was the sight of a mountain dead ahead, looming out of the murk, which persuaded us to skirt around the Alps. Pisa's military airfield didn't help by refusing landing permission to refuel, but we landed anyway. You tend to do that when the fuel tanks are almost empty.

After our belated arrival in Naples we made a beeline for *Andes* and a late evening conference. The Chief Officer proudly told us the funnel had been washed for our benefit, but then, closeted with Capt. Fox and the radio operator, we learned that shipping and aviation radio frequencies were poles apart and we wouldn't be able to talk. Thus we instantly created a new language – principally wing-waggles on our part to tell John Fox what we wanted.

In the morning a taxi took us to the airport, but when we were greeted by a US Marine snapping to attention and giving us a karate-chop salute it dawned on us we weren't at the *right* airport. So we left the US military base and eventually were reunited with our Cherokee. The port door was removed and stowed behind the back seats. Then we were away. In due course we spotted the island volcano of Stromboli, and then the tiny speck of *Andes*, steaming past right on cue. The Cherokee's nose dipped. Through the roar of the wind I heard the pilot shout that he was going to make an initial pass of the ship 'just to look at her'.

The blue waters rushed towards us. How close did he need to be to look at her? – I could see her perfectly well from 5,000 feet. The dive went on... and on. Finally he levelled out just fifteen feet from the sea, banked to starboard and roared past the ship at a level well below the main deck. What on earth did the passengers think?

A specialist aerial photographer focuses on Andes (II) *steaming through the Mediterranean, photographed from a Piper Cherokee which was skimming the wavetops. The pictures were for the 1969 cruise brochure.* (Author's photograph)

The plane then climbed steeply, turned on a wing-tip and swooped for a second pass, this one above the masts. Then the serious stuff began, with constant tight figure-of-eight movements, swooping, passing, climbing, turning; non-stop for three-quarters of an hour. The afternoon offered the mixture as before, except that *Andes* was in the Straits of Messina.

The return flight through the night to England was magical. In our private little world, lit by a red glow over the instrument panel, we exchanged pork pies, sandwiches, biscuits and chocolate, seeming more a part of the world of the stars than of the black void below. Down there was the Mediterranean; then we crossed the coast near Nice and turned north to cross the Alps. This eventful weekend had one more drama up its sleeve, for Southend Airport was covered with low cloud and fog. When you are sitting beside the pilot for a blind talkdown landing – touching down barely a second after first seeing the runway – you are left in no doubt as to how utterly you are in the hands of ethereal voices on the ground, and on the coolness of a pilot responding precisely to instructions.

And all of that was a but a tiny part of a strategy to keep a thirty-year-old ship in business for a little longer.

Back On Dry Land

Royal Mail House – the Company's heartbeat for almost four decades – has been described from the viewpoint of its later years, but let us hark back to its construction. During my time there I imagined that the building occupied by Royal Mail and the area which had once been the underwriting regime of Lloyd's had been parts of the same massive building, joined by a rabbit warren of corridors and annexes. That wasn't so, though the adjoining buildings seem to have been erected at the same time, for RMSP and Lloyd's each moved into its new premises in 1928.

In a 1995 Royal Mail Association newsletter, the Company's one-time Assistant Secretary, Geoff Penny, shed a little light on that. The whole block on which stood Royal Mail House and Lloyd's Building, he recorded, once formed the site of the old East India Company. Presumably that meant it supported East India House, which would have made it one of the most important land-based spots in British maritime history.

He continued:

Much to the annoyance of Lloyd's the RMSP bought a half share in the site and it was only some time later, in 1923, that Lloyd's were able to buy for £500,000 land on the site behind what was to be Royal Mail House; they did at least have a passage through to Leadenhall Street to provide a dignified entrance!

Royal Mail House was, like those magnificently outfitted liners *Asturias* and *Alcantara*, the public face of RMSP's years at the top of the shipowning tree. After so many decades in Moorgate, Lord Kylsant decided that the Company's stature needed an appropriate image focal point, and Royal Mail House was the result. As the chapter on Kylsant describes, the firm's halcyon years were by then behind it and it was largely living off its reserves. A large sum of money was borrowed for the new head office, and the difficulties in paying it back became part of the precarious financial position which led to Kylsant facing court charges.

The liquidation of RMSP resulted in Royal Mail House being sold in 1936 to Lloyd's, who promptly built a corridor which, for the first time, provided a link between their original building and Royal Mail House. That was how RML staff were able to walk through the buildings to a back entrance which was little more than a delivery point. What a change of character that exit was from the imposing grandeur inside. It took us into Leadenhall Place and Leadenhall Market, the latter a dim, full-of-character poultry and game market which by then was largely retail but originally had been a wholesale market. In the 1960s, incidentally, it was operated in conjunction with Billingsgate fish market, whose sights and aromas assailed me on those occasions when I had business at the Customs House, for Billingsgate was next door, spanning the block from Lower Thames Street to the riverfront.

The combined Royal Mail House/Lloyd's Building with which so many of us became familiar had earlier held, in the Lloyd's portion, items of interest which were described in the official booklet for a Coronation Reception held in the building on 1 June 1937. The Underwriting Room:

...is a large hall, domed and supported by marble pillars. Its floor area is 16,000 square feet, and from the floor to the highest point of the dome is a distance of 55 feet...Apart from the marble itself and the frescoes round the dome, the decoration of the Room consists partly of ceiling pictures and partly of medallions on the walls, and the visitor, as he passes into the Room on the west side – the side of the War Memorial – will notice a ceiling panel painted to depict 'Industry'. It is the work of Fred Taylor RI, and represents a scene in Venice with the Port Captain conducting the Doge round a shipyard...

On the east side of the Room there is another ceiling picture also painted by Fred Taylor RI. It represents 'Peace', symbolised by a party in medieval Venice going on board ship, accompanied by allegorical figures of Peace and Prosperity...

The painting on the ceiling of [the northern] end of the Room is the work of William Walcot FRIBA, and shows Neptune holding the Lutine Bell in his left hand, while with his right he spears the marine monster which brings havoc to shipping. On the opposite side of the Room another Walcot picture on the ceiling represents Mercury, the God of Commerce, pouring gold and scrip over the City of London...

The artist Fred Taylor is referred to later in this book – as a marine artist and friend of Kenneth Shoesmith he 'filled in' as artist for Royal Mail around the time of the Second World War, between the time of Shoesmith's death and the introduction of Howard Jarvis as contract artist after the war.

Equally interesting was the Nelson Room in the basement. I never discovered the full extent of that underground labyrinth, which was on two levels. There are memories, in the sub-basement, of small, musty strongrooms which held untold files and thick-covered ledgers. Their unbelievably thick steel doors were so heavy that they had to be leaned on with every ounce of strength before they grudgingly opened.

How different is that vision from the Lloyd's side in the 1930s:

In the basement a room is devoted to the Lloyd's collection of Nelson relics. It includes a number of original letters written by Lord Nelson and visitors will be interested in the change in his handwriting that followed the loss of his right arm. Even more interesting, perhaps, is the original log of HMS Euryalus. This 36-gun frigate fought at Trafalgar, and her log records the receipt of Nelson's famous signal to the Fleet...

The Underwriters at Lloyd's awarded two gifts of Plate to Lord Nelson to commemorate the Battles of the Nile (1798) and Copenhagen (1801), and portions of both these services have at various times been presented back to Lloyd's, and form a fitting basis for the Nelson Collection...

So much for these two grand buildings in their heyday. Things changed dramatically for Royal Mail House following the Company's acquisition by Furness, Withy. Most departments moved to Furness House, leaving a 'city passenger office' on the ground floor (the passenger headquarters were moved to Cockspur Street) and the Publicity and P&I (insurance) departments perched at the top of the building on the sixth floor.

In our sixth floor semi-isolation we explored portions of the building we scarcely knew existed, and quickly discovered the stairway leading to the roof. Some of us would spend lunch-hours up there when the weather was benevolent, relaxing in the sun and gazing across the length and breadth of the City of London. Such moments are my last significant memories of the building.

After leaving the Company in 1971 I was rarely in England. On one occasion I came back for a holiday with my family in the early 1980s. We caught a number 15 bus from the city to the West End. As it trundled along Leadenhall Street, past Lime Street, I gazed open-mouthed at where Royal Mail House used to be. There was nothing but a gigantic hole in the ground. In ten short years the Royal Docks had gone, Royal Mail's ships had gone, Royal Mail House had gone, Royal Mail Lines had gone.

Those were the days, my friend; We thought they'd never end... That philosophic, rather poignant song became a hit through the pure tones of Mary Hopkin during the years I worked for Royal Mail. Its lineage, though, I understand was from a Russian folk song dating from the years when RMSP was still young; its sentiments were timeless and mirrored the fortunes of Royal Mail, whose people, for so long, had no inkling that their working world would end so abruptly.

Generations of Royal Mail folk had periodically faced crises and won. The Company could have collapsed within its first two years; it was in financial straits later in the century; it survived a takeover bid in 1902; it overcame the collapse of the early 1930s. All of that, I suspect, created a special character which strengthened with the years, passed from one generation to the next. There was probably no occasion when there were not staff who had passed through one or other of the crises. Even in my time there were many who had joined in Lord Kylsant's day and had weathered the storms and enjoyed the calms ever since.

Then, in 1965, came the announcement that Royal Mail had been taken over by Furness, Withy & Co. The demise was not outwardly instantaneous, but it was the time when we stopped believing that 'those were the days' which would 'never end'. The Company steadily lost its individuality, and when it was deeply embedded in the Furness Withy Group it became part of the parcel sold to Hong Kong shipowner C.Y. Tung. Later still it migrated to Germany, in the hands of one-time rival Hamburg-Süd.

My mind reels back to an afternoon in the 1960s when a group of us wended our way to the Half Moon in Leadenhall Market for some long-forgotten reason (did we need a reason?). We all had our taverns where we 'raised a glass or two' and dreamed of a carefree future. More than three decades on, we from the younger set of that time have shaped our futures in a multitude of ways. The men and women who shared the late days of Royal Mail's independence are now scattered far and wide. In the year 2001 there are still hundreds, settled across Britain and spread among most of the continents. They still get together to raise a glass or two and reminisce, for the Royal Mail bond will be unbreakable until the last of us have gone.

Macqueen's Legacy is a tribute to these people, and to those who preceded them, for it was the people who made Royal Mail the proud and unique company it was.

1
Raising Steam

During the first half of the nineteenth century such giant strides were made in the world of the steamship that it is easy to envisage the whole picture. It is perhaps more difficult to place within that broad framework the pre-eminent position in which the Royal Mail Steam Packet Company (RMSP) found itself when it began operations.

Looking at that period – spanning either side of 1840 – three British companies stood out as the most dominant in overseas mail steamer services: RMSP, Cunard and P&O. The core of Royal Mail's 'first fleet' comprised fourteen steamers of generally between 1,800 and 1,900 tons. P&O, which had been operating for several years at this stage, had only one ship exceeding 1,800 tons and most were less than 1,000.

Cunard Line, starting operations in 1840, began with a group of four ships, the largest being 1,175 tons. None of its vessels topped 2,000 tons until 1850, by which time RMSP had ordered new ships of almost 3,000 tons.

The advent of RMSP was thus a cornerstone in the development of ocean steam navigation, and it is worth a brief look at the years which led up to that time – little more than two decades after steamers had been at the 'kindergarten stage' of experimental river trips and short coastal services.

Early Days

Among the names which loom out of the mists of early steamer experiments late in the eighteenth century is that of William Symington. His work formed, in Scotland, the first elements of what became the major area of early steamship development.

Symington was an engineer, and his early engines were fitted into hulls built by Patrick Miller, the laird of Dalswinton in Dumfriesshire. The first, in 1788, was successful and a year later the next was hailed by cheering crowds as it reached nearly 6mph on the Forth and Clyde Canal. Miller then lost interest, leaving Symington to wait ten years for another sponsor. Lord Dundas, who had a close involvement with the Forth and Clyde Canal and was anxious for steamboats to replace horse-drawn vessels, provided the opportunity. Symington, delighted to resume his pet project, came up with the famous *Charlotte Dundas* in 1801. Named after his benefactor's daughter, its hull was built by Alexander Hart at Grangemouth. The engine was of 10hp, placed horizontally on deck with the boiler beside it. The paddle wheel was in a cavity at the stern, ahead of double rudders. A second *Charlotte Dundas*, appearing in March 1803, towed the laden sloops *Active* and *Euphemia*, of seventy tons each, a distance of $19\frac{1}{2}$ miles in six hours.

While we must acknowledge the contributions of many others, Symington may justifiably be regarded as the father of the practical steamboat. So much of his own money and energy went into those brief spells of activity that his financial position became perilous. He died in London in 1831 and was buried in the churchyard of St Botolph's, Aldgate. What he had achieved for Britain had already been largely forgotten in an era of dynamic progress. No-one cared enough to arrange for his burial back home in Lanarkshire; there was not even a tombstone erected over the pauper's grave. It was left to a more recently-erected tablet in the church to remind us that he is there – within a cable's length of what would become shipping's 'golden mile', Leadenhall Street.

A stonemason turned carpenter named Henry Bell had followed Symington's efforts with interest; indeed some of the woodwork for Symington's early boats was his workmanship. Bell had prepared a plan for a steamboat and submitted it to the Admiralty in 1800, yet they turned it down and, like Symington, ten years passed before he had another chance. It wasn't until 1811 that the *Comet* was ordered from John Wood & Co. of Port Glasgow and was launched the following July.

With its engine producing only 3hp, *Comet* travelled rather grudgingly at about 3mph, with smoke belching from a funnel which acted as a mast for the sail as well. New paddles were fitted later, and the ship was lengthened. More advanced vessels superseded her on the Clyde and she took to voyaging elsewhere around Scotland, to Fort William and Inverness.

The name of Lewis MacLellan has some relation to the *Comet*, though he in fact founded a different company in 1814. MacLellan, it seems, was initially associated with Henry Bell in operating the *Comet*, but in later years he was forced to leave Scotland. MacLellan was skippering his own steamer when it collided with and sank the *Comet*. Not only was this popular pioneer steamer lost, but lives too, and MacLellan was made a scapegoat even though the inquiry found him to be blameless. He left the country and could be found for years afterwards, described as a 'gruff, sulky old Scotsman, especially when the wind was contrary', skippering a schooner in Australian waters. The *Greenock Advertiser* commented that 'It is fantastic to suggest that he was compelled to flee the country, but he probably left it in order to make life tolerable'.

That sequence, seemingly remote from RMSP, demonstrates that the Company's lineage had a number of strands emanating from those early days of steamship development, for MacLellan's company became Laird Line, and ultimately Burns & Laird, a company RMSP would control in later years. There were more direct pioneer links to Royal Mail's early days, as will be seen shortly.

Comet's hull was lost after she sank, but the engine survived. More than forty years later it was still working, on land, when the marine engineer Robert Napier bought it and presented it to the Science Museum in London. Napier's cousin David Napier had taken over the family's foundry at an early age after his father died. Henry Bell, at that time a housebuilder, had been a friend and customer of David's father, and when he decided to build the *Comet*, David Napier was given the contract for the boiler and castings. David was likely aided in this endeavour by memories of a visit, when still a boy, to the declining remains of Symington's *Charlotte Dundas* in the Forth and Clyde Canal. The extent to which nineteenth century steamship enterprise was inspired by the tangible presence of Symington's early work will never really be known. However, another instance came from the American President Line, which grew from the Dollar Line founded by Scotsman Robert Dollar. Towards the end of his

David Napier (left) and Robert Napier – cousins whose shipbuilding and engineering skills were crucial to the early development of ocean-going steamships, and helped place the River Clyde at the forefront of the industry.

life Dollar recalled that three-quarters of a century earlier he used to play on the deck of *Charlotte Dundas*, abandoned in the mud of the Forth and Clyde Canal at Top Hill Entry. Her deck was just above the water, an ideal position for the lads to strip off and go in swimming.

David Napier went on to build many ships and engines and operated some himself, while Robert became just as highly regarded when he took over David's Glasgow yard. David's fertile mind produced all sorts of innovations, among them surface condensers, steeple engines, twin screws and feathering paddles. Robert Napier built the machinery for three RMSP ships – *Magdalena* of 1851, *La Plata* of 1852 and *Shannon* of 1859 (hull and engines for this one). They clocked up fifty years of service between them – no mean performance for those days.

Long after Robert Napier's death a further ten RMSP ships came from the Napier yard at Glasgow, among them the four superb clipper-bowed steamers *Atrato*, *Magdalena*, *Thames* and *Clyde*, completed between 1888 and 1890. *Magdalena* survived for over thirty years. How easily the Royal Mail story slips into the pioneer days.

Early in his career, in 1826, Robert Napier built a steam vessel which he named *Eclipse*. He owned the ship in great part as well, and she operated on G. & J. Burns' service between Glasgow and Belfast. A report described her as

> the most complete vessel of her size ever built on the Clyde; built of the best British oak, copper-sheathed and fastened, with double side-lever engines, having cylinders 35 inches in diameter, warranted equal in construction and workmanship to the best engines made.

That is perhaps the most succinct comment with which to summarise the Napiers, two talented men who could claim inspiration from the very earliest practical steamboats.

Atlantic Pioneers

A Portuguese ship, *Conde de Patmella*, has been proposed by some historians as the first steamer to cross the Atlantic westbound – not to North America, but from Lisbon to Brazil. Eastbound, the 350-ton *Savannah*, an American full-rigged ship with auxiliary steam equipment, voyaged in 29 days 11 hours from Savannah to Liverpool in 1819. However, only eighty hours or so of steam power were used because of a lack of storage space for coal.

A small steamer sailed from Gravesend to Valparaiso in Chile in 1821, and six years later the Dutch-owned 438-ton *Curaçao* made the first of several transatlantic crossings. She was built on the Clyde when James Macqueen, RMSP's founder, lived in Glasgow and was editor of the Glasgow Courier.

Another 'first' is credited to the 830-ton *Royal William*, built at Quebec in 1831 and recorded as having made the first Atlantic crossing by steam power alone. Her 200nhp side-lever engines came, like so many from that era, from Boulton & Watt. James Watt's engineering achievements in the eighteenth century had been greatly influential in bringing the steam engine into consideration for sea power. Despite *Royal William's* achievement of non-stop steam power, steamers until then – and for years afterwards – were designed to use both steam and sail. The time had not yet come when owners were sufficiently convinced of the new system's impregnability to rely on machinery alone.

Letter from James Macqueen, who was by then almost 85, to a member of the Blackwood family, 1864.

It should also be said that until the invention of the triple expansion engine by A.C. Kirk (who by 1880 was running the Napier shipyard), steamers on long-distance ocean voyages continued to suffer from a shortage of coal spaces and normally utilised sail whenever possible to conserve fuel. The supporting role of sails became so ingrained that long after they had been dispensed with, the terminology in ship specifications suggested otherwise. As recently as 1938 the specification book for Royal Mail's *Andes*, under the heading of 'Rig', stated: 'The vessel to be rigged as a fore and aft schooner, having two pole masts'.

That said, when *Asturias* was torpedoed in 1943 and was being towed to West Africa, the tug was heading to Freetown while the bow of *Asturias* pointed towards Capetown. In the hope of improving matters, a sail was rigged on the forecastle, and while the prospect of a sail assisting a 22,000-ton waterlogged liner seemed ambitious, reports suggest it might at least have assisted the navigation.

By the 1830s, the spring-time of the steamer years had arrived, immediately blossoming in a bewildering array of developments and improvements. It can be no coincidence that the three major mail steamer companies mentioned earlier – RMSP, Cunard, P&O and more besides – all went through their birthpangs during that decade.

2
James Macqueen and the Embryo RMSP

James Macqueen was born in 1778, when experimental steamboats were in their infancy. Indeed, they can be said to have grown up together. His birthplace was Crawford, a small farming community among the Lanarkshire hills about fifty miles from Glasgow. The local Register of Births and Baptisms records that 'William McQueen and Peggy Cranston had a son born 21st June 1778. He was baptised before several witnesses and named James'.

At this point we should come to grips with the spelling of Macqueen's name, which varied even within his own signature. The spelling on his birth certificate is 'McQueen', the style used by James early on when signing his name. Most often in published accounts it is spelt 'MacQueen'. The style used in this book – Macqueen – has been selected for two reasons. It is the form used in his signature during his more mature years and it is the form used in his entry in the 1893 *Dictionary of National Biography*.

James spent his childhood not five miles from the home of William Symington, who was experimenting with his second craft on the Forth and Clyde Canal when Macqueen was aged eleven. Symington's work, and the exciting prospects of steamships, surely ingrained themselves on the impressionable mind of the young Macqueen.

The Man and His Life

James Macqueen left the quiet of Lanarkshire while still in his teens and embarked on a sea voyage to the Caribbean where he was to manage a sugar plantation on Grenada. It was a job which indirectly shaped his future thinking for it brought him, for the first time, in contact with slaves.

During the next twenty or thirty years he travelled a great deal, largely through the areas loosely defined as the West Indies and Spanish Main. He learned about the islands and their inhabitants and, almost inevitably in this part of the globe at this time, the subject of slavery quickly became important to him, and his feelings on the matter were deep. In 1824 he wrote:

> *An enemy to personal slavery in the abstract, still I cannot shut my eyes to the fact that it has always existed, and still exists to a prodigious extent amongst mankind. Much as I should rejoice to see only free men in every country on earth – still I am not so sanguine as to imagine or believe that either the present generation, or the children's children of the present generation, will witness that consummation.*

The methods being adopted by governments in the 1820s for the abolition of personal slavery were considered by Macqueen to be rash and unjust, that they would 'give reign to barbarism to utterly destroy civilisation'. A quite unexpected side to his character then stepped in:

> *Genuine Christianity will accomplish, and it only can accomplish, what its Great Author intended, namely, such a reformation (where reformation is sought) in the human character and manners as should lead to a safe amelioration in political institutions, and a more equal distribution of civil rights amongst nations.*

This was the only occasion on which I have found a demonstration of his Protestant faith – he showed no outward signs of religious zeal.

He was back in Scotland around 1813, living in Glasgow and writing for a living. His imagination was captured by Africa, and the ubiquitous 'Black Continent' always remained his greatest interest. The River Niger, particularly the location of its source and mouth, was important to him from the 1790s when fellow-Scotsman Mungo Park searched the African interior for the river.

Astonishingly for a man who had apparently never set foot in Africa, Macqueen was, in 1816, the first person to plot the exit of the Niger into the Bight of Benin. In identifying the Niger's course he was helped by his slaves on Grenada – some were Mandingos who had once lived on the river's banks. Not only did he quiz them, he talked also with the slave agents. Later he plotted a map of the African interior which was regarded as 'the first approaching to correctness'.

Africa – its peoples, agriculture, trade, topography and slavery – were all subjected to his passionate pen. Several observations were considered important enough to take their place in the annals of African geography, and in 1845 Macqueen was elected a Fellow of the Royal Geographical Society, proposed by no lesser person than the renowned cartographer John Arrowsmith – who had drawn the map of Africa devised by Macqueen.

From 1824 to 1830 Macqueen was editor and part-owner of the thrice-weekly 'ultra-Tory' newspaper *Glasgow Courier*. However, his interest and influence in the paper pre-dated this, for he earmarked some stories as early as 1821 as 'interesting me for the Courier'. Subsequently he was registered in Glasgow for some years as a merchant – a partner in Macqueen, McKay & Co.

His grasp of world commerce was demonstrated through a long association with the Edinburgh publishers William Blackwood & Sons. In 1819 he accepted the first payment of £1 1s per month to supply a Commercial Report for Blackwood's *Edinburgh Magazine*, which had started publication a year or two earlier. In a letter to William Blackwood he said: 'I flatter myself that I shall be able to make the Commercial Report an useful and not the least interesting part of your magazine[sic]'.

By the following year he was venting his feelings on Africa through the magazine. He told Blackwood that his objective with regard to Africa was publicity, and he considered the magazine to be the best way of obtaining it. Having thus flagged his desire to publicise a pet subject, Macqueen, with uncharacteristic diplomacy, added: 'Your magazine is really improving. The last two numbers were highly entertaining'.

Much of the entertainment came from Macqueen's own pen. The February 1820 issue contained his annual review of trade and commerce. Apart from some vigorous and single-minded comments (Macqueen, in such a mood, was no-one's idea of a diplomat), it showed his broad grasp of international affairs; the depressed state of the markets, the 'bullion question' forcing the Bank of England to reduce the note circulation by £6 million, discussion on Mediterranean trade in competition with France, how future trade ought to be conducted and the areas best suited for development – all were investigated.

The East Indies, he claimed, would not provide rapid trade expansion, and warned:

We cannot change the customs and pursuits of nations in a day, and till we can change these completely, we cannot anticipate any wide consumpt for our manufactures in that portion of Asia. Any premature attempt to effect such a change in sentiments, manners and customs, may terminate in a moment our empire in the east… It is a trade that will not be forced.

The Americas received even closer scrutiny:

The swarms of adventurers drawn to that quarter of the world, the system of piracy to which it has given rise, with the convulsed state of these countries, has almost annihilated the trade which our merchants in Jamaica carried on across the Isthmus of Darien to Peru and Chili in the south and to Mexico and California in the north and, we greatly fear, that the trade is gone for ever from that island.

Our trade with the Brazils may continue to improve, but from the nature of the population and Government there established [he had earlier referred to them as 'mostly savages' or 'near-savages'] *it is obvious that the increase must be slow, and that other nations will come in with us for a share of it. Many of the provinces of Spanish America are so desolated, that were peace established at the moment, years must elapse before any considerable and advantageous commerce could be carried on with them.*

Macqueen closed this astonishing annual review with a stirring paragraph about Britain's future in world trade: 'There are many markets in the world', he insisted, 'yet to be opened, and which can be opened to our commerce. Masters of the ocean, we can gain access into every country, and to every land'.

The purpose of looking so closely at that review has been to emphasise the breadth of Macqueen's knowledge of and enthusiasm for overseas trade. It becomes important when examining his Plan for mail steamer services. There was, however, still time to pass before he turned his attention to shipping. His interest in African affairs kept him particularly busy and he was still fighting vigorously for the cause of the West Indian slaves, attacking the colonial system for all he was worth.

More than just giving voice to a passion, he was calculatedly manoeuvring in order to gain influence. He made forays to London and before long had made himself known to the likes of the Duke of Wellington, the Marquis of Lansdowne, Lord Brougham and a number of other Parliamentarians. The trenchant nature of his writing brought less welcome attention – hardly surprising when he was wont to declare to William Blackwood:

First page in RMSP's directors' minute book, 24 July 1839 (two months before the Company's incorporation).

Censure and condemnation ought alone to fall on the head of that profligate imbecile Government who patronises and protects such worthless reptiles to the destruction of the property in a large appendage of our empire, and to the ruin of the characters of those ill-fated British subjects who have unfortunately settled in the British tropical colonies.

He became so deeply involved in the subject of slavery and wider issues concerning Africa and the West Indies that even this resilient Scot was moved to write, in an outburst of a letter in 1827: 'I am sick to death with fatigue and the odorous black subject'. On top of all that, he continued to write commercial reports and sometimes recorded the proceedings of the House of Commons for Blackwood's *Magazine*, published independent works and continued his involvement with the *Glasgow Courier*.

Macqueen's 'Plan'

While nothing appeared on the surface for some time, it is clear that James Macqueen was piecing together his ideas for mail steamer services through much of the 1830s. During 1837 he finally placed before the Government his 'General plan for a mail communication by steam between Great Britain and the eastern and western parts of the world; also to Canton and Sydney NSW, westward by the Pacific'.

The nature of the Plan precluded the usual Macqueen style of writing; it was laid down in great detail and with a conspicuous lack of emotion. Statistics on trade, costs and itineraries were all carefully – if a little optimistically – thought out. Building costs were based on a statement made to the Post Office Commissioners in 1836 by 'that able and practical engineer Mr Napier of Glasgow'. He didn't say which Mr Napier but it was almost certainly Robert. The cost quoted by Napier for a vessel of 240hp and 620 tons burden was 'between £24,000 and £25,000'. In the final analysis, of course, both the size of the ships and their cost escalated enormously.

Macqueen claimed that the cost to extend the proposed West Indies service westwards across the Panama isthmus and the Pacific to Sydney, NSW and Canton, China, 'would not be prohibitive'. Westwards through the isthmus would be a better description, for Macqueen was convinced a passage between the Atlantic and Pacific would be a reality 'at no distant day'. He favoured a passage via Lake Nicaragua, where the distance was far greater than any route through Panama, but by subtracting the lake itself and a considerable length of navigable river, it was not quite such an absurd suggestion. There was only the rather chilling prospect of Lake Nicaragua itself – three volcanic cones rising from waters inhabited by swordfish and sharks. The closest a canal concept came to success during the nineteenth century was at the hands of Ferdinand de Lesseps. The disasters of the attempt – particularly in terms of loss of life through raging disease – illustrates the horrendous difficulties of taming the isthmus.

Macqueen provided reasons why the Government should be involved through a mail subsidy. A simple reason which he didn't spell out was that such a mighty undertaking was unlikely to find sufficient private investors. Even if the money was potentially available, the gamble was gigantic with ocean-going steamer services still so young. Macqueen's raison d'être was his concern that, without mail steamers, the 'channels of British intelligence' as he described them would soon be split among a number of companies; even (probably his biggest fear) under foreign ownership.

An aspect of the Plan which affected the design of the early steamers was their potential in time of war – a factor which might have been put to the test during the Crimean War, though in the event they were restricted to carrying troops. The Plan emphasises that:

It is scarcely necessary to point out the immense advantages which the Government of Great Britain would possess in the event of hostilities, by having the command and the direction of such a mighty and extensive steam power and communication, which would enable them to forward, to any point within its vast range, despatches, troops and warlike stores.

It was eventually made a condition that RMSP's ships be designed to accept heavy armament, but over the years the Admiralty, after inspecting various ships, proclaimed them ineligible to become ships of war. Despite the conditions of construction, a lack of strength was sometimes cited; speed and power were other factors. Thus the Company's ships were restricted to troop-carrying roles when needed until the days of the armed merchant cruiser in the twentieth century's great conflicts.

Meanwhile, the first steamers to be used in the mail service should, Macqueen insisted, be broad in the beam, of a light draft (to negotiate rivers and small harbours), and in speed, accommodation and security be unsurpassable by vessels of other powers.

Towards RMSP

What was James Macqueen's object in promoting such an ambitious project? On paper it was the postal service, but his driving force was, surely, trade and commerce. That contention seems at odds with the very criterion expounded by Macqueen – that an efficient mail service could not be maintained with ships whose primary role was the time-consuming carriage of cargo. Perhaps, then, it was a more adroit manoeuvre, to set up a mail ship network from which satellite trading operations would be generated once the infrastructure was in place.

His writings for Blackwood's *Magazine* emphasised his preoccupation with trade and the prospects for improving it. There is precious little to suggest a burning desire in Macqueen to create a great fleet of ships or to remould the workings of the Post Office. He was keenly aware of the ways and extent that the Industrial Revolution was changing the face of Britain; turning the nation from an agrarian economy to an industrial one. The Caribbean regions were well known to him, while the Indian sub-continent, South Africa, Canada, Australia and New Zealand were at various stages of vigorous growth. It was probably not lost on him that while he was creating the Plan, the new colony of South Australia came into being and was attracting more people than it could support.

Though Australia was a minor player in his ideas it was included, and reference to South Australia has a particular edge to it. With his close watch on the British Parliament, Macqueen would have been aware of the progress of the Bill which established the colony – not least because of his acquaintance with the Duke of Wellington, one of the principal supporters of the South Australia Bill. Support was also given in the House of Commons for the Bill by the fiery Irish Colonel, Robert Torrens. It may have been a matter relating to Torrens which underpinned the Macqueen philosophy. The Colonel was taken to task in later years by Karl Marx who, in his 'Bible of communism' *Das Kapital*, claimed that Torrens had supported the Industrial Revolution even though he knew that it would throw countless people out of work.

Marx got it wrong. Torrens did support the Industrial Revolution, and knew well enough that the number of jobs it created would not match those lost. He also knew that a switch to an industrial economy meant that Britain would be progressively less able to supply its own primary produce. His philosophy, therefore, was the establishment of British colonies in lands well suited to agriculture and pastoralism. The displaced workers – especially those from the land – should settle these new lands where the prospects were so good, and in turn provide the foodstuffs and other staple produce which Britain would increasingly need.

The ships needed to bring this produce would then find freights in the reverse direction with manufactured products from Britain, and there would be plenty of opportunity, too, for passenger operations, both from well-to-do and professional people and labourer migrants. All of that could have provided a ship operator with profits. However, if you were going to outlay the vast sums projected by Macqueen for an immensely complicated schedule, the income from a mail subsidy was crucial.

The scale of his proposed operations was so huge that it was quite impracticable. In the event they were scaled down to initial services which covered the Caribbean islands and rim, New York and Halifax, and even that had to be quickly culled. Macqueen's vision was far ahead of its time, for only in much later years were many individual operations gradually melded into fewer but larger enterprises – almost a hundred years hence there were two British groups (RMSP and P&O) collectively dominant in the kind of world regions envisaged by Macqueen.

When his Plan talked about ships, the style returned to the old, typical Macqueen. Ships for the 'torrid zone' had to be more roomy and airy, and yet secure against hurricanes, than anything yet in service. To provide an idea of what life was like in a ship on the West Indies station in the 1830s, he asked the reader to imagine a small, ill-contrived boat such as the 100hp ten-gun brig *Carron*, with thirty to forty tons of coal on her deck and a cabin 13ft x 10ft, unventilated except for a narrow and miserable hatch.

There are fifty people on board, battened down in bad weather to roll and pitch with the waves. Sleeping berths adjoin the boilers; there is nowhere to stow the passengers' luggage, and mail bags are stuffed under tables and in cabins – wherever there is a little space. The occupants of this hell-hole choke with coal dust and are reduced to the choice of being broiled or suffocated.

He proposed the following areas of operation: Falmouth – Fayal – Halifax; North America and the West Indies, the Brazils; Madeira; Barbados; the West India station; the Pacific station to Canton and Sydney; the Mediterranean and East Indies by the Red Sea; and the eastern world by the Cape of Good Hope. Dealing with the Pacific station, Macqueen paid tribute to William Wheelwright. He was already involved in the affairs of the Pacific coast of South America and was working towards a line of steamers for a service along the coast which resulted in the formation of The Pacific Steam Navigation Company in 1840, a company which was to become closely linked with RMSP in the years ahead.

For the South American section, having chosen Fayal, in the Azores, as the terminal for the transatlantic crossing, Macqueen selected Pernambuco for the first call on the other side. From there, mails would be trans-shipped to a sailing ship for the 670-mile journey north to Maranham (São Luiz) – a six-day journey north and four days back again in order to catch the steamer on its northbound call.

From Pernambuco the mail steamer would call at Bahia and Rio de Janeiro, its southern terminus. At Rio, two sailing ships would be stationed as trans-shipment vessels to Buenos Aires and, on the return passage, Montevideo, round trips of some 2,100 miles taking seventeen days, returning to Rio in time for the following homeward mail steamer.

He planned a twice-monthly transatlantic service requiring three steamers, insisting that one a month would defeat the whole object of speeding up mail deliveries. The round trip from Fayal to Brazil and back would take forty-five days, thirty-nine of them at sea.

In the event, a South America service was not included at the start. Comparing Macqueen's 1837 Plan with the Brazil service which opened fourteen years later, we find that three ships were indeed used; each took just over two months from Southampton to Brazil and back (by 1851 Falmouth was no longer used as a packet station) – but the recommended twice-monthly service took much longer to come to fruition.

The principal Brazil calls were as Macqueen planned, though the time in port was different. The Maranham trans-shipment was not used and the connecting ship to the River Plate was a steamer – as the Brazil run was monthly, only one connecting vessel was needed. Fayal was dropped as the starting point for the transatlantic steamers and, in fact, was ignored, calls being made in the Canary Islands, Cape Verde Islands and Madeira, but starting from Southampton.

By the time that was happening James Macqueen was no longer involved with the Company – he had long since (in mind if not in body) returned to his beloved Africa. During his time with RMSP, his title was initially General Superintendent of Affairs. Why did the man who masterminded the company not have a more senior position; why was he not at least a director? Where did the balance lie between Macqueen's possible desire for a hands-on involvement rather than a boardroom appointment, and the feelings of an upper crust Court of Directors that Macqueen was not suitable material for a director? There is a sense that the directors found him something of an embarrassment; he was not an accountant or an administrator, but a visionary and a thinker.

This juncture, in fact, shows how enigmatic Macqueen was. He had been instrumental in guiding the creation of the Company through Parliament, and before that had been at his persuasive best in gaining the commercial support it needed. That came largely through the West India Committee, with whom he would have been closely in touch since his days on the sugar plantations.

The initial directors included some influential men. John Irving MP, the first Chairman, was a merchant banker and also Chairman of the Colonial Bank, the other institution for whose foundation Macqueen was largely responsible. Irving's son, John Jnr., was also one of the original directors. There was a further merchant banking connection with Thomas Baring, who was an inaugural director, a post he held for the better part of twenty years, some as Deputy Chairman. For many years Baring was responsible for the financial operations of Baring Bros & Co, the financial institution founded by his grandfather.

His brother Francis Baring (later Sir Francis and later still Lord Northbrook) was the Secretary to the Treasury to whom James Macqueen wrote a long letter in August 1838 which is looked at shortly. The Baring influence, then, was significant, especially since Francis had become Chancellor of the Exchequer by the time RMSP was sanctioned in Parliament and Thomas, who was also an MP, remarkably also became Chancellor of the Exchequer.

RMSP's first Deputy Chairman (and, later, the second Chairman) was Andrew Colvile from Fife, whose wife, the Hon. Louisa Colvile, was the daughter of Lord Auckland. Their younger son, Eden, succeeded his father on the Court of Directors after Andrew's death in 1856. George Hibbert was less well known, but his family had been deeply involved with West India merchants for three generations, and he was primarily responsible for the creation of London's West India Dock.

The enigma stems from the relationship between such people and Macqueen; the seeming disparity between his ability to persuade them to found the Company and his subsequent role as an employee.

Such was the case, though. A month before the Company was officially formed, it was agreed that:

> contingent upon the formation of the Company, Mr James Macqueen be engaged on behalf of the Company as from the 1st of September in the capacity of General Superintendent of Affairs of the Company…That, in consideration of the services already rendered by Mr Macqueen in framing the Plan of Operations of the Company and carrying through the contract with Her Majesty's Government, he be paid the sum of £5,000, and that he be further paid the annual sum of £1,000 for his future services, to date from 1 September.

The Baring Letter

Some matters relating to James Macqueen and his Plan, and of the struggle to create RMSP, are contained in a long letter which he wrote to Francis Baring MP, Secretary to the Treasury, on 23 August 1838.

The Plan had by then been approved by the Post Office and Admiralty and now, after time in the public forum, was about to begin its passage through Parliament. The letter was not an introduction to the Plan; rather, it was a response from its creator (detailed and restrained in parts and typically blunt in others) to those who had criticised it and were peddling an alternative.

The rival scheme had been devised by a committee comprising commercial and political interests from certain areas in the Caribbean, notably Jamaica. According to Macqueen, this was 'a plan devised by Mr Phillpotts, which took Bermuda as the central point of communication between Britain and the West Indies'.

Macqueen made no bones about his reaction to proposals like the inclusion of Jacmel, Haiti, on the schedule (a port not included in his Plan) and the use of Bermuda as the centre of operations:

> *Jacmel is an exceedingly dangerous place; frequently steamers cannot venture to approach it, and when they do make it after dark, they lay off and on till day-light. In the night it is scarcely possible to distinguish the place.*

Assembly of the first fleet at Southampton – capturing the time when RMSP's directors, after a rough ride for two years, were able to take new heart. Only two of the ships are identified – Teviot *(I) is on the extreme right and* Clyde *(I) is the dominant ship towards the left.*

As far as Bermuda was concerned, Macqueen listed numerous sound reasons for not having chosen it (though it had been considered) – they ranged from six additional days' sailing to Barbados and other scheduling disadvantages, to the fact that:

> *Bermuda is a place well known to be the most difficult and dangerous to approach at all seasons... Bermuda is $4\frac{1}{2}$ degrees of longitude to the westward than Barbados, and wholly and considerably within the sphere of the variable winds, which winds every navigator knows may be said to blow nine months of the year from the south-westward, directly in the teeth of every thing proceeding from England to Bermuda...*
>
> *Moreover, as regards the distance from Bermuda to Barbados, be it remembered that for nearly half the year, from June to November, the course in the trades is directly in the teeth of the south-east trade wind; and in going from Barbados to Bermuda, during the other portion of the year, the course will be opposed to the strong northerly winds...*

In considering such factors it must be remembered that early steamers still relied heavily on canvas for support.

He cited, too, the objection of the rival committee to calling at Puerto Rico and Santiago de Cuba, implying that the schedule should not include any islands or countries not under British rule. Macqueen's long-established knowledge of trade and commerce quickly demolished such arguments with a detailed account of current trade patterns and levels.

Clearly frustrated by what he viewed as either incompetence or vested interests, Macqueen pointed out to the Secretary of the Treasury:

> *Such was that 'standing committee', which in nautical affairs considered itself wiser than the Admiralty of Great Britain, and who took upon themselves, without considering the question, or allowing any commercial interest in London connected with these quarters, or the great commercial interests in the United Kingdom connected with the Western World, to examine the facts or offer an opinion on the points at issue... It would be a waste of time to dwell on points so clear and obvious to every geographer and navigator; and how Mr P. Cruickshank, who, I presume, represented St Vincent on this committee, can answer to the people of that colony for sending their British mails in a route by which they will be seven days longer in receiving them, is his business, not mine, to look after; while those in Antigua will also be kept back at least three days, which will enable Sir W. Colebrook to retaliate upon Sir H. Martin, that during his attendance on this committee, he must have been labouring under some mental hallucination.*

This letter is essentially a defence of Macqueen's Plan, which he clearly felt was necessary as a deputation from his rivals had recently been received at the Admiralty. The fact that he emphasised in detail the great improvement in arrangements for Jamaica which his own Plan provided suggests that the opposition was centred there.

Since this letter to Francis Baring played its part in stifling the opposition scheme, it is unnecessary here to outline all of Macqueen's argument. A number of other issues were raised, however. There was, for instance, the fact that while James Macqueen was overtly planning an operation for the benefit of mail services, he was ultimately more interested in trade and commerce. A number of comments bear this out. In referring to Baring's original reaction to the Plan, he wrote about:

> the very pointed manner in which you declared that the commercial interests of this nation were entitled to receive the utmost accommodation in mail communications that Government, consistent with its general duties, could afford unto them.

And then 'the very great anxiety which every one evinced, to give the commercial world every facility and accommodation.' Macqueen next established his own position, in the process not only giving us the genesis of his Plan in his own words, but also taking a swipe at those who would scuttle it:

> The plan, in all its parts, is, permit me to say, my own. I received assistance and sought assistance from no one. Aware of the paltry jealousies which disturb West Indian interests on almost every question, it was not considered proper, as it was certainly not considered necessary, to seek assistance in that or any other quarter. Further, as regards the West Indies, I have known them and studied their interests for 40 years; visited repeatedly – the last time only 15 months ago – every colony, port, and place, British and foreign; and made, with a view of perfecting such a plan as has been alluded to, their geographical positions, their seas, winds, currents and harbours, my particular study. Without patronage, and without any personal interest or object in view, I approached Her Majesty's Government with an arrangement of great importance and of great extent, dependent only on its merits and its accuracy.

The core priorities of mails and trade were joined by a third factor – the potential for services to end up under the wing of foreign operations. In dealing with that he also explained why he had included the West Indies-New York extension which, on the face of it, seemed to be something of an anomaly:

> …If not pre-occupied by Britain, this line would be occupied by parties from the United States; when not only an unconquerable competitor would be found in the way, taking away passengers &c, &c, but that all the correspondence of the western coasts of South America, to come through the New Steam Navigation Company established in that quarter, by the isthmus of Panama; all the correspondence of the South American continent, to the westward of the Gulf of Paria, and all the colonies westward from St Thomas to Vera Cruz, would come through the Havannah to New York, and thence to England; nay, even much of the Windward Island correspondence, through St Thomas, would come by the same route.

All told, then, this letter, whose prime purpose was to nullify opposition plans, probes also into Macqueen's philosophies for establishing a shipping company, the manner in which he did it and the immense detail of considerations for routes and schedules. Macqueen, it must be said, was not blameless in the matter of scheduling and many problems were to arise from that. The actual networking of Caribbean routes, though, was based on sound knowledge and it was his optimistic view of timekeeping (influenced by the Admiralty's mail contract demands) which made the first schedules unworkable.

The Mail Contract and its Influence

Royal Mail's reputation over the years was excellent. Reliability, service and seafaring qualities stood out prominently and lapses in any of these areas were dealt with harshly. After some initial setbacks, the company's name became established as a solid and dependable shipping line. Reputations like that were not built overnight and we must look back to its genesis to find the nucleus of Royal Mail's success.

Before the Admiralty would enter into a mail contract it insisted on a set of clauses to ensure, as far as possible, the safe arrival of its precious cargo. The contract, signed in 1840, thus formulated the rigid code of discipline which was the backbone on which the Company's reputation was built. A document of nearly 7,000 words, it described in detail the services to be operated and conditions to be upheld. It also listed penalties: a £500 fine, for instance, for every twelve-hour delay in the scheduled sailing time.

The Royal Mail Steam Packet Company, it began, should

provide, maintain, keep seaworthy, and in complete repair and readiness, for the purpose of conveying... all Her Majesty's mails, a sufficient number (not less than 14) of good, substantial and efficient steam vessels of such construction and strength as to be fit and able to carry guns of the largest calibre now used on board of Her Majesty's steam vessels of war, each of such vessels to be always supplied with first-rate appropriate steam engines, of not less than 400 collective horse-power; also a sufficient number, not less than four, of good, substantial and efficient sailing vessels, of at least 100 tons burthen each'.

The prospect of large penalties led to the start of an unprecedented naval-style tradition. Such discipline was necessary to meet the demands, helping to explain a strong Naval influence. That this should be more noticeable than in other lines holding mail contracts was probably due to the make-up of the Court of Directors in the early decades.

The strictness of the mail contract, which would have inspired confidence in the travelling public, had a sting in its tail. A naval officer travelled in each ship, in charge of the mails. Clauses in the contract made it clear that they had immense powers which at times over-rode those of the captain in matters which could be critical to the safety of the ship.

The naval officer, for instance, had 'full authority' in questions 'relative to proceeding to sea, or putting into harbour, or to the necessity of stopping to assist any vessel in distress, or to save human life...'. And in the case of vessels being prevented from calling at a port through stress of weather or 'other unavoidable circumstance', it was the naval officer who would decide how the problem would be overcome, and 'any directions or orders which he may give...shall be strictly obeyed by the master'.

Such whittling away of a shipmaster's authority seems astonishing. We do not know to what extent the Admiralty men used those powers, beyond reports from the first year of operation which do not indicate significant interference. The Government would naturally wish to have someone on-site to ensure the safety and prompt delivery of mail, but one of the great criterions of the sea is that a ship's captain holds ultimate responsibility.

The contract goes on:

All such steam and sailing vessels always to be supplied and furnished with all necessary and proper apparel, furniture, stores, tackle, boats, fuel, oil, tallow, provisions, anchors, cables, fire-pumps, and whatsoever else may be necessary…

It was clauses like that which provided the highest possible reference for passengers – and that, too, became part of the reputation.

A crucial paragraph insisted that:

The company shall, at all times during the continuance of this contract, make such alterations and improvements in the construction, equipment and machinery of the vessels, as the advanced state of science may suggest and the said Commissioners [of the Admiralty] may direct.

One direction from the Admiralty was that no ships carrying mails should be built of any material other than wood. At first that was understandable, for iron was only accepted by a few commercial operators during the late 1830s and 1840s. There was still widespread scepticism about its use, and even once that was overcome, many years inevitably had to pass before its longevity could be established.

When RMSP placed orders for a group of steamers in 1850 – by far the largest yet in the fleet – the Admiralty insisted on wooden hulls despite RMSP proposing iron. The corollary of that came, frighteningly, only a day or two into the maiden voyage of the first of them, *Amazon*, when she was consumed by fire. The ship and over a hundred of her people were lost. That disaster was responsible for the Admiralty changing its mind and permitting iron hulls for mail ships.

The vast job of piecing the company together steadily came to fruition. On 26 September 1839 – regarded as the foundation date of the company – RMSP received its Royal Charter of Incorporation. On 20 March 1840 the mail contract was signed. On 22 May 1841 the first ship of the fleet, *Forth*, was launched at Leith and on 3 December 1841 the little schooners *Lee* and *Larne* departed from the *Thames* for placement voyages which were the company's inaugural operations.

What of the Founder?

James Macqueen maintained a pointed lack of interest in ships, even during the years surrounding the genesis of his brainchild. There is an impression that his duties as General Superintendent of Affairs were regarded as an obligation towards kick-starting the company of which he had been the progenitor. Even before there was anything tangible to deal with – during 1838 – he wrote to William Blackwood: 'I have been so plagued with West Indian mail communications that I have never had a moment's leisure'. He nevertheless found time to publish in 1840 an exhaustive study of the land and peoples of Africa, and was also instrumental in the formation of the Colonial Bank (later merged with Barclays DCO).

It is difficult to imagine that Macqueen enjoyed his short period of employment with RMSP. Despite the sweeping title of General Superintendent of Affairs, his principal task was to work out routes and schedules. To this end he spent the better part of a year among the islands and ports which the ships would visit. That happened between December 1840 and about October 1841; Macqueen was then in his sixties, and this task would have been gruelling for a man half his age. So complex was the job that Macqueen was not able to present his schedule to the directors until less than two months before the start of services.

However, once the directors saw it, they had some grave misgivings. There was a feeling that Macqueen's estimates of ship speeds were too generous, especially when factoring in the times when speed would be reduced in adverse conditions, or approaching a port after dark. Part of the blame for that, as mentioned earlier, lay with the Admiralty, whose mail schedule demands were optimistic and intransigent. Ships would visit ports whose approaches were downright dangerous in daylight, let alone in darkness – and that led to the most serious concerns.

A minute of 4 November 1841 read:

The Committee are compelled to state that the navigation of the Bahamas, but particularly of Turk's Island and New Providence, present dangers of the most formidable description. It is true ships of a large size, proceeding with great caution and caring nothing for loss of time, have occasionally visited these places, but such instances offer no criterion by which to judge of the difficulty attending a constant navigation in all seasons around these islands.

They pointed out that soundings were not always possible close to reefs. If you look at a chart of that fractured mass of islands which form the curving line of the Bahamas it is clear that a ship could be in 1,500 to 2,000 fathoms one minute and in two or three fathoms shortly after. 'It would seem almost a miracle,' the report concluded, 'to make 112 voyages each year, through these countless rocks and shoals, without the occurrence of disasters'.

So concerned was RMSP that they immediately made contact with Capt. Beaufort, Hydrographer to the Navy. Beaufort gave it 'as his decided opinion that there was nothing to prevent the Company's ships with proper care from… carrying out the course of operation contemplated by Mr Macqueen'. Two matters were relevant to that. Firstly, within five months of services starting, the Company had lost its first ship, *Medina*, after grounding during a night-time approach to one of the very spots which had so concerned the directors – Turk's Island. Secondly, there was an implication that Macqueen was recommending these routes without qualification. Far from that being the case, Macqueen was the person who first alerted the Company to the dangers. It had been reported on 19 October that

in a conversation with Mr Macqueen the Committee were informed by that gentleman that he [had] always calculated upon the establishment of pilots and lighthouses as forming part of his plan; it does not appear that proper steps have as yet been taken to carry out this most essential part of the undertaking.

The Company strenuously advocated the placement of lights at Turk's Island, Barbados and in the North West Providence Channel, adding that 'leading lights also to the Turk's Island anchorage would be highly beneficial'. They stressed that lighthouses were needed in many locations, and those quoted were just the most urgent.

While all of that was being sorted out, James Macqueen was put to work establishing passenger fare tariffs – and with so many combinations of routes and ports, that, too, was no simple task. It was now one month before the commencement of services – fares were still to be finalised and the directors were still mulling over aspects of Macqueen's schedule, portions of which were so tightly knit that steamers (and their crews) would be expected to operate without a break, and with no buffer for delays, for six months at a time.

Somehow, everything came together in time for the first placement voyages in December 1841. That didn't mean the problems had all been ironed out, as will be seen, but the point was reached where a company in preparation became an operational company – and at that moment there came a need for re-structuring the staff. In essence, the planners were now operators.

Before explaining what happened, we should briefly look at another employee, Capt. Edward Chappell RN. He was appointed in December 1840 as a replacement for Lieutenant Kendall, who had been Macqueen's assistant. From the start there was a difference in status between Kendall and Chappell, for the latter's appointment stemmed from a debacle over construction of the First Fleet (looked at in Volume 2), which was largely caused by the lack of a qualified marine superintendent.

Chappell was therefore appointed as Marine Superintendent, placing him much closer in status to Macqueen. The moment services began, the directors abolished the titles of both men. Chappell was appointed Secretary and Macqueen became Superintendent of the Foreign Agencies. A nineteenth century Secretary was a company's senior employee, the equivalent of today's Chief Executive. Macqueen's new role, on the other hand, eroded his status, for he was now responsible solely for overseas matters. The two positions, in terms of seniority, had been reversed. With the expectation that James Macqueen would now simply handle problems in the Caribbean region, one can't avoid feeling that he was being gently edged out.

Early in 1842 Macqueen was hard at work in his new role. Numerous matters were referred to him and his task now was to effectively re-mould the operation to make it workable. His revised plan was submitted in May and he was then instructed to prepare a further revision, but in collaboration with Capt. Chappell. A small point, perhaps, but now his responsibility was further eroded by effectively working under the guidance of the Secretary.

There was no let-up in the workload as 1842 progressed; rather, the reverse happened as report after report poured in from captains and agents – the nature of the problems involved a mix of unworkable timetables, obstreperous crews, negligent captains and officers, and navigational dangers. James Macqueen, embarking on this new and arduous role at about sixty-four years of age, could hardly be expected to have relished it.

When he resigned in August 1842, the response from the directors was clear. They accepted his resignation without comment and decided that as his duties would now devolve on Capt. Chappell, an assistant would be needed for the Secretary. Of the man whose brainchild RMSP was, whose years of hard work planning, producing and organising had been so crucial to the advent of this great undertaking, there was no word. And when he died in 1870, the demise of the Company's founder was not even acknowledged.

Wreck of Forth *in 1849, one of several units of the first fleet lost that decade. The picture, from Illustrated London News, was based on a sketch made at the scene by Midshipman Alfred Varndell of RMSP's* Dee *(I).*

Possibly this disinterest was mutual – Macqueen's involvement lasted only long enough to see the initial operation click into gear. He then took up the threads of subjects dearer to his heart and continued to write profusely. Glasgow had long since lost him to London, of course and there were addresses at Hammersmith and Kensington, and almost certainly others. Though his lifestyle seemed to stamp him as a die-hard bachelor, he had been married. One report suggests that his wife had been with him for at least part of his time in the Caribbean in 1841; however, an obituary notice in a Glasgow paper recorded the death of his wife Eliza on 18 March 1826. I have found no evidence that he remarried.

In 1851 he produced a significant work on commercial matters: *Statistics of Agriculture, Manufactures and Commerce*. Three years later came a piece with more than a hint of his interest in politics: *The War – Who's to Blame?* Having studied official documents on the Crimean War, he 'proves the folly of England in going to war with Russia' as the *Dictionary of National Biography* put it. In the aftermath of that war he embarked on something quite extraordinary for a man nearly eighty years old. Australia had lost its mail steamer services during the conflict, and immediately afterwards set out to have the service re-instated; the Post Office called for tenders and Macqueen tossed his hat in the ring. His 1830s Plan had included an extension to Australia via Panama, and now he resurrected the idea. The bid was not successful.

The years were now catching up with Macqueen, and so was the financial drain of an octogenarian living on a sparse income. For the only time after his resignation from RMSP, his name appeared in the directors' minutes on 7 August 1861: 'Letter of 30 July from Mr Herapath, submitting the circumstances of Mr Macqueen for consideration. Resolved: £50 to be given'; £50!

His life perhaps became more sedentary, but his mind lost none of its enthusiasm. At the age of eighty-six there was an understandable fluctuation in his health, evidenced by a vivid contrast in writing styles. A short, staccato letter to a member of the Blackwood family (his old friend William Blackwood had by then died) reflects a man of tired mind and tired body. A shaky hand recorded: 'While you are in town I should be glad to have some conversation with you for this purpose I will call upon you at any time place that you may appoint any day early next week [sic]'.

Yet, resilient to the last, in his ninetieth year he addressed to Lord Brougham some 200 column inches of lucid and vigorous open letters, filled with compelling statistics and tables, which were reproduced over a period of several days in a newspaper – probably the *Morning Advertiser*. The subject, I need hardly add, was African slavery. Interestingly, Macqueen and Lord Brougham were both born in 1778 and were therefore around ninety when this literary jousting took place. Both were Scots, Macqueen from Lanarkshire and Brougham from Edinburgh. While Macqueen was one of the earliest contributors to Blackwood's *Edinburgh Magazine*, Lord Brougham played a similar role with the *Edinburgh Review*.

Henry Brougham pursued a successful political career with the Whigs, at one stage being Lord Chancellor and making a name for himself with his support for the Reform Bill. To complete the parallels, both men appear to have been somewhat irascible; Macqueen's writing style is evidence of that, while Lord Brougham in later years lost much of his parliamentary influence through his 'eccentric ways'.

Lord Brougham died later that year while James Macqueen still had a couple of years left to enjoy. He died a month short of his ninety-second birthday. *The Times'* death notices recorded: 'On the 14th May at 10 Hornton Street, Kensington, in the 93rd year of his age, James Macqueen Esq, KC Tower and Sword of Portugal, FRGS. Friends will please accept this intimation'. (The entry was incorrect regarding his age – he had been born in June 1778 and was thus not quite ninety-two.)

News of Macqueen's death reached another great geographer, Sir Roderick Murchison, shortly before he was to address the Royal Geographical Society. He said:

I received the news of the death of that distinguished veteran geographer, my old and respected friend, Mr James Macqueen, who died on the 14th inst. at the very advanced age of 92... During the time he was resident in Grenada, in the West Indies, as manager of a sugar plantation, whilst reading an exciting narrative aloud to a friend one night, he noticed that a negro boy in the room stood listening very attentively, especially to those passages in which the Joliba was mentioned. The boy being asked afterwards why he showed such interest, said that he knew all about the Joliba, and that he was a Mandingo, born in the country of the Upper Niger.

The information gained from this intelligent boy was afterwards of great use to Mr Macqueen, when he was engaged in bringing together all that was known about the geography of the Niger, a subject on which he became a leading authority.

He was the first, I believe, who demonstrated, before the discovery was actually made, that the Niger emptied itself into the Bight of Benin. Subsequently he published, through Mr Arrowsmith, the first map approaching to correctness, of the interior of Africa. He was a trenchant and vigorous writer and a keen critic; but his literary productions were chiefly confined to articles in newspapers and periodicals. Some of his geographical memoirs were read before our own Society and published in the 'Journal'...

Number 10 Hornton Street, Kensington, photographed in the 1960s. This is the address at which James Macqueen died in 1870, though it is unlikely to have been the same building.

As a man of action, he distinguished himself in the projection and organisation of two of the most useful and prosperous chartered companies, the Colonial Bank and the Royal Mail Steam Packet Company. In making the preliminary arrangements for the latter, he visited the various countries embraced in the intended operations and, on his retirement, received the most flattering testimonials from the Company.

His memory and interest in geography and public questions were preserved, in scarcely diminished freshness, almost to the hour of his death, and his last moments were passed in great peacefulness. In him the Society has lost one of its most attached members.

This son of the bleak Lanarkshire hills, who travelled uncountable miles across the oceans, became a newspaper editor, worked his way into influential London circles and gave vent to his feelings so tellingly with pen and ink. A man, who possibly used the Government to subsidise, through its mail contract, a great vision which looked far beyond its immediate parameters; this man, James Macqueen, has been under-rated all these years because he remained half-hidden in the shadow of the very company he created.

Because of his very brief involvement in RMSP after its formation we can only make informed guesses at the extent of his influence, direct and indirect, in Britain's early leadership in steamship commerce. He began with an interest in the West Indian and African colonies; their peoples, economies and trade potential and those interests never wavered and never extended to maritime matters beyond shipping's ability to perform a task.

In that slightly enigmatic way he acted as a catalyst to bring into being one of Britain's biggest and most respected shipping companies.

3
The Caribbean: Cradle of RMSP

During the colonial era, the West Indies formed one of the jewels in the British Crown. Through the colonial hierarchy a particular lifestyle developed, and the climate, the scenery and the appeal of scattered islands in tropic seas gave the West Indies lifestyle a decided advantage over some parts of the Empire. But the jewel grew from something more; from a strategic location and the promise of economic benefits, particularly the production of sugar.

This was where RMSP began its trading story. While the core of *Macqueen's Legacy* deals with South America services, for so long the Company's major routes, it is as well to look first at the regions where RMSP began; where its growth was nurtured before branching out on a long road of expansion.

Though British possessions in the West Indies were the main focus of early services, the two biggest Caribbean islands were *not* British. Cuba and Hispaniola were controlled by Spanish and French influences, and while we are used to Hispaniola being divided into two republics, Haiti and Dominican Republic, when the Company began operations the whole island was controlled by Haiti.

The Caribbean rim was also important, and involved some of the longest voyages outside the transatlantic crossing. The Guyanas, Venezuela, Colombia, the Panama isthmus and around the Gulf of Mexico to ports of the southern United States – these expanded the potential greatly, further enhanced by an extension to New York and Halifax.

The nature of the mail contract prevented RMSP's ships from remaining in port long enough to take great advantage of freight opportunities. Even if time had been of no matter, there were limits to the amount of cargo they could carry because their hulls were well occupied with passenger accommodation, engines and coal. From the time Royal Mail started operating, forty years passed before steamers on long ocean hauls became truly viable as cargo carriers. To gain significant income from freight in the 1840s, the company had to rely on items which were small in size and large in value – specie was the most notable, ships sometimes carrying treasure several times the value of the ship; another item was quicksilver, destined for the Mexican mining industry.

When you consider the magnitude of RMSP's first fleet (and perhaps question whether some of the inter-colonial routes actually needed such large and expensive steamers) it is clear that a mail contract to the value of around a quarter of a million pounds was a necessary incentive to establish and maintain the operation. If the Company had been developed on purely commercial grounds, it would surely have begun with a far more modest fleet.

Why the Caribbean?

Part of the answer was simply the presence of colonial establishments with a constant traffic to and from Britain and Europe. The reasoning, however, went further. With numerous islands, dozens of ports and quite a few nations within its scope, the operation seemed to hold more options than, for example, a North Atlantic schedule where only a handful of ports and two nations would be serviced.

Other regions were not viable because of their lack of development of which South America is an excellent example. RMSP was trading to Brazil and the River Plate after ten years and did so for some decades. However, it was periodically on the borderline of profitability, and on at least one occasion operations were scaled back. The potential was there, but only after 1900 did South America's development surge ahead.

Other colonial regions in the 1840s had the trade potential but were too distant for effective steamer services; India, Australia and New Zealand for instance. The P&O network to those areas required massive investment and a quite astonishing infrastructure – it was clear that steamers would not be economically viable until they were much larger and their coal consumption a great deal less. Even P&O didn't extend its services to Australia until almost a decade after RMSP had begun operating.

With Cunard contracted to service North America, that probably left two major choices for James Macqueen – the Caribbean regions and Africa. While he was intensely interested in Africa, his personal experience was in the West Indies, his many years of involvement with the people who ran the island businesses stemming from his own time managing a sugar plantation, placed him in a fine position to judge the possibilities of steamer services. Thus, when his original ambitious Plan had to be culled to manageable levels, this was the region on which he and those with whom he was negotiating concentrated.

The Routes

The services were laid down in the Mail Contract of 20 March 1840. There were eleven separate schedules, not one of which could suffer delays without influencing others. In the event, though, there were precious few routes which could be completed without delays – that was the knife-edge on which RMSP lived in its early days. The routes were as follows:

1. Transatlantic service:
UK – Barbados – Grenada – Santa Cruz – St Thomas – Nicola Mole – Santiago de Cuba – Port Royal – Savannah la Mar – Havana – Savannah la Mar – Port Royal – Santiago de Cuba – Nicola Mole – Samana – UK.

2. Barbados – Tobago – Georgetown – Berbice – Paramaribo – Berbice – Georgetown – Tobago – Grenada – Barbados.

3. Grenada – St Vincent – St Lucia – Martinique – Dominica – Guadeloupe – Antigua – Montserrat – Nevis – St Kitts – Santa Cruz – Tortola – St Thomas – San

Juan PR – Samana – Curaçao – Puerto Cabello – La Guaira – Trinidad – Grenada.
4. As given for 3, in reverse direction.

5. (Schooner): Curaçao – Santa Martha – Cartagena – Santa Martha – Curaçao.

6. (Schooner): Nicola Mole – Crooked Island – Rum Island – New Providence – Rum Island – Crooked Island – Nicola Mole.

7. Port Royal – Chagres – Cartagena – Santa Martha – Port Royal.

8. (Schooner): Savannah la Mar – Trinidad de Cuba – Belize – Trinidad de Cuba – Savannah la Mar.

9. Havana – Vera Cruz – Tampico – Mobile – Havana.

10. As 9, in reverse direction.

11. Havana – Matanzas – New York – Halifax – New York – Matanzas – Havana.

When services began, two minor changes were made – New Orleans instead of Mobile, and Turk's Island instead of Samana. The latter change was particularly interesting, for it

A number of RMSP ships were chartered for service in the Crimean War. Here, Trent *(I) lies in Malta refitting late in 1854 after a mammoth stint steaming back and forth through the Mediterranean and Black seas.*

left only one port of call on the very large island of Hispaniola – the comparatively minor town of Nicola Mole. To help explain why this island, then entirely controlled by Haiti, had so little involvement, it is worth quoting from the 2001 edition of the Caribbean Islands Handbook:

The Haitians are almost wholly black with a culture that is a unique mixture of African and French influences. Haiti was a French colony until 1804 when, fired by the example of the French Revolution, the black slaves revolted, massacred the French landowners and proclaimed the world's first black republic. Throughout the nineteenth century the Haitians reverted to a primitive way of life, indulging in a succession of bloody, almost tribal wars. Even today, African cults, particularly voodoo, play a large part in everyday life like nowhere else in the Caribbean. The country is desperately poor and the standard of living is the lowest in the Americas.

That state of affairs goes some way to explaining the brief reference in Royal Mail's centenary history to the 'refusal of permission to use Samana Bay as the northern transfer station'.

The other change – New Orleans for Mobile – was made on purely commercial grounds.

Having a schedule of routes was one thing, but maintaining it was another matter. The printed schedule meant little from the moment services started. Ports were omitted because the schedule couldn't be maintained – and sometimes non-scheduled ports were visited in attempts to patch up the problems. The captains (and perhaps the naval officers in charge of the mails) developed ways of overcoming unworkable schedules. A report, for instance, was received from the schooner *Lee* from Turk's Island, which was not an official port of call for any of the sailing ships.

By May 1842, James Macqueen had mapped out a reduced schedule. The directors' recommendations included dropping Halifax and Dutch Guyana altogether, reducing calls at Tampico, Vera Cruz, Cartagena and Chagres (which were among the longest routes) to one voyage per month, and cutting out the visit to Berbice by arranging for its mails to travel overland from Demerara.

Generally, the regions listed became the Company's principal stamping ground for many years. To understand the nations, islands, people and trade idiosyncrasies with which Royal Mail was so irrevocably bound, we have to reach further back in Caribbean history.

The Caribbean's Development

Until Columbus discovered the New World, the spoils of discovery and colonisation, and the subsequent trade benefits, had largely gone Portugal's way, particularly in Africa and Asia. In the opposite direction, their neighbour and great rival, Spain, then made its own discoveries, spearheaded by Columbus, and set about negotiating a pact with Portugal.

In the resulting treaty, an imaginary north-south line was drawn down the Atlantic, '370 leagues west of the Cape Verde Islands'. Portugal was given rights to all unexplored regions east of that line and Spain those to the west. Interestingly, the line passed through the bulge of Brazil, bringing that portion of South America into Portugal's 'territory' and explaining why Spanish is the adopted language throughout South America except for Brazil.

Lithograph of La Plata *(I), which spent almost twenty years in the RMSP fleet from 1852.*

Spanish settlers flooded through the Caribbean regions, discovering the Panama Isthmus, Yucatan Peninsula and more. These people expected to find riches, but most discovered instead that they had to till the land to make a living. However, with the knowledge that there was gold at least on Hispaniola, the Spanish searched endlessly for more, colonising as they went. By 1512 they occupied Cuba, Hispaniola, Jamaica, Puerto Rico and the Panama Isthmus.

Though there had been earlier visits to Cuba by the Spanish, Velásquez founded the first settlements there from 1511 onwards. By 1526 they were importing African slaves and over the next 200 years the island established trades in sugar, coffee and cigars. By the early nineteenth century Cuba had entered a long era of unrest, rebellion, dictatorships, blockades and other mayhem – such was the backdrop to much of Royal Mail's years there, which finally saw an American-influenced autonomy from Spain near the end of the century.

With so much violence going on in Cuba, it seems almost odd to record that the locals were unhappy with the behaviour of Royal Mail crews as early as 1842: 'Forth –… Havana authorities complaining of crew's rowdyism; they want a stone wall built around the depot to keep them in'. Cuba's current 'chapter' began in 1959 with Fidel Castro being installed as dictator, a position he still holds as I write more than forty years later. In a strange parallel with the report from *Forth* quoted above, Royal Mail's freighter *Teviot* loaded cargo at a Cuban port three months after Castro took power. Capt. J.F. Anderson reported that during their first morning at the island 'we were boarded by the Navy'. He opened his cabin door to find what looked like a firing squad awaiting him. A sailor waving a sub-machine gun said 'You will tell all your crew that they will behave themselves'. Cubans, presumably, had exceptionally long memories.

The Caribbean basin became a regular hunting ground for the buccaneers – the likes of Henry Morgan, John Coxon and Bartholomew Sharp had their haunts on the islands. Colony-hungry nations, who didn't take kindly to Spain having one half of the world and Portugal the other, moved in after the pirates. The British, French and Dutch began a tug-of-war with island after island. yet one group of islands managed to avoid the see-saw of occupation, the Bahamas. They were under British rule until gaining independence in the 1970s.

The Bahamas is a particularly fractured line of islands, mostly small and often rocky. The nature of the seabed made shipping vulnerable in the days of inadequate charts – in places the sea plunges to 15,000ft within a mile of the shore. The Bahamas also had precious little to contribute in terms of cargoes. Only in later years, with the advent of refrigeration, did its varied fruit plantations provide support. Early on it was the stability of British settlement and its strategic proximity to the United States which provided its importance.

On the northern coast of the South American mainland, the French, Dutch and English each took up adjacent portions which were collectively known as the Guyanas. They developed agriculture, with sugar ultimately the predominant crop, and later discovered pockets of gold, diamonds and bauxite. However, precious little land could be cultivated – this was forested tropical country with high rainfall pouring out of the rugged Guyana Highlands.

The Guyanas changed ownership periodically as one nation or another dominated, until at last there was a settlement, known as the Peace of Breda, which established the sovereignty of the Guyana lands. Indeed, as part of this settlement, Britain ceded part of Guyana to the Dutch in exchange for New York – an interesting deal.

Things were more settled by the time RMSP came on the scene, and ports in British and Dutch Guyana were included on the first schedules. The lengthy sea passage to the mainland provided precious little return and much the same applied to Venezuela, but for different reasons. Venezuela has a long Caribbean shoreline and, like Guyana, comprises tropical lowland areas nearer the coast and highlands inland. Originally settled by Caribs and Arawaks, the country was taken up by the Spanish, who used native Indians as their labour force for the plantations. A broad shift later saw greater integration of those peoples, with African slaves brought in, but in time there was unrest and a growing demand to oust the Spanish. This reached its climax early in the nineteenth century under the leadership of Caracas-born Simón Bolívar.

Venezuela gained its independence in 1821 and Bolívar enjoyed the fruits of that until his death in 1830 but the cost had been huge – a quarter of the population reportedly died in the struggle and the country lay in ruins. So, again, RMSP could expect, only two decades later, to gain little trade from a nation just beginning to haul itself back into shape – yet Puerto Cabello and La Guaira were ports of call on two separate routes.

Throughout the Caribbean, in the wake of each new wave of conquerors and settlers came shipload after shipload of slaves from Africa. The agricultural industries for which the islands were so well suited began to flourish. Sugar plantations in particular had a stamp of richness, due in great part to negligible labour costs through the use of slaves. Laws to abolish slavery, at least in British possessions, came in the early 1830s, shortly before RMSP was born, and would have had an immediate impact on the economies of the islands. At much the same time, spiralling development began in other regions, not least British interests in Africa, India, Canada, Australia and New Zealand. Then came

Eagle *was purchased in 1846 to operate Caribbean intercolonial services.*

improvements in shipping technology – ships of larger capacity and, in 1881, the triple expansion engine which was the point of progress at which steamers became economically viable as long-distance cargo carriers. That decade also saw the first tentative steps in the development of refrigerated cargo equipment in ships.

Thus during RMSP's first half century great changes affected the West Indies and, consequently, Royal Mail. The Caribbean was at an immediate disadvantage in dealing with the increasing competition it then faced – a large scattering of islands had difficulty in accumulating enough produce to be financially rewarding, while shipping companies like RMSP (especially as mail subsidies were whittled away, leaving the firm increasingly reliant on freight for profits) were faced with voyages from island to island to pick up small parcels at each.

It was during this period, and into the 1890s, that RMSP reports regularly alluded to the ongoing economic woes of the West Indies. In 1903 the annual report referred to 'the action taken by the Colonial Office, in conjunction with the Imperial Department of Agriculture, for the development of the industries of the West Indies, which it is hoped will help to restore these Colonies to their former prosperity'.

South America, meanwhile, for all its woes of war and seasonal fevers, was developing its trade, commerce and industry significantly.

This look at the Caribbean's development has been brief and selective, but sufficient to provide an inkling of RMSP's ambitious task – operating a huge mileage in order to link innumerable small islands and nations. The later advances in South America, coupled with the decline in Caribbean fortunes, brought about the shift in emphasis by the company and found South America taking over as the premier region.

Parker's View

Declining fortunes in the Caribbean formed such an important factor in the evolution of RMSP's operations that it is worth briefly looking at the last years of West Indies mail and passenger services. Capt. Walter H. Parker commanded ships in the Caribbean region from 1907 – these are some of his observations:

It is no exaggeration to say that there can hardly be an anchorage from Demerara and Trinidad, along the Spanish Main, up the Mosquito Coast, across to Jamaica, Santo Domingo, Porto Rico, the Virgin Islands, the Leeward and Windward Islands, that the steamers of the RMSP Co have not served regularly or, as required, at some time or another.

The cargo steamers took out and brought home full cargoes and were economically run – but I have often been told they did not pay. There was certainly a lot of steaming about for small parcels of cargo, on which the freight was not high. There was as much trouble given to the ship's people, and cheerfully taken by them, over the humble little shipments by the small native planters of two, four, or any small number of bags – each lot under their own marks and numbers – as there would be with a large shipment.

We had to make out the manifests on board during the passage home, and it can be understood how irritating it was sometimes to have to fill a whole sheet of the manifest with different marks, the whole only totalling perhaps less than a hundred packages. Without a doubt, the Company served the West Indies faithfully and well for over 80 years, and there must be many who sadly regret the discontinuance of the old West Indian Packet service to and from England, since the Great War.

In 1907, however, we in the ships could not – and it is questionable if anyone else could – foresee this happening for, at that time, the British West Indies was still the domain of the RMSP Co. We were identified as practically part and parcel of those Colonies...

On my first voyage to the Antilles – confirmed since by many subsequent ones – I found that, at last, and unexpectedly, I had truly reached the nebulous dream seas of my boyhood's imagination: entrancing tropical islands in smiling waters, glorious coconut palms swaying in the salt-laden breeze of the north-east trades that tempers the heat of the sun, and carries the sweet scent of vegetation far to leeward...

My ship's business... took me to the various agents and, once ashore, I was often able to make a day of it, driving out in somebody's gig to lunch or dine at their plantation houses. I enjoyed their open, if simple, hospitality; nobody was extremely wealthy, some, in fact, the reverse! Many of these old plantation houses bore unmistakable traces of the former opulence of the English families who settled there two hundred years before – now, alas, finding it a hard struggle to make ends meet...

In a walk or drive about the countryside, one may be arrested in some lovely spot by the sight of a pair of handsomely carved stone gateposts, bearing the traces of a family crest, now obliterated by weather and moss. Somewhere near, no doubt swallowed up in a jungle of small undergrowth, is hidden the ruined foundations of a one-time handsome mansion – long ago the residence of the owner of a prosperous sugar estate surrounding it, now fallen on evil days, and reputed amongst the negroes to be infested by duppies [ghosts]...

Two early commanders. Left: Capt. James Tolman Moir, who went to sea at the age of eighteen and joined RMSP as second officer of Thames *(I) in January 1852, at the age of thirty-two. His first command was* Tay *in 1855 and he subsequently commanded more than a dozen ships before retiring in 1880.*
Right*: Lt. Charles Matthew Chapman, who joined the Royal Navy at the age of thirteen and served in many ships while rising from the rank of volunteer midshipman to lieutenant. He also served as Agent for Transports in* Redpole, Lord Cochrane, Amity *and* Horatio *before joining RMSP in December 1841 as one of its original captains. His first command was* Actaeon *and he was subsequently in charge of* Forth, Great Western, Tay, Orinoco *(I) and* Severn *(I).*

> *With the exception of the Company's own offices in the principal ports, all our agents in the numerous outports, combined with their offices that of general merchants and storekeepers. The office was usually only a railed-in enclosure in a corner of the retail shop, wherein the population could buy nearly anything they required. Rope, canvas, cloth, dress material, ironmongery, oil, paints, provisions of all sorts, even to confectionery.*

It isn't difficult to divine that Capt. Parker was captivated by the West Indies. Emerging just as strongly from his words, though, is a reflection of the steady decline. At the time when the first 'A' ships and many smaller vessels were sailing six or eight to the month to Brazil and the River Plate, the West Indies lost its mail service. The trigger was the First World War and its aftermath, when Britain's Government decided it could no longer afford to subsidise expensive mail services to this scattered region of islands, and Royal Mail could not afford to operate mail and passenger ships without a subsidy.

Ironically, the two finest mail ships ever built for the service – *Essequibo* and *Ebro* – had been completed at the start of the war. *Essequibo* operated for less than a year, and *Ebro* for a single voyage, before they were taken up for war service. They did not resume the mail service. There were spasmodic passenger sailings during and immediately after the war with smaller ships, but by 1919 even that was in trouble.

The 1919 annual report stated:

> *The contract for a mail and passenger service between the United Kingdom and the West Indies...having terminated, the Company has been providing, without subsidy, sailings of passenger vessels of smaller and more economical character than those previously employed. Since these sailings were established, advances in the price of coal have been imposed by Government Control, resulting in considerable losses being incurred, even by these small vessels. Unless relief in this respect can be secured it may be necessary to discontinue passenger sailings to the West Indies, a course which the Court of Directors would take with great regret.*

Conditions did not improve and RMSP's passenger line services to the West Indies closed with the arrival home of a small chartered ship in the autumn of 1920. As long as Royal Mail continued to exist, the West Indies always saw the Company's houseflag – but it flew from freighters mostly, and from cruise liners once or twice a year.

4
South America – the Early Years

The Royal Mail Steam Packet Company had been established a dozen years, and its ships operating for a decade, before the first significant expansion took place. For the first time its ships crossed the equator and sailed the South Atlantic to the east coast of South America.

From that statement it may be thought that RMSP took that long to overcome its early problems in the Caribbean regions before contemplating expansion, but that wasn't so. In August 1840 the Admiralty invited the company to tender for a mail service to Brazil and the River Plate. RMSP was anxious to do so and the Chairman, John Irving MP, and James Macqueen talked the matter over with the Chancellor of the Exchequer. He, however, was more circumspect than the Lords of the Admiralty; while the Chancellor liked the idea, branding a Brazil and River Plate service based on 'a junction with our West India line…the most economical and in all respects the most eligible' means of operating the service, he nevertheless decided that 'in the present state of our financial and political affairs, its adoption now might be inconvenient'.

In 1844 the Company proposed an extension of West Indies services to Brazil, but the Admiralty declined. The matter was resurrected in 1848, this time with a Government initiative for a direct England-South America steam mail service. RMSP's tender was the lowest, but then the Government delayed signing the contract. At the core of that was parliamentary concern over the cost of mail contracts, which resulted in long-winded investigations into the South America proposals and a complete review of the current West Indies contract. These hurdles were not cleared until the 1850s.

The new mail contract for South America was signed in July 1850, and in preparation for the new service a tiny schooner with auxiliary screw propulsion became the first vessel selected to take part. RMSP had taken her over during construction in Scotland in 1849 (with the proposed name of *Regulus*) to replace the schooner *Lee*, which had been lost. She was completed as *Esk*. Her initial movements were almost certainly operating local Caribbean services.

During the early years of the South America run, ships operating the transatlantic service ended their passage at Rio de Janeiro. For the smaller amount of business further south, a connecting steamer plied from Rio to Montevideo and Buenos Aires. That was the job assigned to *Esk*. Even by mid-nineteenth century standards she was small for such a long passage – only 231 gross tons. With a saloon little bigger than a cabin on a present-day cruise liner (indeed, the whole hull would have fitted into the restaurant in the last *Andes*) she nonetheless carried six hardy passengers from England to Brazil on her placement voyage. She was equipped to carry twenty-nine passengers as well as cargo and mails.

References to endless problems in the River Plate caused by shallow water and the silting of shipping channels pepper these pages. As late as the 1960s, the Company's ships were known to drag across silt banks from time to time. When *Esk* pioneered the service, matters were so bad that even this tiny ship could not get close to shore. The daunting prospect for arriving passengers was a transfer to an even smaller steamer some seven miles from Buenos Aires, then transferring again after five miles to a whaleboat. This brought them close to the shore for the final transfer to a horse-drawn cart.

Esk sailed from Southampton in November 1850 but carried no mails. The honour of inaugurating the mail service went to *Teviot*, which left the Hampshire port with forty-five passengers on 9 January 1851. *Teviot* was by then almost ten years old and the Company decided it was a good time to implement one of the Admiralty's clauses, advocating the use of technical advances. Thus before she left Southampton she was fitted with new 'patent feathered paddle floats', and was also given new boilers.

The South America service slipped smoothly into a routine of one steamer per month, *Teviot* being followed by *Tay* in February and *Medway* in March. There was an interesting appraisal of those early days in the report of directors that April: 'It would be premature to hazard any conjecture at so early a period, as to what may prove the eventual advantages to be derived from this portion of the service, but it is sufficient to state that the prospects so far are of an encouraging character'. It is easy to smile at a phrase like 'an encouraging character' for a service which, for so many years, would be Royal Mail's pre-eminent operation. So soon after its launch, though, there was uncertainty about the potential.

STEAM COMMUNICATION with the BRAZILS and RIVER PLATE.—ROYAL MAIL STEAM-PACKET COMPANY.—On the 9th January, 1851, the "Teviot," Captain Revett, and thenceforward on the 9th of each month, one or other of this Company's Steamers, will leave Southampton, with Mails, Passengers, &c., for Madeira, Teneriffe, St. Vincent (Cape de Verds), Pernambuco, Bahia, and Rio de Janeiro, and from thence by branch steamer to Monte Video and Buenos Ayres, returning by the same route to Southampton.

Particulars, as to rates of fares, freights, &c., may be had on application at the Company's Offices in London, or at Southampton, where parcels, packages, and publications will be received for the places above mentioned.

Goods taken on moderate freight outward to Rio de Janeiro, and homeward from the same place, as well as from Pernambuco, St Vincent (Cape de Verds), Teneriffe, and Madeira.

Passengers are recommended to make early application for securing proper berths.

E. CHAPPELL, Secretary, No. 55, Moorgate-street, London.

The first advertisement publicising the advent of RMSP's service to South America. It appeared in Illustrated London News *at the beginning of 1851.*

The supplemental Royal Charter dated 29 August 1851 which authorised RMSP to expand its region of operations. This related to the introduction of the service to South America, which had begun under a new mail contract earlier in the year.

The immediate success of the service was due to the confidence with which passengers and freight shippers embraced it, and that factor shouldn't be taken for granted. The travelling public and freight shippers had to place their trust in a ship operator, often with no knowledge of the ship and its management. How well was the ship constructed? What was the standard of accommodation? Was the machinery reliable and effective? And in management – were the captain and officers competent and diligent? Were the provisions of good quality and quantity? Was all of that supported by the best of modern technology?

This was not academic hypothesis. Passengers had good reason to be suspicious, for countless migrants were at sea on their way to new lives, and the ships in which they travelled were in too many cases barely seaworthy or were appallingly run. Cargo carriers could get away with much worse – leaky ships, incompetent crews, drunken skippers, potentially disastrous cost-cutting measures and the like. Rumour has it that some of the timber ships crossing the Atlantic were held together by judiciously wrapping anchor chains around the hull!

Therefore, if a company's credentials were guaranteed by no lesser means than the strict demands of an Admiralty mail contract, its ships would be viewed with confidence. In that lies the core reason why RMSP's South America service was able to immediately flourish and operate from the start with few hiccups.

For such an early era of ocean steam navigation, the achievements during the first five years were astonishing. Up to 31 December 1855 there was scarcely a single late arrival at Southampton. That proud record was pre-empted by the pioneering outward passage of *Teviot*. A Rio de Janeiro newspaper announced her arrival, pointing out that RMSP had:

> *announced that the voyage from Southampton would be made in the short space of 28 days and 19 hours, and in accordance with this announcement the* Teviot *would arrive yesterday at 1 p.m. Large was the number of incredulous people, and in the city everyone consulted his watch with a sardonic smile. But at the hour indicated the telegraph hoisted the signal for an English steamer, and one hour afterwards, with almost mathematical exactitude, the* Teviot *entered this port...*

Teviot, at the end of her third Brazil voyage, in fact steamed into her home port six days early.

There was immediate prosperity from the new association with Latin America, with a steady climb in passenger and freight receipts during the first year. The value of specie carried outward from June to November 1851 reflected the trend: £35,000, £47,090, £88,000, £73,000, £115,000, £232,000. In today's terms those figures are astronomical. The November figure, for example, exceeded four times the value of the ship carrying it. They were mostly investment infusions supporting economic development in South America, in which British business was heavily involved. Nearly £200,000 from the November figure was gold contributed by British business houses towards the foundation of a commercial bank in Rio de Janeiro.

General cargo from England, mainly manufactured goods, rose in similar proportion and by the autumn of 1851 the hulls (limited in their capacity) were filled and cargo was at times shut out. Homeward, the ships carried gold and silver (usually in smallish quantities), diamonds (often to the value of £20,000 or £30,000), coffee, ipecacuana, grapes, lemons, tomatoes, oranges, tapioca and a wide variety of other produce. How the likes of grapes and tomatoes were carried wasn't recorded – presumably picked well before ripening, they may have been packed in sawdust, a method adopted later with ships from Australia.

At first the number of passengers on southbound voyages were quite small, usually between thirty and seventy, but it picked up steadily. During 1855 some totals approached 200 – close to the limit for those small ships. From the start, homeward lists were better, usually a hundred or more making the voyage, of whom a considerable number disembarked at Lisbon – all classes from ambassadors to deported slave-traders.

In this age of phone, fax and e-mail we have to remember that in the 1850s it was the mail steamers which once a month brought news of events across the ocean; world affairs reached the ears of the public in this leisurely way, weeks later. 'Intelligence Reports' from early voyages told of the short war in which the popular Brazilian leader Dom Pedro II crushed Argentina's Juan Manuel de Rosas – an outcome favoured by Britain since it was a blockade of Asunción by Rosas in 1845 which prompted Britain and France to mount a three-year blockade of Buenos Aires. A war with Paraguay also ended in Brazil's favour. The results of those conflicts were encouraging for the prospects of trade development.

No. 4.

1858

ROYAL MAIL

STEAM PACKET COMPANY.

UNDER CONTRACT WITH HER MAJESTY'S GOVERNMENT.

Brazil and River Plate Route.

OFFICES:

55 MOORGATE STREET, LONDON,

R. T. REEP, *Secretary.*

CANUTE ROAD, SOUTHAMPTON,

CAPT. W. VINCENT, *Superintend*

Office Hours, from 10 a.m. till 4 p.m.

FOREIGN AGENCIES:

PARIS	F. REDFERN, Esq., 8 Rue de la Paix.
HAVRE	Messrs. DAVIDSON & Co.
HAMBURG	E. HUNDEIKER, Esq.
OPORTO	W. A. TAIT, Esq.
ANTWERP	B. KENNEDY, Esq.
COPENHAGEN	Messrs. FIEDLER & Co.
LISBON	A. VAN ZELLER, Esq.
CAPE DE VERDS	Messrs. VISGER & MILLERS.
PERNAMBUCO	Messrs. ADAMSON, HOWIE, & Co.
BAHIA	Messrs. WILSON, SCOTT, & Co.
RIO DE JANEIRO	J. J. C. WESTWOOD, Esq., H.B.M. Consul.
MONTE VIDEO	F. SUSINI, Esq.
BUENOS AYRES	A. ROBINSON, Esq.

ONE of the Company's Steam Ships is appointed by Her Majesty's Government to leave Southampton at 2 p.m. on the 9th of each month (unless it should be a Sunday, and then on the following day), with Mails for LISBON, CAPE DE VERDS, PERNAMBUCO, BAHIA, RIO JANEIRO, MONTE VIDEO, and BUENOS AYRES.

Passengers, Specie, and Parcels are booked at the Company's Office, 55 Moorgate Street, London. At Southampton, Passengers are booked by Mr. J. T. DUFFELL, and Specie, Goods, &c., by Mr. F. A. COLLIER, the Company's Cargo Superintendent.

First page of the RMSP Brazil and River Plate Handbook, 1858.

Of the ships which inaugurated the Brazil service, *Medway* was the first to leave, being switched to the West Indies route after two voyages. Her place was taken by *Severn*, and with *Teviot* and Tay she maintained the service with splendid regularity. After the near farcical scheduling of West Indies voyages in the early 1840s (looked at in Volume 2), important lessons had been learned, though South Atlantic crossings had less potential for scheduling problems than the intricate Caribbean network.

On the ninth of every month (delayed twenty-four hours if it was a Sunday) a ship left Southampton; two months and a few days later her bows were seen once more on the horizon, with several days often lopped from the schedule. It was as well for the company that those early years were free from disaster, for seven ships in less than a decade had been lost on Caribbean routes. One of the few teething troubles concerned the time in South American ports – calls were not long enough to reply to arriving correspondence before the ship sailed. So with *Teviot's* 9 July 1851 departure a revised timetable was introduced. Prior to this, outward voyages to Rio de Janeiro took 28 days 19 hours; this was now increased to 29 days 5 hours. Homeward voyage times were extended to 31 days 8 hours.

The extra two days northbound were accounted for by prevailing currents and north-east trade winds, which assisted southbound passages. From the frequently early arrivals at Southampton, though, it can be deduced that the South Atlantic is often a docile stretch of ocean, much favoured in later years by follow-the-sun round-voyagers escaping the English winter.

By reducing time at Madeira by six hours, Tenerife by two and St Vincent (a coaling port) by twelve, the time at Pernambuco, southbound, was raised from six to eighteen hours and Bahia from six to twenty-four hours. On homeward passages, six hours at Bahia became sixteen and six at Pernambuco twenty-one, with a resultant drop at St Vincent from thirty-six hours to twenty-four and at Madeira from twelve to six. An increased stay at Rio de Janeiro was sanctioned, from three days twenty-two hours to six days nine hours. Thus from a Southampton departure on the ninth of the month, a ship would arrive at Rio de Janeiro at 11 p.m. on the eighth of the following month. The homeward arrival at Southampton was put back from the twelfth to the sixteenth.

The new itinerary allowed for twelve hours of daylight at each port on the South American coast. Whatever time of day the vessel arrived, she was not to leave until the statutory twelve hours of daylight had elapsed unless she was anchored by 8 a.m., in which case they could depart the same evening provided mail and passenger business was completed.

The ships coaled at Rio de Janeiro, and captains were instructed to sail at 8 a.m. on the thirty-sixth day after leaving Southampton. If the connecting steamer hadn't arrived from the River Plate, the transatlantic steamer waited up to eight days. After that – connecting steamer or no – she was to depart. The connecting steamer, too, had her schedule amended, allowing a longer stay in Montevideo.

The specifics of those schedule changes have been given to indicate how precise was the timekeeping – and if delays occurred, RMSP was subject to penalty payments.

New Ships

When services to South America began, little new tonnage had entered the fleet. In 1851 the first major construction programme began with five large barque-rigged steamers being built. They incorporated several developments from the original fourteen, as one would expect at a period of rapid technological change. They were a thousand tons larger, had greater coal capacity and passenger accommodation and more powerful engines. The West Indies routes were of much more significance than South America, and so these new 'flagships' were intended for the West Indies transatlantic service – yet they were all were named after South American rivers: *Orinoco, Amazon, Magdalena, Parana* and *Demerara*.

In next to no time this quintet of steamers was almost halved. *Amazon* was lost by fire early in her maiden voyage and *Demerara* didn't even reach that stage – she stranded in the River *Avon* while being towed to the Clyde to have her engines installed and was so badly damaged that she never entered Royal Mail's service. At the time of *Demerara's* launching at William Patterson's Bristol shipyard, a newspaper pointed out that she was second only in size to the world's largest ship, *Great Britain*. The *Great Britain* came from Patterson also, as did her smaller consort on the North Atlantic, *Great Western*. When *Great Britain* stranded in the 1840s, her owners could not afford repairs, and this led to the demise of the company with *Great Western* being put up for sale – that was how she entered the RMSP fleet.

Of the three surviving new-builds, *Magdalena* and *Parana* in time switched to the South America service and made many voyages across the South Atlantic. All three were used as troop transports during the Crimean War, with no significant ordnance for support – a surprising state of affairs considering the lengths the Admiralty went to have them strengthened for carrying heavy armaments.

The scene near Falmouth, Cornwall at the beginning of February 1852 when a portion of the wreckage of Amazon *(I) drifted ashore. The ship had sunk a month before after catching fire off Ushant early in her maiden voyage.*

Before *Magdalena* and *Parana* joined the South America service, other vessels were used to replace some of the original fleet. The first was *Great Western*; then came *Solent*, perhaps the most handsome of the Company's paddle steamers. She was built at White's yard at Cowes on the Isle of Wight.

Of her launching, the *Illustrated London News* wrote: 'The launch of the Solent, from the circumstance of her being the largest steamship constructed at the port of Cowes, appears to have excited more than ordinary interest. The town and more immediate neighbourhood had every appearance of a country fair'. Possibly it wasn't just the ship which 'excited more than ordinary interest', for the lady invited to launch her was the daughter of Manuel de Rosas, the former tyrant dictator of Buenos Aires, who spent a quarter of a century, in exile farming quietly near Southampton until his death. How Manuelita de Roxas y Tivierro came to be invited to grace the occasion is not recorded – it hardly seemed the height of diplomacy.

As for the 2,230-ton *Solent*, it is curious that she appeared sleeker than her consorts, for there was little difference between them. Apart from slightly finer lines, one of her best features was the paddle box design, resembling a rising sun motif with the Royal crown at its centre. Even the directors, in their usually staid annual report, in October 1853, called her 'a new and beautiful vessel'. More down to earth was their assessment of her frugal fuel consumption, allowing her to steam 3,622 miles without coaling. At the time that was a critical matter, for there had recently been such a massive increase in the world's steamer fleets that coal prices had gone through the roof. John Scott Russell was at that time building mail steamers for the Australia run; he placed great emphasis on reducing coal consumption (which worked better in theory than in practice) 'because,' he said, 'fuel has risen to famine price'.

Until now RMSP had used Welsh coal exclusively, but in 1853 it made a block purchase of 10,000 tons from the United States, to ensure the continuation of all services. By 1854 and 1855 matters were even worse, for in addition to the natural shortage it was now almost impossible to charter colliers as they were supplying the steamers involved with the Crimean War. The cost of coal freightage rose accordingly, exacerbated by increased insurance premiums because of the wartime conditions. The war made matters difficult for RMSP in other ways, as it had to cover the temporary loss of ships taken up for trooping duties – they included *Orinoco, Medway, Severn, Trent, Tamar, Magdalena* and *Avon*, while *Parana* and *Thames* carried French troops to the Black Sea.

The Jellicoe Years

Solent left Southampton on 11 February 1855 for her first voyage to Brazil. She was commanded by Capt. J.H. Jellicoe, whose first transatlantic mail ship command this was. Born at Southampton in February 1825, Jellicoe was appointed a midshipman in the first fleet, leaving his home town on board *Clyde* for her maiden voyage in December 1841. He couldn't have joined the Company much earlier, for the first departure had been that of *Forth*, just twenty-four hours earlier.

John Henry Jellicoe received his second class Master's Certificate at the Portsmouth branch of Trinity House on 12 February 1846 – the day after his twenty-first birthday and little more than four years after embarking as a midshipman. He had his first class certificate a year later. When he first joined *Clyde*, incidentally, he had already been at sea for four and a half years, three as midshipman in *Duke of Bedford* followed by a year and a half as 4th officer of *Lady Flora*.

The scene for a very long career with Royal Mail was set during his time in *Clyde*, under Capt. Symons – his career card was filled with reports from Symons like: 'Jellicoe – midshipman: If it meets the approbation of the directors, I would solicit his appointment as 3rd, he having performed the duty most satisfactorily for some time', and 'An excellent second officer. Conduct most satisfactory'. Not one report was in any way critical of him, and a listing in 1886 – when Jellicoe had been a commander for thirty-five years – gave him an 'A' rating, indicating that while a vessel under his command had been aground or in collision, he was not held to blame. I can find only one such instance, when *Moselle* was involved in a minor collision – at a time when such occurrences were almost a weekly happening, his was a superb record.

His first two commands were *Prince* and *Esk* in 1851 and 1852, the ships which pioneered the connecting service between Rio de Janeiro and the River Plate. Following Jellicoe's promotion to command *Solent*, his sea-going career included a dozen further commands. Those years were split by an interlude when he was shore-based as the Company's Superintendent at Southampton, from late 1869 to January 1872. At that point he resigned the position, saying he 'wished to go afloat again', a decision in part caused by a decline in his health (though I suspect the sea was too strongly in his veins for him to be happy ashore).

In time he was appointed Senior Captain – the term Commodore did not come into official use until Owen Philipps became chairman, but it was used as a courtesy title throughout, and he was allowed to fly the 'Commodore's flag', a swallow-tail houseflag rather than the standard rectangular one. That appointment came in 1882, for that February the incumbent Senior Captain, Richard Revett, notified the Court that he would retire at the end of the current voyage.

Capt. Richard Revett. He went to sea at the age of fourteen and joined RMSP in September 1842 as second officer of Forth. *After six months he was promoted to first officer of the same ship and soon gained his first command. He held command of fifteen RMSP ships over a period of more than thirty years, the last four years as master of* Medway *(II), from which he retired in April 1882 at the age of sixty-six. He was Senior Captain from 1868 until his retirement, and in 1883 was elected a director, a post he held until shortly before his death in 1896.*

In February 1892 Capt. Jellicoe retired, receiving a gratuity of £1,000, his final command being *Para*. Biographical accounts generally credit Jellicoe with no less than seventy-three years of service with RMSP (or, to be precise, seventy-two years and nine months), for he was still serving the firm as a director at the time of his death on 7 September 1914, at the age of eighty-nine. For the sake of accuracy it should be mentioned that from his retirement in 1892 he had no official connections with the Company until elected as a director in May 1896.

However, this didn't mean he wasn't in touch. From time to time the Court discussed communications from him with suggestions for this and that, while in 1893 he was granted a free round-voyage to the West Indies 'for the sake of his health'. The irrepressible old salt had his appetite whetted by that, for on his return he enquired whether he could return to service afloat. The response was a diplomatic 'suitable letter to be sent, declining'. Does it not seem unfair that such a man should generally be remembered just as the father of Admiral of the Fleet, Earl Jellicoe of Scapa?

Information Handbook 1858

The RMSP Handbook dated August 1858 contained a detailed account of the operational mechanics of the Brazil and River Plate services:

Fares: Saloon passenger fares included the use of bedding and linen, steward's fees and all other charges except for wine, spirits, malt liquors and mineral waters.

From Southampton to	After Lower Deck and all main Deck Cabins		Lower Deck Fore Cabins	
	Single each berth	Double	Single each berth	Double
St Vincent	£45	£30	£35	£25
Pernambuco	£50	£35	£45	£30
Bahia	£52	£37	£47	£32
Rio de Janeiro	£60	£45	£50	£35
Montevideo	£70	£55	£60	£45
Buenos Aires	£70	£55	£60	£45

Northbound fares for the transatlantic crossing were uniformly £5 higher than for southbound. While such a difference had been logical earlier, because extra voyage time was scheduled northbound to cater for the often absent adverse winds and tides, the schedules for each direction were now practically identical.

Second class:

'A limited number of artisans, emigrants &c, to be victualled and accommodated on the same footing as the ship's crew, finding their own hammocks and bedding, will be conveyed, when there is room for them, from Southampton to the Brazils for £20 each, and from Lisbon to the Brazils for £15 each. By payment of £5 additional, passengers of this class are provided with bunks and bedding, and are allowed to mess on the Warrant Officers' scale.'

Intermediate first class seems to have been employed for Peninsula passengers, with fares to be paid in silver dollars 'or their equivalent in other coin'.

Deck passengers:

Only troops, common sailors, labourers, or others not superior to those classes of society, to be conveyed as deck passengers. To find their own provisions and bedding, and not admitted abaft the chimney. To pay one-fourth the cabin fare; and only to be conveyed intermediately. The fare, however, for deck passengers between Buenos Aires and Montevideo to be four silver dollars each way'.

A long list of passenger regulations included the following:

1) Passengers were not allowed to bring alcohol on board, 'an ample stock thereof being provided on board, at moderate prices.'
2) Although ladies may have sleeping berths allotted to them in the Ladies' Saloon, 'it is to be open for the use of all the ladies on board between 9 a.m. and 9 p.m. every day'.
3) Passengers making the transatlantic crossing were able to break their voyage at an intermediate port of call.
4) Transatlantic passengers are always to have priority of choice of cabins over intermediate passengers, whether previously booked or not.'

That 'privilege', as it was described, had potential problems. Firstly, the stopover was a specific one-month period (i.e. until the next ship arrived). When they boarded the new ship, they 'must be content with inferior accommodation, if there should be none vacant similar to that originally engaged'. And if the ship had no accommodation at all, they waited for the next one which did.

Children of cabin passengers were charged as follows: under three – free. Between three and under eight – quarter fare 'and four such children to be entitled to one berth'. Eight years to under 12 – half fare, and two to a berth. Dogs were charged at one-eighth of their owners' fares.

Passengers showing symptoms of infectious disease at the time of embarkation were refused passage, but if symptoms appeared during the voyage, they were disembarked at the first port of call, at their own expense. When recovered, they could board the next RMSP steamer to resume their journey.

The Woolward Years

With a view to speeding up the mail service, calls at Tenerife and Madeira ceased with the May 1858 departure of *Tamar*. The time scheduled from Southampton to Rio de Janeiro was now 26 days 6 hours; homeward (by now realising that winds and currents made little difference) it was actually one hour less. The itinerary was now:

Port	Arrive	Depart
Southampton	9th, 6 p.m.	
Lisbon	13th, 1 p.m.	14th, 8 a.m.
St Vincent	21st, 4 a.m.	22nd, 4 p.m.
Pernambuco	29th, 4 p.m.	30th, 8 a.m.
Bahia	2nd, 3 a.m.	2nd, 8 p.m.
Rio de Janeiro	5th, midnight	9th, 8 a.m.
Bahia	12th, noon	13th, noon
Pernambuco	15th, 7 a.m.	15th, 6 p.m.
St Vincent	22nd, 6 p.m.	24th, 6 a.m.
Lisbon	1st, 2 a.m.	1st, 6 p.m.
Southampton	5th, 1 p.m.	

By returning to Southampton four days before the next departure, there was time for mail recipients to provide answers for immediate despatch.

Capt. Robert Woolward. Embarking on a seagoing career at the age of fourteen, he spent most of his apprenticeship in Joseph Somes' East India armed transport La Belle Alliance. *He joined RMSP as fourth officer of* Tweed *in October 1844, aged eighteen, and progressed rapidly to be appointed master of* Medway (I) *in May 1853 (though he had already temporarily commanded* Great Western *after her master had died from yellow fever). Including* Great Western *he commanded fourteen ships, the last being* Atrato (II), *and he was Senior Captain for the last two years until retirement in 1894.*

The branch steamer's round voyage was now: Depart Rio de Janeiro 4 p.m. on the 8th; Montevideo arrive noon 13th/ depart 4 p.m. 14th; Buenos Aires arrive 6 a.m. 15th/ depart 4 p.m. 28th; Montevideo arrive 6 a.m. 29th/ depart noon 1st; Rio de Janeiro arrive 8 a.m. 6th.

Screw propulsion made its debut on the Brazil transatlantic route in June 1859 in the shape of the 2,253-ton *Tasmanian*. She made only one further voyage to Brazil, in January 1868. Her place, after the 1859 voyage, was taken by *Oneida*, which had been purchased a year earlier as RMSP's first large screw steamer. *Oneida* and *Tasmanian* came into the fleet through the Company's involvement in the failed European and Australian Royal Mail Co, whose story is told in Volume 2.

The first Brazil voyage by one of the remaining 1851 quins, *Magdalena*, occurred in March 1860. She made twenty round voyages across the South Atlantic, all but one under the command of Capt. Robert Woolward. The voyage not taken by Woolward was in the hands of Capt. Thomas Sawyer, who should have taken the ill-fated maiden voyage of *Amazon* at the beginning of 1852. At the last minute he had been replaced by William Symons whose exemplary leadership in that horrific affair, in which he and many others were lost with the ship, drew much admiration.

Robert Woolward (Capt. Jellicoe's successor as Senior Captain) was thoughtful enough to put his reminiscences in print. Of his switch from the West Indies station he wrote:

I first sailed in the Magdalena *on 9 March 1860…This was a new experience for me, as hitherto my service had been mostly in the West Indies. I did not get on very well at first, as the people did not like me and I did not like them. I had never been used to such dirty people, and it took me some time, and a good deal of scolding, before I could get them into anything like tune.*

It also took considerable space in the local newspapers to publish the abuse lavished on me. However I stuck to it, and before I left the [Brazil] line I was reputed to be as much of an angel as I had been reckoned a devil to commence with.

Early in my coming on the line, I took out HRH the Duc de Nemours and his son, Comte d'Eu, who was to marry the Princess Imperial of Brazil. On arrival at Rio de Janeiro, I had the honour of being introduced to His Majesty, Pedro II, the Emperor, and Her Majesty the Empress. I found out that the Empress was very fond of rhubarb tart, so whenever I was in Rio I had a large one made on board and sent to the Palace; in return I received, on the morning of sailing, a large cake with the Brazilian arms and colours on it. HRH the Comte d'Eu also presented me with a black pearl scarf-pin when he was leaving the ship.

These honours seemed to cause a turn of tide in my favour and I grew more popular. After the marriage the Comte and Comtesse d'Eu visited Europe and took their passage in the Magdalena all the way to Southampton. Having landed them safely, I was a made man in the opinion of the Brazilians, and was no longer abused in the newspapers.

Magdalena's last voyage began at Southampton on 9 December 1864. Of the return leg, Woolward wrote:

We had very bad weather in the Bay of Biscay, and I again had fears of the ship going down with us, as she worked so much she drew the starboard discharge pipe away from the ship's side, and every time she rolled it under, vast quantities of water poured in.

When we arrived at Southampton, I told the superintendent I should not go to sea in her again, as she was not safe. He said, – "My dear fellow, we shall send someone else". I answered, "All right sir, you are the resident manager, and when the ship has gone down, I shall be left to give evidence that the ship was unseaworthy!". She did not go to sea again; instead she was sold to the shipbreaker near Vauxhall Bridge, and broken up.'

She was actually sold between June and December 1865. Capt. Woolward perhaps took a little too much credit for ending *Magdalena's* career, though he was no doubt a major influence. An Admiralty surveyor took a careful look at her, in dry dock, before that final voyage. They passed her for one voyage. When that was over Woolward made his uncompromising comments; the Post Office then ordered a further survey 'before allowing her to proceed on another voyage to Brazil'. Her spot was taken for a couple of voyages by *La Plata*, before *Rhone* and *Douro* entered service – clearly *Magdalena* failed the survey.

On 9 October 1865, still on the Brazil run, Capt. Woolward took command of *Rhone* for her maiden voyage.

The change from the old style of ship to the new was much the same as one would experience if, having been in the habit of riding a cart-horse you were all of a sudden put on the top of a racer. The Rhone *was to all intents and purposes a steam-yacht fitted with every modern improvement and convenience, and I was very proud of being her commander. She was not too successful on her first voyage as we were much troubled with hot bearings, and could not run at the top speed. Nevertheless we had a much faster passage than usual, and the passengers were so pleased they presented me with a valuable pair of diamond solitaire earrings for my wife to wear.*

Woolward added that *Rhone* possessed the first surface condenser seen in Brazil, which so intrigued the Brazilian Emperor that he came aboard to examine it, apparently quite at ease in *Rhone's* engine room while Capt. Woolward was close to fainting with the heat. That was when the Emperor arranged for Woolward – now such a familiar face at Rio – to be presented with Brazil's prestigious Order of the Rose.

During 1866 *Rhone* travelled through severe weather as she headed out into the Atlantic. 'I am sorry to say,' Capt. Woolward wrote to his employers from Lisbon, 'the two lifeboats on the port side and the cutter were lost, the starboard cutter and mail boat damaged, the rails and deck furniture much injured, two horses killed, and one of the crew had his leg broken. I have never before experienced such a gale…' This, believe it or not, was welcome news in Britain. Other ships were passed during the storm and signals exchanged. One, to a ship on her way to England, reported the loss of the boats, but in the confusion it was interpreted by the other ship as the loss of four people; by the time the story had circulated, the number of people lost stood at sixteen. Small wonder that Woolward's letter from Lisbon was a relief.

After taking the January 1867 Brazil sailing, *Rhone* was transferred to the West Indies route. This was no surprise, for she was a fine ship and the West Indies was very much the premier route. Woolward was transferred from her, which almost certainly prevented a premature death, for *Rhone* and many of her people were lost later the same year in a hurricane at St Thomas.

In April 1869 Woolward returned to the Brazil route in command of *Rhone's* sister ship *Douro*, and soon got himself in a spot of bother when he broke Company's regulations by leaving scuttles open at night in hot weather. One cabin was occupied by a Portuguese family with a number of children. While they were sleeping a flying fish managed to launch itself expertly through the open scuttle, landing among the children and 'floundering about'. The terrified children, not knowing what was going on, began screaming.

> *The neighbouring people rushed out to see what was the matter and, not being able to find out, started screaming also, and the ship got into a terrible state of commotion…The passengers in general had become fully persuaded that, at least, the ship was on fire, if not sinking. I have never known a greater scare in a ship than that one.*

On the return passage he had as passengers the Duke of Saxe and his family; one of the sons was, by all accounts, a little devil, allowed to throw whatever he wished overboard and generally leaving a trail of devastation. When they reached Portugal the ship was placed in quarantine because of fever in Brazil; nevertheless the King of Portugal came on board to visit the Brazilian Royal passengers. When he was about to leave, Capt. Woolward stopped him with the news that he couldn't leave because the ship was in quarantine!

The king had previously travelled under Woolward's command, and they had known each other years before as midshipmen in the British Royal Navy. In spite of that, it seems the King was not amused, and promptly arranged for the port Health Officer to release the ship from quarantine.

RMSP was the choice of many illustrious travellers; passenger lists were peppered with barons, counts, ministers, peers, princes and princesses. Capt. Jellicoe, in *Tamar*, hosted Prince Augustus of Saxe-Coburg Gotha for a voyage to South America in 1859, while Woolward brought His Highness Prince Hohenzollern from Lisbon in *Magdalena* two years later. Also in 1861 *Oneida*, under Capt. Bevis, carried their Royal Highnesses the Duke of Oporto and the Duc d'Rega. These are but a fragment of the higher echelon of the clientele. Rarely, though, was there reference to the third class migrant European families heading for a new life in South America – but they contributed hugely to the Company's success.

5
Chaos Amid Consolidation

After 1863 mail contracts no longer concerned the Admiralty. On 13 July that year the first RMSP contract was signed with the Postmaster General, for the carriage of mails once a month to Brazil and the River Plate. The contract was for seven years, starting 1 January 1864, with a subsidy of £33,500. After four years it was extended until the end of 1874, following which – reflecting a worldwide trend – the subsidy was withdrawn and payments were made on a poundage basis.

The recollections of Capt. Woolward have already drawn attention to *Rhone* and *Douro*. The maiden voyages of both ships were to Brazil, *Douro* leaving Southampton on 10 July 1865 and *Rhone* on 9 October. *Rhone*, in particular, was a handsome craft; though they were officially sister ships, *Rhone* appeared to possess slightly finer lines (they did come from different builders).

Another vessel which entered the South America service at this time was the 2,404-ton paddle steamer *La Plata*, which had been laid down for Cunard Line. Royal Mail bought her prior to completion to replace the lost *Amazon*. *La Plata* made her first Brazil voyage in 1865, after thirteen years on West Indies routes. Her service then fluctuated between the two until she was handed over to Denny Bros in December 1871 – valued at £7,600 – in part payment for the new *Boyne*. Having commenced her South America service in 1865, *La Plata* did not join the Brazil route in 1866, when, for the first time, screw ships were used exclusively for a full year – it didn't happen again until 1872. On almost every ocean route paddle propulsion was outmoded long before that – it was, for RMSP, a mirror of the conservatism which haunted so much of its world in the second half of the nineteenth century.

Douro left Southampton on 9 October 1869 to inaugurate a through service from Southampton to the River Plate. This was a crucial development, for in time the River Plate – particularly the meat trade – played a pivotal role in keeping the service profitable. Oddly, there is uncertainty as to why the through service began at this time. It was influenced by the operations of a French competitor, Messageries Imperiales, but was it RMSP's response to MI inaugurating a similar service or a move in co-operation with them? The Company's annual report for 1869 refers to the matter only in terms of 'the existing competition', but there are a couple of (slightly enigmatic) items in the directors' minutes suggesting there was more to it:

On 16 June: 'The Post Office objects to the new arrangement for the Brazil and River Plate service as the French vessel will not be due at Bordeaux early enough'.
And on 14 July: 'Capt. Wilson to go to Paris to endeavour to arrange with the Messageries Imperiales authorities as to the timetable of arrivals for sailings for the through service to and from the River Plate'.

Deck scene on an RMSP steamer. The painting is undated but is most likely from the 1870s.

The most likely scenario is that MI planned a through service and RMSP, through the Post Office, decided to match the competition and at the same time attempted to negotiate a mutually beneficial timetable to ensure that the voyages of the two companies were compatible. The new arrangement provided for a round-voyage of two months and a few days – almost exactly the same as a voyage to Rio de Janeiro and back had taken fifteen years earlier.

That inaugural voyage by *Douro* was taken by Capt. Woolward, who wrote:

> We were very well received at Buenos Aires and a public dinner was given to mark the occasion. We sat down at seven o'clock, and at two the next morning the doctor of the Douro and myself left the table, but we were the first to do so. I can't say when the talking came to an end, but I was told it went on some time longer.

As a mail service, that route was to last exactly a century, for the last voyage, by *Aragon*, occurred in 1969.

The years of the Brazil mail service up to 1869 were times of quite astonishing regularity – only once did the monthly departure fail to take place either on the allotted day or within a day or so of the scheduled sailing. The hiccup involved *Thames* in December 1854, whose departure was cancelled because the ship was requisitioned at short notice as a troop transport for the Crimean War. The directors were less than pleased at being given so little notice that a replacement ship could not be arranged. The first they knew of it was a letter from the Comptroller of Transport Service dated 11 November, and before the end of the month *Thames* was at Toulon embarking French troops.

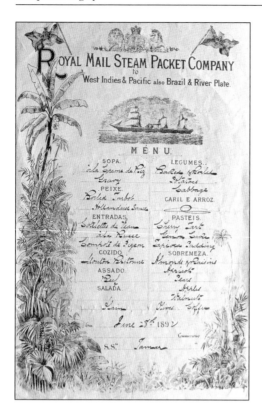

An 1892 menu from Tamar *(II), in Spanish. The labour-intensive nature of that era is reflected in the fact that every menu for every meal had to be hand written.*

The Legacy of PNZA

Hot on the heels of *Douro*'s pioneering voyage to the Plate came the first hint of expansion on the South Atlantic, though it was a one-off event and, on the face of it, quite mystifying. On 22 November 1869 a vessel named *Rakaia* left Southampton and called at Lisbon, St Vincent, Pernambuco, Bahia, Rio de Janeiro, St Thomas and New York, returning to Southampton on 20 March 1870. No reason for that itinerary was quoted. However, *Rakaia* and her consorts *Ruahine* and *Kaikoura* entered the RMSP fleet a few years later, renamed *Ebro*, *Tiber* and *Liffey*. Their presence in the fleet was an immensely convoluted story, and the surrounding events were arguably the trigger which set RMSP on a downward spiral during the decades that followed, leading to the 'new era' at the hands of Owen Philipps.

Rakaia's one-off voyage in 1869/70 was probably a speculation by the managers to test the viability of a long, triangular, cargo-only voyage, using a ship for which no more permanent employment could yet be contemplated. Of greater significance was the opposition shown towards the Company's involvement in the Panama, New Zealand & Australian Royal Mail Company (PNZA), which owned those three ships, by the directors James Mathieson and John Greenwood. During the 1860s both had frequently objected to Company initiatives and this was the matter which brought things to a head – both directors resigned because of it.

The story began innocuously in 1866 when PNZA, a new company, gained the UK-Australia mail contract, operating for the first time via Panama. RMSP was heavily involved from the start, for it provided the England-Panama portion of the service while the PNZA ships operated the Pacific half after a land crossing of the Panama isthmus.

Within a year the service was showing signs of trouble – Royal Mail provided a hefty loan and from that point on became inextricably bound up in PNZA's affairs. That was the matter which concerned directors Mathieson and Greenwood. The three PNZA ships were used as security for RMSP's financial injections and thus entered the Company's fleet when PNZA collapsed a year or two later. It was a remarkably similar tale to the manner in which *Oneida* and *Tasmanian* had been acquired some years earlier.

In its early decades RMSP seemed to be operating from an enviable position. The initial massive funding, the unprecedented magnitude of the first fleet, the possession of mail contracts and a Royal Charter, the apparently bottomless pocket for new-buildings and improvements, all things that must have given rise to a degree of complacency. In the 1860s and 1870s shipping was becoming more competitive and by the 1880s it was an entire new world, with steamer companies springing up almost weekly. Soon there were too many ships for the volume of trade, with the larger and more efficient among sailing ships still able, with their smaller overheads, to corner significant portions of the freight markets.

On the deck of Moselle, *departing Southampton in 1888.*

In such conditions a company had to be constantly alert, aggressive in its pursuit of increased business to ensure continuing prosperity – whether by increasing its share of existing business, opening new routes or making its fleet more efficient and more attractive to passengers and freight shippers. RMSP's failure to do this during the latter decades of the century was the core reason for its decline towards 1900. During this the period spanning 1870 the first signs of that malaise could be seen. Until this time the company's enviable starting position had propelled the company ; developments were largely within the parameters of the original framework, the only significant exception being the inauguration of the South America service.

Now, through PNZA, there were signs that the directors realised they had to diversify. While the general mood seemed to be to gain a new arm to the business by entering the Australia trade, Mathieson and Greenwood took a seemingly ultra-conservative stance by opposing every move of the expansion. We will probably never discover whether that was the case, or if they alone could see that this operation wouldn't succeed.

However, the directors would have taken stock when PNZA collapsed – with the words of warning from their former colleagues ringing in their ears. Never again through the remainder of the nineteenth century did RMSP attempt to enter the Australian trade or, indeed, attempt any major expansion beyond a short-lived Brazil-Caribbean-New York operation. For that reason the PNZA affair was crucial in establishing policies which, over time, weakened the Company's position, particularly with the progressive reduction in mail subsidies placing more emphasis on commercial success.

New Ships, New Services – New Problems

One modest development at that period occurred because of the three PNZA ships. Royal Mail would rather not have had them, but now they were here, how should they be used? The answer was to introduce a 'B' route to South America, thus doubling the frequency of sailings.

The new service began in August 1872 with *Ebro*, under Capt. G.E. Parkes. Departing from Southampton, she called at Cherbourg, Lisbon, St Vincent, Rio de Janeiro, Montevideo and Buenos Aires. The return itinerary was the same until Lisbon, but then Cherbourg was omitted, allowing a direct return to Southampton before proceeding to Antwerp for a four-day stay to discharge cargo; then she returned to Southampton and had approximately three weeks before the next voyage. *Tiber* and *Liffey* followed her, at first departing on the twenty-first of the month, but soon moving back to the twenty-fourth. That placed their departures precisely mid-way between the front-line mail steamers.

The flexibility provided by the second service quickly became evident, with experiments being made with different European ports. One, for instance, called at Antwerp outwards instead of Cherbourg; *Tiber*, on her second voyage, called at Bremerhaven and Hamburg home instead of Antwerp. In February 1873 *Ebro* substituted Santander for Cherbourg outwards. While she was there a rope from the tug fouled the propeller – the boatswain was lowered from the deck to unravel the mess, for which the grateful directors in London gave him a £10 'thankyou'. It was to be expected on a South America service that ports in northern Spain would be tried – Santander, Vigo and Coruña. From those experimental beginnings Vigo in time became established as a permanent call, though at first Coruña was officially substituted for Cherbourg.

Ebro's fouled propeller seemed to presage a long period of accidents and incidents. Three months further on *Tiber* collided with the schooner *Humility* at Antwerp, and a year later *Liffey* stranded on rocks at Point José Ignacio (between Rio de Janeiro and Montevideo) and was lost – Capt. Donne and Chief Officer Parkin were called on to resign. This first serious accident to a South America service ship was followed by further troubles, showing how much shipping was still at the mercy of wind, weather and fate. The accidents through this period were not in themselves out of the ordinary for the time; rather, they highlighted the unusually accident-free years enjoyed previously. *Boyne*, a fine screw steamer, grounded and broke up near Brest in August 1875 on her way home from Brazil. In much the same vicinity *Douro*, on her 62nd voyage, sank after colliding with the Spanish ship *Yrurac Bat* and there was much loss of life.

During 1878 two vessels were acquired from China Transpacific Co, the 2,900-ton *Vancouver* (renamed *Tamar*) and *Vasco da Gama* (renamed *Trent*). Both entered the South America service, the first voyage of *Trent* starting on 27 December 1878 and calling at Cherbourg, Carril, Vigo, St Vincent, Montevideo and Buenos Aires, and visiting Bahia on the return passage. It was a voyage which added to the Company's woes – near St Vincent the engines failed and she had to accept a tow from Allan Line's *Manitoban*; at Bahia the bunker coals caught fire; and at Antwerp she suffered another fire.

At this time the Company's Superintendent at Rio de Janeiro, Capt. May, advocated running a cargo line from Brazil to New York. The Company didn't reject the idea, but it was shelved for some time. After further agitation from several quarters it finally began in 1884, bringing into effect the trial itinerary made by *Rakaia* over fourteen years earlier. One of the first to embark on this long schedule was *Dart*, an intermediate steamer of about 2,600 tons which made her maiden voyage to Brazil in 1883 and her second to the West Indies. Returning to Brazil for her third voyage, with the St Thomas/New York extension added, she struck a reef off the South American coast and broke up.

Worse was to come. *Humber* took the December 1884 departure for the same route, travelling to Brazil, Barbados, St Thomas and New York. She left New York on 15 February 1885 and two days later was spoken to by the steamer *Amerique*. She was never heard of again. Five months later the Brazil/New York sailing was taken by *Guadiana*, which grounded on the Abrolhos Rocks, off Brazil, and was lost. That was the last straw for this apparently jinxed service – after July 1885 the service ended.

The next year, following a more conventional South America schedule, *Tagus* went ashore between Rio de Janeiro and Bahia – this time, after jettisoning cargo, she was refloated.

This difficult period (and the West Indies ships weren't exempt from problems, either) was compounded by a long period in which the scourge of yellow fever in Brazil sapped even more resources. The Company's centenary history considered this the major reason for declining fortunes by the turn of the century, on the basis that many extra ships had to be used to operate a complex series of schedules. While other factors already referred to probably influenced RMSP's wellbeing as much, there is no doubt that the 'fever season' joined that other epidemic of the period – ship losses and damage – in setting the Company back on its heels. From 1878 a constant re-arrangement of sailings coped with quarantine needs, beginning an almost mesmerising variety of itineraries. They began with the introduction of a third monthly sailing. Departures on the ninth and twenty-fourth of the month called at Brazilian ports only, while on the twenty-seventh (later put back to the thirtieth) a vessel sailed direct to the River Plate. The clockwork regularity of past operations had ended. On occasion the separate River Plate trips were withdrawn or delayed as conditions changed.

One alteration introduced an entirely new schedule, starting in November 1880. On the seventh a ship left for the River Plate and called at Brazilian ports on the way home. Two days later another left for Brazil only, and on 24 November a third followed the same route as the first. After eight months of that schedule, yellow fever quarantine (which was seasonal) was temporarily lifted and RMSP reverted to the standard two ships per month for all ports.

A temporary increase in trade prompted a fourth monthly departure from November 1881: now they were on the first of the month to Brazil and River Plate; the ninth and twenty-fourth to Brazil only and the twenty-seventh to River Plate only, the latter journey operating spasmodically until 1883. An innovation during this confusing period was the inclusion of London as a loading and discharging port – a modest introduction to the Port of London, with Southampton still very much the fleet's home port. The calls were discontinued after a few years, then re-instated permanently for cargo ships early in the twentieth century.

Out of this rash of schedule changes (which must have caused havoc among ship programmers and passenger offices), the South America services in August 1885 emerged with exactly the same schedule as the one prior to those seven chaotic years of change. There were departures from Southampton on the ninth and twenty-fourth of each month, calling at Brazilian ports both south and northbound, and the River Plate.

An extra burden at the time was an alarming depression in South American trade. The economic downturn was underscored by the kind of unrest characteristic of the continent in the nineteenth century. A long and debilitating conflict saw Paraguay pitched against the triple alliance of Brazil, Uruguay and Argentina. By 1880 trade was also affected by a war between Chile and Peru, while the economic effects of the War of the Triple Alliance had not ended a decade after fighting had stopped.

So seriously was all of this regarded that the Chairman, the Rt Hon Hugh Childers MP, travelled throughout the West Indies, Panama and Spanish Main regions with a view to attracting new business. As a result, in April 1880 shareholders were told of 'the advisability of increasing the service in the West Indies, should it turn out that the service to the River Plate was not as remunerative as had been anticipated'. The directors opted to 'withdraw some of their ships from the South American route, with a view to their employment in the West Indies'.

The company was in a dilemma. They knew only too well how enormous the potential of this vast land was and yet it was being stifled by wars, revolutions and pestilence to the point at which it would have been tempting to withdraw from the region. When we look at the huge growth of RMSP's services to South America almost from the moment Owen Philipps came on the scene, we are apt to give the new chairman all of the credit. Indeed, much of it belonged with him, but he was dealing with a South America which was then sailing through calmer and more productive waters. Before the First World War it was not unusual for RMSP to be sending eight or ten ships a month across the South Atlantic.

The 1890s – The Woes Continue

In 1890 yet another change was introduced when *Tagus* opened a new route to the River Plate, starting the voyage at Rotterdam and sailing via London and Southampton. From that point until the introduction of the 'A' ships from 1905, the South America services could either be described kindly as complex or less kindly as haphazard. Matters weren't helped by a series of events around 1890 – Portugal adopted anti-British attitudes, for instance, and its people refused to travel in British ships. Specie shipments to Buenos Aires were hit by a high Argentinian premium on gold, and to top things off a revolution was in progress in Brazil.

In a minor change, two sailings a month became fortnightly. Then, for a number of years, the schedules seemed to make little sense. Extra departures were added randomly, apparently scheduled at the last minute when sufficient passengers or cargo were forthcoming. On several occasions two ships left Southampton on the same afternoon, one sailing direct to the River Plate and calling at Brazilian ports northbound and the second to Brazil only – that situation, at least, was explained by yellow fever in Brazil, but further sailings bore signs of unplanned timing and routing.

This sequence suggests that in this new era of competitive shipping the directors had insufficient knowledge of their markets and therefore no strategic plan; instead there

'Selling the pool tickets' on the poop deck of Moselle, *during a transatlantic voyage in 1888.*

was dissention among the directors and the ad hoc nature of operations should hardly be flattered with the term 'flexibility'. To have ships at hand for extra voyages at a moment's notice was an expensive way of operating. The fleet, by 1895, comprised twenty-nine ships; perhaps more telling was that, in a Company renowned as one of the major passenger and mail lines in Britain, the average gross tonnage was 2,771, and the largest were less than 6,000.

At the start of this story a comparison was made between the early fleets of RMSP, P&O and Cunard. Royal Mail at that stage was the front-runner. Now P&O was ordering up to half a dozen newbuildings a year, the largest over 7,000 tons. Cunard, with shorter voyage times, did not require so many ships, but in terms of size they were now streaking ahead, newbuildings by the 1880s and 1890s all exceeding 7,000 tons and some approaching 13,000. Comparisons among such different trades shouldn't be taken solely at face value, but the difference was so marked that it does in part reflect the state of RMSP.

While a broad range of steamers serviced South America in the 1890s, the degree to which RMSP lagged behind was emphasised with the regular use still of the *Elbe* of 1869 and *Tagus* of 1871. Old they may have been, but there were few more reliable workhorses for the Company and both exceeded 100 voyages. *Elbe* had been RMSP's first compound-engined ship, and she was the last unit in the fleet to use square rig. On the afternoon of 3 November 1892 those two grand veterans left Southampton for South America within an hour of each other, *Elbe* on her ninetieth voyage and *Tagus* on her ninety-first. *Tagus* eventually left the fleet in 1897 but *Elbe* remained beyond the turn of the century.

Trent and *Tamar*, acquired second-hand in 1878, and *La Plata*, also second-hand when purchased in 1882, were also becoming a bit long in the tooth. The newest, as the 1890s began, were *Magdalena*, *Clyde* and *Thames*. Many people regard them as the most handsome ships Royal Mail ever owned. With their clipper bows, fine counter sterns, three raked masts and two slim, raked funnels, they have been nominated as being among the most beautiful merchant steamships ever built. It is a curious paradox that such exceptionally fine ships should also have been an indictment against the directors in the very matter which has been under discussion, being tempted by tradition and conservatism to return to outmoded design characteristics.

Another vessel from that group, *Atrato*, was more often seen in the West Indies but her maiden voyage was to South America, leaving Southampton on the afternoon of 17 January 1889 and calling at Carril, Vigo, Lisbon, Pernambuco, Maceio, Bahia, Rio de Janeiro, Santos, Montevideo and Buenos Aires. In addition to mails, a large number of passengers and a full cargo, *Atrato* had on board £120,000 in sovereigns for discharge 'optionally at Rio or the River Plate' (curiously off-handed), £400 in bar silver and jewellery valued at £2,000.

Her transfer to West Indies routes has brought varied explanations – that she was built for West Indies routes and made one South America voyage 'for operational reasons' or that she was to have been used permanently to South America but on her maiden voyage took yellow fever on board and was thereafter switched to the Caribbean. There *was* sickness on board at Rio, but neither story can be correct, for she made at least five more

Magdalena (II), one of the best-looking steamers ever built. The photo is undated but was taken in the decade prior to the First World War.

trips to South America before her transfer. She returned for the occasional later passage south of the equator, including the last departure of the old century – that was a voyage originally allocated to *Thames*, then *Nile*, but both were withdrawn. Why *Thames* was withdrawn is not known, but *Nile* was taken up by the Admiralty for 27/6 per gross ton per month for trooping service in the Boer War. *Atrato's* transfer from the River Plate route coincided with the start of a new West Indies mail contract which required a 1 knot speed increase over previous arrangements. She may have been selected for her superior speed over one of the existing ships on the service.

Nile and *Danube* were sister ships built in 1893 for the Brazil and River Plate service. That period provided the first clear indication that South America services were gaining an ascendency over West Indies routes – at last South America was starting to display its potential. *Nile's* maiden voyage to Buenos Aires began on 19 October 1893. The graceful appearance of *Thames* and her sisters was partly gone; in its place were the beginnings of the 'liner look' which reached its classic form in the 'A' ships of the next two decades.

In 1896, services were supplemented by three new, smaller cargo ships. *La Plata* – third Royal Mail ship to bear the name – left for Santos in August, and two months later Capt. Coff took *Minho* from Southampton on her maiden voyage. Her ports of call were extraordinarily numerous: Coruña, Leixões, Vigo, Villagarcia, Las Palmas, Pernambuco, Maceio, Bahia, Ilia Grande, Rio de Janeiro, Santos, Montevideo, Buenos Aires, Montevideo, Santos, Rio de Janeiro, Bahia, Maceio, Pernambuco, Las Palmas, Lisbon, Southampton, Antwerp and Southampton again, berthing finally at the Hampshire port at lunchtime on 12 January 1897.

Maceio, incidentally, had been a thorn in RMSP's side for some time, for with a decline in mail contracts from the Post Office, the Company gained contracts with South American Governments for the carriage of their mails northbound. The local government at Maceio approved a contract but was so reluctant to pay that RMSP would withdraw the call; when some arrears were paid and a plea came to resume calls, the merry-go-round began again. Given that situation, it is a mystery why Maceio was persevered with for so long in addition to the larger city of Recife (Pernambuco) little more than a hundred miles along the coast.

The final ships of significance built in the nineteenth century were *Tagus* and *Trent*, 5,500-ton steamers built at Glasgow by Robert Napier in 1899. Their designed service, however, was to the West Indies.

Thus did RMSP see out the nineteenth century. There was no great energy evident to welcome the new one; one century, it seemed, simply slid into the next. If things seemed quiet, however, what was happening behind the scenes represented the most crucial events in the Company's history.

They were matters which began in earnest in the 1890s and were not resolved until the 1930s. By 1932, Royal Mail had changed out of recognition. Because the events of those decades were so important, they are looked at in isolation, before resuming the South American service story.

6
The Kylsant Years:
An Overview of the Years 1903-1931

Twice during this span of years there were matters which threatened Royal Mail's very existence. At the centre of the first – in 1902/3 – was a little-known shipping man, Owen Philipps. At the centre of the second, some three decades later, was Baron Kylsant of Carmarthen, the most powerful man in the world of shipping.

The fact that we are talking of the same man in both instances suggests that those years were perhaps the most remarkable for any shipping company. They began with RMSP in disarray, seriously in threat of being absorbed and dismembered, rose to a peak as it became the largest shipping combine in the world and ended in far greater disarray than had been the case thirty years earlier. This, then, is the story surrounding a rags-to-riches shipping tycoon; a corporate highflier whose career came to an ignoble end at the Old Bailey.

Owen Cosby Philipps was born on 25 March 1863 at Warminster in Wiltshire, the third son among five sons and five daughters of Sir James Philipps, twelfth baronet, vicar of Warminster and later prependary of Salisbury Cathedral. Though the family lived in southern England, its origins were in South Wales and there was evidence that they had been prominent since Norman times, even that their descent could be traced back to Maximus, Emperor of Rome. Owen Philipps felt his Welsh links strongly enough to make his home there in later years.

Despite such a seemingly illustrious history, by the middle of the nineteenth century the family had little to show for it but the title. There was no monetary inheritance and so Owen embarked on a career as an £80-a-year shipping clerk with the Newcastle shipowners Dent & Co. Six years later – still as a clerk – he moved to a shipowner in Glasgow; then in 1888 he was ready to branch out on his own. It was a path trodden by many a nineteenth-century shipowner, but most had been in earlier years when sailing ships were still king. By 1888 there was a strong tendency towards larger steamship companies – the role for a fledgling shipowner was now that much harder.

Philipps' initial venture was a company started with his elder brother John; the firm of Philipps & Philipps bought its first ship and began the operation of King Line, which in much later years became part of the British & Commonwealth group. John Wynford Philipps should be introduced here, for his influence was very significant. In time he was knighted and later became the first Viscount St Davids; it was his money which formed much of the finance for King Line.

Late in the century John Philipps gained increasing influence in financial and business circles. An early success was to sort out problems connected with the bankers Baring

Brothers. Then he turned his attention to railway companies in South and Central America. After revitalising the railways of Costa Rica he was appointed chairman of the Buenos Aires and Pacific Railway, a poorly-run line with barely 400 miles of track and deplorable finances. Under the hand of John Philipps the company was expanded to a 2,500-mile network which included the Argentine portion of the Transandean railway, arguably the most spectacular rail journey in the world.

His appointment as chairman of BA & P came at the turn of the century – it was thus in the years immediately preceding his brother's appointment to the helm of RMSP that John Philipps gained great influence in South America. In the meantime Owen Philipps was cementing his place in the shipping world, first in Glasgow and then London. He founded the London Maritime Investment Co. and was its chairman; by 1898 he was chairman also of London & Thameshaven Oil Wharves.

The year 1902 was important for Philipps. Still something of an unknown quantity to many, he made the move to base himself in London. It was the year, also, in which he married, his wife Mai being the daughter and co-heiress of Thomas Morris from Coomb, Carmarthenshire. And on the last day of the year – at the very last minute – his name appeared on the list of candidates for two vacancies on RMSP's Court of Directors.

RMSP's head office for many years, 18 Moorgate Street, London. Note the Royal coat of arms carved above the entrance.

RMSP on the Brink

By 1902 RMSP was flowing with the tide; such initiative as there was largely comprised catch-up measures against the progress of competitors. How different that was from the first decade or two. Now, phrases like 'not desirable' and 'not considered practicable' peppered the Court minutes. In 1895, for instance, a submission to provide 'artifical ventilation' for the carriage of fruit from Jamaica was 'not considered practicable'. Before long Sir Alfred Jones (Elder Dempster Line) did just that and gained enough inroads into the trade through his Elders & Fyffes company to become one of the biggest threats to RMSP's future in the Caribbean.

The next year saw a more specific proposal to fit refrigerated space in *Atrato* for bananas; it was termed 'not desirable'. In 1897 there was an offer (at a time when line voyages were often not profitable) to make three Norwegian cruises with *Elbe*: 'Not to be sent'.

It must be said that RMSP faced increasingly tough times in terms of its mail contracts, for the Government was hell-bent on reducing the subsidy as much as it could, while rival German, French and Italian lines were heavily subsidised. That volatile politician Joseph Chamberlain (father of Neville) was a particular thorn in the Company's side, even attempting to persuade RMSP to move its West Indies headquarters from Barbados to Trinidad (which it eventually did a few years later).

Thus was the backdrop for a crisis which deepened as 1902 progressed. Receipts were down and costs were rising and voyage after voyage returned a deficit. In May the Company's cash flow reached a point where one director implored that voyage accounts should be provided at the earliest possible moment – implying that a thousand pounds either way on a voyage could be crucial. That same month, the vacating of office bearers did not take its normal, pre-ordained course. There was much discussion before the Chairman was re-elected.

A Special Court was convened for 9 June to discuss a takeover bid from Sir Christopher Furness. Given the parlous state of RMSP, the directors, feeling powerless to overcome the difficulties, recommended the takeover. It would, of course, have been left to the shareholders to make the final decision, but in the mood of the day it would probably have been approved. As it was, Sir Christopher disagreed with one of RMSP's figures in its list of assets, which the Company placed at £1,920,322. Of that, the majority (£1,528,364) was the estimated value of the ships and was based on a depreciation of 5% per year. Sir Christopher felt it should be 4%. RMSP stuck to its guns, claiming 5% as more realistic. Sir Christopher then attended the Court and 'handed in a letter'.

The contents of the letter are not known, but it spelt an abrupt end to the deal. Two unexplained factors stem from that. Firstly, if a shipowner was serious about a takeover, why would he abort the deal at the first sign of a hurdle, apparently without any negotiation on the disputed 1% depreciation? Secondly, if Sir Christopher believed 4% was more appropriate, he was being offered the company at a lower price with the depreciation being calculated at 5%. Thus if the minutes are to be believed, there was no business rationale in the developments. Did Sir Christopher Furness, then, really want to buy the Company? Or was this the start of a carefully-planned takeover of a different kind? The bid (coupled with rumours that Sir Alfred Jones of Elder Dempster was making moves to acquire all RMSP's interests in the West Indies trade) had the effect of destabilising RMSP's Court of Directors. Before the end of the year one director had resigned, the Chairman had resigned both as Chairman and as a director and the Deputy Chairman had resigned that position, and not long afterwards resigned his directorship too.

There were, then, initially two vacant directorships. The intrigue was made greater with the knowledge that the Chairman who resigned at this time, Admiral Chatfield, had recently had discussions with the influential John Philipps, and those discussions were a major talking point at a later meeting at which the Court resolved to seek two new directors.

A brief glance at Admiral Chatfield helps explain some of what was happening. Born near Salisbury in 1831, the son of a Church of England vicar, he entered the Royal Navy as a teenager and served for more than half a century. He commanded HMS *Amethyst* at the Ashanti War in 1873 and HMS *Thunderer* in the Mediterranean. He saw service also in the Crimea, Baltic, Caribbean and North American sectors. During the 1880s he was Superintendent of HM Dockyard at Pembroke. A man whose entire career – however illustrious – had been as an officer in the Navy, and without experience in the private sector, was appointed a director of Royal Mail in 1891, and in 1898 became Chairman at the very time when the Company desperately needed a leader with a sound commercial background.

The meeting to elect the new directors was set for 7 January 1903. In the two months prior to this a steady stream of candidates was registered. Owen Philipps was not among them. One of the candidates was C.F. Tufnell, believed to have been a son of Thomas Tufnell who had been chairman during the lean years from 1893 until his death five years later. Another contender was Wilhelm Lund, a shipowner whose Blue Anchor Line operated in the Australian trade. Neither was successful.

At the very last moment, on 31 December, Owen Philipps announced his candidacy for each of the vacant positions. The timing appears to have been significant, for this young man of thirty-nine would hardly have been the choice of the directors and he thus lobbied and manoeuvred in the background to gain shareholder support, leaving his nominations to the last minute in order to minimise the chance of a counter-offensive.

The volatile meeting on 7 January was mostly taken up with shareholders expressing their displeasure. One had been a shareholder for thirty years and 'gets nothing' (a reference to the recent lack of dividends) while the directors took their salaries. More than one wanted to know what remuneration the directors got. Another, Gen. Dunne, not only asked about directors' salaries but also enquired 'which of the Board know nothing about shipping'. Cost-cutting measures, like signing on crews on the morning of departure instead of the day before, had already been implemented. Now they announced salary cuts – the Superintendent at Southampton, for instance, would receive £850 per year instead of £1,000, and the captains' pay scale would be similarly cut.

Out of all that the one shining light was the appointment of Owen Philipps to one of the directorships. As a new director his power was limited, but it was almost certainly his idea, only a month later, to begin negotiations for a new Royal Charter – one which would 'enable them to deal with the share capital, as the amount of the share cannot be altered under the existing charter'. It wasn't difficult to see that RMSP needed more money to make itself competitive again.

On 18 March it was announced that the recently-appointed chairman, Thomas Dence, was resigning due to ill health. A week later, Owen Philipps – on his fortieth birthday – was elected to the now vacant postion. It all sounds very simple. Here was a man of modest reputation, a young 'whipper-snapper' in terms of men in senior positions with a company like RMSP, who had been elected a director and now, after two months and little opportunity to display his professional qualities, was unanimously elected to chairman. All of this was so illogical that it must be assumed that John Philipps' conversation with Admiral Chatfield the previous year was relevant somewhere. Was the non-eventuating takeover by Sir Christopher Furness also involved? We will never know what machinations may have been plotted outside the boardroom, but it is quite certain that, from late 1902, Owen Philipps' destiny was to find himself at the helm of this company.

Royal Mail's hierarchy in its early decades had been something of an old boys' club. There were inordinate numbers of merchant bankers, captains, admirals and right-honourables. It took the advent of Owen Philipps to seriously grasp the nettle of the new generation of shipping, which had been growing for some decades. By whatever means he reached the top job, Owen Philipps was a stunningly appropriate choice. Practically overnight the running of the company changed. Previously the Court minutes had been peppered with reports from captains on happenings during their voyages, suggestions from people ranging from the Southampton Superintendent to agencies in South America and so on. It seems that the Philipps regime placed such matters where they belonged – with the appropriate managers. This cleared the decks for the directors to concern themselves with policy matters, and here Philipps immediately placed his personal stamp of energetic leadership. An amazing proportion of the minutes now began with 'The Chairman reported…'.

Owen Philipps during his early
years as chairman, c.1909.

On 1 April 1903 the system of calculating and presenting the Company's accounts was significantly changed. On the same day, several transatlantic ships were authorised to employ bands for the entertainment of passengers. On 8 April an invitation was sent to Mr and Mrs Rudyard Kipling for a free round voyage to South America – here, surely, Philipps' entrepreneurial instincts came to the fore. Kipling was immensely popular, and during the previous year, 1902, he had published one of his most enduring works, the *Just So Stories*. Embedded among matters like how the elephant got its trunk was a poem which began:

> *I've never sailed the Amazon,*
> *I've never reached Brazil;*
> *But the* Don *and* Magdalena,
> *They can go there when they will!*
> *Yes, weekly from Southampton,*
> *Great steamers, white and gold,*
> *go rolling down to Rio...*

What a masterstroke – to offer the master writer the chance to 'reach Brazil'. Regrettably it was not to be, as he was unable to accept. Some years later, though, the Kiplings did make the journey to South America with Royal Mail – but in one of the fine new 'A' ships.

On 24 June a fleet modernisation programme began with orders for three freighters – *Parana*, *Pardo* and *Potaro*. The significance of this extended beyond new ships – two came from Harland & Wolff and were the first RMSP ships built by the Belfast firm in which Philipps already had a significant interest. Few of its more important ships were built elsewhere from that point on.

During August 1903 auditors were brought in to examine the company's internal finances. They discovered that the Company's accountant had for years been drawing money from the cash box in exchange for IOU notes – he simply hadn't got around to replacing it. On the basis that he hadn't tried to defraud the Company, he was let off with a stinging interview with Philipps and a £75-a-year reduction in salary.

Three small cargo ships for West Indies routes – *Caroni*, *Conway* and *Catalina* – were ordered from Armstrong Whitworth in October 1903; in the same month an agreement was signed for frozen meat to be carried from the River Plate in the new 'P' ships. By November changes announced in RMSP's overseas network included upgrading the Buenos Aires agency to an RMSP office.

Finally, on 25 November, Owen Philipps addressed for the first time the most important issue of all: the question of new mail steamers. He:

> briefly stated the result of the interview with the Hon. Charles Parsons, the inventor of steam turbine engines which would probably be the engines of the future for speeds of 15 knots or over. It will not be possible to obtain any results from the new Allan liner, just fitted with turbine engines, before October/November 1904, and under these circumstances it will probably be advisable to proceed with one mail steamer with ordinary engines at once.

With those words *Aragon* effectively came into being, a vessel more than 60% larger than anything RMSP had previously owned. In the following decade eight similar ships followed, most a little larger than the last. By 1913 *Alcantara* had raised the size to almost 16,000 tons.

In September 1904 Philipps instigated major changes to the West Indies services. During March 1905 the issue of the West Indies mail contract came to a head – this was a matter in which even Owen Philipps couldn't overcome the intransigence of a Government determined to get something for as near to nothing as it could manage. In the end no contract was issued, and for two years the West Indies mails travelled in pretty well any steamer which was heading in that direction.

Later that year he travelled to the West Indies and New York. He had visions of New York playing a more important part than its rather spasmodic role so far, particularly in the passenger trade with the West Indies. He negotiated to lease half of Pier 50 from the Morgan combine, a splendid frontage which came to an abrupt end two years later at the hands of a large American rail company. A slightly inferior berth then had to be settled on, but the Company was by then well established at New York. Part of that arrangement was to bring Americans to the Caribbean and onto the inter-colonial steamers for a cruise.

By December 1905 Philipps was home again, seeking the Court's approval to purchase The Pacific Steam Navigation Co.'s portion of the UK-Australia Orient-Pacific service. This went ahead, at a cost of £254,734, and Royal Mail then owned the four 'O' steamers which operated PSN's portion of the service – *Oruba*, *Oroya*, *Orotava* and *Ortona*. Royal Mail's involvement was short-lived. The other partner in what now became Orient-Royal Mail Line – Anderson, Anderson & Co.'s Orient Line – wanted to go it alone. They began negotiating mail contracts without reference to RMSP, complained about the RMSP ships

RMSP's New York base from 1907 – Pier 42. At that time Royal Mail was fostering the Caribbean cruise market from New York.

and finally sought and won a mail contract on their own. The major issue was that while PSN had a financial interest and supplied ships and officers, the operation of the service was in the hands of Orient. It wouldn't have been in Owen Philipps' nature to let another line control the operation of his ships.

Though the joint venture was short-lived, it paved the way for a number of captains and officers to enter RMSP through the side door. One was Walter H. Parker, who was chief officer of *Oroya* at the time. He spent a good many years with RMSP, and when he left it was again more of a transfer, for he moved to White Star Line in the late 1920s after RMSP had gained control of the company. In view of what was said above about the operation of the Orient-Royal Mail service it is worth considering Parker's views:

> *The four ships belonging to [Royal Mail] were managed as before in all respects, except the appointment of commander and officers, by Messrs Anderson, Anderson & Co. and Messrs F. Green & Co., the founders of the Orient Line. In passing, I will only be voicing the unanimous sentiment of seafarers if I say "Better people one would not wish to serve".*

That uncompromising testimonial seems greatly at odds with the manner in which Orient appeared to be dealing with its joint venture partner, but a company's treatment of its officers was a different matter from facing a man like Owen Philipps with the bit between his teeth.

Capt. Parker provided an interesting word picture of the traditional 'taking leave of the Court of Directors' which had been in vogue with RMSP for so long, when commanders met with the directors at 18 Moorgate on the eve of departure to receive final instructions and discuss points of concern. Of his first voyage in command he had this to say:

> *On the eve of my first voyage in command of the Oroya, Mr Owen Philipps – now Lord Kylsant – was in the chair, and having given me some precise instructions relative to the comfort of the passengers, with a good deal of latitude in the way I might exert myself on their behalf, he, followed by all the directors, shook hands and wished me a safe and pleasant voyage.*
>
> *The last director I came to – a rather short, elderly gentleman – as he shook hands said "Are you a Royal Naval Reserve officer, captain?"*
>
> *'I replied, "Yes, sir!"*
>
> *"Oh, where have you served?"*
>
> *I told him, mentioning that I had served through the Boxer Rising in China.*
>
> *"Oh!" he said, "did you meet my boy John there? John Jellicoe?"*
>
> *I replied that I knew Captain Jellicoe, Flag Captain of the Centurion, by sight only.*
>
> *"Yes, that's him! That's him! Good boy, John!" smiling. "He's an Admiral now! Well, goodbye captain" – patting me on the back – "a pleasant voyage to you!"*
>
> *This was the first and only time I ever had the honour of meeting old Captain Jellicoe...'*

The parting of RMSP and Orient Line allowed Philipps to transfer the 'O' ships to the New York service, which they operated until new tonnage was built. Because the 'O' prefix had become something of a trademark on the New York run by then, the new ships followed this style – which explains why RMSP ships on the New York route bore the same naming style as Orient Line used for the Australia trade.

On 20 December 1905, following a proposal by Deputy Chairman Sir James Fergusson, Owen Philipps was elected Managing Director and from that point on the momentum was stepped up. In February 1906 a five-year mail contract to Trinidad was signed, the chairman negotiated with Harland & Wolff for a new 'A' ship on 'improved terms' and he strengthened the cargo fleet by purchasing Union-Castle's *Greek*. In May the same year Philipps proposed increasing RMSP's involvement in the migrant trade from Spain and Portugal to Brazil and the River Plate, and this led to new philosophies with passenger arrangements. In the same month, with *Amazon* almost ready for delivery, the chairman proposed a short pre-maiden voyage cruise for invited guests and a press luncheon. In June 1906 Philipps announced that he wanted another new 'A' ship built, this time for the Australia service. At the same time, the Court authorised him to purchase more Union-Castle 'G' ships; *Gaul* was purchased three weeks later.

Briefly coming up for air during June, Owen Philipps unexpectedly turned his attention to the office staff, at home and abroad. Because of 'the great pressure of work in the Company's offices…it was agreed to grant a small gratuity to each – total value less than £1,000'. Then it was back into the fray. In July 1906 he proposed the purchase of Larrinaga & Co.'s Cuban Line – in the event this deal didn't go through, but Philipps had flagged his intention of acquiring ships or companies which he felt would be beneficial.

In August 1906 the 'Chairman reported on negotiations he has had with Mr Jenkins of the Shire Line respecting the Company obtaining an interest in the eastern trade. Court approved steps so far taken and authorised their progression'. September 1906 saw *Araguaya* enter service and at the chairman's instigation a short cruise was made for shipping clerks and the Press. Philipps, on a working tour of Brazil and the River Plate, missed that. Also around this time the Australia service 'O' ships were progressively sent to Harland & Wolff for improvements in their electrical system and accommodation.

On 16 January 1907 there were two important announcements. The first was tragic – RMSP's Deputy Chairman, Sir James Fergusson, had died as a result of a severe earthquake in Kingston, Jamaica. He was there, ironically, for a conference on 'the development of the West Indies colonies'. A cable received in London reported:

serious earthquake followed by fire, wrecking Kingston and most of wharves and burning of warehouses, destruction of Company's office and death of Captain Constantine, Company's Representative, Captain Young of the Arno, and that Sir James Fergusson was amongst the missing.

Having absorbed all of that, the Court turned its attention to a different part of the world. Following negotiations with Jenkins & Co., Owen Philipps announced he now had an opportunity to break into the eastern trades, 'with rights and privileges of Conference' by taking a one-third interest in Jenkins' Shire Line. The Company would initially take over *Monmouthshire* for £62,000, and pay a further £21,000 for a share of the goodwill in Shire Line. Later, the chairman negotiated a purchase of Shire Line shares as part payment; in July, it was announced that Jenkins & Co. was in liquidation. This led to further purchases of its steamers and, indeed, of the company.

Royal Mail's Buenos Aires office in 1909.

On 15 May 1907 Philipps reported on an interview with Winston Churchill (then Under-Secretary of State for the Colonies) and the Financial Secretary to the Treasury, Mr Runciman. An inter-colonial mail contract was about to expire and the Government wanted RMSP to extend it for a short time until a new long-term contract could be finalised. This was a business opportunity made for Owen Philipps. The transatlantic West Indies service had survived without a mail contract for two years. Philipps bargained with Churchill and Runciman and emerged with a transatlantic mail contract paid on a poundage basis and a ten-year inter-colonial contract for £25,000 per year.

In June 1907 there were more developments in the third-class passenger trade, for which alterations were approved in *Thames*, *Magdalena*, *Clyde*, *Nile* and *Danube*. Three months later a new contract was signed to carry chilled meat from New York to Colon, for which extra refrigerating equipment had to be installed in *Atrato*, *Orinoco*, *Tagus* and *Trent* – boosting freight shipments was an increasingly important matter.

January 1908 saw *Asturias* ready for service. Because she was initially going to Australia, as part of the remnant Orient-Royal Mail joint venture, she came to Tilbury instead of Southampton. Philipps, as expected, sent invitations to editors and city editors of leading papers and arranged a luncheon for Australian shippers and shipping clerks. His entrepreneurial nature realised that the proximity of *Asturias* to London was an opportunity not to be missed in promoting the Company's fleet: a public inspection day was organised, at a charge of 1/- per head, all proceeds to go to Tilbury Hospital.

In June 1908 – with Forwood Bros in financial trouble – Owen Philipps steered RMSP into purchasing the company and the ships *Agadir* and *Arzila*, together with the resulting inroads into the Moroccan trade. *Amazon* was preparing to undertake a cruise to Norway, RMSP's first single-ship cruise and another pivotal milestone.

Four months later the chairman raised a matter which in the event came to nothing – but it showed that in the short time Philipps had been at the helm, RMSP's progress had not gone unnoticed within the industry. The Bucknall Steamship Co. was the subject of a takeover bid by Sir John Ellerman; while some members of the Bucknall family favoured the deal, others didn't and approached Owen Philipps with a proposal for RMSP to take them over instead.

The Philipps philosophy, then, had taken root. After less than six years at the helm, he had started RMSP on a climb to dizzy heights. He couldn't have achieved that, of course, without reversing the poor trading results which existed prior to his arrival. They, more than anything, reflected his energy and ability. The South America service mail steamers in 1902 showed a trading loss of £9,369. Philipps came on board at the beginning of 1903, and in that year the service showed a trading profit of £21,901; in 1904 £49,640 profit; there are no figures available for 1905 but in 1906 there was £107,354 profit; in 1907 £115,296 profit.

The Halcyon Years

The halcyon years for Philipps and RMSP were the 1910s. They were hectic, almost mesmerising times, with Owen Philipps taking on more and more responsibility. As companies were acquired, or major shareholdings purchased, he became a director of most and chairman of many. He was appointed KCMG in 1909 and GCMG in 1918. Now as Sir Owen Philipps he sat as Member of Parliament for Chester and for Pembroke and Haverfordwest from 1906 to 1922. In 1923 he was created Baron Kylsant of Carmarthen.

Lord Kylsant, pictured in the 1920s when he controlled the world's largest shipping group.

Capt. Walter H. Parker, who was commanding RMSP passenger liners during the Kylsant era.

At various times he served as President of the London Chamber of Commerce, the Chamber of Shipping of the United Kingdom and the Federation of Chambers of Commerce of the British Empire. He was Lord Lieutenant of the County of Haverfordwest and Vice-Admiral of North Wales. He became closely involved with the Order of St John of Jerusalem and was Vice-Chairman of the Representative Body of the Church of Wales. As a financier, he continued to involve himself personally as a shareholder and stockholder in his growing list of companies.

In this manner did RMSP, as the core company, develop during the 1910s and into the 1920s. An integral part of Kylsant's ambition was that RMSP should control a network of services and allied industries, so that the finances to ensure the Company's viability would accrue from a variety of sources and not rely solely on ship trading profits. In that, Philipps demonstrated the importance of an issue which would become crucial in the court case of 1931 – the cyclical pattern of trade. Over a period, freight earnings dropped from a crest to a trough, and then began the climb to the next crest, a cycle generally lasting about seven to ten years. Essentially it was a predictable pattern, but it could be influenced by outside matters like natural disaster or war. Owen Philipps, then, was thinking of the trade cycle as much as anything with his policy of diversification; so that he could, as it were, switch to emergency fuel tanks if the main tank ran dry.

A further factor in his complex make-up was an uncompromising British patriotism – a strange remark, perhaps, but it played a part in his decision, in 1927, to buy the Oceanic SN Co., returning White Star Line to British hands after a quarter of a century under American ownership. Many people claimed that, in the economic climate then existing, it was a foolhardy thing to do. For Lord Kylsant, as he was by then, it was no such thing, for he knew that the trade cycle was on the rise. He had demonstrated his concern for British ownership as far back as 1903, when he spearheaded the creation of a new Royal Charter. The phrase 'It is to be regarded as a cardinal principle of the Company that it is to be and remain under British control' appeared in the Supplemental Charter of July 1904. That Charter, in fact, was in some ways so radically different from what had gone before that it prompted the Official Receiver handling the liquidation of RMSP in 1936 to say: 'It is significant that the Charter of 1904, which authorised the company to acquire interests in other companies, was obtained some eighteen months after Lord Kylsant became a director of the company. I regard this as a crucial point in the company's history'.

The general magnitude of RMSP at its zenith is well known; when Lord Kylsant purchased Oceanic in 1927, RMSP controlled the world's largest shipping group. Its combined fleets comprised some 2.7 million gross tons of shipping, notwithstanding that over one-hundred of its vessels had been lost in the First World War. The ever-growing giant ultimately controlled dozens of companies. Major acquisitions were commonplace, and it is worth taking a brief look at some of the more significant investments within the shipping area.

One of the first companies acquired was The Pacific Steam Navigation Co., which was bought for £1$\frac{1}{2}$ million. In 1912 Union-Castle Line was purchased for about £5 million. H & W Nelson, Nelson Steam Nav. Co., David MacIver and MacAndrews were all wholly-owned. RMSP held more than 400,000 of Elder Dempster's ordinary shares and 10,000 6$\frac{1}{2}$% 'A' cumulative preference shares, and in the same company the 'Kylsant-Pirrie' group held nearly a million and a half shares (of which 596,000 were in Lord Kylsant's name). By 1928 RMSP and companies it controlled held one third of Harland & Wolff's shares, and following the death of Lord Pirrie in 1924 Kylsant took on the role of chairman.

In Hull, Blyth & Co., RMSP held 55,000 £1 shares, with ten other group firms also shareholders. The Jamaica Coaling Co. was purchased outright, while £21,000-worth of stock was held in Kaye, Son & Co. Ltd (Jamaica Banana Producers). A large shareholding in Lamport and Holt was held by RMSP itself and most of the remainder was distributed among other companies in the group (Kylsant had a personal investment of £50,000). In one of the many firms of which he was chairman, the London Maritime Investment Co., RMSP owned some £45,000 of stock. McGregor, Gow & Holland, in later years loading brokers for Royal Mail, was wholly owned within the group and Lord Kylsant was a director. About £250,000 of Moss Line shares were held by RMSP, and three other group companies were also shareholders.

Glen and Shire lines were both wholly owned. Kylsant formed Coast Lines Ltd in 1917 after purchasing all the ordinary share capital and much of the preference in Powell, Bacon and Hough Lines Ltd. Other coastal lines acquired were British & Irish SP Co., The City of Cork SP Co., Belfast SS Co., Burns & Laird Line and, through the latter company, nearly 50% of David MacBrayne's shares.

Then there was Lord Kylsant's biggest coup, the Oceanic Steam Navigation Co. – White Star Line – purchased in 1927 for £7 million.

Those landmarks show what a load Kylsant had taken on by 1927 (the Group as a whole at that time is looked at in Appendix III). With its interlocking components, the operation of the RMSP Group eventually became too much even for him. There are two viewpoints from which his situation can be judged. One was put forward in the *Dictionary of National Biography*:

> *It was at that time that, reviewing the enormous responsibilities shouldered by Kylsant, his friends began to fear that he was carrying a burden which no single individual was capable of bearing: in 1924, on the death of Lord Pirrie, he had added greatly to his commitments by assuming control of the vast concern of Messrs Harland and Wolff, of Belfast. The position, already difficult, was aggravated by a severe depression of trade instead of the revival upon which Kylsant, optimist as he was, relied. Rumours were so rife that it became impossible to conceal the true nature of the position. He was given leave of absence by the Royal Mail Steam Packet Company, and on his return was arrested.*

The opposing view was that Kylsant was a businessman *par excellence* and on the basis of the trade cycle, things should have steadily improved during the late 1920s. Had they done so, and RMSP emerged unscathed – if it had not reached a point of crisis through the severity and length of the Depression – it is interesting to speculate just how large the group might have grown. Kylsant's counsel at the trial put it this way:

> *…If the cycle of trade had returned as many people in 1927 and 1928 thought it would, if things had gone on an even keel and risen again, then instead of Lord Kylsant sitting in the criminal dock here, he would be acclaimed as one of the steady sober men of British business who, in prosperous times, pursued a conservative policy and who in evil days took advantage of that conservative policy in order to maintain his dividend, and who had got his fleet and his company out of a period of difficulty.*

Clearly the word 'conservative' was used to describe not Kylsant's mode of operation, but his habit of 'salting away' some of the profits to be used in leaner times.

The question of whether or not that situation – as the basis on which two annual reports and a debenture prospectus were allegedly 'false in a material particular' – constituted a criminal offence was the crux of the case made out by the Crown against Lord Kylsant in 1931. On 13 May that year he was summonsed on two counts. The wording of each was identical: that as a director of a public company – the Royal Mail Steam Packet Co. – he:

> *did make, circulate or publish, or concur in making, circulating or publishing, a certain written statement of account, to wit, an annual report of the directors of the said Company, which he knew to be false in a material particular with intent to deceive shareholders of the said Company contrary to Section 84 of the Larceny Act, 1861.*

The annual reports involved were those for 1926 and 1927.

On the same day Harold John Morland, a partner in Price, Waterhouse & Co., was charged with aiding and abetting Lord Kylsant with the same two reports. Morland was RMSP's auditor.

They appeared before the Lord Mayor of London at the Guildhall on 2 June 1931 for a preliminary hearing. The opening day began badly when, early in the morning while Kylsant was still in his office, a third summons was handed to him. Its wording was similar to the earlier ones except that it referred to a share prospectus and alleged 'intent to induce persons to entrust or advance property to the said Royal Mail Steam Packet Company…' Mr Morland was not concerned with this charge, for there were no audited figures involved.

The Crown's case was essentially this: for a number of years during the First World War and up to 1920, RMSP reaped enormous profits, a large proportion of which it held on to in various hidden or undeclared reserves. From 1921 to 1927, it was claimed, large losses were made and in order to show a favourable balance each year the reserves were systematically 'milked' until by 1927 little or nothing remained in them.

The prosecution claimed that Kylsant did not make RMSP's true position sufficiently clear, that by covering seven bad years with the use of old reserves, and issuing dividends each year, he was, in effect, saying 'hold on to your shares because your company is doing very well, making profits even during the trough of the trade cycle'. The Crown insisted that, having transferred some £5 million from reserves to continue this veneer of profitability, the group was sailing into the storm of the Depression in such a poor state that it was inexorably being drawn onto the rocks, and the shareholders were entitled to know that. The last straw was the issue in June 1928 of a prospectus offering for sale £2 million of 5% debenture stock. The same kind of 'misleading information' was contained in it to ensure that the issue was fully subscribed.

That is a simplified account, seen through the eyes of the prosecution. The first two days of the hearing were heavily charged with legal argument; there were bitter clashes and biting remarks, particularly from Sir Patrick Hastings (defending Harold Morland), who couldn't discover any reason for the charges against his client. Defence and prosecution, with the Lord Mayor in the middle, waged a fierce battle about the evidence of Lord Plender, an eminent chartered accountant. The astonished witness, innocently interrupting to explain why he was there, was told to shut up; then the Lord Mayor shrugged helplessly and observed 'I don't think I have ever been up against anything like this before'.

Temperatures rose further when Sir William McLintock was called. He was another chartered accountant and had been instructed by the Government to examine RMSP's finances. Points of law which cropped up, added to those with the first witness, made Sir Patrick very unhappy. Lord Kylsant's defence counsel – another famous man of law, Sir John Simon – was equally dissatisfied, and the two of them told the Lord Mayor that the case was being handled so badly from the Bench that they felt they could not continue their tasks in that court. Having delivered carefully worded explanations they gathered up their papers, walked out of the court and took no further part in the preliminary hearing. Their exit meant that the hearing reached a predictable conclusion: both men were committed for trial on all counts.

Central Criminal Court.

1

SESSIONS HOUSE,
OLD BAILEY, E.C.4.
Monday, 20th July, 1931.

BEFORE:
MR. JUSTICE WRIGHT.

REX

— v.—

OWEN COSBY PHILIPPS, Baron Kylsant of Carmarthen, and HAROLD JOHN MORLAND.

[Transcript of the Shorthand Notes of Messrs. GEORGE WALPOLE & Co. *(Shorthand Writers to the Court), Portugal Street Buildings, Lincoln's Inn, W.C.2.]*

Counsel for the Prosecution : The ATTORNEY GENERAL (Sir WM. JOWITT, K.C., M.P), Mr. D. N. PRITT, K.C., and Mr. EUSTACE FULTON (instructed by THE DIRECTOR OF PUBLIC PROSECUTIONS).

Counsel for Lord KYLSANT : Sir JOHN SIMON, K.C., M.P., Mr. J. E. SINGLETON, K.C., and Mr. WILFRID LEWIS (instructed by Messrs. HOLMES, SON & POTT).

Counsel for Mr. MORLAND : Sir PATRICK HASTINGS, K.C., Mr. STUART BEVAN, K.C., M.P., Mr. C. J. CONWAY, K.C. and Mr. F. J. TUCKER (instructed by Messrs. SLAUGHTER & MAY).

FIRST DAY.

The CLERK of the COURT : Owen Cosby Philipps, Baron Kylsant, and Harold John Morland, you are charged——

1st DAY

20 July, 1931

Sir JOHN SIMON : My Lord, before Lord Kylsant is asked to plead may I say this——

Mr. Justice WRIGHT : Is this a matter which you desire to discuss in the absence of the Jury ?

Sir JOHN SIMON : No, my Lord, it is a matter which your Lordship will be able to deal with. My Lord, I call your attention to the Indictment which, as you will see, consists of three Counts, and I ask your Lordship to consider whether or not in fairness to the Defence greater particularity should not be shown in making the allegations which the Indictment contains. The matter to which I wish to draw your attention to is what the particulars of each of the three Counts mean. Your Lordship may take the first one as an example. Your Lordship will see that the first Count refers to an annual report of the board of directors of the Royal Mail Steam Packet Company for the year 1926, dated 11th May 1927. You will find that is

The moment which changed the course of RMSP: the opening page of the trial transcript for Lord Kylsant in 1931.

The Trial

The Kylsant trial lasted for nine days and has come down through the years as a landmark case of company law. The extent to which it taxed everybody in the courtroom may be gathered from two comments made at its conclusion. The Attorney-General, Sir William Jowitt (who led the Crown's prosecution) told the jury: 'I have finished in what I may say I think has been for me the most anxious and the most worrying case I have ever had since I have been at the Bar'. Then Mr Justice Wright, the Judge under whom the case was conducted, said: 'Members of the Jury, you have had a very trying and arduous duty in this very long case, and under the circumstances I desire to recommend that you be excused from further attendance on any jury service for a period of ten years. That is the only form of compensation which it is in my power to give you'.

On all charges both defendants pleaded 'not guilty'. Kylsant had already stressed that he had attempted to deceive no-one and that every action he had taken had been in good faith, aimed at RMSP's continuing prosperity. Mr Morland, like Sir Patrick Hastings, was puzzled throughout as to why he was there at all.

How did the prosecution shape its case? We could begin by posing a question: what does a public company do with its profits at the end of the year? If the profits are at least reasonable a proportion will be paid out as dividends to shareholders. A further portion will be ploughed back into the company – purchasing new equipment, perhaps, or some other means of increasing the firm's efficiency. But if its management is prudent, it will hold on to a certain amount, as investments, so that there is a fund to meet unexpected liabilities or to help pull it through difficult times.

For a British shipping company at that period, there were specific instances where reserve funds were essential. Firstly, RMSP held an Excess Profits Duty reserve, dating from 1914 when abnormal trading conditions commenced and there was a potential for gigantic profits. To ensure that profits did not reach too absurd a figure the Government said, in effect: 'If your profit exceeds what we consider a desirable limit, we will tax you on everything over and above that figure at anything from 40% to 80%'. The 'desirable limit' was a threshold calculated on an average of results in pre-war years.

It was a most complex arrangement. RMSP could not know in advance what its liability would be for any one year, and with such a vast concern the final figure decided on by the Inland Revenue was not calculated for a long time. Thus a fund, building to more than £2,000,000, was set up to meet the contingency when it came. Then the Government relented and said: 'Although you made large profits during and after the war, we realise that when it came to newbuildings afterwards, prices were abnormally high and so we will repay a portion of the excess profits duty'. They further complicated matters by announcing that those repayments were subject to normal income tax as earnings for the year. With a group the size of Royal Mail, which had lost 104 ships, post-war buildings were huge.

Income tax was not a simple deduction at the end of the year. The Income Tax Act specified that if a company, after a run of good, taxable profits, then made substantial losses, it would receive back a proportion of the tax it had paid earlier. This was used to augment the Income Tax Reserve.

Royal Mail's longstanding West End passenger office in Cockspur Street, London, pictured shortly after RMSP first occupied it in 1913. It underwent major rebuilding in the 1920s.

Then there was a deferred repairs reserve, created early in the First World War against the large repair bill that the Company would face when the war ended. It did not cater simply for damage caused by the war. During hostilities the continuance of trade was essential, so every ship which was serviceable continued to operate as far as possible without routine repairs and maintenance, allowing the maximum utilisation of ships and keeping building and repair yards free for more urgent work.

Shipping companies did not disclose those reserves. Several terms have been used to describe them, the most common being 'hidden reserves', and they were perfectly legal. An obvious benefit from their use in shipping was that a stabilising effect was achieved during the trough of the trade cycle, permitting dividends to be maintained and keeping competitors as much in the dark as possible about the Company's current position.

The Trade Facilities Act, passed in 1921, was a means by which companies could raise money on advantageous terms and came with a Government guarantee for its repayment. It was an enquiry into a request by Lord Kylsant in 1929 for an extension of credit beyond the agreed expiry date that alerted the Government to RMSP's position, for by then the facilities had been closed. Concerned at RMSP's inability to repay, the Government appointed Walter Runciman, Sir William McLintock and Brigadier General Sir Arthur Maxwell as Voting Trustees to investigate the Company's affairs.

The Act remained in force until 1927 and RMSP used it to raise money for, among other things, two much-needed mail liners for the South America service – *Alcantara* and *Asturias*. Royal Mail was faced at that time with powerful competition from the Vestey Group (in the shape of Blue Star Line) which, also under the Trade Facilities Act, built five passenger liners for the River Plate service. *Arandora Star* and her sister ships entered service in 1926 and 1927; they were Blue Star's entry into the passenger trade and Kylsant described them as 'very keen competition'.

Another example of competition involved the wholly owned Pacific Steam Navigation Co.'s services between New York and the West Coast of South America. During the 1920s the American ships competing with PSN received a Government subsidy of £10,000 per voyage – at a time of depressed trading conditions, that subsidy allowed American ship operators to discount freight rates and thus boost its percentage of available cargoes. A similar situation faced another Group company, Lamport & Holt. That was the kind of thing RMSP had to contend with when it could least have done with it, and why it was in its interests to disclose no more than it had to of its financial position.

The Crown also directed its attention to a better-known example of hidden reserves. The term 'fleet depreciation' is a familiar one, but its usage was not as simple as it may appear. It involves writing-down the book value of a ship by a certain percentage each year so that the sum of money shown against 'book value of fleet' in the balance sheet represents a true picture. Most authorities agreed that 4% per year (i.e. a life-span of twenty-five years), or $4\frac{1}{2}$% at most, represented a true depreciation; producing the closest figure to the current market value of ships. Royal Mail's depreciation was based on 5% over a life expectancy of twenty years, thus over-allowing for depreciation so ships generally realised a higher price than their book value when sold. (That was the inexplicable sticking point in the proposed takeover bid by Sir Christopher Furness in 1902.) RMSP's depreciation rate amounted to another, perfectly legal, 'hidden reserve' which, with such an enormous fleet, involved a large sum of money.

The absence of those reserves from the balance sheet was also quite legal. What the Government inferred was that transfers from those funds were made over a period of years in which trading losses had been made. But there can be no difficulty in realising, firstly, that the amounts of various liabilities could not be calculated in advance and, secondly that, with the complex revenue payments and the depreciation system, large sums of money would not become available for use by the Company until several years after they first came into being. This was one of the principal lines of defence, that the majority of the 'old reserves' transferred to the profit and loss account, creating a favourable balance, were not free to be used by the Company until the years in which they were used.

Up to 1927 there were, as Sir John Simon put it, 'three heads of controversy and possible dispute in settling up this excess profits duty business'. First there was the Government's claim for excess profits duty. Next came the obsolescence allowance, the name given to the Government's allowance against the high price of post-war building. And lastly there was a deferrred repairs allowance, which was made by the Government in view of high prices for repairs which had been deferred in the national interest.

All three factors were transformed in 1927 into physical credits and debits of the company. When the two credits were subtracted from the excess profits duty, the net result was that Royal Mail owed the Government £340,417. Not having known earlier that they would be granted any allowances, the Company had built sufficient reserves to allow for the maximum duty on excess profits: the fund amounted to £2,260,000. This, as it turned out, was a quite realistic figure, for the Government claimed £1,769,000; the allowances which finally reduced the figure to £340,417 were matters which could not be counted on until much later. Only during the year or two prior to 1927, when there were indications that the claim would not be as high as expected, could a certain amount be safely drawn from the fund and transferred to the profit and loss account. Then, in 1927, when the figures were finally fixed, the balance was credited as profit for the year. The term used to indicate those transfers in the annual reports was 'adjustment of taxation reserves'.

The prosecution insisted that this phrase, a standard accountancy term, was misleading as it told the man-in-the-street shareholder nothing about the manner in which the reserves had suddenly appeared. The Attorney General continued to insist that RMSP lived off its 'old fat' during lean years which went on so long that the Company should have given a clear indication of its true position.

Many other factors were drawn into the case. One which was regarded equally seriously by both sides was Lord Kylsant's salary. The arrangement was that he should receive a basic annual salary of £3,000. However, when business was good it was reflected, naturally, in the size of the dividend. It was decided early in Kylsant's time as Chairman and Managing Director that if the annual dividend was 5% or higher, he would receive – instead of his £3,000 – 0.5% of the Company's gross earnings for the year. Thus from 1920 to 1927 his salary from RMSP amounted to £213,619 – an average of more than £26,000 a year. It was a vast salary, and the Crown accused Kylsant of arranging for transfers to be made to allow the 5% dividend to be paid and thus allow him to gain his commission.

Lord Kylsant revealed at the trial that in 1902 Sir Francis Evans (an influential director of the newly-formed Union-Castle Line, and formerly chairman of the component Union SS Co.) was to have been appointed Chairman and Managing Director of Royal Mail, an arrangement which fell through principally because of a technicality which resulted from Sir Francis requesting a 1% commission. When Kylsant later received the senior appointment he thought 1% was excessive and reduced it to 0.5%. This arrangement was unanimously agreed to at a general meeting of the Company, and was therefore not a decision made by the directors but by the shareholders themselves.

Whether or not this was an answer to the Crown's challenge, the jury clearly took note of it – and that in 1928, though entitled to his commission, he decided not to claim it. The feeling was, clearly, that whatever Lord Kylsant might have been doing from a business point of view, his manoeuvres were not for personal gain.

Closely involved in the trial were six companies described as the '100% subsidiaries' – The Pacific Steam Navigation Co., RMSP Meat Transports, H & W Nelson, Nelson SN Co., David MacIver and MacAndrews. It was claimed that their annual figures were arranged in a misleading way, by various technically legal methods, to improve the apparent position of the parent company. This was leading up to the third charge against Kylsant, regarding the prospectus, for the Company must appear to be in a sound position if the public could be expected to subscribe to new stock.

The most telling of those matters involved the two Nelson companies. There was an apparent show of strength by RMSP when, in 1927, it announced the purchase of one million new shares in the Nelson SN Co. The prosecution claimed that the purchase would have given RMSP shareholders confidence in the Company's financial position, but that, in fact, no money changed hands.

It worked like this: RMSP applied for the one million £1 shares in Nelson SN Co. during December 1927. Half were paid for (on paper) in full – £500,000. The remainder were acquired to the extent of 10% – £50,000; thus RMSP owed Nelson £550,000. The Nelson companies that year paid out bonuses of £300,000 to their shareholders – the only one being

No Underwriting Commission has been or will be paid on this Issue

The Subscription List will open on Tuesday, the 3rd July, 1928, and will close on or before Wednesday, the 4th July, 1928.

THE ROYAL MAIL STEAM PACKET COMPANY.

(Incorporated by Royal Charter, 1839.)

Capital Authorised by Royal Charter £25,000,000

CAPITAL ISSUED AND FULLY PAID	£8,800,000
4½ per cent. DEBENTURE STOCK	£1,400,000
5 per cent. DEBENTURE STOCK (not including present issue)	£3,100,000
RESERVE FUND	£1,450,000
INSURANCE FUND	£1,311,755

ISSUE OF

£2,000,000

Five per cent. Debenture Stock at the price of £92. 10s. per cent.

Payable as follows :

On Application	5 per cent.	Applications must be made in multiples of £10
„ Allotment	5 ,, ,,	
„ 25th July, 1928 ..	22½ ,, ,,	
„ 19th September, 1928 ..	30 ,, ,,	
„ 17th October, 1928 ..	30 ,, ,,	
	92½ per cent.	

Payment in full may be made on allotment, under discount at the rate of five per cent. per annum. Thereafter payment in full can be made at any time under discount at the same rate, as at the due date of the instalment following date of payment in full.

Scrip Certificates will be issued in exchange for Letters of Allotment as soon as practicable after allotment and will be exchanged for registered Debenture Stock Certificates after the date of payment of the final instalment.

The Stock will be issued in multiples of £10, and after registered Stock Certificates have been issued will be transferable in any amount not involving a fraction of £1.

Present Stockholders will receive preferential allotment if they apply on the special coloured form provided for the purpose.

Interest will be payable half-yearly, on 1st January and 1st July. A first interest payment of £1. 15s. per cent. (less Income Tax) will be made on 1st January, 1929, after which the Stock will rank for interest equally with the existing five per cent. Stock.

The Company may at any time redeem the whole or any part of the Stock at par on giving six calendar months' notice to the Stockholders, but otherwise the Stock becomes redeemable only when the security created by the undermentioned Trust Deeds becomes enforceable.

The debenture stock prospectus of 1928 which was the subject of the third charge against Lord Kylsant - the one on which he was found guilty.

Royal Mail House, Leadenhall Street - the grand headquarters built in the 1920s when RMSP was at its zenith – photographed during the 1960s. (Author's photograph)

RMSP. That amount was credited to RMSP's profit and loss account, but, again, was not paid in cash. RMSP then sold to Nelson SN Co. the whole of the share capital of H & W Nelson for £250,000, thereby (added to the £300,000 bonuses) covering the whole of the new capital in Nelson SN Co. Having sold H & W Nelson, RMSP still had total control of it by being the sole shareholder of its new owner. All of this seemingly vibrant investment, which would have made potential investors happy, occurred without a penny changing hands.

The prospectus charge, in effect, said: 'In 1928 you decided to issue £2 million of 5% debenture stock. If, at the time, it was known that the Company had been for a number of years making heavy trading losses, no-one would have handed over their cash to buy the stock. Therefore in the years leading up to 1928 those ingenious methods of creating a favourable balance and a favourable appearance of investment activity were employed to ensure that the issue was fully subscribed. And then, in the prospectus itself, an equally misleading resumé of the ten years up to 1927 was given so that prospective investors would be in no doubt that they were buying into a company blessed with healthy finances'.

Why was a public issue made at that time? The Royal Charter, in its most recent form, authorised a maximum capital of £25 million, of which there was ample not yet taken up to cover this extra £2 million. A large portion was required for the building of the new head office, Royal Mail House in Leadenhall Street. Also, for a number of years RMSP had held a £300,000 overdraft from Barclays Bank. In 1926 it was increased to £500,000 on the understanding that the extra £200,000 would be repaid within three months from the proceeds of a public issue. The period was extended several times, but clearly could not continue indefinitely.

The Crown's case particularly targeted the following sentence in the prospectus:

Although the Company in common with other shipping companies has suffered from the depression in the shipping industry, the audited accounts of the Company show that during the past ten years the average annual balance available (including profits from the Insurance Fund), after providing for depreciation and interest on existing debenture stocks, has been sufficient to pay the interest on the present issue more than five times over.

The ten years referred to were 1918 to 1927. The Crown, in its most powerful argument of the case, laid an assault on Kylsant based on those ten years. The figures from that decade, it was claimed, were absolutely abnormal and that to take an average was misleading because all the profit had come in 1918, 1919 and 1920, when the Company was doing splendidly in the aftermath of war. The last seven years, though, and right up to the time when the prospectus was issued in June 1928, showed poor results and bore no relation to the phrase which had been put in bold type; a phrase which aimed to persuade the would-be investor that that was what the Company had achieved in the past and was therefore what it might be expected to achieve in the future.

No-one suggested that any individual statement or figure was false. As Mr Justice Wright said in his summing-up:

In the main it is quite obvious that this [the prospectus] *is, letter by letter, word by word, an accurate document, so far as it goes, and it can only be found the basis of a charge of fraud if you are satisfied that there was this deliberate and wicked and criminal intent to concoct a false and misleading document.*

It is worth pointing out that Lord Kylsant was happy enough with the debenture issue to subscribe to it on his own account.

Who would envy the jury their duty to decide on a verdict? Harold Morland, ably defended by Sir Patrick Hastings, was acquitted on both counts. Lord Kylsant was found not guilty on counts one and two (the annual reports) but guilty on count three, the issue of the prospectus.

With the technical nature of the case, built on figures and odd phrases about which opinion differed so widely, it is a wonder that any verdict could have been reached with certainty. Lord Kylsant worked during his entire career with RMSP for the benefit of the very shareholders whose interests the court case was intended to protect. When you look at the gigantic personal investments he had in those companies, he could have aimed at nothing less.

At all events, the humiliation of this highly-respected sixty-eight-year-old man of business can be imagined as he began a jail term of one year. The humiliation was scarcely mitigated by the judge – clearly impressed by his irreproachable attitude throughout the case and his equally irreproachable business record over forty years – passing as lenient a sentence as he could.

The White Star Connection

No company in the group other than RMSP and the six subsidiary companies mentioned earlier came within the framework of the *prima facie* case. The implication of the Attorney-General was that the financial structure of RMSP and its wholly-owned subsidiaries had become emaciated due to a run of poor years. That was all there was to it. Losses had been made since 1921, he said, and shareholders were entitled to know that. Surely there was more to a long and very expensive court case than that; more than a series of damaging submissions by the Crown, many of which were proved to be without foundation. What, as the *Dictionary of National Biography* put it, the 'true nature of the position was' has never come to light. Was there – in the background – something more? There was, for RMSP's financial obligations at that time included one of frightening proportions – that was White Star Line.

When Kylsant announced his surprise purchase of Oceanic Steam Navigation Co., from 1 January 1927, for £7 million, he did not pay the previous owners (the International Mercantile Marine Co.) from the Company's funds. It was to be paid over a period of time, at an interest rate of 4%, which raised the purchase price to almost £8 million. To finance the deal a new company was set up – White Star Line Ltd. Their capital was £9 million, 5 million in preference shares (which were offered for sale, half at a time, in January and July 1927) and 4 million in £1 ordinary shares. The latter were divided among companies in the RMSP group.

Lord Kylsant did not confine himself to White Star's traditional North Atlantic service. For almost three decades White Star had also operated steamers to Australia; Kylsant already held an interest in Shaw Savill and in George Thompson & Co., managers of the Aberdeen Line. He wanted to build up his interests in Australia because, he said, 'I believe in its future'. Aberdeen-White Star offered both passenger and freight services to Australia. A year after his purchase of White Star, Kylsant committed nearly £2 million to buy the Australian Government's Commonwealth Line, and within weeks had spent a further £1 million to gain a controlling interest in Shaw Savill. Both purchases were made by White Star, not RMSP.

Not yet content, on 18 June of the same year, again using White Star, he startled the shipping world by announcing that an order had been placed with Harland & Wolff (of which he was still Chairman) for an Atlantic super-liner of 60,000 tons. She was to be named *Oceanic* and would cost about £3,500,000. Thus in the space of eighteen months he had committed more than £14 million in connection with White Star alone.

Much of his capital came from Treasury loans whose repayments began in 1928, and we have already seen the use he made of the Trade Facilities Act. His immense faith in the trade cycle, his boundless optimism that by 1927 the pendulum was on the upswing, convinced him that his huge financial commitments would be absorbed splendidly on the crest of another wave. That they were not – that a killer slump lay just around the corner – may be viewed either as sheer misfortune or as financial recklessness. Criticism of his management at this time ran deeply through the companies involved. It seemed as though, in the twilight of his business life, he suffered from a form of megalomania; that his steady empire-building over the years would not satisfy him at its earlier rate of progress.

Was he simply an opportunist, buying and investing as opportunities arose, or was there a final target at which he was aiming? Could this acceleration of asset-building have been caused by a realisation that his days in control were finite and that he needed to accumulate sufficient resources in order to achieve one final coup – to take over P&O?

At the end of the First World War Lord Kylsant had headed a syndicate which attempted to buy all the British-based interests of the International Mercantile Marine Co., but the deal was vetoed by the US President. Kylsant had to wait nearly a decade for the 'consolation prize' of White Star alone. When President Wilson blocked the original offer, Kylsant turned his attention instead to P&O. His opposite number there was Lord Inchcape; the two of them stood metaphorically on a pedestal high above anyone else in British shipping, and there was no love lost between them. A shipping journal recorded on one occasion: 'After the Armistice he assisted Lord Inchcape in the disposal of standard steamers, a deal in which, apparently, he was not sufficiently in the limelight, and his soreness even became a public matter'.

In 1918 P&O was still the larger group, but Kylsant, undaunted, set about gaining control of it. His bid was frustrated when Lord Inchcape arranged an injection of new capital. There were suggestions that Kylsant's purchase of White Star, with which he displaced Inchcape as controller of the greatest tonnage in Britain, was partly a move to give him greater latitude for another attempt to acquire P&O.

Whatever the answer, his handling of White Star drove his brother John (Viscount St Davids), who was a director of White Star, to resign and circulate to shareholders a notice essentially saying that 'all was not well with the group'. After Kylsant had been convicted and his giant group lay in ruins, the unhappy White Star was merged (at the Government's insistence) with its former rival Cunard Line; the great *Oceanic* never progressed beyond the keel. Neville Chamberlain, as Chancellor of the Exchequer, dangled a juicy carrot to ensure that the merger was agreed to – if they joined forces, he said, the Government would advance the large sum of money needed to complete Hull 534, soon to become *Queen Mary*, on which work had been suspended two years earlier because of the depressed Cunard coffers.

The Royal Mail group was left, after the trial, with a complex and massive list of debts in its wake. There were creditors with claims amounting to millions of pounds. The International Mercantile Marine Co. alone was still owed £2,700,000 of the White Star purchase price – in the end they received something like $4\frac{1}{2}$ d in the pound.

Epilogue

When the court's decision was handed down, Sir John Simon lodged an appeal on behalf of Lord Kylsant, essentially a legal technicality on the interpretation of the Larceny Act. It was held early in November and was dismissed.

In the meantime, on 1 September Lord Kylsant resigned all his directorships of Royal Mail group companies. Exactly when he began his term in Wormwood Scrubs is difficult to pin down, but it seems likely to have been about 4 November, immediately following the dismissal of his appeal. He was released on 18 August 1932 – with remission for good conduct he served less than ten months of the sentence, reportedly spending the time working in the prison library. He also risked his life to help a fellow prisoner when he spotted a block of slates falling from the roof and rushed forward to push the man out of the way before they smashed on the ground.

Those months of incarceration allowed much time for thought. As well as pondering the past, he must surely have mulled over the reception he would get after his release. Over the years he

Lord and Lady Kylsant, almost certainly taken after his release from prison in 1932. The photo shows well the great height of the men in the Philipps family – of the five brothers, all over six feet, Lord Kylsant was the tallest, at 6ft 7in.

had been dubbed 'the Napoleon of shipping'; an immensely powerful businessman who had fallen from grace. Did the world at large think of him as a common criminal, a con man of the first order; or was he an ambitious person caught up in economic events beyond his control?

When the moment came, the response was emphatic. *The Daily Mail* recorded that 'he was met by his wife and, after a few hours spent at his London home, the scene years before of many brilliant parties, he travelled with her to Coomb, his beautiful country home overlooking the Bay of Carmarthen'.

The Morning Post took up the story: '…He received a remarkable welcome at his Welsh home, the tenants of his Coomb estate attaching ropes to his car and dragging it in triumph to the house'.

The Times explained that 'Lord Kylsant was owner of 6,000 acres in Carmarthen and Pembrokeshire, and of the historic castles of Llanstephan and Amroth'.

From *The Financial Times*: 'On 14 February 1933 he attended the House of Lords and took the oath and subscribed the roll. He was given a very warm welcome by many of his fellow Peers'. For the most part, though, Kylsant saw out a peaceful, if short, retirement at Coomb. He had by his side his wife Mai; they had three daughters but no son, which meant that on Lord Kylsant's death the peerage would be extinguished.

The death of the 'Napoleon of shipping' occurred on 5 June 1937, less than five years after his release from prison; and hastened, surely, by the five previous turbulent years. The *Times* opened its obituary notice with these words: 'Lord Kylsant, who died in his sleep on Saturday night, at Coomb, his Carmarthenshire seat, at the age of 74, was for a long period an outstanding figure in British shipping. He accomplished much, and it was largely because he attempted too much that his later years were clouded. During the past year his health had been failing, and for the last month he had been confined to his bed.'

He was laid to rest at the local Llangunnock parish church, where a memorial tablet to him was unveiled later that year. It seems appropriate that the final word related to finances. In March 1938 his estate was finally settled, being valued at £116,137, the bulk of it in property. He was, then, far from being a pauper; but that was a telling figure, just a handful of years after his investment assets alone had been valued at more than £5 million.

The rise and fall of Owen Philipps was complete.

7
'...The Question of New Mail Steamers'

Having examined the years of Lord Kylsant from the broad front of the company's overall position, a closer look at South American services under his direction is equally compelling.

Before his arrival it was already clear that the pendulum had swung towards South America as the major sphere of operations; soon after he became chairman that shift was confirmed in no uncertain terms.

Just two weeks after Owen Philipps (still two decades away from his baronetcy) had been made chairman, it was reported that details and drawings for new '6,000 tons deadweight steamers suitable for Brazil cargo trade' were being prepared. Orders for three of this class were placed on 24 June 1903, one with Workman-Clark and two with Harland & Wolff. They were named *Parana*, *Pardo* and *Potaro*. Describing them as 'suitable for the Brazil cargo trade' didn't do them justice. The 'P' ships were more concerned with the River Plate than with Brazil, for they became the company's first custom-designed ships for refrigerated meat. While they were essentially cargo ships, they could carry many migrants to South America – both factors promised increased income.

New cargo ships for the West Indies trade were also ordered at that time – *Catalina*, *Caroni* and *Conway* were smaller at just over 2,600 tons gross. On 14 October 1903 the directors were informed that 'Armstrong, Whitworth & Co. Ltd offer to build three cargo vessels for the West Indies trade. Carrying capacity about 4,200 tons and a sea speed of 10 $\frac{1}{2}$ knots. One extra main boiler available for possible fruit carrying arrangements, and fitted with a derrick for weights up to about 35 tons; they agree to take the *Ebro* in part payment, plus £80,000 cash'. The offer was accepted, though a month later the builder agreed to take *Minho* as well as *Ebro*. Despite being built for Caribbean service, all of the 'C' ships served at times on the Brazil cargo run.

Generally, though, the 'P' ships were of more interest, not only because they pioneered Owen Philipps' decision-making career with RMSP, but because they cemented the company's South American meat trade, which would become a vital element of its operations. A new contract was negotiated with the River Plate Fresh Meat Co., signed in October 1903 while the ships were under construction.

A further development at this time was an arrangement for River Plate-bound freighters to load in London. Little has survived on previous arrangements in this regard, but there was an agreement with other lines which precluded RMSP from using London as a loading port on this route. One of Philipps' first tasks was to have that changed, and before the 'P' ships were in service, the Company had gained a share of the London trade. The 'P' ships operated from London and Hull to Brazil and the

River Plate for their first few years. Designed to cater for the shallows of the River Plate, they navigated upriver as far as cattle stations at Campana.

By March 1918 enough export meat became available in Patagonia to warrant an extension southwards to this remote land. Even today few people live at this 'uttermost end of the earth'; at the end of the First World War was almost as desolate as the moon, with just a scattering of large sheep stations occupying an empty landscape. The ships made their way south towards the Magellan Straits, letting down their anchors at Rio Gallegos, Punta Arenas, Gregory Bay and Rio Seco in latitudes high enough for near permanent night during the middle of winter. There, in the glare of crude electric arc lamps and in bitter cold, meat cargoes were loaded. So remote was this country that the dying breed of square-riggers, homeward bound from Australia with cargoes of wheat, rounded the Horn and then met with the astonishing sight of arc lamps where nothing ought to be. It was not unknown for a windship to turn west on a rescue mission – for it was assumed this must be a ship piled up on the rocks – only to find her happily taking in cargo.

The first ship to visit Patagonia was *Pardo*, under Capt. G.F. Huff. Sailing in March 1918 from Newport Mon. and Milford Haven, she called at the River Plate and then loaded meat in the far south. After coaling later at Rio de Janeiro, she re-crossed the Atlantic and discharged at a strange selection of ports – Cowes, Le Havre, St Helens Roads, Plymouth and Newport. On her second Patagonian voyage, in August the same year, her itinerary included another unfamiliar name, for she bunkered at Dakar instead of Rio de Janeiro.

The '*P*' ships carried migrants (generally Spanish and Portuguese) in the 'tweendecks for the transatlantic voyage. The company's agent at Bilbao, in a fit of enthusiasm, once designed a poster to attract emigrant passengers for *Pardo*. He grandly depicted the ship with enough topsides to rival the biggest Cunarder, and gave her five funnels – four more than she actually had. He was predictably asked to withdraw it.

When *Pardo* and *Parana* were taken out of service and sold in the 1930s (*Potaro* had been lost in the First World War), the Patagonia service came to an end. There were occasional visits later, when cargo warranted, but no regular scheduled calls.

Chartered Tonnage

Before the arrival of Owen Philipps, successive generations of directors, managers and superintendents had, one suspects, held the blinkered vision of men reared during the Company's early years. Their thinking was of a company supported by Royal Charter and mail contract subsidies – of established route schedules which only needed minor adjustments now and then.

There was, for example, Admiral Whish RN, who had become a director in 1854 and was either chairman or deputy chairman for most of the period from 1873 until his death in 1883. Thomas Tufnell joined the Court in 1856, and was either deputy chairman or chairman from 1881 until his death in 1898. Eden Colvile also became a director in 1856 and was chairman from 1880 until his death in 1893 – and in his case there was a family tradition dating back to the original Court in 1839, for his father Andrew was on the first

The poster produced by RMSP's Bilbao agent, depicting Pardo (I) with *five funnels.*

Court of Directors, originally as deputy chairman and then chairman for a decade from 1846. Eden joined the Court following his father's death. Two former Commodores were also in decision-making positions late in the century, both having joined RMSP in its earliest years – Capt. Revett and Capt. Jellicoe were directors in the 1890s, and the latter continued well into the twentieth century.

Those examples provide an understanding of how the company's early operations became ingrained in the decision-makers of the 1880s and 1890s. Owen Philipps was affected by none of that tradition. He could (and did) come in with a purely objective vision. While he might fight tooth and nail for a mail contract, he regarded freight carriage as the principal element of the company's future, followed by passengers.

While the 'P' ships were still under construction, a new facet of RMSP's story began – a mixture of increasing trade opportunities with South America and Owen Philipps' ability to take advantage of them. The company began to charter cargo ships; the trickle became a flood, and as the years passed Philipps periodically urged the construction of new cargo ships to reduce chartered tonnage. Many loaded at UK west coast ports, others at east coast or Continential ports, for Brazil only. Though departures were irregular, there were often two or three a month. Numbers built up to a peak from 1909 to the start of the First World War. In the busiest four years nearly seventy charter voyages were made (mostly southbound only), with thirty-five being the highest number in a single year. They were principally carrying manufactured goods during a boom era for Brazil's industrial growth – for railways, buildings, factories and the like, not least in the Sao Paulo area; there was probably coal, too, to fuel these new industries.

The ships were mostly between 2,500 and 4,500 gross tons, often typical tramp ships of their day, products of the Clyde, Sunderland, West Hartlepool and the like, yards for which such vessels had become the bread and butter since technology advances made ocean tramping viable. Most are now long forgotten, but a few names and owners are remembered: Raeburn & Vérel's 4,003-ton *African Monarch* of 1898, for instance; Leyland's *Albanian*, a Sunderland-built ship of the same vintage; *Crown of Castile* and *Crown of Cordova*. There were Glasgow vessels belonging to Prentice, Service & Henderson; Glen Line's *Glenfarg*, 3,647 tons and among the oldest as she dated from 1894; G.M. Steeves' *Labuan*; Irish Shipowners' *Lord Ormonde*; Larrinaga's *Maria de Larrinaga*; Elder Dempster's *Melville*; Furness, Withy's *Persiana*; and J.P. Corry's *Star of Ireland*.

These vessels were used during the peak period around 1910, but from as early as 1905 RMSP used *Cheviot Range* and *Pennine Range*, 3,400-ton steamers from the Furness, Withy-owned Neptune SN Co. Leyland's *Planet Mars* was another. Typical of the earlier charters was the Plate SS Co's Oroño, a 2,891-ton steamer built at the Middlesborough yard of Sir Raylton Dixon in 1898 – she belonged to the fleet of Rochester-based ships managed by Gellatly, Hankey & Co. This astonishing surge in cargo trades and voyage charters declined gradually as new cargo ships were built for the company and as South America's industrial expansion inevitably slowed.

The Mail Ships

On 25 November 1903, Owen Philipps was at last able to devote some attention to the inadequacies of the mail ship fleet. On that day, the directors' minutes recorded the interview between Owen Philipps and the Hon. Charles Parsons referred to earlier; in the absence of evidence that steam turbines would be satisfactory, they would not yet be used.

The fusion of interests between Royal Mail and Harland & Wolff was already established, for a fortnight later Owen Philipps:

> *resolved to proceed at once with a new mail steamer. It was therefore agreed that Harland and Wolff should build one mail steamer for the Brazil and River Plate [trade], on their usual commission terms – that is, that the builders should render the Company a monthly statement of their expenditure on the ship, plus 5% for profit, and the Company to pay in cash or by bills at three, four or six months after date equal to cash.*
>
> *Messrs Harland and Wolff's books to be open to inspection or verification by any persons appointed for the purpose by the Royal Mail Steam Packet Co.*

Those words heralded perhaps the most momentous operational milestone in the Company's history – *Aragon*, as she was named, would be RMSP's first true ocean liner, by far the largest ship in the fleet to date; a vessel designed to make ocean voyaging a pleasure and not just a function. In short, she pioneered for Royal Mail all of those characteristics of a passenger liner which more recent travellers took for granted. She pioneered, too, the term 'A' ship, which became synonymous both with Royal Mail and South America throughout the remainder of the Company's years as a passenger ship operator.

All told there were nine ships in the class. For all that they followed a common design pattern in general, they varied in too many respects to be called sister-ships. In November 1904 the Court approved two more ships, one each from Harland & Wolff and Workman-Clark – they became *Amazon* and *Araguaya*. Then in September 1905 Philipps stressed the 'urgent necessity of ordering another mail steamer for the protection of the Company's River Plate route. With this object the Court authorised him to enter into negotiations with Messrs Harland & Wolff on more favourable terms regarding payment'.

Some time passed before that order was placed because Owen Philipps made a working trip to New York and the West Indies. He told the directors in February 1906 that satisfactory terms had been arranged, and so the order was placed – she would become *Avon*.

The final vessel in the initial group was a curiosity, for she was ordered for the Orient-Royal Mail service to Australia. She was to be 'similar to but somewhat larger than the *Amazon*, the details to be left to the Chairman'. When built she was named *Asturias*. If intended for permanent service to Australia, this was a curious name. The vessels RMSP had inherited for the service were 'O' ships; whether or not the Company retained the 'O' nomenclature, an 'A' ship name seems odd, and choosing a Spanish region (so appropriate for the South American trade) even more odd.

The fact is that by early 1907 cracks were showing in the arrangements with Orient Line. In January Philipps had told the Court that 'it might become necessary to give notice to the Orient company to terminate the agreement'. A name for the Australian service ship was not decided until May 1907. Although Philipps hadn't at that stage ended the agreement, there must be a suggestion that he already suspected this would happen and therefore planned that this ship would follow the others into the South America trade.

Following this giant three-year investment in five liners – each a little larger than the one before – there was a gap of some four years before the final four were initiated; they, too, were staggered over a few years. They were larger again, the first of them jumping 3,000 tons from *Asturias*. The overall increase from first to last was thus significant. From *Aragon's* 9,588 tons the size reached 15,831 tons before the group was complete.

The 'A' ships revolutionised passenger comfort and pleasure as far as RMSP was concerned, and under the entrepreneurial eye of Owen Philipps, more new ground was broken in terms of advertising and promotion. The Company aimed to increase its share of passengers who were going to travel anyway, and it wanted to tap into a new market – those who would simply take a sea voyage for pleasure. The 'A' ships were making seasonal cruises before 1910. They provided for the first time a quality of accommodation space and public rooms which would justify the expansive

117

promotion to which they were subjected – but it shouldn't be suggested that previous ships were functional freighters with a bare minimum of facilities for passengers. RMSP's front-line ships had been well regarded from the start; and especially from the time of the *Thames* class, around 1890 (when superstructures provided improved options), the Royal Mail ships were good enough to hold their own in the face of European competition.

Now, though, the upper decks were greatly extended, and with major size increases as well there was sufficient space to provide cabins and public rooms of great spaciousness; that, in turn, lent itself to fixtures, fittings and décor of breathtaking quality and craftsmanship. All of that was like a magnet to those who had the money to travel first class.

Promoting passenger ships through printed matter quickly became part of Philipps' philosophy. In earlier years 'promotion' comprised a factual Information Handbook, supplemented by discreet newspaper advertising. Barely a year after Philipps became chairman, the pages of schedules, tariffs, freight rates, regulations and the like which comprised the Handbook, came wrapped in a full-colour graphic cover.

In the same year – 1904 – RMSP published a lavish guide promoting Royal Mail voyages to Brazil and the River Plate. It talked of ports being sufficiently close to avoid monotony; a range of land tours from eight days to seven weeks (which could be extended to a year by staying at ports *en route*); first class return fare to Vigo £12 or to Rio from £45; first class tickets valid for steamers of The Pacific Steam Navigation Co. (on the other side of South America) and the Messageries Maritimes Cie; a string band of 'skilled musicians' was carried on all passenger ships (another of Philipps' initiatives) and was used for dances, concerts and private functions. Another matter for which Philipps was responsible was the addition of libraries on the ships – a recommendation for that some time before he arrived had been vetoed.

A further year later – as *Aragon* was ushered in – the era of the marketing-style descriptive brochure was introduced. Here, then, was a revitalised Company offering travel facilities previously unknown in RMSP, and doing an effective job of telling the world about it.

8
Harland & Wolff and Pirrie

The strength of the bond between Royal Mail and Harland & Wolff was so great that the two companies became irrevocably intertwined. Not only did Owen Philipps forge a strong link with Harland & Wolff from the start of his time with RMSP, in later years he was its chairman.

The first ships built for the Company by Harland's were *Pardo* and *Potaro*, ordered in 1903. It isn't known whether the arrangement for Harland's to bill RMSP monthly on the basis of costs plus 5% was at first a long-term contract or on a ship-by ship basis, but in later years – from 1917 – an Agreement was in place in which Harland & Wolff automatically received first offer for any new tonnage, with pricing on the same arrangement.

The Harland & Wolff story began with Edward Harland, a doctor's son born in Scarborough, Yorkshire in 1831. His childhood ran parallel with a period of rapid technological advancement and from the start Harland held an interest in engineering. He joined the staff of the Glasgow marine engineering company, J & G Thomson. Not long after Thomson began to build ships as well as engines, Edward Harland became its Naval Draughtsman; then he moved to the Tyne as manager of a shipyard there. In 1853 – in his early twenties – he was appointed manager of a Belfast shipyard which had been started by Robert Hickson on four acres of land leased from the Belfast Harbour Commissioners. The area became known about that time as Queen's Island, following a visit to the shipyard in its early days by Queen Victoria.

The ambitions of Harland were not satisfied with the management of a promising new business at so young an age. He began looking for land to develop on his own account. This worried Hickson, for he relied heavily on Harland; eventually he agreed to sell the business to him. Harland raised the money largely through the help of a Bibby Line partner – Bibby subsequently had many of its ships built there.

That same Bibby Line partner had a nephew with an un-Bibby-like name – Gustav Wilhelm Wolff. Three years younger than Harland, Wolff was a native of Hamburg who had come to England at the age of fourteen as an apprentice with a machinery company in Manchester. Later he became a draughtsman with Robert Hickson's enterprise. He was appointed assistant to Edward Harland, who subsequently made him a partner in 1862.

Under those two men the firm of Harland & Wolff prospered. When White Star Line (in the shape of Oceanic SN Co.) switched to steamers, Bibby Line recommended that they build at Belfast; they did – exclusively – until the merger with Cunard. The completion of White Star's first steamer, *Oceanic*, in 1871 was thus one of Harland's milestones. By this time an individual style was beginning to emerge. The firm favoured

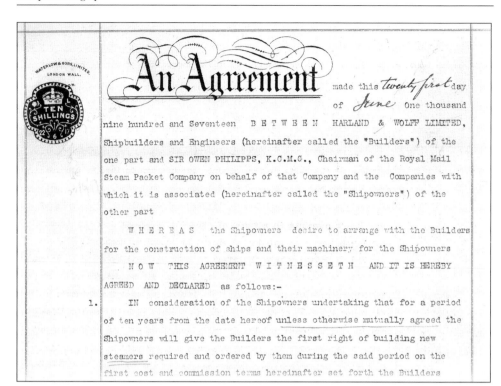

Part of the Agreement between RMSP and Harland & Wolff, 1917, in which the builder was given first option to build all new tonnage.

Sir Edward Harland.

Lord Pirrie.

long hulls with narrow beam, for instance (Bibby's *Persian* exemplified that, having a length of 362ft and beam of 34ft). They were often fitted with four masts and some featured a flat bottom which became known as the 'Belfast Bottom'.

In 1874 two new partners were appointed. Walter Wilson was one – he had little involvement with RMSP. The other new partner, though, became very closely associated with Royal Mail – he was William James Pirrie. Once the new partners were on board, Sir Edward Harland, as he was now titled, devoted increasing time to civic and public duties, and Gustav Wolff later did much the same. Sir Edward died suddenly on Christmas Eve 1895.

By this time Pirrie had virtual control of the firm, since Wolff spent nearly twenty years from 1892 as a Conservative MP for Belfast East. The cosmopolitan Pirrie came from an Irish family of Scottish descent, but had been born in Quebec in 1847. His father died not long after William Pirrie was born, as a result of which the family returned to Belfast. He was apprenticed to Harland & Wolff at the age of fifteen and was made a partner at twenty-seven.

His later years displayed a list of business, civic and public appointments which outdid the firm's founder: Lord Mayor of Belfast; two years as Chief Magistrate of Belfast; a Freeman of the City of Belfast from 1898; High Sheriff for County Antrim and County Down; Justice of the Peace. In 1906 he was created a baron, and three years later a Knight of the Order of St Patrick. Then in 1921 came the crowning honour when he was created Viscount Pirrie of the City of Belfast.

The Pirrie Years

Pirrie's reign took Harland & Wolff through its finest years. Ironically his greatest triumph and greatest setback concerned two sister ships, *Olympic* and *Titanic*. Their construction was an amazing achievement. Pirrie never wavered in his opinion that *Olympic* was his firm's masterpiece and his own personal favourite. By a twist of fate he died on board a ship built by the rival Belfast builder, Workman-Clark, and his body was transferred at New York to be carried home in his beloved *Olympic*.

As for *Titanic*, Pirrie had wanted to sail on her maiden voyage, but having had an operation shortly before, wasn't able to join her. This was the other side of the *Titanic* story – how many people should have been on her but weren't? One was a stoker who was about to sign on but didn't when his fiancée complained bitterly at the prospect of him vanishing over the western horizon a month before their wedding. I can vouch for that tale, for the stoker was my grandfather.

Lord Pirrie's business interests spread far beyond shipbuilding and, by comparing his interests with Kylsant's, it is clear how closely involved he was with the RMSP group. He was chairman of the African SS Co. and Ocean Transport Co.; a director of White Star Line, the International Mercantile Marine Co, Frederick Leyland & Co., the British and North Atlantic SN Co., the Mississippi & Dominion SS Co., Wilsons and Furness-Leyland Line, Elder Dempster, Lamport and Holt, Burmeister & Wain (Diesel System) Oil Engine Co, and Union-Castle Mail SS Co. In addition he was a member of the Committee of Lloyd's Register, member of the Advisory Committee to the Board of Trade on New Lighthouse Works, and Vice-President of the Institute of Naval Architects. He held further positions outside the shipping sphere.

Eden *(II), a freighter for West Indies services, after launching at Harland's Belfast yard in 1956.*

One of the directorships was particularly relevant to RMSP, for Burmeister & Wain pioneered the manufacture of marine diesel engines. Rudolph Diesel's work on engine development resulted in the first reliable diesel engine in 1897. Six years later, in France, he completed the first marine diesel. Its instant success found manufacturers building diesel machinery across Europe, with an English factory at Ipswich. The Danish firm of Burmeister & Wain fitted a diesel engine in the East Asiatic Company's *Selandia*, the first ocean-going vessel to receive one. Her historic maiden voyage, in February/March 1912, was from Denmark and London to Bangkok, and she created a lot of interest in the *Thames*. Among many visitors were members of the Royal Family; another was Winston Churchill, then First Lord of the Admiralty. He was quoted afterwards as saying 'As a result of this visit I have given instructions for investigation of the possibility of using diesel engines for propulsion of warships'.

It was unusual for a major new facet of technology to gain such instant across-the-board approval. The enthusiasm was emphasised in July 1912 when Lord Pirrie and the chairman of Hamburg-Amerika Line, Albert Ballin, visited Selandia's brand-new sistership, *Fionia*. Ballin was so impressed that he asked the East Asiatic Co. to sell the ship to Hamburg-Amerika – immediately. With the prestige that would flow for diesel engines and Danish engineering, East Asiatic agreed. Lord Pirrie was equally impressed, convinced that diesel machinery was the way of the future.

Harland & Wolff expanded dramatically between 1907 and 1921 with additional shipyards, engine works, foundries and repair works at Southampton, Liverpool, London, Glasgow and Govan. It was the Finnieston works at Glasgow, purchased in 1915, that housed Pirrie's new diesel engine works; here the first diesel for a Royal Mail ship was built a few years later. The firm of Burmeister & Wain (Diesel System) Oil Engine Co., of which Pirrie was a director, was formed in 1912 and took over all the patent rights in the UK for the engine.

The fact that Royal Mail had virtually every one of its diesel engines built by Harland & Wolff was due to the close relationship between Lord Pirrie and Lord Kylsant. Their association probably began around the time of the formation of the International Mercantile Marine Co. (IMMCo). In later years Pirrie did his best to break up IMMCo, which had been the brainchild of American financier J. Pierpont-Morgan, and was formed in 1902 as a combine consisting of the White Star, American, Red Star, Leyland, Atlantic Transport and Dominion lines. Thus a large slice of Atlantic shipping came under US control.

A company which possessed significant links with Harland & Wolff was Holland-America Line (HAL). The Dutch firm may well have closed its doors during those early years of the century had Harland & Wolff not held 51% of its shares when IMMCo was born. With Pirrie on the IMMCo board, an agreement was reached on behalf of HAL which saved it from being squeezed out by the American group. By the end of the First World War HAL was better placed to buy back its shares from Harland & Wolff. That association was no doubt reflected in the joint service which sprang up in 1922 between RMSP and HAL, operating between Britain, Europe and the Pacific coast of North America. The first RMSP vessels for that service were those for which Pirrie's firm provided the early diesel engines.

In March 1924 Lord Pirrie headed to South America:

in the interests of the Royal Mail Steam Packet Co, to examine the harbours and the facilities of the various ports; to observe in what respect modifications were necessary in new ships so that they would suit the proposals which the authorities had under contemplation for improvements of ports and harbours.

The ships alluded to were the recently-ordered *Asturias* and *Alcantara*, destined on their completion to be (albeit briefly) the largest motorships in the world.

Lord Pirrie travelled to the River Plate in *Arlanza*. At Buenos Aires the British Chamber of Commerce organised a banquet which was attended by representatives of commercial interests in South America. Lord Pirrie told them he was sorry not to see their completed deep-water port with a minimum depth of 30ft at low water, plus deep approaches. Failure to provide this, he stressed, would cause British and Continental shipowners to shelve their ambitious plans for the future and would place Argentina in a second-rate position for trading. 'Commodious dock facilities' was the theme he drove home wherever he went.

Feeling that doing nothing but criticise Argentina's port facilities was not entirely diplomatic, he added that the butter on board *Arlanza* was so good he thought it must be Irish...but it turned out to be Argentinian!

Pirrie left *Arlanza* at Buenos Aires and travelled to the west coast, where he joined the 8,480-ton *Ebro*. She had been built for RMSP by Workman Clark in 1915, but in 1922 was transferred to The Pacific Steam Navigation Co. It was thus as a PSN ship that Pirrie joined *Ebro* in Chile. After his visit to Antofagasta, the seventy-seven-year-old caught a chill. His schedule called for a stopover at Iquique but he didn't leave the ship and his condition suddenly deteriorated when he contracted double pneumonia. It was the feeling of the ship's doctor that he was better off on board than anywhere he could be placed ashore before the ship reached New York.

When they reached Panama his condition rallied and he insisted on being brought on deck to see that wonder of modern engineering, the Panama Canal. It was a fatal mistake, for he quickly suffered a relapse and died shortly before midnight on 7 June 1924.

Messages of sympathy reached Lady Pirrie (who was travelling with her husband) from King George V and Queen Mary, from Queen Alexandra and from Prime Minister Ramsay MacDonald, among many others – an indication of the esteem in which he was held. Lord Pirrie had cabled RMSP in London, with his last report on matters of mutual interest, just seven days before his death.

His body was embalmed, and when *Ebro* reached New York he was transferred to his first love among the ships he had helped create, White Star's *Olympic*. After the passage to England his body was taken home and he was laid to rest in Belfast City Cemetery.

In a tribute, Lord Kylsant said: 'As a shipbuilder he stood by common consent head and shoulders above all the other shipbuilders either in this country or abroad, and was recognised by all as the leading shipbuilder in the world'.

Far from jeopardising the RMSP/Harland & Wolff relationship, Lord Pirrie's death seemed only to strengthen it. After that time practically every new ship ordered by RMSP, and then by Royal Mail Lines from 1932, came from Harland's. The splendid 'A' ships of 1959/60 were the last units completed for Royal Mail before the Company entered the Furness Withy Group.

9
Burgeoning Markets

The large number of chartered ships being usefully employed by RMSP early in the twentieth century was a clear sign that there was much opportunity for the Company's own ships during a period of economic expansion in South America. That this was taken advantage of is evident in this chapter, which looks at ships and voyages – many of them from the growing fleet of modest freighters – as the new regime set RMSP on its revitalised course before the First World War.

Shortly before Owen Philipps came on the scene, the small cargo steamers *Tyne*, *Tamar* and *Teviot* were built. *Tyne*, 2,902 tons, came from Robert Napier at Glasgow in 1900. At about the same time Napier was building two mail steamers of about twice the tonnage – *Tagus* and *Trent* – and there is no hint as to why this smaller ship was tacked on. The directors, it seems, were a bit bemused themselves, for a week before her launch they were discussing selling her 'if £10,000 net profit can be got'. It couldn't, and so *Tyne* remained in the fleet until her loss after being torpedoed in 1917.

Tamar and *Teviot* were sister ships of about 3,200 tons built by Craig, Taylor & Co. at Stockton in 1902, their order coupled with the smaller Dee for an all-up cost of £117,902. Little about the ships appeared at the time of construction beyond a most extraordinary directors' minute: 'As to the use of liquid fuel. Recommending that the builders of the new ships furnish plans etc'. Whether or not this was a reference to diesel machinery is uncertain – a working engine had been produced by Rudolph Diesel by 1897, but it wasn't first fitted to an ocean-going ship until a decade after those remarks, which were made in November 1901.

It Happened in 1906

Tyne, *Tamar* and *Teviot* were engaged in South American services for most of their careers. Far removed from the express mail liners, they plodded across the ocean at a steady eight or nine knots. A voyage by *Teviot* in 1906 saw her load at Southampton, Hull, Antwerp and London for Brazil, then return to the UK; it occupied her from 15 September until 22 January the following year. At that rate she would have scarcely completed three round voyages a year; the square-rigged sailing ships of the period, without the expense of operating machinery, would have competed favourably with that.

The year 1906 also saw the mail ship Trent on the Brazil and River Plate route for the only time in her career. Built for West Indies services, she was on her way there when a machinery breakdown forced her into Plymouth. She managed to then reach Southampton, burning 200 tons of coal in the process. *Magdalena* was hurriedly organised to take her place, and so Trent, after repairs, took *Magdalena*'s River Plate sailing.

1906 also saw the first voyage for RMSP of the recently purchased cargo ship *Manau*. Together with her sister ship *Marima*, her purchase was part of Owen Philipps' desire to reduce the number of chartered ships. *Manau* had been the *Transvaal* and *Marima* the *Zulu*, both 2,740-ton steamers with Bucknall Line. On 30 March 1906 Manau departed for Brazil under Capt. Fookes. She had voyaged 6,833 miles, and was approaching Bahia, when she grounded on rocks just after midnight on 22 May, broke up and was a total loss.

Still in the same year, another purchased ship, *Segura*, made her first RMSP voyage, a round trip to Buenos Aires. This ship held three names during her RMSP years alone, as well as her original name of *Greek*. She had been built over a decade earlier for Union Line, one of ten 'G'-class ships designed and built by Harland & Wolff. The Belfast builder was as closely linked with the component companies of Union-Castle Line (the merger occurred in 1900) as it was with Royal Mail, and Gustav Wolff had been a director of the Union Line. That helps to explain why Owen Philipps, as he scoured the market for more tonnage, negotiated with William Pirrie at Harland & Wolff for purchase of *Greek* for £35,000 and, in the same year, her consort *Gaul* for £39,500 (she became *Sabor*).

Manau's sister-ship *Marima* made her first River Plate voyage during the latter months of 1906, under Capt. G.A. MacKenzie. These smaller cargo ships enjoyed a greater flexibility than was possible with liner schedules and utilised a wide range of ports, particularly discharge ports in Britain and Europe. On two of her early voyages, for example, *Marima* discharged at Sligo Bay and Fleetwood.

By this period the fleet was becoming very large. In 1908 it comprised forty-six ships and ten steam launches, tenders and the like, with a combined gross tonnage of 200,077; many chartered ships were swelling operations. Six sailings a month to South America were not uncommon. The departures for August 1907 were exceptional for the period: 2nd – *Nile* to Buenos Aires, 7th – *Tamar* to Brazil, 8th – *Tyne* to Brazil, 9th – *Aragon* to Buenos Aires, 16th – *Magdalena* to Buenos Aires, 22nd – Charter voyage to Bahia Blanca, 23rd – *Araguaya* to Buenos Aires, 30th – *Danube* to Buenos Aires, 31st – *Potaro* to River Plate. The build-up of trade reached a climax in 1913 – during the first six months there were forty-eight voyages to South America, ten of them in February alone.

A further event in 1906, though it involved a vessel on the West Indies mail run, had such an important outcome for Royal Mail staff that it should be recorded. There was a collision in fog at Cherbourg between RMSP's *Orinoco* and the crack German North Atlantic liner *Kaiser Wilhelm der Grosse*. Though the *Kaiser* was more than double *Orinoco's* tonnage she came off second best, with a great rent in her hull (made worse by the sharpness of *Orinoco's* clipper bow) and the loss of four lives. *Orinoco* suffered principally from bow damage, the forepeak area being crumpled, bowsprit destroyed and rigging damage. One seaman was lost. A court of enquiry found the *Kaiser* wholly responsible and, after a long delay, her owners paid over the cost for *Orinoco's* repairs.

The collision and its immediate consequences were serious enough, but there was an unhappy sequel. *Orinoco's* master was Thomas Pearce, and after the accident he was given command of *Trent*. The events at Cherbourg affected his health, and though only in his forties, less than two years later he had to be taken from his ship after becoming ill. His health deteriorated further and he died in the latter part of 1908.

The damaged Orinoco (II) *in Cherbourg Harbour, 1906, after collision with the German liner*
Kaiser Wilhelm der Grosse *(below)*

The stress from *Orinoco's* accident wasn't the sole cause of this; rather, it was the last straw in a quite amazing run of family accidents at sea. They began off the Australian coast in the 1870s when his father, commanding the steamer *Gothenburg*, went down with his ship. A few years later Tom Pearce was an apprentice with Aitken and Lilburn and was one of two survivors from the wreck of *Loch Ard* – the other survivor was a teenage passenger, Eva Carmichael, whom he pulled to safety from the treacherous waters of southern Australia.

A year later, in Loch Sunart, Tom was wrecked again, this time on the Irish coast. After that he left sailing ships and spent most of his career with Royal Mail, climbing through the ranks until he gained command. By that time he had two sons – the eldest joined Aitken and Lilburn for his apprenticeship and, in 1905, was in *Loch Vennachar* when she was lost with all hands off South Australia's Kangaroo Island.

Is it any wonder that Tom Pearce buckled under the accumulated years of stress? When news of his death reached the Court of Directors, one of their number was deputed to represent the Company at Tom's funeral. There is no record of that having happened before. His widow (still with one son to support) had precious little money. It was proposed that RMSP provide an ex-gratia payment of £500. Not all of the directors agreed and the matter was discussed at a special meeting – out of that came not only an agreement to pay the £500, but also the more far-reaching decision to establish a superannuation fund. Thus the superannuation arrangements which benefitted so many Royal Mail employees over the years owed their existence to the death of a man who is still best remembered as young hero, Tom Pearce, the Loch Ard's apprentice who saved Eva Carmichael on the rugged Victorian coast.

The Pearce story still hadn't ended. Tom's younger son, Robert Jun, despite the way the decades had treated his family, elected to go to sea and joined Aitken and Lilburn for his apprenticeship. He had his share of dramas but survived to find himself in a minesweeping trawler during the First World War; they accidentally hauled aboard a live mine, which exploded on contact. As with Loch Ard, only two people survived – Robert Pearce was one of them, blasted high into the air but otherwise unharmed.

Robert joined Shaw-Savill Line, another company enmeshed with the Kylsant empire. During the 1930s, when he was chief officer of *Pakeha*, he received an unexpected letter from Mrs Townsend, an elderly lady in Bedford. The letter explained that she had been the Eva Carmichael whose life Robert's father had saved. She would like to meet Robert and 'talk over the old days' – she had tracked him down with the aid of a London newspaper after reading a not entirely accurate account of events after the Loch Ard tragedy in Basil Lubbock's recently published book Colonial Clippers.

There is no record of whether the meeting took place – one hopes it did, because Eva did not live very much longer. As for Robert Pearce, by the First World War he was commanding the Shaw Savill freighter *Waimarama*. He took her, with a cargo of high octane fuel, into the Mediterranean as part of the Malta Convoy. There was an air attack, and a bomb made a direct hit on *Waimarama*; with her volatile cargo the result was predictable. She exploded in a ball of flame and sank. Oddly, for the third time in the Pearce family saga, there were two survivors from a devastating scene. This time, though, a Pearce wasn't among them.

1. Cover of the very large cruise brochure for 1969 (347mm x 247mm) whose importance for RML is described in the Introduction. The photo forming the cover was taken during the flight of the Piper Cherokee described in the story.

ANDES
Cruises 1969

Royal Mail Lines

THE ROYAL MAIL CO.

S.S. NILE LEAVING SOUTHAMPTON.

2. Postcard of *Nile* (II) leaving Southampton, from Raphael Tuck's Oilette series. The artist was Neville Cumming and the card was produced during the decade from 1905.

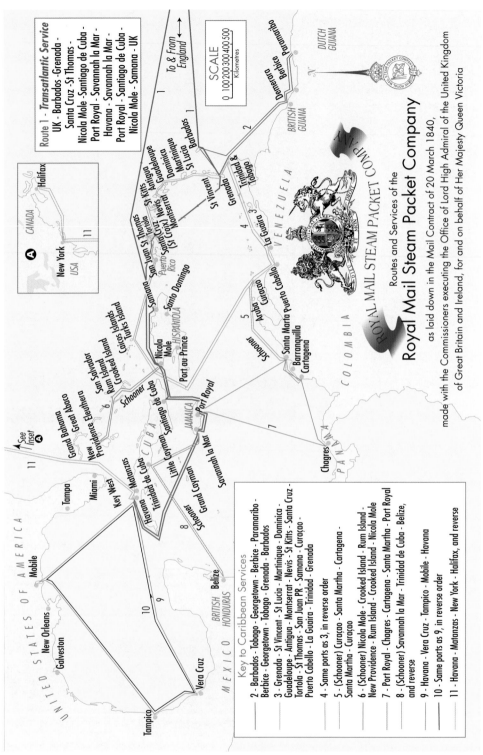

Route 1 - *Transatlantic Service*
UK - Barbados -Grenada -
Santa Cruz -St Thomas -
Nicola Mole -Santiago de Cuba -
Port Royal - Savannah la Mar -
Havana - Savannah la Mar -
Port Royal - Santiago de Cuba -
Nicola Mole - Samana - UK

SCALE
0 100 200 300 400 500
Kilometres

To & From
England

Routes and Services of the
Royal Mail Steam Packet Company
as laid down in the Mail Contract of 20 March 1840,
made with the Commissioners executing the Office of Lord High Admiral of the United Kingdom
of Great Britain and Ireland, for and on behalf of Her Majesty Queen Victoria

ROYAL MAIL STEAM PACKET COMPANY

Key to Caribbean Services

2 - Barbados - Tobago - Georgetown - Berbice - Paramaribo -
Berbice - Georgetown - Tobago - Grenada - Barbados

3 - Grenada - St Vincent - St Lucia - Martinique - Dominica -
Guadeloupe - Antigua - Montserrat - Nevis - St Kitts - Santa Cruz -
Tortola - St Thomas - San Juan PR - Samana - Curaçao -
Puerto Cabello - La Guaira - Trinidad - Grenada

4 - Same ports as 3, in reverse order

5 - (Schooner) Curaçao - Santa Martha - Cartagena -
Santa Martha - Curaçao

6 - (Schooner) Nicola Mole - Crooked Island - Rum Island -
New Providence - Rum Island - Crooked Island - Nicola Mole

7 - Port Royal - Chagres - Cartagena - Santa Martha - Port Royal

8 - (Schooner) Savannah la Mar - Trinidad de Cuba - Belize,
and reverse

9 - Havana - Vera Cruz - Tampico - Mobile - Havana

10 - Same ports as 9, in reverse order

11 - Havana - Matanzas - New York - Halifax, and reverse

3. RMSP's original route network, as laid down in the mail contract of 1840.

4. RMSP's operations handbook for 1904. Only after Owen Philipps joined the Company in 1903 did this regularly updated publication gain its attractive colour cover – an early tangible sign of the new chairman's influence.

5. This 1913 joint venture booklet between RMSP and the Pacific Steam Navigation Co. was a detailed ninety-page guide book for travellers. A small amount of information about the companies and their ships was included.

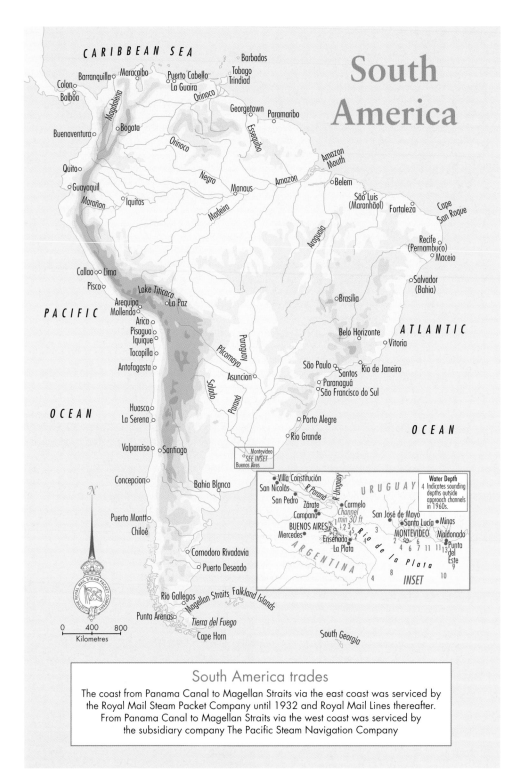

6. Places served by RMSP and Royal MailLine in South America.

7. The breathtaking first class dining saloon in *Asturias* (II), one of the illustrations in a particularly lavish booklet produced when the ship entered service.

THE ROYAL MAIL LINE

8. Third class brochure for the 'A' ships dating from the early 1920s. The entire artwork and design was produced by Kenneth Shoesmith.

THIRD CLASS TO SOUTH AMERICA
BY TRIPLE SCREW STEAMERS
"ALMANZORA"   "ANDES"   "ARLANZA"
(15,551 Tons Gross)   (15,620 Tons Gross)   (14,930 Tons Gross)

9. A portion of a 1937 brochure cover for use in South America, publicising the coronation of King George VI. The rich artwork came from Kenneth Shoesmith, showing that his talents extended beyond maritime subjects.

10. Page from a booklet issued to passengers in 1953 to mark the coronation of Queen Elizabeth II. This picture shows *Tagus* (I) at the Spithead Revue of 1887 for Queen Victoria's Golden Jubilee. Artist Howard Jarvis adopted a unique style for this booklet.

11. Voyaging down the southern European coast during 1970 in idyllic conditions is *Derwent* (III), one of the freighters brought into the Royal Mail fleet to maintain the River Plate meat trade after withdrawal of the 'A' ships in 1969. (Author's photograph)

12. Food and service were paramount matters throughout the company's life — this was a small portion of a first class buffet on *Aragon* (II) in the 1960s. (Author's photograph)

13. A timeless scene on a fine day at sea, photographed from *Derwent* (III) during a passage to Lisbon in 1970. (Author's photograph).

Cruising

THE
ROYAL MAIL
STEAM PACKET
COMPANY

NEW ROUTE TO
THE WEST INDIES

14. In 1905 RMSP began promoting its cruising holidays to North Americans. This booklet, issued that year, was produced for the United States, detailing voyages from New York to the Caribbean linked with cruises on intercolonial steamers between the islands.

The principal tour was forty days New York to New York, including a fortnight's cruise in *Solent* (II) – $280 per person for a twin share cabin.

R.M.S.P.
"ARCADIAN"
CRUISES de LUXE

15. A detailed eighty-page cruise booklet covering *Arcadian's* (I) holiday voyages in 1914. Much of the contents comprised detailed descriptions of the ports of call. There was, though, ample description of the ship, starting with these enticing words:

'The twin-screw ocean cruising yacht *Arcadian* possesses marked advantages, differentiating her from any ordinary mail steamer, or even from the palatial 'A' steamers of the RMSP. Specially arranged for pleasure voyages, the whole of her six decks is devoted to the pleasure and well-being of passengers.'

R.M.S. "ALMANZORA" - SIERRA LEONE

16. Postcard produced during the 1930s of *Almanzora*, showing her at Sierra Leone during a cruise. During the inter-war years *Almanzora* principally operated South America services, but was withdrawn on occasion for cruises. The artist was Kenneth Shoesmith.

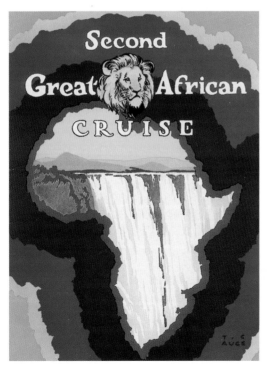

17. Without reference to company or ship, this cover introduced the reader to the most ambitious cruise ever made by a Royal Mail ship - the 101-day Second Great African Cruise by *Asturias* (II) in 1927. The cruise is described in Appendix II.

18. Perhaps the most classy brochure cover produced by Royal Mail, cool and elegant. It was produced to promote the 1938 cruise season before itineraries had been released, for it comprises a photographic study of the ship and the cruising scene in general. The painting of *Atlantis* was by Kenneth Shoesmith.

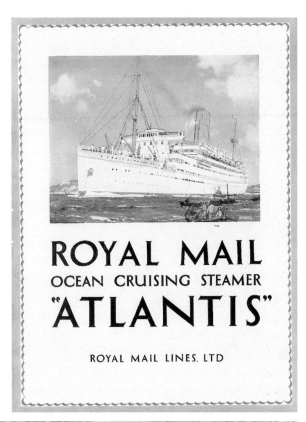

ROYAL MAIL
OCEAN CRUISING STEAMER
"ATLANTIS"

ROYAL MAIL LINES, LTD

ROYAL MAIL CRUISING STEAMER "ATLANTIS" OFF MIAMI.

19. The work of artist Kenneth Shoesmith dominated Royal Mail's promotional literature through the 1920s and 1930s. His individual style was displayed well in the flood of postcards of *Atlantis* produced in the 1930s. He rarely depicted a ship 'at sea', preferring settings of places the ship visited. This example shows her off the Florida coast at Miami.

ROYAL MAIL CRUISING STEAMER 'ATLANTIS' IN A NORWEGIAN FJORD

20. A Kenneth Shoesmith postcard of *Atlantis* in a Norwegian fjord. It employed a particularly strong foreground, which became something of a Shoesmith trademark.

ROYAL MAIL LINE TURBINE STEAMER 'ASTURIAS' LEAVING CAPETOWN. CRUISING

21. Asturias (II) at Capetown in the 1930s, a striking painting by Kenneth Shoesmith.

22. *Andes* (II) pictured during a cruise in the 1960s, probably by the ship's photographer. She was in the eastern Mediterranean, either Greece or Turkey.

23. Among the most important but least kept items of shipboard literature were the menus. A range of cover design subjects were used through the 1960s, probably the most attractive being a series of bird paintings, among them this picture of bramblings by an unidentified artist. This particular menu was used on *Andes* (II) on 9 June 1964 at Southampton, for the lunch which preceded the presentation of Miss Pears 1964 by Gracie Fields.

Bramblings

ROYAL MAIL LINES

24. The sitting room and bedroom of Almanzora Suite, one of the four suites on *Andes* (II) during her cruising years. These pictures were from a set of cabin photos taken in the early 1960s for an album used by consultants in the Passenger Department. (Author's photographs.)

Farewell to ANDES
Final Cruise 4th April to 3rd May, 1971

Passenger List

25. Passenger list for Royal Mail's last passenger ship voyage, an *Andes* (II) cruise early in 1971. The stern view of *Andes* steaming away was an evocative masterstroke.

26. *Orinoco* (I), 2,901 tons, built in 1851. A large and fine ship when she was built, her ignominious end came after just eight years, being broken up because she was riddled with dry rot.

27. One of the first postcards issued by RMSP was this Charles Dixon painting of *Trent* (III), used on the West Indies mail service from early 1900.

R.M.S. "LOCH RYAN" 9,904 TONS GROSS
Royal Mail Lines' Cargo/Passenger Service between United Kingdom and North Pacific Coast.

28. Postcard of *Loch Ryan*, 9,904 tons, a cargo ship carrying 12 passengers, issued in the 1950s. The artist was Howard Jarvis.

R.M.S. "LOCH LOYAL" 11,035 TONS GROSS
Royal Mail Lines' Cargo/Passenger Service between United Kingdom and North Pacific Coast.

29. Postcard of *Loch Loyal*, 11,035 tons, the last cargo liner built for RML. She came from Harland and Wolff in 1957. The artist was Howard Jarvis.

Approaching the First World War

The period up to the First World War passed profitably for RMSP. On the South America run the 'A' ships consolidated their position as the premier liners trading to the region. Their operation and timekeeping were rarely at fault. From 1910 their itineraries were occasionally varied to include smaller ports that were generally the domain of cargo ships – Ilia Grande and Flores principally. As early as 1908 *Avon* was discharging passengers (not an inappropriate description) into lighters at Recife by means of a wicker basket slung from a derrick.

Those three old faithfuls *Thames*, *Clyde* and *Magdalena* each reached its hundredth voyage for Royal Mail in the region of 1910. Though all were by then usually employed on the UK – West Indies – New York run, the greater part of their careers were spent on South Atlantic routes.

At this time, with the 'A' ships building healthy business, RMSP sought bigger premises in South America. They signed an agreement just before the First World War for a new property in Buenos Aires, and within two years had also concluded an agreement to purchase at Rio de Janeiro numbers 53 and 55 Avenue Rio Branco from the Benedictine Monastery of Sao Bento, to whom the property had been left for sale to boost the institution's funds.

The October 1911 sailing of *Araguaya* used Villagarcia as a new Spanish port southbound; every third 'A' ship sailing then included Villagarcia, though on one occasion *Araguaya* called at Coruña instead. Those calls were principally to embark migrant passengers.

An important event in July 1912 was the maiden voyage of *Deseado*, first of five 'D' class ships for the meat and migrant trades. One of Owen Philipps' first acts as Chairman had been to order the three 'P' ships for this trade. While they continued to be used (two surviving the war and staying in service until the 1930s) their cargo capacity was too small to be significantly profitable; indeed, there were times when freight rates were so low that they made an operational loss despite being full.

The 'P' ships were around 4,500 tons; Deseado and her sisters were about 11,500 tons and much more economically viable. Apart from vast refrigerated hold spaces, they could carry close to a thousand passengers, principally migrants. They did not need to maintain such a strict schedule as the 'A' ships, providing a flexibility which allowed the freight departments to breathe a little easier. Their final significance was that RMSP based them at Liverpool. This was a complete departure, providing the Company with three UK bases for its meat ships – Southampton, London and Liverpool – which maximised delivery options to centres all over the country.

The 'P' ships had been designed, in part, at a size which allowed them to move upriver from Buenos Aires to load at cattle stations. The 'D's and subsequent meat ships were too large for that, which Royal Mail countered by building the specialist meat lighters *Doon*, *Dart* and *Devon*.

Deseado's maiden voyage itinerary was Liverpool, Coruña, Villagarcia, Vigo, Leixões, Lisbon, Rio de Janeiro, Buenos Aires, Ensenada, Tenerife, Vigo, Liverpool. Essentially the same schedule was followed for years to come by all five ships.

The extent to which business was booming was reflected in the fact that RMSP, still awaiting its last 'A' ships, chartered Lamport and Holt's *Vauban* during 1912 and 1913. At first she retained her name, but after four voyages was renamed *Alcala* and briefly entered the RMSP fleet. After *Andes* had embarked on her maiden voyage in September 1913, *Alcala's* services were no longer required. Late that year she was returned to Lamport and Holt to resume her traditional service between Buenos Aires and New York. The same company's *Vandyck* was also used at this time for some charter voyages.

Tales of the *Tamar*

Early in 1912 *Tamar*, under Capt. R.A. Ellis, was homeward bound from Brazil. During the passage from Rio de Janeiro to St Vincent, where she would coal, it was discovered that the bunkers were unexpectedly low and the stock was exhausted some time before Cape Verde was reached. That kind of story was familiar enough in the middle of the nineteenth century, and there were tales of ships heading in all directions across the ocean in search of islands whose trees could be chopped down. It wasn't the done thing in 1912, and neither was Capt. Ellis's solution of ripping down and burning almost £500-worth of ship's fittings to keep the furnaces fed. At a court of enquiry Capt. Ellis lost £20 contingent pay, while the chief engineer was suspended for three months.

According to the Company's details of service book, Capt. Ellis was merely docked the £20, but he was nevertheless replaced on the next voyage by Capt. Walter H. Parker, who had hitherto served on West Indies services. He was not particularly pleased with this command, for he had just returned home for leave. He recorded in his autobiography that his urgent call to *Tamar* was 'to supersede a man who had been called on to resign command of the *Tamar*', which he described as an 'ultra-cargo steamer' in the Brazil and River Plate trade. He joined her so close to sailing from London's Royal Victoria Dock that he hadn't even time to unpack a uniform before they were moving down the dock.

Already unhappy at the rude break-up of his holiday, Parker was even less pleased when he looked around. The deck and engine room hands had been shipped in Antwerp and were apparently less than desirable exports from Germany and Scandinavia; they turned out to be the worst crew he ever sailed with and the ship got in a filthy state. When, at the end of the voyage, Capt. Parker gave many of them bad discharges, they asked him why. His response was emphatic: '*Because I can't give you anything worse, damn you!*'.

Subsequent voyages, he said, were better in every way – though that hardly seems to have been the case on her next homeward passage. The service report read: 'On 16 January 1913, on voyage from London to Newport, Mon., in lat 50°30' N, long 1°08' W, the Chief Engineer reported the propeller working loose. Course altered to Nab Lightship, which was passed at 1.10 p.m., and at 6.05 p.m. ship berthed alongside 41 quay, Southampton. She was there five days, then proceeded Hull to load for Voyage 33 to South America'. How much worse that story would have been had the ship not been successfully nursed to Southampton.

Tamar loaded for Voyage 33 and departed for Brazil and the River Plate early in 1913. Shortly after leaving Montevideo homeward the officer on watch reported receiving a curious message by morse from a German steamer nearly four weeks out from Hamburg. Had England, the ship wanted to know, declared war against Germany? Having been assured by the Officer on Watch that the request hadn't been provoked by manoeuvring too close, Capt. Parker warily asked what reply had been sent. The laconic answer had apparently been: 'Not yet'.

10
War and Post-War

Just as the approach to war has slipped into this story without warning, so, one suspects, the war itself was thrust on the people in a way that left them less prepared than they would be for the next great conflict. The assassination of Archduke Ferdinand at Sarajevo on 28 June 1914 provided the grim sequel to the exchange of messages involving *Tamar* a year earlier. This conflict would change the destiny of Royal Mail, as it changed the destiny of the world.

As early as 16 August, *Arlanza* was at the mercy of an armed German liner, *Kaiser Wilhelm der Grosse*, and survived to tell the tale. This was the *Kaiser's* second brush with a Royal Mail ship, coming eight years after her collision with *Orinoco*.

By the end of August the 'A' ships had moved their home terminal to Liverpool. Southampton was closed to commercial shipping by the Admiralty. For some of the 'A' ships, Liverpool's unfamiliar surroundings did not last long for they were soon requisitioned. On 6 September 1914 *Aragon* went to an equally unfamiliar port – London – then sailed to Southampton, Gibraltar, Alexandria, Port Said, Suez and Bombay. Her return passage ended at Devonport. *Avon* made a similar voyage at much the same time.

Aragon had been at Buenos Aires when war was declared. At the next berth was the German liner *Cap Trafalgar* – two of their respective country's most modern and large South America service liners eyeball to eyeball. *Aragon* quickly sailed; the German ship was larger and a low tide prevented her from following *Aragon* out of port.

Aragon left the River Plate and sailed without lights up the coast. At Pernambuco a man claiming to be from a local radio station came on board and offered information completely the reverse of what the ship had previously learned about the location of a German squadron. His eagerness to learn what course *Aragon* would take was not terribly subtle – Capt. Mason carefully explained that he would take the normal course, west of Fernando Noronha, as this would take his ship well clear of the squadron's position so kindly provided by the gentleman.

Once out of sight of land a quite different course was set, and Capt. Mason was rewarded by learning that his radio operator picked up German voices which were rapidly becoming fainter.

Left: *the dust jacket of H.W. Leslie's First World War history of RMSP.*

Below: *the original photo from which the jacket took its design - a blurred but evocative picture taken from a lifeboat by a survivor of the sinking of* Arcadian *(I) from torpedo attack in April 1917.*

Arcadian, *on trooping duty, had just left Salonika for Alexandria and had 1,335 people on board when she was torpedoed. How quickly she sank can be gathered from the report (even if it was perhaps not quite accurate) that the final plunge captured on the photograph occurred 'little more than five minutes after the explosion'. About 270 men were lost.*

Pardo's Tale

Aragon wasn't Royal Mail's only ship at Buenos Aires at that time. On the day war was declared, *Pardo* reached Buenos Aires and was promptly rammed in number two hold by an out-of-control steamer in the approach channel. Capt. Parker grounded her on an adjacent mudbank as she was in danger of sinking. At length she was brought to the port and entered drydock. With the prospect of lengthy inactivity, Capt. Parker decided to make a few observations around the port. He noted that *Cap Trafalgar* had a new crow's nest high on her foremast, and there were 'feverish coaling operations'. He was sure she was being converted into an auxiliary cruiser and succeeded in temporarily having the bunkering stopped.

As Europe quickly plunged deeper into crisis, the Argentine authorities ordered all ships in the port to be searched 'for contraband of war'. At first *Cap Trafalgar* refused, 'an officer at the gangway actually declaring her to be a ship of war'; then the German Minister announced that that had been a mistake and the ship could be searched.

The delayed search, predictably, uncovered nothing sinister and she was allowed to resume coaling. Capt. Parker estimated between 4,000 and 5,000 tons were loaded before she departed for 'Las Palmas'. Before long she was off Montevideo with a request to load bunkers as she was short of coal! There was little doubt that she was supplying other German steamers, but she was allowed to load more at Montevideo. It would be nice to imagine that Capt. Parker's observations did their little bit towards the demise of *Cap Trafalgar* at the hands of the auxiliary cruiser *Carmania*, but that wasn't the case: she was discovered in September 1914 providing coal to German freighters in the shelter of a remote South Atlantic island and was sunk by Cunard's *Carmania* after a fierce battle – and *Carmania's* people didn't know what ship they had sunk for several days.

Capt. Parker, meanwhile, was still at a loose end in Buenos Aires while *Pardo* was being repaired. He spent the time walking round the docks, 'observing and deducing', and from his comments it seemed not to have been the safest occupation. It was a telling introduction to what the Company, its ships and its personnel would face over the next few years.

Hostilities Escalate

So many tales were already there for the telling – and the war had only been underway for a matter of weeks. In this chapter we are concerned with the South America service and how it fared at this time. Traffic suffered immediate disruption. By 11 August the Argentine meat contracts with Swifts and La Blanca had been suspended, and it was expected that the River Plate Fresh Meat Co. would soon follow. The suspensions took immediate effect; meat already on the high seas was suddenly not bound by contract and RMSP was obliged to negotiate a settlement with the consignees. Alternatively, a vessel could return her cargo to the port of shipment, but would not earn freightage. With cargoes not yet loaded, shippers were prepared to negotiate new terms.

Within a week of the start of hostilities, southbound freight Conference rates were abandoned. 'Special rates of freight will be quoted on application', a notice to shippers said. In fact the shipping industry as a whole, not knowing quite how to react, did much the same thing, and the Brazil Steam Lines (RMSP, T & J Harrison, Lamport and Holt and The Pacific Steam Navigation Co.) were among many British lines to place a 50% surcharge on tariff rates. When conditions sorted themselves out, the percentage was gradually reduced.

Different facets were, in this respect, paradoxical. Normal trade corridors were disrupted as traditional trade patterns broke down. Many exports were vetoed because materials and manufacturing facilities were needed for the war effort. Imports were still vitally needed, but they were troublesome, too, because there was less money to pay for them once exports had declined. The paradox was that when the sums were done at the end of the war, it was clear that Royal Mail and its other group companies had made enormous profits – that, as we have seen, was a factor in the court case against Lord Kylsant.

You would hardly have expected that result early in the war, with vessels like *Andes*, *Amazon*, *Aragon*, *Demerara*, *Parana* and *Pardo* lying idle in foreign ports waiting for cargo and hopeful of embarking some passengers. They retained full crews, which further exacerbated the finances, and such cargoes as were carried attracted soaring insurance rates. Often a month or more passed between 'A' ship departures, and sometimes double that period separated general cargo voyages. Only the 'D' ships maintained something like a regular service – never had the meat trade been so important. During 1917 the freighter scene almost disintegrated; there was one sailing each in January, February, March, September and November – two each by *Pardo* and *Parana* and one by *Monmouthshire*.

The war displaced many ships from their normal routes and among the strangers to ply the South America trade were Shire ships, now in RMSP ownership. *Denbighshire* was the first to switch routes, though she made her first passage to South America shortly before the war. It wasn't a good start, however, for she put in to Lisbon to replace a lost propeller. During 1915 two more entered the trade – *Carmarthenshire* and *Pembrokeshire*, both of which made their maiden voyages on the route. *Carnarvonshire*, *Cardiganshire* and *Monmouthshire* joined the service in 1916.

Most other ships on South Atlantic routes were familiar, though *Dee*, making a single voyage to Brazil in March and April 1916, was an exception. Another was *Sorata*, a 4,606-ton freighter built in 1897 and owned by The Pacific Steam Navigation Co., which was used for several east coast voyages under the Royal Mail flag. Also in 1916, *Danube* returned to the route after an absence of some years.

By no means all of the ships with which South America was familiar came through the war unscathed. *Potaro* was captured by a raider in January 1915, was used as a scout and then scuttled. The same raider, *Kronprinz Wilhelm*, captured and sank *Tamar* that spring, while in September 1915 *Caroni* was sunk by shellfire from a German submarine.

During February 1916 *Alcantara* fought her famous duel with *Greif* – which resulted in both ships sinking – and a year later *Drina* and *Arcadian* were torpedoed and sunk. Another transport, *Tyne*, met a similar fate in June 1917, as did *Aragon* that December. *Amazon* was lost early in 1918.

So the terrible roll-call of people and ships went on. Not surprisingly, as the war progressed and more and more ships were lost, those which remained were at a premium. That was where much of the First World War profits came from. Whether or not the Government thought they were excessive, they were earned the hard way.

Post-War Times

Beyond the Armistice, there were still too few ships, too much cargo, too many passengers. The Royal Mail group alone had lost around a hundred ships. In 1918 shipyards were building as many standard design cargo ships as they could churn out. Some of them were for Royal Mail, modified for the carriage of meat. To operate them, a new company was established – RMSP Meat Transports. In March 1918 the first of those ships left North Shields, sailed to the *Thames* and then Plymouth before setting off on her maiden voyage to the River Plate; she was *Navasota*. Three sister ships followed in 1919 and 1920, and a group of slightly smaller units was built at the same time.

The larger ships had 440,000ft^3 of insulated space divided into forty-one chambers, and they were driven by twin-screw reciprocating engines. Apart from *Navasota* they were *Nagara*, *Natia* and *Nariva*. The smaller ones, *Narenta*, *Nebraska* and *Nictheroy*, were single-screw ships with steam turbines.

March 1918 also found Capt. G.F. Huff taking *Pardo* from South Wales for the first meat-loading voyage to Patagonia, a service described earlier. That May *Larne* made a rare voyage to Brazil, and returned by way of Sierra Leone. *Segura* (formerly *War Pansy*) began operations to the Plate in May 1919, while that summer and autumn saw the maiden voyages of *Severn*, *Somme* and *Siris*.

So the war losses were gradually made up. RMSP gained the use of some ships in an unexpected way, for in the wake of the Russian Revolution many ships were impounded by nations not recognising the new Soviet regime, Britain among them. Twelve of the steamers came to Royal Mail for management and operation, most remaining until the early 1920s. With services now so far-flung, only one of the twelve is known to have been used on South America routes, the 4,784-ton *Vologda* voyaging to the River Plate in 1919. Generally these ships were staffed by company personnel, but as there were not enough to go round, some skippers were supplied by the Ministry of Shipping through master mariners whose ships had been lost.

A larger vessel completed in 1919 was The Pacific Steam Navigation Co.'s *Orbita* which, in conjunction with other 'O' class ships, was to operate to the west coast of South America. When that trade suffered a downturn in the 1920s, RMSP took them (in exchange for the two former West Indies mail ships *Ebro* and *Essequibo*) and opened a North Atlantic service with them. *Orbita's* maiden voyage in September 1919, though, was under the Royal Mail flag as the company's first post-war express mail liner sailing from Southampton to Brazil and the River Plate. The surviving 'A' liners had not been returned from government service and *Orbita* was chartered for several voyages to help fill the gap.

Other 1919 maiden voyages were *Nagara*, *Radnorshire* and *Glamorganshire*, while *Tamar* crossed the South Atlantic for her first voyage under that name – she had previously been *Denbighshire*. Much of this new tonnage consisted of standard design government-ordered units which were taken over by shipowners while under construction at the end of the war.

For a short time RMSP enjoyed perhaps the most successful period in its history. The war was over, surviving ships were steadily returning to service and new ones joined them; and there was no shortage of cargo and passengers to be moved. The River Plate mail steamers, in particular, were in such demand from first class passengers that on occasion they spilled over into second class accommodation. Such good times, of course, couldn't last. The 1920s saw an expected downturn in trade, and worsened with the onset of the Great Depression. Before dealing with those leaner years, it is worth a closer look at the 'A' ships, which re-established RMSP as a front-line passenger company from 1905 and formed a renowned and integral part of the South American scene for the next two or three decades.

11
All Aboard the 'A' Ships

After so many decades as a passenger ship operator, Royal Mail was at last able, through the advance of technology, to possess in the 'A' ships vessels which made people *want* to travel by sea. The ships are described in some detail in Volume 2. This chapter takes a broader view, starting with matters not confined to the 'A' ships, for it leafs through the Company's regulation book for 1906 to reflect the manner in which the ships were run.

As far as navigation was concerned, long experience had developed a routine which specified that after a junior officer had set a course, it had to be approved by a senior officer and then by the captain. If any navigational matter was approved by the captain but not by the chief officer:

> *he must at once respectfully represent the point to the Captain, and if any difference of opinion then exists, particulars of it, with the reason why each has his view, should be entered in the ship's Log, when the Chief Officer's responsibility in that particular case ceases.*

When the ship's position was doubtful, the captain or chief officer had to be in charge of the bridge for at least four hours prior to the time when land might expect to be sighted. A lookout was always to be posted on the forward bridge and another on the bridge at night, to be doubled in foggy conditions. During daylight the forward bridge lookout was only to be used in thick or foggy weather. Every half hour during the night, when the bell was struck, the lookout men had to 'call aloud their stations', and between the bells the junior officer of the watch inspected side and masthead lights – and inspected the lookouts, reporting if any were asleep.

Until the ship cleared Lisbon outward, officers were divided into two watches instead of three, with only the chief and second officers taking charge. While entering port the officers were stationed as follows: captain on the bridge; chief officer on the forecastle; second officer on the quarterdeck or poop; third officer on the forecastle; fourth officer abaft the bridge to pass on the captain's orders, or at the telegraph when there was no fifth officer; fifth officer at the telegraph on the bridge.

Red and white flags, or a disc, were used by the officer stationed aft to signal to the captain 'whether or not the screw was clear' – the white flag signified 'all clear' and the red one the reverse.

Regulation fourteen said:

> *The Directors desire to impress forcibly on the captains and officers the great importance they attach to the use of the lead at all times when it can be of service; not only should it be used in entering and leaving port, but at night or in thick weather, whenever land is being approached,*

A standard cargo ship after launching at Workman Clark's yard, Belfast during or just after the First World War. Units like this formed a large part of RMSP's replacement tonnage after the war.

or the vessel is likely to be in the vicinity of land, or of anything dangerous. The lead should not be confined to occasions when there is doubt as to the position of the ship, but it should be used, especially at night or in thick weather, to verify the supposed position.

The Officer on Watch had to provide the latitude position to the captain before 1 p.m., while the chief officer took his own observations. When land, lighthouses or other features were in sight, it was the chief officer's duty to make sure bearings were taken every half hour and noted in the log book. No harbours where 'the navigation is at all intricate' could be entered after dark. The compasses – cause of so many accidents at sea – were checked and the errors worked out whenever possible. The result of every check had to be noted in the log book, and even the method of calculation used. If more than twenty-four hours elapsed between compass checks, the reason had to be noted. Even spare compass cards – the direct responsibility of the master – had to be brought out every so often for examination.

Each week watertight doors were tested. Pumps had to be regularly inspected, sluice valves, suctions etc overhauled 'on every available occasion'. On every survey for the Passenger Certificate, the chain cable was got up and examined, and the shackle pins knocked out and coated with white lead.

The captain's inspection was carried out at 11 a.m. every day at sea, while an inspection of the engine-room, engineers', stewards', boatswain's and carpenter's store rooms, empty passenger cabins, officers', engineers', servants', seamen's, firemen's and coal-trimmers' berths was carried out at least once a week. The magazine was inspected with the same frequency, particularly the Drowning Pipe, by which the room could be flooded in the event of fire.

A corner of the first class social hall in Almanzora. *The fine Tudor-style design and artistry extended through this very large and lofty room with stunning effect.*

Regulation eight politely put passengers in their place: the officer on watch was to 'answer civilly any questions put to him by passengers, but are to avoid entering into prolonged conversation, so that his attention may not be diverted from his proper duties'.

Fire regulations were particularly strict. On no account was turpentine to be included in the ship's stores, and paraffin was only allowed in special tanks. Oil for paint thinning had to be kept in iron drums or tin cans and paint was mixed out on the weather deck. Anyone using a naked light in the store room was liable to instant dismissal. At 9 p.m. the cook's fires and ship's company's lights were put out; at 11 p.m. the fires and lights in the saloons were extinguished, with the exception of Police Lights. At his discretion the captain could allow the saloon and smoking room lights to remain on until midnight. That clearly referred to oil lighting and not electric, which had been progressively added to the fleet since the installation of a Siemens system in *Orinoco* in 1886.

In relation to electricity:

The cost of electric lighting in each of the ships will be watched with great interest, and any important suggestion likely to lead to improvements or economy will be gladly received by the Superintending Engineer.

Much must be left to the discretion of the Captain and Chief Engineer to make the lighting by electricity successful, and popular with passengers. With this view, the lights should be regulated as circumstances may require, but it is considered that the 'police', engine and boiler-room lights, should be kept going all night. All other lights may be regulated as may be found necessary or agreeable to the passengers, subject, of course, to the Captain's instructions.

With the exception of the engineers' department, the use of naked lights and candles was prohibited. Smoking in the dining saloon and cabins was also forbidden although, again, the captain was empowered to give permission, on special occasions, 'to smoke after déjeûner and dinner, provided it is not objectionable to passengers'.

Signalling at night to all English Channel stations was compulsory. Mail steamers simultaneously let off a roman candle and yellow light. Cargo steamers (except those from the West Indies, which had a different signal) and passenger-cargo vessels used a roman candle and yellow light fired simultaneously, followed by two roman candles, one right aft and the other just abaft the bridge, also fired simultaneously. On busy nights it must have been quite a show, and if officers at shore stations had a weakness for fireworks, they could conceivably sit back and watch rather than acknowledge the signals, for if there was no answer within five minutes the operation had to be repeated. When passing Hurst Castle approaching Southampton at night the steam whistle was sounded, and the signals remained up until answered with a green light from Hurst.

Rules regarding discipline were interminable. In mail ships, 'no captain or officer of any grade is to make any public room a place of resort', and the captain, chief officer, chief engineer, purser and surgeon were the only members of the ship's company allowed to eat in the saloons. Divine service was to be 'duly and reverently performed' every Sunday by the captain when circumstances permitted. Swearing and bad language were strictly forbidden; so was card playing among the officers. Regulation forty-five stated that 'no female, except passengers and the stewardess, is to be allowed to sleep on board any of the

Company's ships'. Officers and crew were not only prohibited from using passenger accommodation as 'a place of resort', they were not even allowed to use the passenger decks unless it was unavoidable. Dismissal faced any stewards or servants 'soliciting fees from passengers'. No liquor or mineral waters were allowed in the ship except those in the ship's store.

The discovery of smuggling resulted in instant dismissal. With a view to preventing smuggling and the 'secret carriage of freight', the captain searched the ship shortly before arrival in the United Kingdom and principal ports abroad. Together with two 'executive officers' (one being the chief or second officer) and a warrant officer, the master searched his ship from stem to stern, including the engine room, forecastle and the sea chests of any seamen who gave cause for suspicion.

The black hulls, buff funnels, pink boot topping and white upper works which distinguished Royal Mail ships for many years was a distinctive combination, but some found it bland – and from the regulation of 1906 which forbade painting abroad to be in different colours from those in which the ship left England, it leads one to wonder if any masters had their own ideas about aesthetic appeal.

Regarding hurricanes and the dreaded Colon 'norther':

> With good sea-room, sails or awnings furled, funnels additionally secured, boats well lashed, hatches on and ready for battening, a ship may be considered secure from danger, being at all times more or less hurricane-rigged.

Despite that assertion, the operative phrase was 'more or less'.

Matters to be entered in the ship's log included when guns were fired, especially at night, and why; when ports and deadlights were barred in during the hurricane season; when compartment wells were sounded and the depth of water found; the deaths of animals on freight or provedore account; marks of turtle which died or were thrown overboard.

Even though the comfort and well-being of passengers were primary concerns, any who didn't conform to the accepted dress code (or, at least, departed too drastically from it) at mealtimes were talked to by the captain, as was anyone in good health who didn't come to the saloon for meals but asked for them in their cabin. Card playing was allowed among passengers (except on Sundays), but if it reached a level of out-and-out gambling, the captain had to step in 'firmly but respectfully'.

The status symbol for a first class passenger of being invited to dine at the captain's table was handled differently in 1906; the captain and purser changed their seats regularly so as to satisfy the majority of passengers. I have, however, seen at least one instance on an 'A' ship where this wasn't the case, suggesting either that captains had a degree of autonomy or that the rules changed not long afterwards.

Passenger bookings were quite haphazard. If a passenger boarded without having booked a passage, the booking could be done there and then, but with a 10% surcharge. The principal problem involved third class passengers, whether in the 'tweendecks in the time-honoured style for migrants, or as deck passengers. Hundreds at a time could pour on board, creating mayhem for the purser's staff. The purser, stated the regulations, should adopt the best method 'for preventing deck passengers from travelling without tickets, or from going beyond the point to which they have paid'. With the best will in the world, plenty slipped through the net. Problems with berthing arrangements in first class led to officers at times giving up their cabins for the use of passengers, though this was frowned on by Head Office unless the circumstances were most exceptional. 'It is very undesirable in any circumstances,' the book emphasised, 'for the captain to give up his cabin to a passenger'. I'm sure the Company found no argument from its captains on that.

Maiden Voyage of Andes

During 1913 the seventh of the 'A' ship series was completed at Belfast. Her maiden voyage was, for the most part, incident free. As her log book has survived, the opportunity is taken to reproduce brief extracts to provide an officer's-eye view of the ship's operation. It provides, in a voyage notably lacking in drama, an overview of ship's routine. This was the first voyage of a ship which would still be in operation, on Ministry of Transport service, in the 1950s; the ship which became the cruising queen for thousands in the 1930s as *Atlantis*. The log began as she left the fitting-out basin, steaming into Belfast Lough for trials:

Amazon (II) at Southampton. During 1906 she became the second 'A' ship to enter service.

[GENERAL FORM.]

Not Transferable. **B. & R. P. FIRST-CLASS SINGLE TICKET.**

PASSENGERS ARE MOST STRONGLY ADVISED TO INSURE THEIR BAGGAGE, AS THE COMPANY ACCEPTS NO LIABILITY FOR PASSENGERS' EFFECTS.

Baggage can be insured at the Company's Offices in Great Britain, and their Agencies abroad.

The Royal Mail Steam Packet Company.

REMARKS.

Berth No.

*Min. Rate £*_____

*Supplement £*_____

*Total £*_____

No. LDN. 3799

LONDON   Head Office, 18, MOORGATE STREET, E.C.

Issued subject to the Conditions and Regulations on front and back hereof.

First-Class Single Passage *from*_____

*to*_____ *by Steamer "*_____*" sailing*

*about*_____*191 (unless prevented by any unforeseen occurrence), with liberty to the*

Company to substitute any other Steamer or Steamers for the whole or any part or parts of the passage.

Name of |_____
Passenger |

Portion of a first class Brazil and River Plate ticket, 1913. The full ticket was about A4 in size and the entire document larger than A3 as it included a set of on-board vouchers.

11 September 1913

07.10 Left dock and proceeded towards Lough assisted by two tugs (*Hercules* and *Jackal*).

08.00 Cast off tugs and proceeded to Lough for compass adjustments.

10.45 Compass adjustments completed. Proceeded full speed.

Noon Moderate breeze; smooth sea, showery weather.

14.25 Stand by.

14.30 Stopped.

14.34 Half astern.

14.38 Stopped and let go port anchor.

14.40 Hove up port anchor and let go starboard anchor in 6 fathoms off Carrickfergus.

17.42 Skulmartin Lt ship passed.

Average speed on trial run: 16 knots.

Draft leaving: fore 17ft 4in; aft 24ft 1in.

12 September 1913

01.30 – 02.00 Passing through banks of fog.

13.05 Lizard Lt Hse psd.

15.38 Eddystone Lt Hse abm 7 mls.

17.03 Start Point Lt Hse abm 1½mls.

18.00 Moderate wind and sea. Cloudy and clear.

19.50 Portland Lt abm 4 mls.

21.52 Needles Lt abm.

22.05 Hurst Pt abm. Signalled.

Average speed from Start Point to Portland Bill on a distance of 49 miles: 17.6 knots.

23.12 Anchored.

Capt. James Pope, possibly in the wheelhouse of Arlanza *(I) before the First World War.*
Capt. Pope was Commodore from 1910 until his retirement in 1913.

13 September 1913

06.15 Hove up anchors and proceeded.

06.55 Stopped to receive docking pilot
and proceeded to Ocean Quay, assisted
by tugs *Neptune* and *Ajax*.

07.25 All fast alongside Berth 47.
Finished with engines.

Average speed Belfast to Southampton:
15˙85 knots.

13 – 25 September 1913

At Southampton.

26 September 1913

12.15 Sent lines to tugs. Let go from wharf
five minutes later. Tugs *Neptune* and *Ajax*
in attendance. Pilot W. Nicholls. Draft
leaving: fore 22ft 6in; aft 25ft.

13.00 Accident boats swung out. Passed
Calshot Castle.

18.25 Entered Cherbourg Harbour. Let

go port anchor in $7\frac{1}{2}$ fthms. Brought up
and rang off engines.

18.40 Commenced embarking
passengers, mails and baggage.

20.45 Hove anchor, turned and
proceeded slow. Discharged pilot

21.00, then full speed.

27 September 1913

07.51 Ushant Lt Hse abm 14 miles.

Noon Fine and cloudy, moderate wind,
slight sea. Position: lat 43° 4' N;
long 9° 22' W.

Distance steamed in last 24 hours: 321 mls.

28 September 1913

06.55 Passed Company's *Flintshire*
opposite way. During morning passed
Company's steamer SS *Demerara*.

11.00 Divine Service held in Social Hall.

12.52 Stopped. Starboard anchor

dropped. Arr. Vigo.

13.30 Commenced cargo work & embarking passengers & baggage.

18.20 Finished cargo work. Fire gear placed. Ship detained through four cases of trachoma among 3rd class passengers, who were refused passage, which necessitated all baggage being turned over to find theirs.

18.55 Shifted moorings to clear buoy.

21.17 Proceeded full speed.

Distance steamed 24 hours to noon: 358 mls. Draft leaving Vigo: fore – 22ft 6in; aft – 24ft 10in.

29 September 1913

13.16 Berthed Lisbon. Commenced coaling, embarking passengers & baggage.

14.40 Commenced cargo work.

18.40 – 19.50 Taking in mail.

21.24 Anchor aweigh. Slow ahead.

21.39 Full speed & proceeded course N 80° W.

Distance steamed to noon: 225 mls.

30 September 1913

Mdnt to sunrise: Frequent rain squalls; fresh wind and rough sea. Heavy rain at intervals.

Noon position: lat 28° 36' N; long 16° W.

Distance steamed to noon: 245 mls.

Speed set at 16 knots.

1 October 1913

Distance steamed to noon: 384 mls.

2 October 1913

Fine and clear. Light winds. Smooth sea. Making 16 knots.

Noon position: lat 23° 6' N; long 18° 38' W.

Distance steamed to noon: 394 mls.

3 October 1913

Distance steamed to noon: 385 mls. Solar

observations unobtainable. Moderate wind and sea. Overcast and showery. Wind later strong.

Speed reduced from 16 to 14 knots.

4 October 1913

14.00 Exercised crew at boat drill.

15.00 position: lat 12° N; long 24° 4' W.

Distance steamed to noon: 354 mls.

5 October 1913

11.00 Divine Service held in Social Hall.

15.00 position: lat 6° 25' N; long 26° 58' W.

Distance steamed to noon: 374 mls.

6 October 1913

00.20 Passed Company's SS *Potaro* same way one mile east. Fresh wind and moderate sea. Fine and clear. By 08.00 changed to overcast & rainy. Southerly swell.

14.23 True bearing St Pauls Rocks S 73° E, distant 8 mls.

Position: lat 0° 58' N; long 29° 30' W.

Distance steamed to noon: 372 mls.

7 October 1913

15.00 position: lat 4° 55' S; long 31° 59' W.

Distance steamed to noon: 372 mls.

8 October 1913

Mdnt – 00.50 Port engine stopped for engineroom purposes.

15.00 position: lat 10° 48' S; long 34° 50' W.

Distance steamed to noon: 390 mls.

Speed 16 knots.

9 October 1913

15.00 position: lat 16° 44' S; long 37° 42' W.

Distance steamed to noon: 392 mls.

10 October 1913

Noon Passed German SS *Cap Roca* bound same way.

The central well and dome of the first class dining saloon in the 11,000-ton Avon (III) of 1907. The most momentous occasion to grace this room was a gala dinner to celebrate the engagement of ballet maestro Vaslav Nijinsky, who was the star performer with the Imperial Russian Ballet travelling to Buenos Aires for a tour in 1913.

Distance steamed to noon: 405 miles. Speed 17 – 18 knots.

21.35 Ft Villegagnon abm. Reduced speed. Rio de Janeiro. Anchored & received pratique by 22.30. Commenced discharge passengers & baggage.

23.30 Commenced cargo work & coaling, and taking in fresh water.

11 October 1913

04.00 Ceased cargo work. 05.50 Finished coaling.

06.13 Aweigh slow ahead & proceeded to berth.

07.55 Commenced discharging mails and cargo.

10.40 – 11.00 All cranes stopped for engineroom purposes. Cranes working very unsatisfactorily.

15.45 Received mails.

20.45 Finished all cargo. Unmoored $\frac{1}{2}$ hour later.

12 October 1913

11.00 Held Divine Service in Social Hall.

15.00 position: lat 26° 40' S; long 46° 4' W. Distance steamed to noon: 228 mls. Speed 16 – 17 knots.

13 October 1913

Lead cast eight times during day; depths ranging 56 fthms to 11 fthms.

Distance steamed to noon: 411 mls. Speed 17 knots.

14 October 1913

10.42 Stopped. Discharged Monte Video mail, also mail for HMS *Glasgow*. Embarked pilot & proceeded full speed 11.28.

Distance steamed to noon: 398 mls.
  Speed 17 – 18 knots.
Afternoon: In approach channel for
  Buenos Aires.
15.24 Passed *Punta Indio* Lt abm.
16.40 Passed *Intermedio* Lt Vssl.
17.37 Passed *Banco Chico* Lt Vssl.
19.05 Passed *Ensenada* Lt Vssl &
  Company's SS *Deseado* at anchor.
21.10 Stopped & made fast, tugs ahead
  and astern.
21.30 Passed breakwater.
22.00 Made fast alongside, Buenos Aires.
22.15 Commenced discharging mails and
  passengers.

15 October 1913
In North Dock, Buenos Aires
00.45 Finished discharging mails.
06.00 Hands mustered: all present. Night
  watch relieved.
07.30 Commenced disembarking
  emigrants & discharging baggage and
  parcel post.
Cargo work proceeding until 14.30.

16 October 1913
06.15 Sent lines to tugs Thiers and
  Nelson. Shifted berth, operation
  completed 11.30.
13.00 Recommenced cargo work.

17 – 18 October 1913
Cargo work proceeding; completed 09.15
  eighteenth.

19 October 1913
Coaling proceeding.

20 October 1913
Finished coaling 05.00.
am Shore labour painting overside.
J. Brampton (Boatswain) and J. Best (AB)
  placed on sick list.

21 October 1913
Shore labour painting ship and preparing
  insulated holds. Afternoon:
  commenced loading meat into
  numbers 3 and 4 holds.

22 October 1913
Cargo work proceeding.

23 October 1913
Cargo work proceeding with
  interruptions on account of rain.
22.50 Finished & closed down number 2
  hatch.

24 October 1913
01.30 Recommenced work at No 5 hatch.
  Finished & closed down 04.10.
08.00 Commenced embarking passengers
  and baggage.
10.38 Let go from wharf & proceeded.
  Tugs *Dona Catalina* and *Thiers* in
  attendance. Courses and speeds to
  pilot's orders.
20.51 Reduced speed. Stopped off Monte
  Video. Discharged pilot and received
  mails.
21.10 Proceeded full speed.
22.13 Flores Isl Lt abm.
22.45 Set in thick fog; speed reduced.
Distance to noon: 7 miles. Draft: fore –
  20ft 6in; aft – 26ft 2in.

25 October 1913
Mdnt – dawn: Patches of fog at intervals.
  Light wind & smooth sea. Lead cast at
  frequent intervals – 15 to 20 fthms.
15.00 position: lat 33° 43' S; long 52° 15' W.
Distance steamed to noon: 302 mls.
Speed various 10 – 15 knots.

26 October 1913
03.15 J. Brampton, Boatswain, departed
  this life.

11.00 Divine Service held in Social Hall.

Noon – distance steamed 387 mls.

12.30 The remains of J. Brampton, Boatswain, were committed to the deep, lat 28° 58' S; long 48° 7' W.

27 October 1913

Noon Speed 15 knots. Distance steamed 375 miles.

17.33 Stopped and let go port anchor. Rio de Janeiro.

20.00 Commenced coaling

28 October 1913

Mdnt – dawn Finished coaling and pressure shut down.

05.45 Weighed anchor & proceeded to quay.

09.00 Received parcels. Embarking passengers and baggage.

12.20 Proceeded, course and speed to pilot's orders.

Departure draft from Rio de Janeiro: fore – 19ft 8in; aft – 25ft 8in.

29 October 1913

Noon Distance steamed 349 mls. Speed 15 knots.

Position: lat 18° 47' S; long 38° 35' W.

30 October 1913

Noon Distance steamed 375 miles.

Speed 15 – 16 knots.

15.00 position: lat 13° 1' S; long 35° 54' W.

Moderate wind, smooth sea.

31 October 1913

Noon Distance steamed 379 miles.

Speed 15 – 16 knots.

15.00 position: lat 7° 15' S; long 33° 22' W.

1 November 1913

Noon Distance steamed 375 miles.

Speed 15 – 16 knots.

15.00 position: lat 1° 36' S; long 30° 43' W.

2 November 1913

11.00 Divine Service held in Social Hall.

Noon Distance steamed 386 miles.

Speed 16 knots.

15.00 position: lat 4° 20' N; long 28° 11' W.

3 November 1913

Mdnt – dawn Continuous and heavy rain, giving way to squally wind and moderate sea. Heavy squalls of rain at intervals. Stellar observations unobtainable – sky overcast.

Noon Distance steamed 383 miles.

Speed 15 – 16 knots.

15.00 position: lat 10° 7' N; long 25° 22' W.

Passed *Highland Rover* opposite way.

Moderate freshening trades. Fine & cloudy.

4 November 1913

Noon Distance steamed 380 miles.

Speed 15 – 16 knots.

Altered course to N 48° E.

15.00 position: lat 15° 45' N; long 22° 33' W.

Moderate trade wind and sea. Fine & clear.

5 November 1913

Noon Distance steamed 369 miles. Speed 15 – 16 knots.

15.00 position: lat 21° 21' N; long 19° 50' W.

6 November 1913

08.00 Strong head wind & rough sea. Ship spraying forward. Fine & clear.

Noon Distance steamed 360 miles.

Speed 15 knots.

Strong wind & rough head sea. Hazy horizon.

15.00 position: lat 26° 43' N; long 16° 56' W.

7 November 1913

Noon Distance steamed 378 miles.

Speed 16 knots.

15.00 position: lat 32° 18' N; long 13° 33' W.

17.00 Exercise ship's company at boat stations.

8 November 1913

Noon Distance steamed 389 miles.

Speed 16 knots.

18.07 Pilot boarded. 18.25 Received pratique & proceeded.

18.35 Let go port anchor. Brought up and rang off. Lisbon. Commenced coaling and discharging passengers and baggage.

21.00 Received thirty-five cases of cargo.

22.00 Finished discharging and receiving baggage. Coaling proceeding with all possible speed.

9 November 1913

03.15 Finished coaling.

03.58 Anchor aweigh. Slow ahead as required.

04.33 Full speed ahead.

04.41 Passed Belem Castle.

Noon Distance steamed 222 miles.

Speed 16 knots.

16.00 Moderate following gale, high confused sea. Overcast & rainy.

17.29 Dead slow.

17.50 Sounded in 58 fthms.

18.09 Full speed.

19.58 Stopped & anchored. Vigo.

20.15 Commenced taking fresh water & discharging passengers and baggage.

20.45 Commenced loading cargo.

22.30 Finished cargo work.

23.00 Weighed anchor and proceeded to sea.

10 November 1913

02.17 Cape Finisterre abm 5 mls.

Noon Distance steamed 324 miles.

Speed 16 knots

14.45 position: lat 45° 52' N; long 7° 35' W.

11 November 1913

02.10 Ushant NW Lt abm 14$\frac{1}{2}$mls.

11.32 Stop engines. Pilot boarded. Full ahead.

Noon Distance steamed 377 miles.

Speed 15 knots

14.07 Stopped & anchored. Cherbourg.

14.20 Commenced discharge passengers, baggage & specie.

15.20 Hove anchor, turned ship, pilot left. Full speed.

19.10 Rounding Needles.

19.37 Hurst Castle abm.

Late evening Berthed Southampton.

So ended the first two months in what would be a very long life. It was a voyage which would have pleased the Company in many ways – precious little in the way of incident reports and no sign of teething problems with the new ship except for the operation of the cranes. The cases of trachoma were not out of the ordinary; an infectious eye disease, at that time it was so prevalent among the poorer classes in Europe and the Middle East that it warranted a special mention in the Company's handbook. No passengers were allowed to land in Brazil, Uruguay or Argentina if they were suffering from 'trachoma or other infectious eye disease, tuberculosis or leprosy'. A special note under the immigration regulations insisted that all applications by 'Syrians, Arabs, Armenians, Turks, Gypsies, Hindoos, Egyptians or Chinese' for passages had to be referred to Head Office.

Perhaps the matter which comes through most strongly was the tightness of the schedule; port operations were around the clock, with the ship departing the moment essential tasks were completed. Montevideo was not even really a port of call, but a twenty-minute 'stop engines' as essential transfers took place. Such was the rigidity of a mail service.

Migrants and 'Swallows'

The number of third class passengers Royal Mail conveyed across the South Atlantic over the years was enormous; not only migrants heading to a new life in South America, but passengers referred to as 'swallows' who seasonally made the journey for harvesting work.

While surviving material provides some data and photos of third class passengers and their world, there is a dearth of diaries, reminiscences and the like to provide first-hand accounts of this aspect of the service. Many were Spanish and Portuguese, but other parts of Europe provided considerable numbers; enough for Royal Mail, in the 1920s and 1930s, to produce 3rd class brochures in Greek, Yugoslav, Danish, Polish and more. Their voyages were remote from the lap of luxury, and it would appear that RMSP and other companies, while catering for staple needs, did so with the minimum of expense. From time to time concerns were expressed by various governments, the most significant of which occurred with the Highland ships, which Royal Mail Lines inherited from Nelson Line. Shortly after RML had acquired them, the Spanish authorities advised Royal Mail that they 'did not comply with Emigration Regulations in Spain and the Company has been warned that Spanish authorities would not continue to tolerate this state of affairs indefinitely', while the Polish Government 'had refused to permit the booking of passengers for these ships so long as they are without cabins, general rooms etc'.

The people themselves, though, made the best of their accommodation and formed something of an island community; their world was so different from the rest of the ship, but I have read many a suggestion that they had more fun than those in the more formal first class. I saw this and realised it was still so in the 1960s.

The Pianist and the Dancer

Inevitably, what has been recorded over the years generally came from first class. Some of the more influential passengers from the early decades have already been mentioned; far into the twentieth century the mail ships continued to carry kings, queens, princes, counts, dukes, ambassadors, generals, politicians and the like. Then came film and theatre people, opera and ballet stars, sports people and pop idols.

One of the most popular passengers from the early years of the twentieth century was the Polish pianist Paderewski – possibly the finest pianist the world has known. Before the First World War he travelled to South America in *Asturias* for a concert tour and in the course of the voyage consented to play at the ship's concert. That, surely, was the ultimate in shipboard entertainment...or was it?

At much the same time the world's most famous ballet company also travelled to South America for a tour. This was Sergei Diaghilev's Imperial Russian Ballet Company, and their star performer was Vaslav Nijinsky, by common consent the greatest ballet dancer of all time. In August 1913 the Diaghilev company travelled from Southampton to Buenos Aires for the start of their tour.

The prospect of the great Nijinsky spending three weeks on board *Avon* was significant enough, but the events which unfolded during the voyage were among the most unexpected and perhaps controversial in the artistic world. Nijinsky was at his peak as a dancer, taking audiences by storm wherever he went. Taken in hand by Diaghilev at about the age of ten, they became inseparable. Even so early in the century, their relationship seems to have been accepted, with Nijinsky's genius over-riding all else.

A Hungarian society girl, Romola de Pulszky, saw Nijinsky dance in Budapest and was so captivated that she followed the company wherever they went. She took ballet lessons herself, and managed to join the Diaghilev company. That was shortly before the South American tour. She had only viewed Nijinsky from afar, and saw the voyage in *Avon* as her chance to get to know him better; to become friends.

That is the point at which she joined *Avon* at Southampton. '...the immensity of the boat impressed me,' she wrote. 'I had never been on an ocean liner before. The Royal Mail Steamship Company's *Avon* was quite the latest novelty in ocean service'. As she settled into shipboard routine she came across the master, Capt. Down, who she described as 'a great stout man, like a kind, big bear, with a long beard'.

Nijinsky and Diaghilev were on the passenger list, but neither could be found. Nijinsky eventually boarded at Cherbourg, but there was no Diaghilev – one report claimed he was detained on business, another that he had a fear of sea travel. For Romola it was a frustrating voyage – day followed day with the great dancer as remote from her as ever. Nijinsky settled into a routine which elevated *Avon* briefly to a special status in the world of the arts. In the 'C' Deck lounge where a piano was placed, Nijinsky and conductor René Baton created, day by day, a new ballet. Every morning crowds of passengers stood admiringly as Nijinsky went through his practice routine in a roped-off area on deck.

There were social events to look forward to – a fancy-dress ball, for instance, and an equator party (with first-timers being 'baptised' with champagne); and hectic shore excursions at Lisbon and Madeira. Quieter moments were spent relaxing in deckchairs and gazing for the first time at the southern constellations. During the last days of the transatlantic crossing, Romola remembered, one warm night they heard 'weird, enchanting Spanish music'. The third class were enjoying a spontaneous fiesta, the kind of exuberant happening which characterised Royal Mail ships as long as they were travelling the South Atlantic. The steerage, Romola explained, 'was full of Italian and Spanish peasants called "swallows", going over to the Argentine for the harvest'. They were dancing the bolero, the tango and tarantella – a mesmerising experience which drew first and second class to the rails like a magnet.

Romola's descriptions reflected an idyllic South Atlantic voyage. She, though, was far from relaxed. Her attempts to get closer to Nijinsky were getting nowhere – they couldn't even talk since he was Russian and she Hungarian. Just a day before *Avon* reached Rio de Janeiro the unbelievable happened. Nijinsky had clearly taken more notice of Romola than she had thought – through an interpreter, out of the blue, he asked her to marry him.

So it was that the maestro of dance became engaged on the *Avon*. When Capt. Down found out, he was all for having a shipboard wedding, but that was not to be – they were married in Buenos Aires. That didn't stop Capt. Down laying on a special dinner for the occasion, 'a gala affair, the dining room beautifully decorated with tropical plants, an exquisite dinner served, and champagne in the real Russian fashion'.

They were not destined for a happy future, but that day, at least, was a joyful climax to the voyage.

Sir Ernest Shackleton

Ernest Henry Shackleton was not intimately associated with the 'A' ships, but from a photograph taken on board Andes, discovered in a file many decades later, has emerged an absorbing tale of the explorer's last weeks.

Shackleton joined the North Western Shipping Co. (the sailing ship arm, in its dying days, of White Star Line) as an apprentice in the square-rigger *Hoghton Tower*. In 1894 he switched to steamers, joining Shire Line's *Monmouthshire* as a junior officer some years before the company was bought by RMSP. Later he was in *Flintshire,* and with Shire Line eventually gained his master's ticket at the age of twenty-four. He left the company then and joined Union-Castle.

Shackleton's merchant navy career ended with a successful bid to join Scott's *Discovery* expedition to Antarctica. Shackleton did much valuable work, but then suffered a haemorrhage and after an agonising trek was invalided out of the expedition. Taken to New Zealand, he joined Orient-Pacific's *Orotava* for the return to England. Like the Shire ships in which he served, *Orotava* would shortly come into RMSP ownership.

Later years involved activity in the Antarctic which has been well documented. Less known, perhaps, is that after returning from the *Endurance* expedition in 1917 he helped with British Government propaganda in South America. However useful his work was, the hot and humid atmosphere caused his health to decline. When the war ended he started planning what would become his last polar journey.

Plans reached a climax in the summer of 1921 when Shackleton bought the wooden auxiliary screw sloop *Foca 1*, built at Risör, Norway in 1917. He renamed her *Quest*. In September the party left Plymouth in high spirits. The first days running south were in less than perfect weather and the ship, with low freeboard and very tall masts, proved an uncomfortable sea boat. Nearly everyone was seasick, Shackleton being one of only two not to suffer. There was trouble with the engines, too, and the great explorer was taxed to the limit, at one stage being on the bridge constantly for almost a week.

Quest put in to Lisbon on 4 October for engine repairs. It was here that a little of Shackleton's past began to catch up with him. RMSP's *Tyne* was in port, and he recognised her as the one-time *Monmouthshire* in which he had served so many years

Sir Ernest Shackleton (left) and RMSP's Commodore, Arthur P. Dix, pictured on Andes *(I) at Rio de Janeiro in December 1921. This was almost certainly the last photo ever taken of Shackleton.*

before. He met *Tyne's* master, Capt. Morris, but had to decline an invitation to visit her as he was trying to get his expedition back on track. Capt. Morris noted a resignation about him. The hardships of earlier journeys had done nothing to improve his health, and Shackleton felt, Morris said, that his time was nearly up. That much was recorded in Royal Mail's centenary history, but it seems likely that Andes was also at Lisbon, travelling northbound, and that Shackleton and others from his party did visit her.

Later *Quest* stopped over in Madeira. There Shackleton saw RMSP's *Saint Margaret of Scotland*, a ship of just over 2,000 tons built for the Company in 1909 as *Balantia*. The un-RMSP-like name *Saint Margaret of Scotland* was given during the First World War, when she was on the Clyde being fitted out as a hospital ship and funds to support this were provided from collections in Scotland made by the Red Cross. RMSP acknowledged the generosity of the Scottish people by renaming her. In 1921 she was operating from Britain to Madeira and the Canary Islands. Shackleton and some of his party dined on board. They apparently spent a 'very jolly evening on board', during which *Saint Margaret of Scotland*'s chief engineer provided help for *Quest*'s on-going machinery problems. Shackleton finally left the Royal Mail ship in a 'bright and cheery mood'.

Though the weather improved after this, Shackleton was ill while they were at St Vincent. Rio de Janeiro was reached on 22 November. The weary explorer had to attend dinners and other functions given in his honour, and all in the conditions he so hated – high temperatures and heavy atmosphere. Speeches and lectures were delivered during early December, and it was during this period that Shackleton gained a brief respite when he again visited *Andes*.

Of all the flashbacks which accompanied his voyage south, this was the most important, for *Andes* was commanded by Arthur Porrett Dix. The visit was a renewal of an old friendship, for they had known each other during Shackleton's years in the merchant navy. Dix was now Commodore and on the verge of retiring. Shackleton's day on *Andes*, then, must have been like a brief calm in the heart of a great storm.

On 19 December he sailed *Quest* out of Rio to a military gun salute and in temperatures well above 100°F. That was his last contact with the outside world. They sailed south and by Christmas had run into the 'most frightful storm in all Shackleton's experience', the little ship rolling 50° to each side and wallowing in 40ft-seas. They reached South Georgia on 4 January 1922, and in the early hours of the following morning Sir Ernest Shackleton suffered an attack of angina pectoris and died.

In this last chapter of his life it was quite uncanny how RMSP was able to virtually 'escort' him from Europe to South America. And the photograph of Shackleton with Capt. Dix, taken at Rio de Janeiro by the ship's photographer on *Andes,* was surely the last picture ever taken of the great explorer.

12
Towards the World's Largest Motorships

At the outbreak of the First World War the Company was operating a two-pronged passenger-cargo operation to South America:

1) Weekly by 'A' steamers from Southampton to Cherbourg, Coruña★, Vigo, Leixões★ (Oporto), Lisbon, Madeira★, St Vincent★, Pernambuco★, Bahia★, Rio de Janeiro, Santos★, Montevideo★, Buenos Aires.
2) By 'D' steamers from Liverpool to Coruña•, Villagarcia•, Vigo, Leixões★ (Oporto), Lisbon, Rio de Janeiro, Montevideo, Buenos Aires. Homeward – Buenos Aires (*La Plata*), Rio de Janeiro, Lisbon, Vigo, Liverpool.

★ signifies calls not made every voyage. • signifies calls made by alternate steamers.

Passenger fares were quite reasonable, especially in comparison with the following decade. These prices were minimum rates from Southampton ('A' ships) or Liverpool ('D' ships): 'A' ships – First class to Pernambuco £31 single/£50 return; to Bahia and Rio de Janeiro £33 single/£53 return; to Santos £34 single/£54 return; to Montevideo and Buenos Aires £39 single/£62 return. Second class to all ports in Brazil, Uruguay and Argentina £22 single/£39 12s return.

Third class fares were not quoted – generally they were migrants embarking at European ports, with fares paid in Spanish or Portuguese currency. The cost of a one-way ticket would have been about £16.

'D' ships – First class to Brazil £25 single/£43 return; to River Plate ports £30 single/£50 return. Intermediate class to all ports in Brazil, Uruguay and Argentina £16 single/£30 return.

While those were minimum fares, even in 1914 it was possible to pay as much as £388 10s for a Cabin de Luxe in an 'A' ship for a round voyage.

'A' ship departures were on Fridays or, occasionally, Saturdays, at noon. The boat train left Waterloo at 9.30 a.m., which left little time to absorb delays during the train journey or in boarding procedures. The Cherbourg call was at about 5 p.m. the same day, and a train left Gare St Lazaire in Paris at 10.50 a.m. to meet the ship.

In the post-war years an 'A' ship voyage from Southampton to Buenos Aires took twenty-two days, followed by six days in Argentina and twenty-two days back. The 'D' ships took three or four days longer in each direction and spent nine days at Buenos

Aires and the meat berths. Their homeward passengers were brought down-river by train to embark at La Plata.

Yellow fever was not yet fully overcome and even the mail steamers, so strictly scheduled, sometimes suffered delays. In February 1920, for instance, *Almanzora* spent eleven days in quarantine at Rio de Janeiro, while *Darro* was held up for fifteen days.

Fares, by 1920, had risen sharply. The minimum 'A' ship single first class passage from Southampton to Rio de Janeiro was now £83 and to Buenos Aires £98.

The concept of interchangeable tickets between companies was already well entrenched. In 1914 first and second class passengers who booked on an 'A' ship could break their journey at any port and continue in ships of RMSP, PSN, Lamport and Holt or Nelson Line. Northbound passengers breaking the journey at Madeira could continue in a Union-Castle ship. 'D' ship round-voyagers had various options. They could, for instance, disembark at Montevideo and later cross the *La Plata* River to Buenos Aires to rejoin the ship (the river crossing paid for by the Company). They, too, could swap ships and companies along the coast. Passengers in any Royal Mail ship to the River Plate could return to the Mediterranean by the Italian Veloce Line or Navigazione Generale Italiana. England-Lisbon tickets were interchangeable with Rotterdam Lloyd. Round voyage passengers in the PSN 'O' ships (interchangeable with RMSP) would normally travel via the Magellan Straits, but an option for them (£5 first class or £3 second) was to travel in one direction overland on the famous Transandean railway.

Cargo-only services were maintained with the 'N' class meat ships and 'S' class general freighters, plus the occasional Shire and chartered vessel. General freighters returned fortnightly from Rio Grande do Sul, Paranagua, Santos, Rio de Janeiro, Vittoria, Bahia and Pernambuco to Le Havre, Antwerp, Rotterdam, Hamburg and the UK. Coffee and timber were among the most significant general cargoes.

The Tinsley Factor

Various booking arrangements for migrant traffic were used through a network of agencies over the years. In the 1920s an unusual arrangement developed to cater for those coming from Eastern Europe. After the Armistice in 1918 a man named Cdr. R.B. Tinsley CBE, RNR launched the Uranium Trading and Transport Co., a Dutch-based concern which planned to establish a migrant steamer service between Rotterdam and the eastern seaboard of North America, and another to South America.

Tinsley then reached an agreement for RMSP to carry his passengers across the South Atlantic. When he learnt that Royal Mail was also planning to open a new North America service he abandoned his idea of a ship-owning company and instead agreed to act as the Company's agent in Russia, Poland, Yugoslavia, Czechoslovakia, Latvia, Estonia and Lithuania. Licences were obtained for all of those countries as well as Germany, Holland and Finland. At all of his offices RMSP's name was the one displayed – the operation penetrated to towns and cities like Warsaw, Lwow, Krakow, Stanislawow, Bialystok, Brazesc, Zagreb, Belgrade, Ljubljana, Split, Prague, Riga, Libau, Reval and Kovno.

Still lacking her final coat of paint, Asturias (II) *nears completion at Queen's Island, Belfast. Her somewhat messy appearance belied the prestige of the world's largest motorship and some of the most exquisite shipboard décor ever conceived.*

The communist bloc was very young and Russia, in particular, was still coming to terms with the mighty upheaval which had taken place. The various governments imposed rigorous conditions on foreign businesses like Tinsley's, which included prohibiting the release of passage money from the country of origin until the passenger had boarded the ship.

Cdr Tinsley needed to establish a central gathering place on which his passengers could converge to collectively undergo emigration formalities and then travel as a group to the port of departure (usually either Lisbon or a French port). He discovered what he wanted at Marktredwitz, a town in upper Bavaria. There was a good railway connection with Vienna via Passau and Regensburg, and from Russia and Poland via Breslau/Plauen along Czechoslovakia's northern border. It was also on the main line from Prague to western Europe. Marktredwitz was therefore ideally situated for an emigrant control centre, but its purchase led to a difference of opinion between Tinsley and RMSP, which resulted in legal proceedings.

The crux of the matter was the extent to which Royal Mail had committed itself financially to the development of this east Europe agency. The Company insisted that the terms of the agreement were fluid as they didn't know how viable the business would be. Tinsley considered himself in partnership with RMSP and therefore expected a good deal of financial help in the purchase of Marktredwitz. Ultimately Royal Mail offered a £5,000 loan and Tinsley bought the station, spending more than £7,000 fitting it out.

The agency came to an abrupt end about 1926 when Cdr Tinsley began using some of the passage money for his own purposes. The Tinsley factor may have ended, but passengers continued to come from Eastern Europe. Poles, in particular, formed considerable groups to the Argentine. When they were added to migrants from western and southern Europe, the numbers were enormous, and migration to South America became stronger still from the mid-1920s because of changes to United States immigration laws which effectively killed off the trade to North America.

The World's Largest Motorships

Despite a worsening trade climate in the early 1920s, Royal Mail ordered two new mail liners for the South America service. They were ordered for two reasons: to replace 'A' ships lost in The First World War (even though that had happened a good few years before) and to place Royal Mail back in the forefront of the South America lines, for some of the existing ships were now the better part of twenty years old. The timing was to an extent dictated by the Trade Facilities Act, which allowed shipping companies to borrow money on favourable terms for this kind of project.

The new ships provided welcome work for Harland & Wolff at Belfast. The order was placed in 1924, with the ships due for delivery in early 1926 and early 1927. They were given the names *Asturias* and *Alcantara*, perpetuating names from earlier 'A' ships. At 22,000 tons, they were significantly larger than previous ships and were, for a short time, the largest diesel-powered ships in the world. All of that mirrored the influence of Lord Kylsant, who was doubtless also responsible for initiating the breathtaking quality of their first class public rooms.

They entered service at a critically bad time, greeted by the crippling General Strike and leading into the years of the Great Depression. How they survived those years in regular service, and emerged as two of the most popular liners in the great list of Southampton-based ships, was a story embracing a long series of day-to-day battles, erudite decision-making and sheer hard work.

In one respect they were *not* a success. Their diesel machinery failed to give them their designed speed and caused serious vibration. Less than a decade later, as the world began to emerge into better times, they were sent back to Belfast to have their engines replaced with steam turbines. Not only was their performance then more satisfactory (allowing reduced voyage times), their external appearance was also dramatically improved.

As with earlier ships, they carried their share of famous passengers. The most eminent were the Prince of Wales and Prince George, who travelled from the River Plate to Rio de Janeiro in *Alcantara* during 1931. A mighty welcome greeted them at Rio, and after their visit to Brazil they crossed the Atlantic to Lisbon in *Arlanza*.

When *Asturias* and *Alcantara* entered service there was a further modification of South America schedules. By the end of the 1920s the established passenger services comprised fortnightly departures from Southampton and from Liverpool. Every fifth sailing from the Mersey was a cargo-only 'N' class ship, often *Nagara*. Together with general cargo services they took RMSP's South Atlantic operation through to the time of Lord Kylsant's arrest.

13
The RMSP/RML Transition

About a year after the July 1931 trial of Lord Kylsant, the Royal Mail Steam Packet Company ceased to operate and, in its place, Royal Mail Lines Ltd was formed and took over the Company's fleet. While the result of the Kylsant trial appeared to provide the trigger for those events, that was not the case – at most, the trial hastened the inevitable.

RMSP and most of its group companies were in debt. In such a situation, shareholders and creditors have the power to close a company down and accept a limited payout from remaining assets, or sanction an attempt for the company to trade out of its difficulties. In the case of RMSP matters were not so straightforward. The size of the group was so great, and its influence in British shipping so significant, that to allow this 'empire' – 15% of the entire British mercantile marine – to simply collapse would have had huge repercussions on the industry and even, one suspects, an effect on the overall British economy, which was already reeling from the Great Depression. Quite clearly, every effort had to be made to prevent this happening.

There were moves in that direction a year before the Kylsant trial; in July 1930 the voting rights attaching to RMSP's investments were vested by the Government in three Voting Trustees – the Rt. Hon. Walter Runciman, Brigadier General Sir Arthur Maxwell and Sir William McLintock. The trigger for that was RMSP's inability to repay government loans and White Star Line's inability to pay a dividend on Preference Shares which became due on 1 July 1930.

Matters showed no sign of improvement – in 1930, for instance, RMSP made a loss of £530,731 16s 11d. Early in 1931 a Preliminary Scheme of Arrangement was put in place, its object to create a strategy to allow the group companies to return to profitability. This could only stand a chance of succeeding with the support of shareholders and creditors, so the organisers (with the sanction of the High Court) gained a period of grace – in which to develop the strategies to the point of adopting a Complete Scheme of Arrangement.

The moratorium had to be extended several times, and a Second and Third Preliminary Scheme adopted during 1931 and 1932, before the Complete Scheme of Arrangement became a legal reality in the High Court on 24 June 1932. Royal Mail Lines Ltd was formed from that document, being incorporated on 4 August 1932. The Royal Mail Steam Packet Co. was not immediately wound up – accountants were given the task of unravelling its finances and investments and a further four years passed before the company could be formally liquidated.

Desna, 11,466 tons, built in 1912 for the meat and passenger (principally migrant) trades to the River Plate. She was sold for scrap after twenty-one years.

RMSP to RML – Spanning the Gap

One of the Voting Trustees, Sir William McLintock, became the voice linking creditors and shareholders on one hand and the Company on the other. In particular he addressed a number of meetings of shareholders of both RMSP and White Star Line (the latter company being the biggest hurdle in the Scheme of Arrangement).

The work which was going on while the moratorium was in place was described in Sir William's address to RMSP's First debenture stockholders on 30 November 1931. He first reminded them that they were holders of £2,900,000-worth of debenture stock 'which is secured by a substantial charge on Royal Mail House, Leadenhall Street' and on other assets.

The core of Sir William's address dealt with the proposed Scheme of Arrangement which was the eventual aim of the Voting Trustees.

> *The general lines of the proposed Scheme, so far as it affects the Royal Mail Company, is that the operations of the vessels directly owned by it and also by those of its 100% subsidiaries which operate with South America will be consolidated and the ships – on which the position of the different creditors so much depends – will be operated in the most economical and efficient manner.*

He was at pains to point out that 'where security is held, that security will be preserved' – but there were two conditions: firstly, creditors and stockholders must agree to an extension of the moratorium. Secondly, financial creditors must agree not to enforce 'the realization of their securities' until (as a provisional date) the end of 1934. No secret was made of the enormity of the task, hence the need to extend the moratorium; this was agreed to.

Extremely Adverse Conditions

About a month later, RMSP held its Annual General Meeting. By then its chairman was P.G. Mylne Mitchell, and part of his address provided an insight into the Company's world at this crucial time:

> *The period covered by the accounts before you (i.e. the year 1930) was one of unprecedented depression, not only on the routes served by your fleet, but throughout all the world's routes, and in considering the company's affairs, and the position in which it is placed at the present time, it should not be forgotten that whatever factors may have operated to bring about present conditions, a contributory cause has been the acute and long-continued depression in trade.*
>
> *The problems arising in the Company's affairs would have been sufficiently difficult even if a moderate improvement in trading conditions had been experienced. Instead of this, it is well known that world trade in general took a further turn for the worse, and shipping in particular has encountered extreme adversity during the past two years, so that more tonnage has had to be laid up, and it has been increasingly difficult to make ends meet even on the much reduced sailings. That this has been a common experience is too well known to need emphasis.*
>
> *You appreciate, of course, that your company's business is almost entirely a liner service – i.e., a service operating to a pre-arranged timetable – and that there is a limit to which the scheduled sailings can be curtailed if the service has to be maintained. There is a very keen competition on these services, mainly with heavily subsidised lines.*
>
> *In face of the extremely adverse conditions prevailing, the efforts of the staff throughout the company's services have been directed towards securing as much as possible of the business offering, and at the same time effecting the utmost economy without impairing efficiency. In spite of these endeavours gross receipts have diminished, although the company's proportion of the traffic available has been more than maintained with restricted services.*
>
> *Drastic steps have been taken to curtail expenditure in all directions, and a reduction in 1931 as compared with 1930 of fully £100,000 per annum has been actually effected in general administration charges. To this saving the whole of the officials and staff ashore and afloat have contributed by accepting drastic cuts in their salaries, and I cannot pass from this subject without speaking of the very loyal co-operation of the staff in closely watching expenditure, and the earnest desire they have shown to assist in every way in keeping the flag flying during these present difficult times...*

Sir William McLintock also addressed this meeting, and if Mr Mitchell's remarks were depressing, what Sir William had to say was a bombshell. He referred to the two main assets of the Company – its ships and its investments (mostly in other shipping lines) – which had a combined book value of £17,493,000. However, because of the various conditions which then existed, it was estimated that the real value of those assets was only about £8,500,000.

Engineroom of Asturias *(II) during her early days as a diesel ship.*

> *A considerable part of the 'drop' of about £9 million is due to the holdings of the RMSP Company in Ordinary shares of White Star Line Ltd, Lamport and Holt Ltd and Elder Dempster & Co. Ltd, being regarded as of no value by the Voting Trustees.*

He turned then to calls on investments totalling £1,138,418 (mostly relating to White Star Line Ltd and Lamport and Holt) already due but still unpaid. Even when they *were* paid, 'the Ordinary shares of the companies concerned will still be valueless'.

He next looked at the most serious matter of all – White Star Line Ltd. RMSP's balance sheet showed identical amounts on both sides of the ledger: £2,350,000. This was the amount White Star Line owed RMSP (the balance of its £7 million purchase price, for after Royal Mail had bought Oceanic SN Co. it then formed White Star Line Ltd and sold the Oceanic shares to it). RMSP, in turn, owed the same amount to the original Oceanic vendor, the International Mercantile Marine Co. (IMMCo). This was where the incestuous nature of RMSP group investments formed a grid-lock – RMSP could not pay IMMCo until White Star had paid RMSP. White Star could not pay RMSP until it was 'able to collect the arrears of calls on its Ordinary share capital'. Its Ordinary share capital was entirely held by RMSP group companies – and so the story came full-circle.

One listed RMSP asset was £325,000 payable by White Star Line – reflecting an instance in which RMSP's directors placed the Company in a position of responsibility which had a sting in its tail. After forming White Star Line Ltd, the new company needed to raise capital and part of this was done through a public issue of 5,000,000 Preference shares. Though this was a White Star issue, the parent company, RMSP, guaranteed both the capital and dividends. The dividend due on 1 July 1930 could not be paid by White Star, so RMSP covered the cost – this was the £325,000 shown as an RMSP asset, for it was an amount now owed by White Star – but, according to Sir William McLintock, 'under present conditions, the possibility of the amount being recovered can, for practical purposes, be disregarded'.

The next dividend fell due on 1 January 1931, and not only could White Star not pay this, neither could RMSP. This gave the preference shareholders a right of action against RMSP, and was the situation which formally triggered the process to create the Scheme of Arrangement.

Finally, Sir William returned to his original point – that ultimately a very large amount would have to be written off the book value of the Company's assets; that 'the effect of this will be to entirely extinguish the reserve account in the balance sheet'.

The shareholders would have gained little joy from all of that.

First class winter garden in Asturias (II), *full of superb intricate detail and modelled on the Cordova Mosque in Spain.*

The Scheme of Arrangement

The bottom line for shareholders was still that if they wished to have any chance of recovering investments, they had to support a further extension of the moratorium and the establishment of the final Scheme of Arrangement. They did.

The Scheme of Arrangement was needed because of the complexity of RMSP group investments. These few examples help explain that complexity. RMSP owned 1,100,000 ordinary and 20,000 preference shares in Lamport and Holt Ltd, while Elder Dempster owned 1,694,997 shares, PSN had 100,000 and Lord Kylsant 50,000.

Though PSN was 'wholly-owned' by RMSP, many of its shares were held by people and companies who were also RMSP shareholders – Viscount St Davids, for instance (Lord Kylsant's brother). RMSP and Elder Dempster each held more than £1,300,000-worth of stock in Union-Castle. An investment in the Argentine-based Swift & Co. was held by Nelson Line, another RMSP wholly-owned subsidiary. Viscount St Davids, incidentally, and the Prudential Assurance Co. were the two petitioners on the basis of which the Scheme of Arrangement was created.

One of the more crucial matters was Lord Kylsant's personal holdings, for at the end of 1929 shares valued at £5,416,210, spread over at least twenty companies, were issued in his name. His RMSP shareholding amounted to £1,682,000, and there was almost as much in Elder Dempster. In addition to this web of shipping company investments, there was much diversification – a comprehensive list of RMSP's interests when the Company was at its zenith is given in Appendix III.

While the unravelling of RMSP involved all investments, the Scheme of Arrangement concerned fifteen companies: RMSP, RMSP Meat Transports, Nelson SN Co., H & W Nelson, David MacIver & Co., Pacific Steam Navigation Co., MacAndrews, Glen Line, Elder Dempster & Co., African SS Co., Elder Line, British & African SN Co., Imperial Direct Line, Harland & Wolff and Oceanic SN Co.

The Scheme required the creation of Operating Companies 1 and 2. Company 1 (which became Royal Mail Lines, Ltd) would operate all of the former RMSP ships and those of other lines engaged in the Brazil and River Plate trades. That brought fifty-two ships under Royal Mail's wing, those formerly belonging to RMSP, RMSP Meat Transports, the Nelson companies and David MacIver & Co. Operating Company No 2 became Elder Dempster Lines Ltd and incorporated the West Africa lines (Elder Dempster, African SS Co., Elder Line, British and African SN Co. and Imperial Direct Line), a total of fifty-five ships. The new companies would take over their respective ships without any liabilities other than those of current trading creditors. The original owning companies were paid for the ships with shares in the new companies.

What of the other group companies? It seems likely that the architects of the Scheme channelled into two baskets those companies which naturally belonged together, then set about individually dealing with those which had no common thread. Their legal and financial factors were all different. MacAndrews, for instance, came under the clause 'Secured loans or issues of securities guaranteed by His Majesty's Treasury or by the Government of Northern Ireland'. For Glen Line, there were Secured and Unsecured creditors and drawers of Bills of Exchange. PSN and Harland & Wolff involved similar clauses but with the added hurdle of unpaid monies to Harland's for the recently-built Reina del Pacifico. Thus, through the great complexity of the matter, those companies were resolved in different ways and left the influence of Royal Mail.

RMSP's Final Days

Royal Mail Lines, Ltd took over the running of the South America trade ships following its formation in August 1932. From that point on, RMSP was in the hands of the accountants and receivers who tried to salvage what they could. In the event, while the continuity of operations had been achieved through the Scheme of Arrangement, the story for RMSP was worse than anyone had feared. The debts were staggering.

The winding-up order was made on 10 February 1936. In June there was a meeting of shareholders and creditors at London's Holborn Restaurant. One report said:

It was disclosed that the total deficiency amounted to the huge sum of £22,481,535. Creditors are not expected to get more than [one shilling in the pound]. *There is not the least prospect that shareholders will receive anything…*

A meeting of shareholders followed. The Official Receiver said that so far as the shareholders were concerned the total amount due in respect of shares – money which had been put up in shares – was £8,800,000.

'If you add that to the total deficiency for the creditors, which is £13,381,535, you arrive at the enormous total deficiency of £22,481,535 which has been lost.'

'I am afraid the only mournful satisfaction you can get out of this is that you have been concerned in a very, very serious loss.'

A clergyman in the front row of the shareholders asked, 'Is it fair to ask you whether in your opinion there is not the least prospect of our receiving anything?'

The Official Receiver: 'I am sorry to say it – not the least prospect.'

The Annual Dividend

The prosperity of any company is reflected in the dividends it pays its shareholders. While there can, from time to time, be an anomaly, this is a good indicator of fluctuating trading conditions and the management of the company's affairs. The dividends quoted below, forming a complete list of dividends issued by the Royal Mail Steam Packet Co., are annual totals, normally comprising two half-yearly dividends announced in the directors' reports in April and October.

Though the Company was formed in 1839, entries begin in 1842, which was the Company's first operational year. 1931 was RMSP's last operational year and there was therefore no potential for dividends in the years 1932 to 1936, the year in which the Company was liquidated.

1842............ –	1845............5%	1848............$6\frac{2}{3}$%	1851............$6\frac{2}{3}$%
1843............ –	1846............$5\frac{5}{16}$%	1849............$6\frac{2}{3}$%	1852............$6\frac{2}{3}$%
1844............$2\frac{1}{2}$%	1847............$6\frac{1}{4}$%	1850............$6\frac{2}{3}$%	1853............$6\frac{2}{3}$%

1854............$6\frac{2}{3}$%	1874............$9\frac{7}{12}$%	1894............$4\frac{1}{6}$%	1914............ −
1855............15%	1875............$4\frac{1}{6}$%	1895............5%	1915............6%
1856............$9\frac{1}{6}$%	1876............$3\frac{1}{3}$%	1896............5%	1916............7%
1857............$8\frac{1}{3}$%	1877............$4\frac{1}{6}$%	1897............5%	1917............7%
1858............$6\frac{2}{3}$%	1878............$6\frac{2}{3}$%	1898............5%	1918............7%
1859............$6\frac{2}{3}$%	1879............$6\frac{2}{3}$%	1899............5%	1919............8%
1860............$6\frac{2}{3}$%	1880............5%	1900............5%	1920............7%
1861............$6\frac{2}{3}$%	1881............$7\frac{1}{2}$%	1901............$2\frac{1}{2}$%	1921............6%
1862............$11\frac{2}{3}$%	1882............5%	1902............ −	1922............6%
1863............20%	1883............$5\frac{5}{6}$%	1903............ −	1923............6%
1864............$24\frac{1}{6}$%	1884............$5\frac{5}{6}$%	1904............ −	1924............6%
1865............$21\frac{2}{3}$%	1885............$1\frac{2}{3}$%	1905............ −	1925............5%
1866............$16\frac{2}{3}$%	1886............$3\frac{1}{3}$%	1906............ −	1926............4%
1867............$6\frac{2}{3}$%	1887............$7\frac{1}{2}$%	1907............$2\frac{1}{2}$%	1927............5%
1868............ −	1888............$9\frac{7}{12}$%	1908............2%	1928............5%
1869............$6\frac{2}{3}$%	1889............$9\frac{7}{12}$%	1909............3%	1929............ −
1870............$11\frac{2}{3}$%	1890............$6\frac{2}{3}$%	1910............4%	1930............ −
1871............$15\frac{5}{12}$%	1891............5%	1911............5%	1931............ −
1872............$17\frac{2}{3}$%	1892............5%	1912............6%	
1873............$13\frac{1}{3}$%	1893............5%	1913............6%	

The absence of dividends in 1842 and 1843 was explained by RMSP's operational difficulties during those years. In 1855 came the first double-digit dividend; in fact, more than double that of any previous year. That was largely caused by the Company being able to repay loans and extinguish other liabilities. Earnings were probably also boosted by Government charters for the Crimean War, especially since some ships had, prior to their charter, been earmarked for sale.

The next unusual period covered 1862 to 1866, in terms of proprietor returns easily the company's most successful period. There was probably no single cause – it was simply the crest of the shipping world's cyclical wave. Nevertheless, it is astonishing to record a dividend of just over 24% in 1864. The directors' report for April 1865 explained the second portion of that dividend:

In presenting the Accounts for the year 1864, the Directors think they may safely congratulate the shareholders upon the satisfactory state of the surplus… This result is due to the steady progress of the Company's earnings from freight and passage money, all the items of which shew [sic] an increase, more or less, over those in the preceding year's Account. It is especially gratifying to notice that in the case of inter-colonial freight and passage money, the excess is very considerable…

In conclusion, the Directors consider that the state of the present Accounts justifies their recommending that a distribution be made of £9/10/- per share, free of income tax; viz: £8/10/- per share out of the balance of Profit and Loss Account, and a bonus of £1 per share from the Insurance Fund.

Nebraska *coaling at Newport, Monmouthshire. Built for the River Plate meat trade, the 'N' class ships later traded also to other regions, including the Pacific seaboard of North America.*

This halcyon state of affairs quickly ended, and for the first time in a quarter of a century, no dividend was paid for 1868. Contributing factors were a general downturn in trade, caused in part by a war in South America, the 1867 hurricane, earthquake and tidal wave which caused such loss of lives and ships at St Thomas and the financial nightmare which accompanied the decline of the Panama, New Zealand and Australia RM Co.

Matters then generally conformed to normal trade patterns until the turn of the century. From a routine 5% in 1900, the dividend dropped by half in 1901, and then became non-existent for the next five years. That reflected the Company's malaise, already dealt with; continuing lack of dividends until 1907 was due to Owen Philipps re-moulding the Company's operations and spending much money on new ships.

The absence of a dividend in 1914 can be largely explained by a general trough in trade conditions accompanied by uncertainty surrounding the outbreak of war. The year 1928 was the last in which RMSP paid a dividend. The fact that none was paid as early as 1929 is indicative of the financial woes which were outlined earlier in this chapter. The Great Depression had set in, there were debts on the new Royal Mail House and Lord Kylsant's ambitious plans were in tatters.

14
RML To South America

When Royal Mail Lines took over the services of RMSP and its subsidiaries in 1932, a curious problem developed with the MacIver fleet. In June 1933 it was announced that David MacIver & Co. was in liquidation, but that 'the Scheme of Arrangement does not expressly provide that the goodwill of the vendor company [MacIver] be transferred to Royal Mail Lines, Ltd. But as soon as the company name is struck from the Register in Somerset House, anyone else can register a company in the same name and use [with] the name an inferred 'goodwill''. Royal Mail moved quickly to acquire the goodwill 'for a nominal sum not to exceed £5'.

The MacIver ships were general freighters which had become familiar on the eastern seaboard of South America. Some continued on those routes as RML ships. The Nelson fleet was more significant, for it included five 14,000-ton passenger-cargo liners which had been built for essentially the same service as Royal Mail's 'A' ships – the main difference was that their UK port of departure was London, a feature Royal Mail retained.

The five were *Highland Brigade*, *Highland Chieftain*, *Highland Monarch*, *Highland Patriot* and *Highland Princess*. None were more than five years old, and *Highland Patriot* had only just been completed. Three other Nelson ships taken over were the only ones not to bear a Highland prefix – *Murillo*, *Meissonier* and *Molière*. They had formerly been meat carriers in the Lamport and Holt fleet and their names were left unchanged under Nelson ownership; RML, however, gave them 'N' class names, though, curiously, not for a year or so.

Thus, while the long-established Royal Mail company had just been decimated, it now emerged even stronger in terms of tonnage. The principal South Atlantic operations were:

Southampton-based ships – *Asturias*, *Alcantara*, *Arlanza* and *Almanzora*. Of the other surviving 'A' ships, *Atlantis* (ex *Andes*) was engaged in cruising and *Arcadian* (ex *Asturias*) was laid up and shortly went to shipbreakers.

The Royal Yacht Victoria and Albert *passing* Alcantara *(II) during the Royal Naval Review at Spithead in 1935.*

London-based ships – the five Highlands.

Liverpool-based ships – *Deseado, Desna, Darro* and *Demerara*. They were sold in 1933/4, by which time they were over twenty years old. That closed the Liverpool service.

Pardo and *Parana* were also sold at this period. The loss of so much refrigerated space was largely overcome with the Highland ships, but meat was also carried in the 'N' class freighters. General freight was carried in *Sarthe, Somme, Sambre, Siris* and *Sabor*, and in some of the former MacIver ships.

Under the chairmanship of Lord Essendon, RML took on a new look in more ways than one. Despite less than ideal economic conditions, it was a crowded decade as the new Board of Directors moulded what they had inherited into a lean, efficient operation. The term Board of Directors, incidentally, was now adopted because the

The wood-dominated bridge on a Highland ship, five of which entered the Royal Mail fleet through the RMSP Scheme of Arrangement. The photo dates from their Nelson Line years, and appears to have been taken before the ship left the builder's yard at Belfast.

title 'Court' applied only for a company incorporated by Royal Charter – that was one thing which had been lost in the transition.

Perhaps the most visible change was the publicity style adopted for passenger services. An avalanche of literature was produced – not only for the growing wealth of the cruising market (there had been plenty of brochures for this in the 1920s), but also for the South America run, which had not seen promotional matter on the scale which now appeared. There is a telling comparison between what was produced in the 1930s and in what one might imagine was the more publicity-conscious 1960s. During the latter decade two different sets (comprising six brochures, two for each passenger class) were the principal support, in addition to one all-class booklet late in the decade and an introductory booklet released before the new 'A' ships entered service. In the 1930s there were no fewer than thirty brochures dealing solely with the South America service, six jointly covering South America and cruising and fifty-one individual cruise brochures.

This was a prosperous period for migrant travel and other third class passengers. Cdr Tinsley may have left the scene but the traffic continued unabated. With third class potential extending beyond British, French, Spanish and Portuguese, RML issued fare structures from Austria, Belgium, Bulgaria, Czechoslovakia, Denmark,

Egypt, Estonia, Finland, Greece, Hungary, Latvia, Lithuania, Luxemburg, Malta, Norway, Palestine, Poland, Romania, Russia, Sweden, Switzerland, Syria, Turkey, Ukraine and Yugoslavia and even Albania – quite an astonishing list. Through bookings were arranged to places along the coast as far apart as Para, Sao Francisco do Sul, Pelotas, Porto Alegre and Asuncion. Manaus was another destination, a thousand miles up the River Amazon and a collecting place in the middle of Amazonas for produce from Brazil, Peru, Bolivia and Colombia.

The business of selling was becoming competitive; today's hard-sell methods had been born, and the new Royal Mail gave the appearance of jumping on this bandwagon and leaving the tradition-soaked RMSP in its wake. If that was the outward face, though, the new company, deeper down, brought a great deal of the old Steam Packet Co. into the new camp; a pedigree of that standard didn't vanish overnight – and nor should it. The new enterprising era was exemplified at the time of King George VI's coronation by a colourful Spanish-language brochure produced to entice South Americans to make the voyage and be part of the occasion.

Arlanza, which had carried the King years earlier when he was the Duke of York, ended her long and satisfying career a year after the coronation, and was deservedly given a great farewell from the South American coast. She was broken up at Rosyth.

The Second World War

Almanzora, alone of the original 'A' ships, now remained on the South America run. On the stocks at Belfast, though, was a new liner for the service; it was planned that she would leave Southampton on her maiden voyage on 26 September 1939 – a hundred years to the day after the foundation of RMSP. As the ship's construction progressed the uncertainties in Europe were rumbling more and more ominously. Already a number of Mediterranean and Baltic cruises were altered to avoid trouble spots. Until war was a certainty, though, plans for the vessel's entry into service had to continue. When Viscountess Craigavon crashed the champagne on the raked bows on 7 March 1939 the new ship was christened *Andes*.

Work on finishing the liner went ahead. Invitations and programmes were printed for luncheons on board on 21 and 22 September; the first brochure for the ship was printed, filled with artist's impressions depicting public rooms and deck spaces as vast – appropriately so for the largest liner Royal Mail ever owned. That historic day of 26 September passed without celebration, though, for on the outbreak of war earlier in the month, work on *Andes* went into reverse as splendid new fittings were removed and stored, and the ship was quickly made ready for war service.

Before setting out on her initial ocean voyage, *Andes* made the short passage to the Clyde. She then moved down to Liverpool and sailed quietly from the Mersey on 9 December 1939. Her maiden voyage took her across the North Atlantic to Halifax NS, where she was to embark troops for the passage back to England. Troop carrying was her allotted task for the whole of the war years and for a time afterwards.

Alcantara and *Asturias* took on the more belligerant role of armed merchant cruisers, *Alcantara* later being converted to a trooper. Troop carrying was also undertaken by the

Highland ships and *Almanzora* (whose last scheduled voyage had ended late in 1939 – she thus had a reprieve during the war years).

On 5 December 1939 the first of RML's South America service vessels was lost; *Navasota* was torpedoed in the Atlantic with the loss of 37 officers and men. The following July saw *Sambre* go in much the same way, and in the space of about a month that autumn *Highland Patriot*, *Natia* and *Nalon* were all lost. *Culebra*, which had made an occasional Brazil voyage as a relief ship, was sunk in January 1942 and all hands were lost.

Somme, *Siris*, *Sarthe*, *Sabor*, *Nariva*, *Nagara* and *Nebraska* were all lost between 1942 and 1944, while *Asturias*, torpedoed off Freetown in July 1943, was declared a constructive total loss but after the war was repaired under the ownership of the Ministry of Transport.

Much-needed meat supplies were maintained from the River Plate as far as possible, augmented by four new 'D' ships completed for the trade during the war. *Darro*, *Drina*, *Deseado* and *Durango*, unlike the earlier 'D' ships, carried only twelve passengers, but the insulated cargo capacity of each was around half a million cubic feet. The need during those years for food supplies and other cargoes hardly needs emphasising. Some ships were able to complete voyages with no impact sufficient to warrant their inclusion in the company's war history. These few snippets from commercial voyages early in the war provide glimpses of the manner in which the war touched them – they cover the period until the spring of 1940, taken from voyage reports to the managing director's committee.

Parima, one of eight 'P' class freighters built during the Second World War. She is pictured in her early days during the war, employed on transport voyages as far afield as India, Africa and Australia.

Highland Monarch, *on the right, in a convoy to the Middle East in 1941.*

Between October and December 1939 *Highland Monarch* made her first wartime voyage, averaging 15.34 knots. Outward passengers in first and intermediate classes numbered 152; only seven were carried homeward. Such loss of earnings deteriorated further with later voyages. Freight, however, was good and she was a full ship on the homeward passage (as were all of the meat ships at this period). At Lisbon on the outward passage the Naval Control Officer ordered her to omit Las Palmas and there were delays at Brazilian ports.

Gascony left England shortly after war was declared and had little outward cargo but was full for the trip home. She managed an average of 9.83 knots. On 3 January 1940 RML reported it had twenty-five ships operating commercially. In addition there was one (*Lochgoil*) undergoing salvage operations after being mined (she was declared a constructive total loss but was repaired under Government ownership), six were requisitioned for Government service and there were four under construction (*Pampas*, *Pardo*, *Potaro* and *Palma*).

Andes, making her first voyage in December 1939, returned to the UK on 1 January 1940 after Atlantic passages which were regarded as her unofficial trials. Run at varying speeds, averaging 15.2 knots, she ploughed through two fresh gales and proved to be very seaworthy, shipping little water, maintaining a good speed and steering well. The machinery also worked smoothly and well.

A different story emerged from the little freighter *Sabor*, which also arrived home on 1 January; however, she had begun her voyage to Brazil on 25 August 1939. Still a coal-burner, she meandered along at an average of 8.84 knots (a speed probably affected by convoy restrictions). Her outward passage was in ballast but she brought home a full cargo. There were complaints about the amount of fuel used, but it

Highland Chieftain *arriving at Durban in July 1945, bringing home South African troops.*

transpired she added 2,621 miles to her voyage through Admiralty routing and zig-zagging. She had been three days out from Barry when an order brought her scurrying back to join a convoy.

Nela averaged nearly 11 knots during a passage to the River Plate and back between October and mid-January, but her daily coal consumption was nearly 70 tons (compared with only 26 tons in *Sabor*), aggravated not only by wartime conditions but also heavy weather almost throughout the voyage. She had good cargoes in both directions. *Highland Chieftain* left London on 13 November and returned on 17 January, commanded by Commodore T.J.C. Purcell-Buret DSC. Freight-wise *Highland Chieftain's* voyage was very good in both directions, including a full meat cargo northbound. Outward passenger numbers were quite good but on the homeward passage carried just eight.

By February 1940 reports were being filed of emergency drills. *Natia*, for example, during a voyage to the River Plate which was extended by 2,391 miles through deviation and zig-zagging, held fire and boat stations ten times during the voyage and gun drill twenty-one times. *Highland Patriot* (21 December to 16 February), on the voyage prior to the one on which she was torpedoed, tested all watertight doors daily, held fire and boat drill fourteen times and gun drill every second day.

The torrid period experienced by shipowners was now setting in. For *Highland Monarch* (January and February 1940) there were delays first off Southend and then in the Downs. She voyaged to the River Plate via Las Palmas for fuel, without cargo and with only thirty-four passengers (she could carry about 500). No fuel was available at River Plate ports and so she had to reach St Vincent in the Cape Verde Islands on the northbound passage before replenishing bunkers. For her homeward passage she had twelve passengers and a full cargo.

A problem was experienced by *Nalon* (16 December – 7 March) with her steering gear. It wasn't a new complaint for the ship but on this occasion it was put down to constant zig-zagging. *Nagara*, also on the River Plate service (23 December – 15 March), had good cargoes both ways. Her master, Capt. T.E. Coombs CBE, RD, RNR, acted as convoy commodore. Another 'N' ship, *Nariva*, made a similar voyage at much the same time and had a packet of complaints to explain her poor performance, averaging $10\frac{1}{2}$ knots on a coal consumption of 64.82 tons per day. The usual course deviation and zig-zagging were compounded by an inefficient crew in the stoke-hold, poor-quality Durham coal supplied at Dakar and bad weather during parts of the voyage.

That selection provides an idea of the new routines, complications and frustrations which accompanied voyages that generally would not warrant a mention. More detail on wartime voyages is given in Volume 2. It should perhaps be added that the shore-based staff were having their own problems, not the least of which involved the logistics of communication as some were moved from war-torn London to the comparative sanctuary of Taunton.

15
The Final Chapter

When the Second World War ended, Royal Mail Lines began the final chapter in a very long book, though no-one could have known then that it would be the last. There was, perhaps, a little writing on the wall, but the directors could hardly be blamed for not divining in 1945 all the factors which would combine to end the mail services in 1969.

The Company managed to acquire quite a lot of new cargo tonnage during the war. In addition to the large-capacity 'D' class meat ships, eight smaller general cargo ships had been built by 1945. They were the 'P' ships, six of which survived the war and were invaluable during the years that followed. The smaller *Gascony* and *Lombardy* joined them at times on the Brazil run, as did the
class Liberty ships *Beresina*, *Berbice*, *Barranca* and *Balantia*, and the *Teviot* and *Tweed*.

As far as passenger vessels were concerned, things could have been worse. Only one Highland ship had been lost, leaving four to maintain the London service. The Southampton schedule was depleted, though, with *Almanzora* sold to breakers in 1948 and *Asturias* no longer available. That left *Alcantara* and the (comparatively) new *Andes*. It was January 1948 before *Andes* began her maiden commercial voyage, after a major refit at Belfast, and *Alcantara* did not resume her old service until October that year.

The Future on the Horizon

As far back as the mid-1930s Royal Mail had been aware of the future threat that air travel might pose to shipowners. Rather than ignoring the challenge, it seemed more sensible to have a stake in it; thus in the 1930s and 1940s the Company twice became involved in new airlines which were formed to provide services to South America.

The first began in 1937 after a two-year gestation. British Airways was the brainchild of Sqn Ldr S.C. Winfield Smith and was intended to challenge the dominant overseas operator at the time, Imperial Airways. Some 25% of the capital (£750,000) was divided among several shipping companies, including Royal Mail, Union-Castle and Bibby Line. RML was offered the sole booking agency in the UK.

The new airline began operating in 1937, with South America as an important component. During the Second World War, however, British Airways was merged with Imperial, the resulting company becoming British Overseas Airways Corporation (BOAC). Royal Mail ended its association at that stage, but it didn't end the shipping industry's concern about or interest in aviation. By 1943 the General Council of British Shipping was urging shipping lines to again develop air services. Royal Mail, Blue Star, Pacific Steam Navigation Co., Booth Line and Lamport and Holt joined forces to help create a new airline to service South America. Formed in 1945, with its headquarters initially in Royal Mail House, it was named British South American Airways (BSAA).

At first RML had a 40% shareholding, but reduced this when the capital was dramatically increased towards the end of 1945. Services began in January 1946, but from the start a cloud hung over the airline's future, for the Labour Government was intent on nationalisation and quickly gave BOAC authority to buy substantial shareholdings.

Matters became worse over the next two years through the loss of three aircraft. A York aircraft, *Star Leader*, crashed near Bathurst, West Africa, killing all twenty-four on board. The Tudor IV plane *Star Tiger* was lost while crossing the Atlantic, and there was mystery surrounding the disappearance of another plane in 1947 during a flight from Buenos Aires and Santiago, Chile. At least part of that mystery was eventually solved, albeit not for half a century. In January 2000 climbers in the Andes mountains stumbled across the wreckage, well-preserved in high-altitude permafrost.

Heated confrontations in Parliament alleged poor training and operational standards. They were refuted by BSAA, but the company's chairman, Air Vice-Marshal D.C.T. Bennett, was dismissed. Within a year BSAA had been absorbed into BOAC, and Royal Mail ended its interest in airlines.

Clearly, competition from aircraft was a major (though not the only) factor which caused the decline of passenger line services during the next two decades. Most lines suffered the same fate at much the same period; there was an inevitability about it all, and ship owners could do little but gauge developments and choose the best time to scale down operations, or switch to the growing passenger ship panacea of cruising. In addition to RML's direct involvement in air services, their potential threat to shipping was under the microscope very early. One RML director, who was also on the board of BSAA, said, as early as 1945: 'If new designs of aircraft and/or engines greatly cheapen costs, there may be a rapid growth of traffic, both in passenger and freight, and considerably greater encroachment into shipping business than at present seems probable'.

During the war comprehensive reports were prepared by the Company's Passenger Manager on post-war competition from aircraft. The most telling of these was written on 12 October 1943 in which he claimed:

> A re-built German and Italian fleet would be a much more formidable obstacle to us than all the other foreign competition put together. My point in mentioning this is to emphasise the fact that our sea-borne traffic should be no less than it has been, even with air competition, provided our German and Italian rivals are kept in check.
>
> If this could be achieved and, say, for the sake of argument, that 50% of the Saloon traffic travelled by air, I feel sufficiently optimistic to think that we should obtain a considerable proportion of the balance. Whether third class, or the emigrant type of passenger, will travel by air is problematical.
>
> To travel by air, in preference to sea, a person will need to be air-minded and wishful of a fast journey. Many people, even when pressed for time, will not be sufficiently confident to travel by air, at least for some years. There will be others, I think the majority, who with time to spare, or for health or pleasure reasons, will desire sea travel. An ocean voyage will never lose its attractions. The restful atmosphere, and life aboard ships, especially in tropical seas, will continue to lure many people.

But to arrive at some sort of conclusion as to who are likely to travel by air in the future, I think it is advisable to give an analysis of the various types who used the sea routes in the past:

1) a) *Chairmen, directors, managers of banks, railways, meat companies etc – 1st class 'A' steamers.*
   b) *Well-to-do Brazilians, Uruguayan and Argentine (including Anglos) passengers – 1st class 'A' steamers.*
   c) *Wealthy British passengers in search of health and pleasure – 1st class 'A' steamers.*

2) a) *Staffs of banks, railways etc – 1st class Highland ships.*
   b) *Commercial travellers – 1st class Highland ships.*

3) *Middle class family type – 2nd class 'A' steamers.*

4) *Superior type of emigrant – Intermediate class Highland ships.*

5) *Purely emigrant types – Third class.*

It is difficult to decide which, in these five classes, will travel by air, but I think air travel will create traffic, and whether a passenger travels both ways by air will depend on his or her experience on the initial journey.

It goes without saying that, generally, tourists or the leisured class will not wish for speedy transportation – they will prefer the restful and carefree atmosphere of an ocean liner rather than an 'express transfer' by air, in addition to which the sea journey ensures a pleasurable voyage with first class 'board and lodging' throughout.

A businessman may go by air, but after accomplishing his task abroad, he may regard himself as entitled to a holiday or rest and choose the 'pleasure way' to return home. In the event, the incitement (through propaganda) to tourists to travel the 'pleasure way' will tend to persuade regular travellers and others to decide upon the sea route when time is not the governing factor.

Under conditions to date, i.e. from the States to South America, air-borne passengers on a 6,000 mile journey have to sleep at a different hotel each night, necessitating packing and unpacking on each day of the journey: this will not appeal to everybody, and as the quantity of baggage is limited, there are many people who dislike being parted from their luggage. During the Graf Zeppelin period, Hamburg-Süd were compelled by the German Government to carry passengers' baggage at a very reduced rate.

It is recognised that the aeroplane is designed to become an important factor in the transportation world, and it may reduce the number of Saloon passengers, but any loss in this respect could be counter-balanced by restrictive measures on the sea-borne activities of our greatest pre-war rivals – the German and Italian lines.

Air competition will be felt more on some routes than on others. If air services were to be operated as a separate entity, and there was open rivalry with the shipping companies, it would involve the latter in advertising their services, and extolling their merits, at much greater length and expense than they have done in the past. The American Shipping Line realised this when they had to face the competition of Pan-American Airways.

Broad-based though those remarks were (and had to be in the heart of a world war), they were remarkably perceptive. Line services did, indeed, continue (largely with good passenger loads) for something like a quarter of a century. And his emphasis on voyaging for pleasure, though clearly concerned with round-voyage passengers, reflected the very factors which governed the eventual renaissance of passenger shipping – cruising.

It is as well, then, during the remainder of this story, to remember that everything which happened in Royal Mail's passenger trades after the Second World War occurred with the expectation, sitting in the background, of increasing air competition.

Andes Joins the Mail Service

The long-term future for the mail service, then, was under the first wisps of cloud the moment the war ended – but one matter which provided the company with great pride was the first commercial voyage of *Andes* in 1948. During January a gathering took place on board the ship at Southampton, an event which had been postponed since September 1939. Royal Mail's chairman, Walter Warwick, made sure that his guests learned not just about the ship they had come to see, but also about her achievements since 1939. There was pride in that, too, as he outlined her world-wide trooping voyages and her record passages. 'In the course of her war service,' he said, 'she steamed over half a million nautical miles and carried no less than 350,000 souls'.

But the focus was primarily on the future:

I think that, having seen the Andes, *you will first of all feel, as I do, that she reflects great credit on her builders, Harland & Wolff Ltd, – on Heaton Tabb & Co., and Hamptons, the contractors who have, between them, been responsible for restoring her furnishings as far as possible to their pre-war condition, – and on all who have had a hand in her design and construction. Speaking for the Company, as her owners, I can say that she well fulfils our aims and expectations, and notwithstanding that it is now eight years since she was first completed, she is thoroughly up-to-date and possesses many characteristics which should make her very popular with the travelling public.*

He had something to say, too, in response to grumblings from South America about how long it was taking to get services back to normal:

Complaints of this kind are quite understandable, especially when so many people even now do not appear to appreciate the extent of the tremendous sacrifices made by this country in the war effort when all our resources were thrown into the fray to ensure a victorious outcome of the struggle…

Under the stress of war it took less than two months to convert Andes *to war service. Her furnishings which were landed into store were unfortunately destroyed by enemy air attack, so have had to be entirely renewed, and it has taken no less than ten months to restore her to her present condition, which is creditable considering all the difficulties encountered.*

So Royal Mail's largest ship embarked at last on the trade for which she had been designed. She disappointed no-one and, for a time, this became a golden era.

The Unthinkable Loss

An interesting situation with passenger operations arose after the war ended. The London-based Highland ships had had their number depleted by one during the war, and in 1946 a replacement for her was ordered – she became *Magdalena*.

However, the major service had been more significantly depleted. Of the three Southampton-based mail ships operating at the outbreak of war, two were no longer available – the badly damaged *Asturias* was repaired and used on government service, and *Almanzora* made her way to shipbreakers. Remember, too, that *Arlanza* had been withdrawn in 1938.

On the other side of the ledger, *Andes* would enter service after her refit, joining *Alcantara*. Thus the premier mail service would have two ships where there had been four prior to the war. Why was the major service deprived of new tonnage, while an immediate replacement was ordered for an intermediate ship belonging to an inherited service?

In view of the research which had gone on during the war, there may well have been a shift of thinking which preferred ships of moderate size and speed (and therefore reduced operating cost), in which freight was important. That would allow them to remain viable if passenger numbers declined. It is significant that the only passenger tonnage built after the war was of the intermediate type, which featured large refrigerated capacity.

So the order was placed in 1946 for Harland & Wolff to build a replacement for *Highland Patriot*. She would be a little larger than the Highlands, but at 17,547 gross tons not greatly so. In May 1948 she was launched, becoming the third Royal Mail ship to bear the name *Magdalena*. In the following March she left Tilbury for her maiden voyage. Apart from the usual maiden voyage welcomes, the outward passage was uneventful. Northbound, however, she grounded near Rio de Janeiro. Holed below the waterline, much of her meat and fruit cargo was soon flooded. Later the vessel refloated and a slow tow began towards Rio; she then made contact with the harbour bar and broke her back. Thus this fine ship was lost on her maiden voyage.

This was the unthinkable loss – a large, up-to-date ship put ashore on rocks in fine weather; a ship with all the latest navigational aids and manned by officers with long experience. What was learned at the Court of Enquiry explained the 'unthinkable', and it caused the company's chairman to display undisguised anger in a letter which is quoted shortly.

The enquiry dealt solely with the initial grounding. It covered many factors, but there were three of particular importance: the level of involvement in navigation from Capt. Lee after leaving Santos, the amount of compass error (coupled with general equipment teething troubles), and the course being steered, particularly in relation to the set of the current. Several astonishing facts emerged.

There was, for example, a lighthouse at Boi Point, whose position was known to be half a mile inland from the position marked on the chart. Capt. Lee plotted his bearings on the charted position of the light, and while this wasn't significant to the stranding, it displayed (counsel for the Ministry of Transport claimed) a slackness in navigation.

First class observation lounge in Magdalena *(III).*

The after portion of Magdalena *(III) after she had broken her back off Rio de Janeiro in 1949. The insurance payment of well over £2 million was thought to have been the largest claim for a ship loss up to that time.*

The master was not aware of his first officer's background:

> 'What experience had the first officer, Mr Senior, of these waters?'
> 'I am not really in a position to say…'
> 'Did you know that he was a submarine officer, was taken a prisoner of war, and was a prisoner for five years?'
> 'No.'
> 'Did you know he had never approached Palmas Island before?'
> 'No, I did not.'
> 'Did you know he had not seen Corcovado Light before? – I could not answer that.'

At 4.30 a.m. the first officer had called Capt. Lee and reported that *Magdalena* was half a mile north of her course line. Capt. Lee was asked:

> 'Did you appreciate that put her in a dangerous position?'
> 'No, I did not.'
> 'But it did, in fact, put her in a dangerous position?'
> 'Looking back at what happened, it certainly did.'

When the senior second officer felt some unease, after plotting a revised course and realising the ship would pass less than a mile from unlighted rocks on a moonless night, why did he not report this to the captain? When he handed over the watch to the first officer and remarked on the closeness of the course to the Tijucas Rocks, why did the first officer not pursue the matter? When the officer on watch recommended to the captain a course change of four degrees to the northward, why did the captain not query the effect, especially as it was already known that something – either the current or an incorrect compass – had already set the ship northward of her original course line? To what extent should the officers have relied on the gyro compass, when it had been faulty earlier and the senior second didn't trust it? Why was the radar not in use; why, indeed, was it not to be used 'unnecessarily', and what constituted necessity?

There existed, it seems, a distinct lack of communication. The evidence was peppered with such matters. Capt. Lee possessed (as he said in his evidence) implicit faith in his officers. The Wreck Commissioner placed matters in perspective when he observed:

> The broad fact remains that these officers, from Boi Point onwards, at any rate, seemed to have a fairly good idea of where the ship was. You can criticise the actual pin-point but, roughly speaking, she must have been where she was put on the chart, if for no other reason than where she ultimately got to.

In this manner did a sorry tale emerge. In the end the verdict was given:

> The report which I am about to read is unanimous. The court having carefully enquired into the circumstances attending the casualty, find that the said casualty was caused by the fault of the ship's master, Captain D.R.V. Lee, and of her first officer, Mr C.J. Senior, and the court suspends the certificate of Captain Lee for a period of two years, and of Mr Senior for a period of one year, both periods to run from today…

After Magdalena

Since management had four years to think about a replacement for Highland Patriot, *Magdalena* was clearly considered necessary. Why, then, was she not replaced? Let Royal Mail's Chairman, Walter C. Warwick, explain. The following was the letter he wrote on 4 October 1949 to his counterpart (Sir Frederick Rebbeck) at Harland & Wolff after *Magdalena's* Court of Enquiry:

> *My dear Rebbeck,*
> *You will, of course, be aware of the findings of the Court of Enquiry issued yesterday in connection with the sad loss of* Magdalena. *This will close a sad and brief chapter of a very fine ship which we had all confidently anticipated would have added lustre to the fine record of this Company in stimulating the further development of trade with South America in accordance with the Company's traditions over a very long period of time.*
>
> *If ever there was a case where a ship should not have been lost, this is it, and I still feel I cannot calmly talk about the astounding lack of care which led to so tragic an end of this fine ship.*
>
> *We, of course, have collected the insurance monies and have considerable funds available for new tonnage but with the very changed conditions with which we are now confronted and the fact that already there is one fine passenger ship* Presidente Peron *recently delivered by Vickers to the Argentine Government, and within the next few months there will be two additional similar ships, these changed circumstances render it necessary that we should proceed cautiously and rather wait on events before deciding upon further very heavy Capital expenditure.*
>
> *These three Argentine ships, each with about 350,000 cubic feet of refrigerator space, will have to be provided with a share of the Meat business which the British Lines have collectively built up over the past fifty years, and a further disturbing factor in the general situation is the uncertainty of this country's general trade relationships with the Argentine.*
>
> *Following upon the recent devaluation of British Sterling, the Argentine Government have now issued a series of complicated regulations regarding a large and wide range of exchange rates varying from about $9\frac{1}{2}$ pesos to $25\frac{1}{2}$ pesos per [pound] Sterling.*
>
> *The quite unrealistic rate of $9\frac{1}{2}$ pesos seems to have been deliberately fixed with a view to securing large increased Sterling payments both for Meat and other foodstuffs to be imported from the Argentine and, in effect, would seem to create a very serious method of discrimination.*
>
> *I have no doubt that this particular matter will form the subject of very serious discussions between the British and Argentine Governments and it is to be hoped that some fair and mutually reasonable basis will ultimately be arrived at but, certainly, the present outlook is distinctly disturbing and I just mention this to emphasise to you the need for caution on our part before seriously contemplating further heavy Capital commitments…*

The matter of changed trading conditions was straightforward enough. After the war there had been frenetic trade, both cargo and passenger. This 'false prosperity' declined after a time, thus the prospects when *Magdalena* was ordered were excellent, but by the time she entered service, trade had slid back into a trough. On its own that would not have prevented a replacement being built. Royal Mail, more than any other company, had good reason to be aware that troughs and crests went in cycles.

More important were the references to Argentina's changed political climate. Juan Perón, an army general, had seized power and became dictator in 1943; three years later – the very time *Magdalena* was ordered – he was installed as President. Mr Warwick highlighted some of Perón's initiatives – these were turbulent times in Argentina, and they were not benefiting British shipping. The 12,500 ton passenger-cargo liners *President Peron*, *17 de Octubre* and *Eva Peron*, for instance, created out of the blue totally unexpected competition. They continued to operate, incidentally, for many years, later under the names *Argentina*, *Libertad* and *Uruguay*, and under the re-constituted ownership of Empresa Lineas Maritimas Argentinas. All of that may also have influenced the status of the Southampton express service, at least to the point of compounding other factors.

An irony of the Perón company's effect on Royal Mail was that RMSP had once held a controlling interest in it. Originally developed by Nicholas Mihanovich, an Austrian, in the 1870s, two-thirds of the firm's stock was purchased by Lord Kylsant in 1917 (by then it was known as the Argentine Navigation Co.) and he was its chairman until forced by the Voting Trustees to sell in 1930. The 300 or so ships in this ocean, coastal and river fleet went to Alberto Dodero and, in another twist, Dodero had to have a London Committee because of the financial arrangements for the purchase. The chairman of the London Committee was none other than Walter Warwick. Needless to say, he resigned when Perón nationalised Dodero's company.

Royal Mail's position, then, returned to status quo at the end of the 1940s, but by the mid-1950s there was a need to consider the future of the mail service. *Alcantara* had passed her thirtieth birthday and the four Highlands were not far behind. This brought the company to the last significant crossroads in the century-old South America mail service. It chose a major policy shift, the culmination of all the factors discussed earlier.

In 1958 *Alcantara* was withdrawn, after thirty-two years of admirable service, and was sold to shipbreakers. Shortly after, *Andes* was also withdrawn and was sent to Holland for the first part of a refit which turned her into a first-class-only full-time cruise ship. The Southampton express Brazil and River Plate mail service – a Royal Mail icon since 1851 – had ended.

Meanwhile, the London-based intermediates were being replaced. During 1959 and 1960 three new liners were delivered from Harland & Wolff. The sister ships *Amazon*, *Aragon* and *Arlanza* were about 20,000 tons, and as they were introduced (before in some cases), the 30-year-old Highlands were sold.

The three new 'A' ships maintained the passenger and mail service, but from London instead of Southampton. Each also had some 500,000 cubic feet of insulated cargo space. The four 'D' class refrigerated cargo ships were still operating, and so were most of the 'P' ships, but by the 1960s there was an increasing tendency for the freighters to be placed on other routes and the 'D' ships were laid up on occasion. First the 'P' class and then the 'D's were sold, and by 1968 the 'A' ships maintained the whole – now much depleted – South America operation on their own.

Even that didn't last. RML had, in 1965, been absorbed into the Furness Withy Group and by 1968 the new management judged the Brazil and River Plate mail service to be no longer viable. During April 1968 *Amazon* was transferred within the group to Shaw Savill Line and renamed *Akaroa* for service between London and Australia/New Zealand. Early the following year her sister-ships followed, utilised on a round-the-world service with the new names *Arawa* and *Aranda*.

To retain at least a portion of the meat trade, other changes occurred within the group. Houlder Brothers' *Hornby Grange* (renamed *Douro*) and *Duquesa* entered the Royal Mail fleet, and shortly afterwards Shaw Savill's *Persic* was switched to RML to replace *Duquesa*. *Persic* was renamed *Derwent*.

That, in a nut-shell, is the story of change so mesmerising, after a hundred years of rock-like stability, that it is still difficult to comprehend decades later. In those few years an operation occupying six passenger/mail/cargo liners and a dozen cargo ships, with enormous combined freight capacity, was reduced to two second-hand cargo ships for use when cargo warranted.

Tales of the Sixties

The South Atlantic ships generally operated without fuss or headlines. To Royal visits mentioned previously can be added Princess Margaret's visit to *Andes* during a British Trade Fair at Lisbon in 1959 (though *Andes* was on a cruise at the time). The cocktail party attended by the Princess was a Royal Mail initiative which reflected the Company's still-

Capt. T.W. Stevens CBE, RD, RNR, ringing off engines in the wheelhouse of Aragon *(II), signalling his retirement in 1963. He joined Royal Mail as a cadet in 1917 and had reached the rank of chief officer when he was mobilised for war service in 1939. He held many positions during the war, including Commodore of Convoys. From his return to RML in 1947 he commanded a variety of ships until being appointed the first master of* Aragon *in 1960. He was Company Commodore from June 1961 until his retirement in March 1963.* (Author's photograph)

Amazon (III) approaches the end of a voyage from South America during the 1960s, pictured in the Thames shortly before arrival in London's Royal Docks. (Author's photograph)

important links with Portugal. RML had a stand at the Fair, which was visited both by Princess Margaret and the Portuguese Prime Minister, Dr Salazar.

Some new ports and itinerary changes were introduced in an effort to increase freight yields. In September 1959 *Potaro* opened an extension southward to the Magellan Straits (which had been frequented by the earlier 'P' ships), calling at the Chilean port of Punta Arenas. Earlier that year heavy rains in southern Brazil had caused floods downriver in *Uruguay* and *Argentina*. For several days the River Plate waterfront was under about ten feet of water. Buenos Aires was badly affected, and *Highland Monarch*, alongside the *Frigorifico Anglo*, was practically isolated. Capt. T.W. Stevens RD RNR entertained influential Argentinians on *Highland Brigade* about the time of the floods. At the same port, early in 1960, Capt. E.A.C. Thacker, in *Deseado*, entertained to lunch Sir John Ward, Britain's Ambassador to the Argentine, after he had inspected the latest Royal Mail arrival in the River Plate, *Yaguarete*.

She and her sister ship *Yacaré* were Dutch-built meat lighters which collected meat from up-river cattle stations and brought it to the ships at Buenos Aires. They replaced *Dart* and *Devon*, which had operated since 1912 and 1914 respectively. *Dart* and *Devon* were built by Cammell Laird at Birkenhead and it was a tribute to the builder that their sale almost half a century later was for further trading.

A juggling act saw the new 'A' ships introduced as the Highlands were phased out. The first to go, in January 1959, was *Highland Chieftain*, sold to a Gibraltar firm. On 17 September *Highland Brigade* was sold to Greek shipowner John S. Latsis; she ultimately went to shipbreakers in 1965.

The sale of *Highland Princess* and the maiden voyage of *Amazon* almost coincided. *Highland Princess* also went to Latsis, and later operated with Czech and Chinese owners. Her sale by RML took place a week before Christmas 1959, and a month later the first new ship – *Amazon* – left Tilbury for her maiden voyage. She was the first white-hulled mail ship since the time near the turn of the century when most ships briefly had white livery. With a gross tonnage of 20,350, *Amazon* and her sister-ships were a little larger than *Magdalena* but generally thought of as being quite similar. In a number of ways, though, they were strikingly different, not least by providing three passenger classes against *Magdalena*'s two.

Shortly after visiting Andes at Lisbon, Princess Margaret launched *Amazon* at Belfast, and on 12 January 1960 visited the completed liner prior to her maiden voyage. *Amazon* was the scene of a succession of parties, luncheons and staff visits, all amid last-minute work to complete the new ship. The only thing to mar those frantic three weeks was an absence of cargo owing to a dock strike. Possibly a unique event during the short voyage down-river to Tilbury was the presence on board of the Board of Directors, managers and company secretary. At 9.30 on the morning of the 22nd the regular meeting of the Board was held afloat.

A rarely photographed part of a ship, the shaft tunnel of a Royal Mail Lines freighter in the 1960s. (Author's photograph)

That afternoon the *Amazon*, festooned with flags of all descriptions came alive as liners only do when their passengers are on board. By car and train they arrived at Tilbury Riverside Station; the boat train was still the maroon, steam-pulled stock, hissing and grunting as it approached the buffers. Through the Customs Hall and up a ramp to notices in English and Spanish telling the different passenger classes which way to go – first and cabin class straight ahead into 'C' Deck Square; third class to 'C' Deck aft.

The bustle and confusion so well-known to the ship's staff (especially in the Purser's Office) was made that much more difficult by the staff having as yet hardly become familiar with the ship themselves. Last minute scampering down the gangway by visitors; tugs ready fore and aft; formalities completed and warning blasts sounded. At 7.35 p.m. *Amazon* moved away from the Stage.

Three months later, *Aragon* entered service, leaving Tilbury on 29 April 1960 – just twenty-four hours after the last Highland ship, *Highland Monarch*, arrived in the Clyde for breaking up. On board *Aragon* at Vigo during her first outward passage, the ship was presented with a splendid representation of the Arms of *Aragon*. Señor Antonio Zubiri, President of the County Council of Saragossa, handed the Arms to Capt. T.W. Stevens. Sr Zubiri represented the three provinces jointly corresponding to the ancient kingdom of *Aragon*. A personal presentation was made to Capt. Stevens – a special copy of a book on navigation written by Martin Cortes in 1551.

Arlanza, last of the trio, began her maiden voyage in September 1960.

Andes had by then completed her conversion to full-time cruise liner. Rarely after that did she return to the South American ports whose people knew her so well. The few occasions when she did were on long winter cruises, the last being after the 'A' ships had been withdrawn, so she was catering cruise-style for passengers who had been in the habit of making an 'A' ship round voyage to escape the English winter.

In 1960 the 'P' ships were still often engaged in the South American trade, and the voyage to Punta Arenas mentioned earlier was followed by others. The six 'P' ships were placed on the sale market in 1965, and they were not replaced. Later in the decade the 'D' ships also left the service, after largely uneventful careers since the Second World War. In 1964 Deseado was 'converted' to a cadet training ship, carrying six engineer cadets in what had formerly been passenger accommodation. She was the last 'D' ship to be sold, going to Hamburg shipbreakers in 1968 after a final charter voyage to war-torn Vietnam.

The 'A' ships quickly settled into the mail service, departing from London on a three-weekly schedule. Their near-perfect timekeeping was only slightly marred by the occasional delay, usually for a minor engine defect or weather conditions. Only once did a serious disruption take place, for whenever there was a dock strike (regular occurrences) the ships sailed without cargo to meet the terms of the mail contract. The one disruption was the seamen's strike in 1966, which did immense harm to British shipping at a time when liner services were struggling to survive. The only bright spot from that affair was that, for the only time in their careers with Royal Mail, all three ships were together in London's Royal Victoria Dock. That curiosity lasted a very short time, for the last to arrive berthed the day before the strike ended.

These liners were rarely in the spotlight. Exhibitions of fine seamanship occurred often enough, though. During a strike, Capt. Grant took *Amazon* out from Rio de Janeiro

The 'A' ships of the 1960s were frequently admired in London's docks, but they were equally impressive at night when few people saw them. This is Arlanza (II), *pictured at her loading berth, No 3 shed King George V Dock.* (Author's photograph)

without tugs or port labour. There were transfers at sea – one for a medical emergency and others, involving two 'A' ships in mid-Atlantic, to transfer stowaways. Sad occasions included amazing efforts in poor weather to get a seriously ill asthmatic to hospital; happy times included the Duke of Edinburgh's visit to *Arlanza* at Buenos Aires for the largest party held on the ships. Events such as those are looked at in Volume 2.

Many well-known faces were seen on board – they ranged from Charlie Chaplin to mountaineers Chris Bonington and Don Whillans; entertainers Dorita y Pepe, Hank Marvin of The Shadows and Keith Potger from The Seekers. These ships bumped whales in the South Atlantic and bumped the shallow River Plate bottom; one retiring *Commodore* managed to bump the gantry at Tilbury Landing Stage but their accidents and mechanical troubles were few as they maintained the century-plus traditions of Royal Mail.

During 1964 the Company carried out what the war had stopped it doing in 1939 – celebrating its centenary. Of course, it was now a century and a quarter, but since the celebrations on board *Andes* had been quashed in 1939, RML decided to make up for it twenty-five years later. On 28 September a Royal Mail Lines supplement appeared in the *Times*. How fitting that this most prestigious of newspapers – which had carried sailing notices in the earliest days, news stories ranging from the loss of *Amazon* in the 1850s to Lord Kylsant's trial, and which had carried the death notice for the firm's founder, James Macqueen – should be responsible for telling the world of the great catalogue of achievement by a company of which most readers would previously have known little.

Arlanza (II) travelling through storm seas, homeward bound from Buenos Aires. (Author's photograph)

The main celebration came that night (two days after the actual anniversary because the 26th was a Saturday), with a dinner on board *Aragon*. The ship looked wonderful, glinting in a new coat of paint and dressed overall. The order for a dressing line had been sent out to all ships in the fleet. At about 6.30 p.m. the guests began to arrive – top men from the business world; MPs; diplomats and ambassadors. The Guest of Honour was the Lord Mayor of London – how appropriate for a company whose head office had been within the City limits since 1839. H. Leslie Bowes CBE (not yet knighted), Royal Mail's chairman, and Capt. W.S. Thomas then mingled with their guests – newspaper magnate Lord Thomson of Fleet, architect Sir Basil Spence, MP for Southend East (past whose constituency the 'A' ships sailed every voyage) Sir Stephen McAdden; ambassadors, *charges d'affaires* for South American nations; directors and chairmen of other shipping companies, and many more.

It was easy, at such times, to imagine the 'A' ships' routine continuing forever, but less than four years later everything had changed. In fact, the changes began in 1965; having so recently celebrated 125 years as an independent company, Royal Mail Lines was absorbed into the Furness, Withy Group. On 11 May that year, Furness, Withy offered terms for the purchase of the 66% of RML shares which it did not already hold.

Although Royal Mail is not at present trading on a profitable basis...there should in due course be considerable scope for improvement from a closer co-operation between the two companies which can only be achieved if Royal Mail is under the complete ownership of Furness, Withy.

Ultimately that confidence was unfounded, and in 1968 *Amazon* was withdrawn from service. During April, while *Amazon* was in the hands of Harland & Wolff for conversion to her new role as a tourist-only ship for Shaw Savill Line, *Arlanza* brought to Britain the first cargo of South American beef since a ban had been imposed following an outbreak of foot and mouth disease. Lamb and mutton shipments were restored later.

Speculation on the futures of *Aragon* and *Arlanza* grew during 1968. That autumn the decision to transfer to Shaw Savill was made known. At the beginning of February 1969 *Arlanza* slipped into London after her last South Atlantic voyage. Capt. G.A. Gibbons, her commander since Capt. T.W.F. Bolland had retired as Commodore in the summer of 1965, wrote in his last voyage report for *Arlanza*:

I was amazed how the name of Royal Mail Lines is regarded with affection, respect and esteem by people in South America. I received numerous letters, visits from people in ports, and even telegrams from people of all nationalities, in Brazil, Uruguay, Argentina and Chile, saying with how much regret and sadness they have learned that Royal Mail passenger ships will no longer serve South America, and wishing us all the best in the future. One was from a Brazilian who had done 76 transatlantic crossings in Royal Mail ships.

16
Aragon Closes the Book

The last mail voyage was made by *Aragon*, which left Tilbury on 4 January 1969. The discharging of cargo from the previous voyage continued until sailing because of time lost over weekends and Christmas. Export cargo totalled 915 tons and there were 1,415 bags of mail. The ship was closed down at 6 p.m. on 3 January, and at 10.30 p.m. she left her berth in King George V Dock for Tilbury Landing Stage, being all secure by 1.20 a.m. on 4 January.

A mixture of mist and hazy sun in the early morning gave way, by 11 a.m., to dense fog. Visibility on the river was virtually nil. Departure time was 2 p.m. and passengers were embarked on schedule. By lunchtime the familiar scene in 'C' Deck square was in evidence – tears, hugs and kisses; a wall of trunks and cases; the abstract babble of voices; children excitedly pushing through a forest of grown-up legs; stewards, officers and purser's staff sorting out endless problems. Away from this vortex of life the ship maintained its usual level of peace, and from the starboard rails one could quietly gaze out at the impenetrable wall of fog.

Altogether 293 passengers embarked. Of the ninety-seven in first class, eighty-eight were making the round voyage, and with the weather which came to see them off they were no doubt thankful they had booked. A quarter of the eighty cabin class were also doing the round trip. The 116 tourist class passengers were busy on 'C', 'D' and 'E' decks sorting out their own piles of baggage. No round voyagers here; Lisbon was the destination for many, Vigo for others, but a good sprinkling were voyaging across the Atlantic. It was usual on this service for passengers to join and leave at every port. This voyage was no different, and while 293 embarked at Tilbury, there were 360 on board at Buenos Aires.

There was confusion as sailing time approached, for the fog remained thick. Just off the Stage the Soviet liner *Alexandr Pushkin* lay at anchor, awaiting *Aragon*'s departure so that she could embark passengers for a cruise. We couldn't see her, but the occasional boom from her siren told us how close she was.

A launch was to take me on the river to photograph the liner as she sailed. At a quarter to two an optimistic Gravesend boatman came on board and asked if I was ready. We cruised along the length of the ship and cut the engine under *Aragon*'s bow. Her bridge wasn't even visible from there. As we rocked gently, the slight swell drifting us out into the river, we were surrounded by a grey vacuum, listening to the throb from the diesel of an unseen passing coaster. Visitors were asked to leave at 2.30 p.m. The shore telephone line was taken down, then hurriedly replaced. At 2.45 p.m. the pilot boarded. At last the fog began to disperse and at 3.30 p.m. *Aragon* moved away into the river, *Alexandr Pushkin*

A misty departure from Tilbury for Aragon *(II) on 4 January 1969 - the start of Royal Mail Lines'*
last mail voyage. (Author's photograph)

slipping in almost before she was away. A glint of winter sun broke through the mist like
burnished gold, and dozens of seagulls wheeled overhead in silhouette, screaming around
the ship as she moved forward at 'dead slow'.

After three hours at anchor off the Nore, because of further fog, *Aragon* finally made the
crossing to Flushing, where she took on 1,140 tons of heavy fuel and twenty-nine
passengers. Sailing at 2 p.m. on 5 January, the ship was soon plunging across the Bay of
Biscay in 'boisterous conditions'. Past the uninviting rocks of Finisterre, she reached Vigo
at lunchtime on 7 January. Vigo can be a pleasant place in summer, but that January day
was bleak and wretched under the influence of a blustery Atlantic, and the ship was
despatched for Lisbon as quickly as possible. She spent 8 January there in fine weather and
sailed at 7 p.m. for Las Palmas, the weather improving with every mile. At Las Palmas
there was a short delay because of another liner in port ahead of her – she was *Alexandr
Pushkin*, which had last been seen somewhat vaguely at Tilbury.

The passage across the Atlantic was splendid, with Capt. Kennedy taking his ship
between the Cape Verde Islands to provide interesting scenery for the passengers. Rio de
Janeiro was reached on time on 19 January. The passage along the coast was made in fine
conditions – the calls were Santos (20 January), Montevideo (23 January) and Buenos
Aires (24 January). On the 25th she shifted to La Plata to load meat. A total of 436 tons
was taken on here and more than 2,000 tons in the South Dock. Passengers and mail came
on board at the New Port on 30 January. Senior officers of the Prefectura Maritima
boarded to say farewell to the last of the Company's mail liners, and *Aragon* sailed at 6.15
p.m. The call at Montevideo next day was uneventful, and departure for Santos was made

just before midnight the next day, after a thousand tons of cargo had been loaded.

Arrival at Santos was on 4 February; 822 tons of cargo was loaded. By the time she had taken on a few tons at Rio, the liner was loaded down to her marks with 5,124 tons of cargo, more than £100,000 in freight earnings. Ironically, this was the most valuable cargo an 'A' ship had ever carried. There were 363 passengers for the transatlantic passage.

Aragon left her berth at Rio de Janeiro at six o'clock on the evening of 5 February. At all ports along the coast there had been lively farewells with balloons, streamers, postcards of the ship and even a few toilet rolls thrown from the ship to a background of music. Tugs gave the traditional farewell of three long blasts on their sirens, acknowledged from the ship. At Santos four tugs accompanied *Aragon* downriver and flew the signal 'WAY' ('wish you a pleasant voyage'). As departure from Montevideo was near midnight there was only a small knot of people to see her off, but what they lacked in numbers they made up with sheer exuberance. Capt. Kennedy hosted parties at all ports for the people who had helped to keep the service ticking over smoothly for so many years.

Fine weather accompanied *Aragon* across the Atlantic to Las Palmas, where she docked at 7 a.m. on 15 February. There was little to be done here; a few passengers embarked or landed, four tons of cargo was loaded and 300 tons of fuel taken on. The ship was held back until one o'clock to give passengers time for shopping.

On the run to Lisbon the approach towards England's worst winter for years began to make itself felt. *Aragon* ran into a heavy northerly swell, accompanied by a marked drop in temperature. During the call at the Portuguese capital on 17 February the day was wet and blustery. She sailed that evening for Vigo in worsening conditions. A strong gale blew throughout the night and the call at Vigo next day was made in conditions as bleak as on the outward passage. In the chill, drenching rain squalls, 40 tons of cargo was handled, nearly 800 bags of mail landed and over 100 passengers embarked and landed.

Aragon took her departure at three in the afternoon in severe conditions. I well remember taking leave of Vigo in 'severe conditions' on board *Arlanza* a couple of years earlier – we were at dinner when the ship emerged from the lee of the headland and instantly began the kind of rolling that causes utter consternation. For *Aragon*, the weather on this occasion was more deceptive, for after passing Finisterre things improved for the remainder of the passage to Southampton.

The Last Homecoming

Southampton would host the final significant scene of a story in which the city had been a background since *Teviot*'s paddles had thrashed the waters of the Solent on 9 January 1851. *Aragon* was due to dock at 8 a.m. on 20 February, and during the previous evening London-based staff who needed to be there made their way by train to the Hampshire city. A few who were perhaps not so urgently needed came as well. If asked why, they would probably not have been able to explain very well – they felt a sense of occasion, a sense of history; above all that an important part of their lives, many years for some of them, was ending.

Capt. W.A. Kennedy (left) of Aragon (II) receives in 1969 a commemorative plaque from Capt. E.J. Kirton, Southampton's Dock and Harbour Master, to mark the end of mail services by a company which had used Southampton constantly since 1841. (Author's photograph)

This last scene was played out in atrocious weather. I joined the 6.30 train from Waterloo that cold evening. As the exodus from London's businesses began, snow started to fall. It became heavy almost at once, driven in violent gusts by north-easterly winds. As we drew out of Waterloo it was already an inch or two thick and whipping down with some fury. It was a slow journey and the deeper we penetrated into Hampshire, the worse conditions became – great drifts of snow in cuttings and a white-out beyond. At Basingstoke the lights went out, which at least gave us a better view of the weather. Finally we crawled into Southampton Central – more like a junction on the Trans-Siberian Railway, with the train covered in slabs of snow which penetrated to the unlikeliest places on the front, back, sides and underneath.

Overnight the snow turned to rain, six inches of snow transforming itself into the most depressing mess imaginable. In the early morning gloom the Calshot Signal Station confirmed that *Aragon* was passing Netley at 7.30 p.m. – right on time.

For the purposes of photographing *Aragon* against the Southampton background, I had arranged, as at Tilbury, to hire a launch. At half-past eight I was at No. 8 steps. The rain fell steadily and hard, straight down through windless air. The gloom, even for a February morning, was terrible. I had a mug of steaming tea in the launch while we waited for the light to improve. After a while we began to steer around the docks towards the ship, cutting through water that was glass-smooth but for the rain's pockmarking. Dozens of black-headed gulls and terns wheeled and screeched above the water.

We passed by *Aragon* to have a look at *Queen Elizabeth II*, lying inert at Ocean Terminal, awaiting her first, triumphant voyage. Back at 38/39 berth, *Aragon* – showing the rigours of her passage from Lisbon in the form of rust and dirt along the hull – was a disconsolate sight in her isolation at the far end of the quay. In those conditions were my photographs taken. Afterwards I was on board for two presentations – a silver salver from the Company's agents at the port (McGregor, Gow & Holland Ltd), and a pewter plaque, bearing inscribed silhouettes of *Teviot* and *Aragon* – the first and last company ships to make the South America mail voyage – presented by the Southampton Docks Authority. Capt. W.A. Kennedy, who was nearing the end of his last voyage, as he would retire after arrival at London, received those mementos.

Passengers milled about in the usual way. Sitting quietly amid the bustle were two Indians, one elderly with a grizzled, grey beard, the other younger, wrapped and belted in an old blue overcoat and with trousers so wide at the bottom as to flap like a ruffled ensign every time he moved. They had been refused permission to land and would be taken to London and returned to their point of departure.

At length all business was completed. The tugs *Chale* and *Calshot* were attached forward and aft respectively by 10.30 p.m., waiting for the Isle of Wight ferry to pass. Still the rain lashed down – pools of water and slush were everywhere, and the gulls, delighted with the whole occasion, stood in regimented lines along the forward ropes. One by one the ropes were released, the last at 10.55 p.m., and the ship edged away from the quay. *Calshot* parted company first, whistling thrice in salute to *Aragon* and receiving a booming acknowledgement. In Southampton Water *Chale* released her hawser and there was a more distant exchange of farewells wafting across the water. The rain stopped, and for a minute or two a watery sun peeped through the clouds, took a look at the scene and disappeared.

The two remaining legs of the voyage were uneventful. Passengers and cargo were landed at Rotterdam and then *Aragon* returned across the North Sea to London, where she docked about 22 February 1969 to unload that maddeningly large cargo of meat.

Aftermath

South America's trade has always been enigmatic. 'Our trade with the Brazils may continue to improve, but…it is obvious that the increase must be slow, and that other nations will come in with us for a share of it' – those were the words of James Macqueen in 1820, long before the Royal Mail flag first flew in South America. In retrospect, he was not wide of the mark.

There is an impression that for such a massive continent, faced with huge population increases and escalating industrial development, the seemingly limitless trade expansion never quite reached its expected potential – that was the enigma.

While the factors which progressively plotted the Company's South American course were many and varied, those which brought down the curtain on the mail service in 1969 are easier to discover. The immediate cause credited for the withdrawal of the 'A' ships was Britain's outbreak of foot and mouth disease in cattle, though that was compounded by unstable trade conditions generally. When foot and mouth was diagnosed in 1967, imported Argentine meat was thought to have been the cause; a ban was therefore placed on this vital part of the ships' income. Without it the liners were not economically viable, despite quite good returns on the passenger side.

The matter was not as simple as that. You don't end a century-old service because of a temporary setback. Over the years the amount of Argentine meat coming to Britain had dropped greatly, and the reduced tonnages were divided among a greater number of carriers. Not least, as mentioned earlier, was Argentina's entry with a Government shipping line – by 1970 this firm was operating a large fleet. More Argentine meat was by then exported to America than to Britain, and markets generally were becoming wider. Part of that emanated from festering differences between the British and Argentine governments, the latter by then placing a reduced 'ceiling' on the tonnage permitted for sale to Britain. As early as about 1970 there were references to serious political differences over the Falkland Islands. It didn't take many more years to bring that matter to a head.

The practise of South American nations, Argentina particularly, insisting on carrying increasing percentages of their freights in their own government shipping lines – known as 'flag discrimination' – periodically incurred the wrath of senior Royal Mail officials; they described it as a serious threat to international trade. The use of flag discrimination should not be confused with the advent of new competition, where everyone is competing on level terms. Here we are talking of a government effectively reducing freight tonnages by diverting what it wished to its own ships. While that matter gained most notoriety in the meat trade, it also affected general cargoes and had a role to play in the closure of Royal Mail's Brazil cargo service. And it was not only by government decree that this happened – a more invidious method was, at times, employed by shippers who dictated where cargo would be stowed – and in the process at times insisting on spots which would cause the ship serious stability problems.

Less easy to explain was the shortfall in outward cargoes. Long gone were the days when Royal Mail ships set out across the South Atlantic with full holds. By the 1960s they rarely carried more than 1,000 tons, and at times sailed in ballast. For such a fast-developing continent that state of affairs hardly appeared logical.

The final 'A' ship voyage did not entirely extinguish the Company's links with Brazil and the River Plate. The cargo liners *Derwent* (ex *Persic*), *Douro* (ex *Hornby Grange*) and *Duquesa* have been referred to – they were ageing and not kept long. On 13 November 1970, in the wake of 'rumour and speculation', the now-infamous Furness Withy Group staff memorandum announced that twenty-three group ships – almost a quarter of a million gross tons – were to be withdrawn. The memo referred to 'an unprecedented rate of escalation in operating expenses during the present year, which shows no sign of abating'. This was re-iterated with the words of chairman John MacConochie, explaining that 'the Group's directors could see no prospect of fares and freight rates being increased within a reasonable period by an amount sufficient to produce an acceptable level of profitability for the ships concerned'.

To what extent a different approach during the 1960s could have produced continued profitability is a matter for speculation. By 1971 Royal Mail's operations – now simply an operational arm of the Furness Withy Group, had become much less meaningful. Ships entered and left the fleet with bewildering speed. There was constant movement with ships of Royal Mail Lines, Shaw Savill, Furness Withy, Prince Line, Pacific Steam

A forlorn sight on a wretched February day in 1969 as Aragon *(II) leaves Southampton to close the Company's mail ship era after almost 130 years.* (Author's photograph)

Navigation Co. and the like swapping ownership. Matters became more misty still with RML featuring among Furness Withy assets acquired in Hong Kong by C.Y. Tung; and then sold to the Company's one-time competitor Hamburg-Süd in 1990.

It was an ignominious slide into oblivion, perhaps made more acute by the news that the company's name was still being used in the 1990s to badge a German refrigerated cargo ship as part of Hamburg-Süd's South America operations. A company's future has always been critically moulded by its decision-makers. In the 1960s this was especially pertinent, for it was a decade of enormous change in shipping development and economics; change which turned the industry on its head. Perhaps, at that time, Royal Mail could have done with the vision of another James Macqueen and the entrepreneurial business ability of another Owen Philipps.

Appendix I:
The Origins of the Meat Trade

Royal Mail's involvement with refrigeration began with the fitting of cool chambers in *Tagus* in 1883 – but while they gave the directors an insight into the system's usefulness, they were purely for provedore purposes. The directors' report for October 1883 stated:

> *She* [Tagus] *has been fitted with a Cold Air Machine and Chamber for the better conveyance of Provisions in connection with the victualling of passengers, and the plan has already met with expressions of approval.*

One surviving report suggests that she *did* carry meat cargo, in which case small amounts were presumably carried in the stores chambers when space permitted.

Through the remainder of the 1880s and 1890s similar installations went into a good many ships. In April 1884, for instance, it was announced that *Neva* and *La Plata* would shortly receive the same installations. Not until 1900 did RMSP take the plunge to modestly enter the meat trade – the directors decided on 20 June 1900 to fit refrigerated spaces *'for the carriage of chilled beef in the five Brazil mail ships'*. A contract was signed with the River Plate Fresh Meat Co. for five years. Before those five years were up the contract was revised, for by then RMSP was under the guidance of Owen Philipps and three custom-built refrigerated ships were being built (*Parana*, *Pardo* and *Potaro*) and the first 'A' ship (*Aragon*) was also on the way. Suddenly, then, the first tentative arrangements turned into a flood.

In terms of the timing of RMSP's entry into the trade, there was no doubt that Owen Philipps influenced the manner and extent of expansion from 1903, but the growth of South America's meat trade largely developed from sources over which Royal Mail had no control – they are looked at shortly.

There had already been some global milestones for this young industry – the steamer *Strathleven* made a pioneer voyage from Melbourne, for instance, and the sailing ship *Dunedin* pioneered large-scale meat cargoes in 1882. When tales from *Dunedin* floated through on the grapevine, they doubtless contributed to the ever-cautious RMSP distancing itself from refrigeration. Before *Dunedin* left New Zealand the refrigeration plant malfunctioned and the entire consignment had to be discharged and sold locally. A new cargo was loaded, and during the voyage the captain had to crawl through the main trunk to adjust the cold air circulation. He became so numb with cold that the mate had to crawl in behind him, tie a rope around his legs and drag him out.

South America established its first freezing plants shortly after this, but they were small. Nelson Line, approaching the situation from a different direction, *did* become involved at that time. The company stemmed from a firm of cattle salesmen who, in the 1880s, expanded its operations into South America and set up a meat plant at Zárate. Then it decided to provide a ship to supply a large chain of retail butchers in Britain.

Thus, until about 1900, the amount of Argentine beef available for export by Royal Mail ships was too small to be tempting. Likewise, until then the inadequacies of early equipment, and the shortage of ships fitted with it, prevented meat suppliers from significantly changing their traditional arrangements. Britain still purchased most of its meat from the United States and Canada, a mixture of canned meat and live cattle. Among the American companies involved, the major ones comprised a group known as the 'Big Six', of which two were by far the most influential; their names would become very familiar to Royal Mail in later years – Armour & Co. and Swift & Co. In 1903 the 'Big Six' had a combined capital of $87,873,000, with $35 million belonging to Swift and $20 million to Armour. It isn't hard to see the stranglehold the two companies had on the North American cattle industry. Britain's imports, then, were largely dictated by those companies and, to a lesser extent, other American concerns.

By 1909 there were seven firms operating in the River Plate area, the oldest being the one with which RMSP signed its first meat contract, the River Plate Fresh Meat Co. This was British-owned and had started in 1882. The Sansinena Meat Freezing Co. was owned in Argentina (but with additional works in Uruguay) and began in 1884. Two more British firms were Las Palmas Produce Co. of 1886 and Smithfield and Argentine Meat Co. of 1904. Frigorifico Argentino Centrale started in 1905 and was Argentinian. The other two firms – La Blanca Argentine

Meat Freezing Co. and La Plata Cold Storage Co. – were both American-owned by 1909, having been acquired by Swifts. At this period Swifts and Armours entered the South America scene in a big way and began to transform the meat supply business.

South America's exports to Britain were at first, then, very minor compared with those from North America, but they increased dramatically after 1900. Between 1904 and 1908, Britain's imports of live cattle dropped by about a third, and there was a corresponding increase in refrigerated cargoes. The origin of refrigerated meat also changed dramatically, as the following figures show:

Country of origin	USA	Argentina	NZ	Australia	Total
1900-04 (Ann. Avg)	134,278	49,354	11,109	8,772	208,539 tons
1908	71,607	179,515	17,394	5,629	281,599 tons

In four years or so, America's tonnage had dropped by almost 47% while that from Argentina had increased by 264%. Small wonder that those were the very years in which RMSP's three insulated 'P' ships and the first 'A' ships appeared.

In the United States, dramatically varying meat prices led to Government enquiries, though little came of them. The claims essentially amounted to price-fixing among the dominant companies. Almost certainly price collusion also existed with British sales outside London (it was regarded as almost impossible to organize price-fixing at Smithfields). With such powerful influences from North America, control of shipments of Argentine beef lay largely in the hands of Swifts and Armours.

If there was collusion there was also rivalry. By the time of the First World War the two men at the helm were Louis Swift and J. Ogden Armour, and in their hands the two companies initiated spectacular growth in South America. To their earlier interests were added features like Swift's first Uruguayan works in 1912 and new Armour works at La Plata in 1915 which could handle 12,000 tons per month. In combination the American companies greatly increased their market share. In 1911 British companies controlled 31% of the River Plate beef trade, Argentina 22% and America 47%. By 1917 Britain had 29%, Argentina 8% and America 63%.

There would, of course, be many more developments over the years, but the foundations had been laid for what would become a familiar and increasingly important backdrop to Royal Mail ships in the River Plate.

Solent (II), RMSP's first dedicated cruise ship. The photo was taken at Southampton during the nineteenth century and may, in fact, have been taken when she was new in 1878.

Appendix II: Cruising

In 1853, RMSP's directors sanctioned the use of *Thames* to visit a Royal Naval Review at Spithead. Suggestions that this constituted the Company's first cruise have been queried in some quarters – did attendance at a Review qualify as a cruise? Possibly not, but this undoubtedly *was* the first Royal Mail cruise for the directors made it clear that a pleasure cruise had been arranged, only one feature of which was a visit to the Review.

Periodically there were further visits to Spithead over many years. Some were instances of hire by the Admiralty, but more than once it was a commercial undertaking – for the 1902 Review, for instance, it was decided 'to send *Elbe* to the Review for a three-day trip with passengers at £21 per head, victualling, light wines and railway return tickets included'.

For mainstream cruising operations, the public's demand was not at first catered for in today's fashion. Early cruising was a simple corollary of people with sufficient funds discovering a means to escape the winters of Britain, Europe and North America. RMSP's South America and Caribbean routes were perfect outlets for that – ships heading for tropical climates, but on voyages short enough to keep the cost reasonable. The ocean cruise concept thus developed from those round-voyage passengers.

Well before 1900, Royal Mail had hit on something of a potential gold mine with the combination of round voyages and intercolonial steamers based in the Caribbean. Passengers travelled from England in a transatlantic ship, then transferred to an intercolonial steamer for a leisurely journey among the islands. In the 1890s a range of tour packages began with UK departures from December to the end of February. Passengers could then join another steamer for an island-hopping voyage or stop off at a port and resume with the next ship. The major option was marketed as the Special West India Tour – £65 for sixty-five days.

RMSP advised:

> Eden, Esk and Solent *are now performing the intercolonial mail service in the West Indies. These fine ships, in addition to the Company's large transatlantic mail steamers from Southampton, form an unequalled means by which passengers can visit or make passages among the West India islands at the best season, and avoid the winter of this country at a very moderate expense. The Company's system of tours will be repeated this season, commencing with the mail steamer leaving Southampton on 18 December, and being continued every 14 days till 26 February next.*

Capt. Robert Woolward was commanding the transatlantic steamer *Don* at that stage and, in his autobiography (published in 1893), he announced that he thought that the cruising timetable was too rigid. The incorrigible old skipper, who was almost seventy by then, provided his own ideas:

> *for people anxious to get away from England for the worst three months of the winter... The best way of proceeding will be to take a return ticket from Southampton to either Savanilla or Port Limon, with permission to remain a fortnight at Jamaica... also to remain a month at Barbados on the homeward voyage...*
>
> *During the month's break at Barbados, return tickets to La Guaira on one part of the month, and to St Thomas on the other, would give opportunity of seeing the whole of the Windward and Leeward West India Islands, and Caracas in Venezuela. The whole could be done inside £100 for each person.*

Caribbean cruising options clearly had enormous potential.

So far that was a means of gaining extra passengers on scheduled line services, but in August 1904 the directors agreed that 'the *Solent* should be placed "intercolonially" at the disposal of tourists during the coming season'. This, then, was the commencement for RMSP of specialist cruising operations. Soon the market was extended to the people of North America – a Company booklet produced in New York by RMSP's North American agents Sanderson & Son had this to say:

> *Recognising the great value and the increasing popularity of the West Indies as a Winter Resort for Americans who desire to escape the rigors of the northern winter, the Royal Mail Steam Packet Company has decided to extend its Southampton – West Indies service to New York, thus, for the first time, offering to tourists from the United States etc an opportunity of visiting these charming tropical islands, with the same luxury and comfort to which they are accustomed in crossing the Atlantic, and voyaging upon palatial steamships, whose size and construction ensure the utmost stability.*

The New York-West Indies-Southampton route was served by *Tagus, Atrato, Orinoco, La Plata* and *Trent*. They brought passengers from New York to Kingston, Jamaica, for a variety of options. The principal itinerary involved *Solent* for a cruise among the islands. The booklet remarked:

> *The cruising yacht Solent, so well and favourably known to English tourists in the tropics, will be equally popular with Americans. She is a beautiful yacht-like passenger steamship, of over 2,000 tons, specially built for the tropics, and regularly employed in West Indian tours. She does not carry any cargo. Her commander has discretion to vary the ports of call and the schedule of itinerary, in order that passengers' wishes may be considered whenever possible, and many interesting places are frequently visited, at which ordinary steamers do not call*

Pictured in the Caribbean during the 1910s is the intercolonial steamer Berbice *(I), used seasonally as a cruise ship.*

From that it appears there was an element of 'choose your own itinerary' – an extraordinary state of affairs. Another feature reflected the growing world of photography, for some of the steamers were fitted with darkrooms for the use of passengers.

At this period a well-known sailor-writer of the day experienced Royal Mail's cruising style. His name was Frank T. Bullen, and he must have found this Caribbean luxury a far cry from from the rugged days, not so long before, when he was second mate in Orient Line's wool clipper *Harbinger*. After praising the transatlantic steamer (*Tagus*) in an RMSP booklet, he turned his attention to three little white-painted jewels in the Caribbean:

> *...of all the companies I know who keep what we call 'station boats' employed, the Royal Mail may be congratulated upon having the prettiest and best kept up for the passenger service. The* Eden, Esk *and* Solent *would be admired anywhere...*

Bullen took passage in *Eden*, and was 'agreeably surprised' at her size and space, and that she was manned as extensively as the transatlantic ships. His reference to 'the prettiest and best kept up [ships] for the passenger service' invites reference to RMSP's West Indies Superintendent Capt. William Owen – 'Hurricane Bill', as he was known. He was the son of a captain in the Honourable East India Co. and joined the merchant navy 'as a midshipman in Green's old *Malabar* and other ships'. After joining RMSP he rose to command quickly, but subsequently spent many years as the West Indies Superintendent. He was, a captain of the period remembered:

> *a stern, strict disciplinarian in regard to the ships; the station ships, in particular, he maintained like men-of-war! If he saw a lower boom not square, or a badly spread awning, or anything in the slightest degree slovenly, the chief officer of the offending ship very soon heard about it in no uncertain manner.*

Inter-island cruising was boosted in 1909 with the arrival of *Berbice*, 2,379 tons, to replace the thirty-one-year-old *Solent*. A booklet issued when she entered service described her as 'virtually a replica of the 'A' ships'; a miniature replica, perhaps, but this product of Harland & Wolff was an exceptionally fine vessel for a small intercolonial steamer.

The booklet emphasised:

> *On a ship intended primarily for traffic in the tropics, ventilation is of great importance, and in this respect the* Berbice *is admirably equipped. All her cabins are furnished with electric fans. The dining saloon, a spacious apartment which extends the whole width of the ship on the main deck, is similarly fitted, whilst the ports are arranged in pairs and provided with jalousie shutters as protection from the sun.*

On the deck above – the Bridge Deck, reserved exclusively for first saloon passengers – is a very fine promenade, the length and breadth of which affords ample scope for the many open air recreations by means of which modern ocean voyagers beguile away the time. There is also further promenading space on the boat deck above. On the bridge deck are situated the lounge, at the forward end, and the smoke room, the latter being a delightfully cool and comfortable verandah, semi-enclosed, at the after end. Both these apartments have large opening teak-wood windows on each side, and are furnished in wicker-wood. The lounge is also equipped with a well-stocked library and a piano.

The state rooms and their furnishing and decoration touch the high-water mark of tropical comfort; their exceptional spaciousness would by itself suffice to keep them cool, even without their electric fans, and the coolness is further emphasised by the exquisite decoration scheme in white satinette enamel. On the main deck aft is a large swimming pool.

The installations of electricity, refrigerating plant and insulated chambers are other important factors in the maintenance of the high standard of comfort.

The emphasis was still on seasonal cruises during the northern winter – that initial *Berbice* brochure covered December 1909 to March 1910. The choice of itineraries included some in conjunction with other companies. *Berbice* Yachting Tour was the main option – fifty-four days at a cost of $350. It began in *Magdalena* or *Clyde* from New York to Port Antonio, Kingston, Colon, Cartagena, Puerto Colombia, La Guaira, Trinidad and Barbados. Passengers then spent eight days based in a Barbados hotel before joining *Berbice* for a little over a fortnight, calling at Grenada, St Lucia, Martinique, Dominica, San Juan, Havana, Santiago de Cuba and Port Antonio, ending the voyage at Kingston. After ten days ashore based in Kingston, passengers joined *Nile* or *Oruba* for the return to New York.

Though *Berbice* was earmarked as the Caribbean cruise ship, her sister ship *Balantia* operated in tandem with her. Many passengers made out-of-season voyages in both ships, for 'voyaging for pleasure' was not confined to the three-month season. For years RMSP's West Indies transfer base had been Barbados, but had now shifted to Port of Spain, Trinidad. *Balantia* and *Berbice* were stationed there to await the transatlantic mail ship. One then left with the Demerara mail and the other, with the 'Northern Islands' mail, departed some time later. They returned after a week, in time for the next homeward mail.

One of *Balantia*'s skippers wrote:

Many English tourists used to come out in the winter months to linger at Barbados or Trinidad and make the week's trip to the Northern Islands – as the Windward and Leeward Islands are called, amongst them many illustrious and well-known people of rank, often repeating the run north several times. They could do it very luxuriously, for the little ships were absolutely up-to-date – more like large, well-appointed yachts than anything else.

Amazon pioneers single-ship cruising

During the summer of 1908, *Amazon* made a seventeen-day cruise to Norway. 'Single-ship cruise' is defined as a pleasure cruise (as opposed to a line voyage) utilising only one vessel from embarkation to completion. Thus *Amazon* elevated RMSP to the cruising style still predominating today. She then made several Norway cruises in one block in 1909, but after that the favoured ship was the slightly larger *Avon*. In June 1909 it was announced that *Avon* would operate New York-West Indies cruises from January to April 1910. Three were scheduled, two of thirty-one days each and one of eighteen days, visiting Bermuda, Puerto Rico, Jamaica, the Panama isthmus, Venezuela, Trinidad, Barbados, Martinique, Cuba and Nassau.

She then had time for one South America voyage before taking a block of four Norway cruises with Grimsby as the terminal port. In 1911 her cruising commitments were about the same – 7 January to 25 April New York-West Indies and 5 July to 5 September UK-Norway. From that point on, most of the '*A*' ships were periodically taken from the South America service for cruises.

How quickly RMSP cemented its place in cruising is emphasised by the speed with which the Company employed a cruise liner full-time. She was *Ortona*, which entered the fleet from the Orient-Pacific service. That operation ceased in 1909 and there seems little doubt that suddenly having a ship like *Ortona* without work was the trigger which prompted RMSP to convert her for cruising. Though only about 8,000 tons, after extensive alterations her tonnage increased to about 9,000. She emerged also with a new name – *Arcadian* – and departed from Southampton for her first cruise in January 1912. It was to take her to the Caribbean and New York, but unfortunately included an unscheduled call on a coral reef near Cartagena. She was hauled off unharmed and thereafter stuck more strictly to her official itineraries. Hers was nevertheless a brief career, for she entered war service and was torpedoed in 1917.

While *Arcadian's* cruising life lasted barely three years, it was a cornerstone for the Company, for all subsequent cruise liners took their conceptual lineage from her. Promotional literature possessed themes and rhetoric repeated year in and year out until 1971, flavoured with specifics which were individual to the day. The 1914 schedule, for instance (though some cruises were cancelled through the outbreak of war), emphasised how particular destinations were selected at the ideal time of year – June to August in Norwegian fjords and Arctic waters; September in the Mediterranean and October to the Atlantic islands.

In that 1914 booklet *Arcadian* was described in some detail. The dining saloon:

Elegant decoration, lofty height, a perfect system of ventilation, and ingenious devices which produce the effect of perpetual sunshine through the lanceolate windows, combine to render this room the finest dining hall afloat. In the fashion of the most up-to-date hotels, small tables are arranged so as to facilitate social intercourse at meals. All passengers are accommodated simultaneously.

Lounges:

The saloons on board ship play an important part in daily life. The dome-crowned Social Hall affords passengers the amenities of an elegant drawing room, fitted with a fine piano; and book-cases, constantly replenished from shore libraries, stand in the Lounge at the further end. Quiet refinement characterises the Reading and Writing Room amidships, and the Smoking Saloon a little further aft.

Keeping fit:

The white-tiled swimming bath, 35 feet long, surrounded by spray baths and dressing cabins, presents irresistible attractions after a warm or dusty day ashore, whilst the covered-in gymnasium, fitted with all sorts of athletic apparatus and appliances for electrical massage, cannot fail to attract those desirous of "keeping fit".

Cabins:

Furnished with electric fans, large wardrobes, full-length mirrors, chests of drawers, reading lamps and restful chairs, the cabins constitute really comfortable bedrooms. An Arcadian *speciality consists in the provision of comfortable bedsteads instead of the old-fashioned berths. The large proportion of single-bedded rooms ensures personal privacy.*

Deck spaces:

Perhaps the crowning feature of the Arcadian *is the exceptional area of the deck space provided for amusements, rest and promenade. The Deck Stewards' domain covers a length of over 500 feet, six circuits equal a mile, and the unencumbered area exceeds half an acre. Unique opportunities are here afforded for all kinds of sports, and the Open-Air Ballroom draped with bunting, and festooned with fairy-lights, proves particularly attractive to all lovers of dancing'.*

First class lounge in Berbice *(I), at the forward end of the Bridge Deck.*

First class dining saloon in Berbice *(I), occupying the full width of the ship on the Main Deck.*

Arcadian *(I) during her brief period as RMSP's first full-time cruise ship. She had been built in 1899 as* Ortona *for The Pacific Steam Navigation Co.*

A rare surviving interior photo in Arcadian *(I). Her late Victorian style of intricate woodwork and detailed domes presaged a new standard for ocean liners which flowered in the early decades of the twentieth century.*

By the time *Arcadian* was operating, RMSP was showing its preference for spending the summer months with northern Europe itineraries. Those who recall more recent cruise seasons in the 1960s will know that generally there was just a single cruise to that region each year; in 1914 *Arcadian's* first five cruises were to Norway, visiting relatively little-known fjords and towns. Two headed further north, to the likes of Trondheim, Tromso, Narvik, Hammerfest and North Cape. Passengers were embarked at Grimsby and Leith to minimise the time spent crossing the potentially rough North Sea.

The last two cruises (most likely cancelled because of the war) were scheduled to use Southampton as the terminal port – cruise six to Spain, Morocco, Algeria, Venice, the Dalmatian coast and Sicily, and cruise seven to Villagarcia, Tangier, Gibraltar, Las Palmas, Tenerife, the Azores and Lisbon.

The ship's launches played an important role. They appear to have been substantial craft, some even being named. At practically every port there were options for 'Shore Excursions' and 'Launch Excursions'. Though they were used on all itineraries, their value was greatest in Norwegian waters, where the steep terrain limited road access. They were used for trips through islets, to the Seven Sisters Waterfall, to a whaling village at North Cape and so on; virtually an extension of the cruising concept, going where the big ship couldn't.

Between the Wars

The years between the two world wars were the pinnacle of Royal Mail's cruising story. Not only did they usually possess a permanent cruise ship, many other ships played supporting roles, particularly in the 1920s. The RMSP group reached its peak at that time and so the Company enjoyed the flexibility of being able to swap ships – either permanently or for a limited time – between fleets, and also had at its disposal a sufficiently large and varied operation to provide many cruising options.

Once trading conditions returned to an even keel after the First World War, cruises were quickly reinstated, the first by *Avon* to Norway in the summer of 1921. That year *Saint Margaret of Scotland*, though operating a line service, was being promoted for cruises to Madeira and the Canary Islands. There were again intercolonial cruise options in the Caribbean basin and further summer cruises to Norway. The Company also offered 'short tours by mail steamers' to France, Germany, Spain and Portugal. Also reinstated was co-operation with

An RMSP publicity handbill made good use
of the rescue in 1910 of the crew from the
Wellman airship by Trent (III) during a
Bermuda – New York voyage – a service
commonly used by Americans for holiday
trips. The airship was attempting to become
the first to make an Atlantic crossing. Capt.
Down had some anxious times during the
hours before the rescue was completed, ranging
from attempting to keep in touch with the
airship's erratic progress through the hours of
darkness to an abortive attempt to grapple its
trail ropes. The occupants of the airship
finally abandoned it by dropping to the water
in their lifeboat and were picked up by Trent
and taken to New York.

The
Royal Mail
Steam Packet Company
Tariff of Fares
New York-Bermuda Service

R. M. S. P. " TRENT "
En route from Bermuda to New York, rescuing crew of Wellman Airship America

Sailing Hour, 10 a.m. ~om Pier 42, North River, near foot of Christopher St.
Reached by Ninth A. nue Elevated; McAdoo Tunnel from 33d Street, New York, or Pennsylvania, Erie and Lackawanna Railroads to Christopher Street station; Ninth Avenue, Eighth Street crosstown and Belt Line surface cars.

Head Office—THE ROYAL MAIL STEAM PACKET CO., 18 Moorgate St. London, E. C.

Bermuda—W. T. JAMES & CO., Hamilton

SANDERSON & SON, General Agents
22 State Street, New York   149 La Salle Street, Chicago
W'   ' /ES, N. E. P. A., 200 Washington Street. Boston, Mass.
K. .u .... VILLE, Toronto and Adelaide Streets, Toronto, Canada

the now wholly-owned Pacific Steam Navigation Co. The combinations there were boundless, with RMSP's services to the West Indies, Panama and the South American east coast, and PSN's operations on the west coast and through the Panama Canal to New York. With such a wide range of possibilities they were marketed simply under the umbrella of 'Tours round South America'.

The Company had by then spent a few years pondering its response to the loss of its full-time cruise liner *Arcadian*. It decided to take the larger but not very much newer *Asturias* and refit her as a cruise liner. Confusingly, they bestowed on her the same name, and so it was as the second *Arcadian* that she emerged for her new career in 1923. In the mid-1920s *Araguaya* was also sent to Belfast for conversion to a cruise liner, and like the others emerged with accommodation for first class-only, of whom she carried just 365. After that, *Arcadian* made further cruises but was often employed on the prestigious New York-Bermuda route.

Late in 1930 *Arcadian* was withdrawn and laid up. Furness, Withy had already introduced the new *Bermuda* on the New York-Bermuda route, against which the ageing *Arcadian* could scarcely compete, and by 1930 two more were being built – *Monarch of Bermuda* and *Queen of Bermuda*. The Depression also caused *Araguaya* to be withdrawn that year, and she was sold after being superseded by *Atlantis*.

Over the years Royal Mail made a number of attempts to establish itself in the New York passenger trade. Its last foray began in 1923. Three liners were acquired from The Pacific Steam Navigation Co. – *Orca*, *Orduña* and *Orbita* – and a fourth came from an unusual source. She was *Ohio*, which had been under construction at Bremen as *München* for Norddeutscher Lloyd in 1914 and lay uncompleted throughout the war. Afterwards she was seized by Britain as reparations, construction was completed and she was purchased by RMSP. *Orca* and *Orbita*, at least, were engaged in cruising during the North Atlantic off-season – *Orca's* introduction to RMSP service was a two-cruise programme from New York to the West Indies from January to March 1923.

She was slightly larger than the other PSN ships acquired at this time, with a gross tonnage was 16,063, and also a little newer, having been built in 1918. The Company issued an unpretentious leaflet to mark her introduction, but it provided a good description of what was clearly a fine ship – in the shadow of some of the Company's more celebrated liners, vessels like the 'O' class tend not to be given the credit due to them.

The leaflet stated:

> Ascending the embarkation gangway the passenger enters a spacious Entrance Hall on the Shade Deck. This Hall, and those of the Awning Deck below, and the Promenade Deck above, are panelled in a refined interpretation of the Louis XVI period, in white tastefully relieved with gold.
>
> Communication between the decks can either be had by the electric elevator, or by the handsome staircase, which is surmounted by an oval dome light, in keeping with the general surroundings. Upon the Shade Deck entrance are situated the Enquiry and Postal Offices, Money Exchange, and also a Shop, where the needs of the passengers can be supplied.

First class smokeroom in Orca, *a former Pacific Steam Navigation Co. ship which created a cruising milestone with her ambitious Great African Cruise in 1926.*

The first class Dining Saloon, on the Main Deck, is decorated in an early Georgian period, the panelling painted white, having the ornamental motifs and members of the cornice and panels picked out in gold. Over the centre of the room a well-proportioned wrought iron dome, illuminated by hidden lights, adds to the general height and decorative effect. The furniture, which includes a cold buffet, is of selected French walnut. On either side of the central sideboard are two excellent reproductions of well-known masterpieces in oil after Raeburn and Romney. The chairs are of William and Mary type, upholstered in soft blue morocco, and the tables are arranged for either small or large parties of diners.

So the description continued. The First Class Lounge, for instance, had white-painted Louis XVI ornamental panelling, 'relieved by heliotrope silk curtains to the spacious windows that occupy three sides of the room'. Walls were relieved with gilt ornamental oval pendants with coloured engravings, while there were centrepieces like a pair of Sévres vases and marble clock. The Smoke Room had floor to ceiling oak panelling in the Elizabethan style with period-style oil paintings above the fireplace.

For *Orbita* a very different brochure was produced a year later for two Mediterranean cruises – a sixteen-page booklet filled with photographs and descriptions of ports of call, but precious little about the ship. The cruises were from Southampton between January and March 1924. The first lasted the better part of a month. There were twelve ports of call, mostly one or two days – Lisbon, Gibraltar, Barcelona, Monaco, Naples, Sicily, Malta, Tunis, Algiers, Tangier and Villagarcia. The second cruise (despite the booklet being headed 'Two Mediterranean cruises') did not quite enter the Mediterranean. The ports were Madeira, Tenerife, Las Palmas, Casablanca, Tangier, Gibraltar, Lisbon and Villagarcia.

The 'O' ships, then, augmented the cruising opportunities, but they were short-lived. The New York service was terminated after 1926 (initially because of the economic downturn, but a continuing involvement followed the acquisition of White Star Line early in 1927). During 1926 *Orduña* and *Orbita* were returned to PSN. When RMSP acquired White Star Line, *Orca* and *Ohio* were transferred to its fleet, becoming, respectively, *Calgaric* and *Albertic*.

Before leaving the fleet, *Orca* made, early in 1926, an unprecedented leap in the cruising stakes with a monster Great African Cruise which targeted passengers from Britain and America. A year later *Orca* had gone, but the almost-new *Asturias* was available. At 22,000 tons she was far larger than any other ship in the fleet except for her sister-ship *Alcantara*, and her décor and sheer artistry were among the finest ever conceived on board ship. In January 1927 *Asturias* departed for the Second Great African Cruise. To place this 101-day extravaganza (the longest cruise ever made by a Royal Mail ship) in perspective, it is worth reading some of the preamble to the tour booklet:

The exceptional success of the first Great African Cruise by the SS Orca was marked evidence of the wide appeal of a cruise that combines the alluring new lands of South and East Africa with old favourite places – West Indies, South America, Egypt and Europe. The Second Great African Cruise will follow the same unique and fascinating itinerary...

Further evidence of that pioneering spirit, for which the Royal Mail Steam Packet Company is famous, is found in the arrangements for the Second Great African Cruise. The itinerary as laid out for the Orca *made travel history – an extension of de luxe travel to lands of beauty and mystery far off the beaten tracks. Now to this is joined another notable innovation – the great new motor vessel* Asturias.

The American Express Company, with its world-wide experience in conducting de luxe cruises, will again co-operate in the management of all cruise features both on ship and on shore. This guarantees constant and varied entertainment between ports and the best possible arrangements for numerous included excursions in the various countries visited, as well as for the optional tours that are offered...

Asturias departed from Southampton and crossed the Atlantic to make New York the first port of call, to embark American passengers – the greater number of her passengers, in fact, were Americans. She made a beeline, then, for warmer climes, visiting Trinidad before heading to Rio de Janeiro, Santos, Montevideo and Buenos Aires.

Next she crossed the South Atlantic to Capetown. Between the two continents lay the tiny speck of Tristan da Cunha. 'Weather permitting,' said the booklet, 'Tristan da Cunha will be approached and a supply of provisions placed on a raft to be floated ashore to the 129 inhabitants. This was done on the first Great African Cruise'. With the decline in sailing ships, Tristan had become more isolated than ever, and the promise of provisions would have filled the islanders with joy. Precious few ships had been there since the occasional square-rigged sailing ship in the nineteenth century. A vessel the size of *Asturias* had to anchor a mile or more offshore. They were lucky with the weather – it was a benign day, though overcast with damp grey sweeps of cloud clinging to the dormant volcano.

It was something of a paradox that the Tristan islanders had chosen their isolation but relied on visits by windjammers. Once their era had passed, any visit by a ship was doubly important. How favourably the visit by *Asturias* was received can be gauged by the fact that a baby girl born at the time of her visit was christened Asturias. During the 1960s Royal Mail learned that the name had been perpetuated, for the baby of 1927 now had a niece, and she had been christened Asturias Connor.

After crossing the South Atlantic, passengers in *Asturias* began a series of options at Capetown – staying with the ship throughout the African portion, with shore excursions included in the itinerary, or making optional port-to-port overland journeys. From Capetown, for instance, they could travel to Kimberley, Mafeking, Bulawayo and Victoria Falls, doubling back to Johannesburg and Pretoria to rejoin the ship at Durban. *Asturias* visited Mossel Bay, Port Elizabeth, Durban, Mozambique, Zanzibar and Mombasa before reaching Aden to transit the Red Sea.

A brief call at Port Sudan was to disembark those taking an optional journey to Khartoum, Luxor and the Nile, joining other passengers at Cairo. Another tour began at Port Tewfik, with passengers travelling overland to Cairo and then to Alexandria while the ship transited the Suez Canal. There was also an optional tour to Palestine and Jerusalem. After transiting the Suez Canal she travelled north west to Naples, Monaco and Gibraltar, before returning to Southampton and New York.

The Second Great African Cruise shouldn't be allowed to overshadow other activities during the 1920s. *Asturias* and *Alcantara* were both used on occasion for Mediterranean cruises. *Arcadian* cruised full-time until her transfer to the New York – Bermuda service, while *Araguaya* joined the cruise scene with less fanfare. *Avon* was still periodically cruising, too, and in 1928 tried a new venture with cruises around Scotland and Ireland.

The increased range of cruises was partly attributable to the construction of *Asturias* and *Alcantara*, not only through their participation but also the ability to withdraw older 'A' ships from the South America route now that new ships were in service. *Araguaya* had already gone in that direction, and at the end of the 1920s, with *Araguaya* maintaining seasonal cruises from New York to the West Indies and Canada, *Andes* was also withdrawn. She underwent major reconditioning, emerging in 1930 as a full-time cruise liner, and with a new name – *Atlantis*. While *Atlantis* and *Arcadian* had both belonged to the original group of 'A' ships, *Atlantis* was six years younger and over 3,000 tons larger at 15,620.

With her introduction, *Arcadian* was laid up and eventually sold for breaking up. As mentioned earlier, the Depression spelt the end of the line for *Araguaya*, which was sold to Yugoslav owners in 1930.

The *Atlantis* Years

There was a continuing use of other ships in supporting cruise roles, but the 1930s was the decade of *Atlantis*. More than any of her predecessors, her name became practically a household word. There were various reasons for that, both operational and marketing, but the achievement was particularly notable as the ship's operations (through the Depression in the early years) spanned the collapse of RMSP and the formation of Royal Mail Lines.

She took the 'Northern Capitals' and Arctic waters cruise concept to new heights. There might be three days, for instance, cruising around Spitzbergen and Bear Island, with landings at various spots. Iceland was added to the itineraries. The 1931 schedule included a seven-day cruise to Bergen and five fjord destinations – a lovely glimpse of this magical country for a price as low as 11 guineas. At the other end of the scale was a twenty-two-day cruise to the Baltic with prices as high as 300 guineas. Thus *Atlantis* catered for all pockets.

Arcadian *(II) and boat train at Immingham in the 1920s. Immingham was used as a terminal port for Scandinavian cruises in order to minimise the passage time across the North Sea.*

Atlantis *cruised to many parts of the world but was best known for her voyages to Scandinavian waters. This picture epitomises the ship and her stamping ground, at anchor in a Norwegian fjord during the 1930s.*

The 1931 Baltic cruise was promoted (prematurely as it turned out) as something of a coup, for at a time when Soviet Russia was immensely difficult to enter, she was to visit Leningrad with an excursion to Moscow. *Arcadian* had earlier been the first British cruise ship to visit Leningrad after the Revolution, but with *Atlantis* the Russian authorities had second thoughts and the visit had to be cancelled.

Very quickly, then, *Atlantis* settled into her new role, balancing old favourite ports with innovative new spots to lure back those who had already sampled her timeless style of luxury. Her reputation spread beyond those who travelled in her, for her promotional material was astronomical. Brochures, booklets, postcards and posters were issued in profusion. A vital part of the *Atlantis* image came from the partnership between Royal Mail and artist Kenneth Shoesmith, whose influence in moulding the ship's very individual character is looked at shortly.

That, of course, was in conjunction with the ship herself; her finely-detailed fittings and appointments made her still a thing of splendour when she was like a graceful old dowager duchess with a quarter of a century of service under her belt. And that distinctive 'A' ship profile, particularly splendid in cruising white, was the epitome of the cruising yacht with raked funnel and masts and graceful counter. Even her name added to the mystique with which she beguiled the travelling public.

So experienced was Royal Mail in the cruise scene now that the annual programmes by *Atlantis* proceeded with little fuss – summer northern cruises, with Mediterranean and West Indies itineraries at other times. The big Winter Cruise concept continued; there were always people with the money to escape the northern winter. They didn't regain the magnitude of the Second Great African Cruise, but they were not voyages to be sneezed at. In 1938, for instance, the voyage was around Africa for fifty-eight days, minimum fare 120 guineas. With visits to spots like the Seychelles, Mauritius and St Helena, in addition to more traditional African ports, it was a tempting menu.

Late in the 1930s the cruising arrangements reached a crossroads. Ever since the formation of Royal Mail Lines in 1932 the passenger fleet had been under review. *Atlantis*, *Arlanza* and *Almanzora* all reached their quarter century. The diesel machinery of *Asturias* and *Alcantara* had not been a success and they were re-engined. Then an order was placed for a new mail liner – she would become *Andes*.

How all of that would affect *Atlantis* was, in the late 1930s, still in the melting pot. *Andes* had been designed for part-time cruising, but it appears not to have been a major concession. Various future options were discussed, and when the order for *Andes* was given, the most favoured seemed to be that one of the other ships (most likely *Asturias*) would become the new full-time cruise liner, with *Atlantis* being pensioned off during 1939.

The artists – Shoesmith and Jarvis

The artists who produced countless items from postcards to brochures, especially from the 1920s, were crucial in helping to establish an image for the Company's cruising operations; indeed, for all of its passenger services. In relation to postcards, there is a paradox between, on the one hand, the dominance of two artists over several decades (Kenneth Shoesmith and W. Howard Jarvis) and on the other an almost mind-boggling variety of styles – monochrome and sepia photographs, pen-and-ink drawing, pencil sketches, a wide array of coloured painting styles and, in later years, colour photographs.

Kenneth Shoesmith was the first of Royal Mail's influential artists. Born in 1890, he started out not in the art world but in the merchant navy – with Royal Mail. He rose to the rank of chief officer before deciding, in 1919, to come ashore as a full-time commercial artist – small wonder that so much of his work depicted Royal Mail's ships. Leslie Walters, for fifty years a member of Royal Mail's Publicity Department (and its head for more than a decade) recalled that Shoesmith's name became known in the department around 1911/1912, while he was serving in a Shire ship on the Far East run. The Company ran a competition among staff for 'ideas for possible publicity items', and Shoesmith won the five guineas for a water-colour study of an 'A' ship in a sunset scene.

Those who know Shoesmith's work recognise it instantly. Defining the style is not easy – it blends aspects of art nouveau and 'pop art', whose periods his work spanned; some (particularly brochures) might be classified as art deco. He drew those influences, however, into his own individualism. At times he over-emphasised an aspect of a ship – usually the hull or funnels – to exaggerate its size. Whether this was Shoesmith's idea or a directive from Royal Mail is not known, but I suspect it was the artist's choice, if only because he was able to achieve it without seeming to make the ships look 'wrong'.

With his stylistic approach, few would suggest any problem with the treatment of people in his work. This, though, was apparently his greatest personal dissatisfaction, and he was reportedly still taking lessons in figure work not long before his death. Few of Shoesmith's paintings depicted a ship at sea – most were set in ports or spots like a Norwegian fjord. There is, then, a lot of scene setting – often bold and attention-grabbing – and therefore the potential for the ship to become somewhat lost among the surrounding scene. It is to the artist's credit that this never happened.

Kenneth Shoesmith's profuse output ended at about the start of Second World War, for he died in 1939. The earliest items which I have seen date from the early 1920s, though according to Leslie Walters he had begun work for RMSP shortly after the First World War. From the time of his death, production dropped away because of the war. Calendars were the principal, and perhaps only, requirement during the period, and this was handled until 1947 by Fred Taylor, an artist friend of Shoesmith's. In retrospect this quiet period was fortuitous, for Shoesmith's bold style would never be challenged, and it allowed a more natural easing in of a new regime. For the second and last time a 'contract' artist was acquired – W. Howard Jarvis.

A senior member of the Society of Marine Artists until his death in the 1960s, Howard Jarvis did a great deal of work for Royal Mail. He was, like Shoesmith, an ex-*Conway* boy and former merchant navy officer. Through sheer volume and variety, Jarvis did for *Andes* what Shoesmith had done for *Atlantis*, producing picture after picture and, in the process, helping to reflect her character. When I first met him in the early 1960s (by which time *Andes* was in her cruising livery), we quickly discovered that we both preferred her the way she was before. I'm not sure, though, that it was for the same reasons – my principal concern was the change of visual balance because of the white hull, while Howard took enormous objection to the addition of two large launches raised high above the foredeck.

However aesthetically distracting they were, those launches were powerful selling tools. They *did*, though, break the splendid lines of the ship. The purist in Howard Jarvis felt so strongly on the matter that he produced two brochures in which they were omitted. He was politely but firmly told that they had to be re-instated. In his final works from late 1961 to 1964 he made every effort to portray the ship in locations where the launches could be depicted ferrying passengers ashore rather than stowed in their davits. That ongoing saga reflected, with one who admired the finer products of the marine architect, the spell cast by *Andes*.

During the 1950s and 1960s Jarvis produced numerous brochures and postcards of every Royal Mail ship which carried passengers, from the 'A' ships to twelve-passenger ships like the 'E' and 'D' classes and the *Lochs*. His paintings for a Coronation commemoration booklet in 1953 were particularly fine and in a style quite different from his usual work. Generally it was not difficult to pick a Jarvis painting, though each picture was given its own character, which ranged from the yellow-dominated boldness of the *Escalante* postcard to almost photo-realism with *Amazon*.

Jarvis saw out an era of painted artworks which had existed for over half a century. The declining range of products after the mid-1960s used colour photography.

Andes – The Last Cruise Ship

The Second World War and its aftermath closed cruising operations for a good many years. After 1945 Royal Mail was far less replete with passenger ships than it had been earlier – there were *Andes*, *Alcantara* and four *Highland* ships, with the new *Magdalena* to come.

The *Highlands* were unsuited to cruising, and with their comparatively small size, limited first class accommodation and fifteen-knot speeds, they could not compete, either, in an express service to South America. That left the major mail service burden with *Andes* and *Alcantara*. Together with the era of post-war austerity that explains why the war had been over for a decade before Royal Mail resumed its cruising programme.

Andes made her first cruise, to the Mediterranean, in June 1955; from then on her schedules became quite complex with cruises sandwiched between South America voyages, cruises becoming more dominant late in the decade. At that time came another crossroads. *Alcantara* was sold for breaking up in 1958, and the three-decade-old *Highlands* were also about to end their useful lives. The Company chose to replace all of them with the newbuildings *Amazon*, *Aragon* and *Arlanza*; they would maintain the mail service, leaving *Andes* free for full-time cruising. Accordingly, late in 1959 she underwent the first portion of a major conversion to cruise liner.

Spanning the period of her metamorphosis from line service to cruise liner, her master was Capt. Geoffrey Fletcher, whose family enjoyed a quite extraordinary bond with Royal Mail. Geoffrey Fletcher served as a cadet with The Pacific Steam Navigation Co. and as third officer with Leyland Line before joining RMSP in 1924. His first command came in 1947. His father, Capt. Robert Fletcher, commanded ships in the Orient-Pacific Line to Australia before moving to RMSP – he died at sea whilst in command of *Darro* in 1915. His eldest brother, Capt. Robert Norman Fletcher, joined RMSP after First World War and commanded several of the Company's ships. He died in 1955. Another brother, Capt. C.V. Fletcher, joined RMSP in *Drina* in 1914. He was in command of *Sambre* when he resigned in 1938.

When *Andes* was retired in 1971, Geoffrey Fletcher, at my request, penned some reminiscences of his time in her. Too extensive to quote in full, the following extracts provide an insight to the changeover period and to her cruising world.

I started my time in the Andes *as Staff Captain. This was not very easy because, for one thing, there had not been such a rank in Royal Mail for a very long time, if ever, and no-one was very clear as to my duties, including myself. . . There was, perhaps, an added incubus in my case as I think it became known pretty soon that I was to succeed the Commodore as captain when he retired at the end of this Winter Cruise; this was a matter of some importance to the passengers, who were mostly 'old hands' and naturally interested in who was to be there in the future.*

The Winter Cruise, in those days before she actually started her cruising life, was something very special, the numbers being kept down to add to the comfort of those who travelled and who were paying, for those days, a high price. Even so, the first class saloon was not large enough to accommodate everyone at one sitting (considered a must), so what was the second class saloon was used to seat the over-flow. This was by no means so ornate or comfortable as the main dining room, nor was it air conditioned; also, being near the waterline, the ports had to be kept closed on occasion which, at times, made it uncomfortably hot. All this made it really appear second class as compared to the other and was a cause of dissatisfaction and murmering to many seated there, as there was, of course, not supposed to be (nor was there otherwise) any distinction.

The majesty of Norway's fjord country, near Merok, dwarfs Andes (II) *during a cruise in the 1950s, before her conversion to full-time cruise liner.*

In consequence, it was a rule that at least one of the senior officers should have his meal there with the hope that the occupants would not think they were being neglected. This was a blessing in disguise to me for it did give me a chance of a definite function...

One of the highlights of this particular cruise was the Mardi Gras at New Orleans; the ship was due to arrive there the day before this event. As we approached New Orleans, the Commodore was laid low with a fever and I had to take over. We arrived off the port to find the entrance to the Mississippi shrouded in thick fog so we had to join the assembly of ships already anchored there... Soon after day-break there were signs of a slight lifting of the fog and a pilot came off... Conditions even now were by no means pleasant and there was an obvious risk in attempting to enter the river. The decision was not made any easier for me (and I had to make it, as the Commodore was in no fit state) as I had never been up the Mississippi before and I would hazard a guess that such a large ship as the Andes had never been as far up it.

All went well, though there were many tense moments but progress was so slow that it took all day and the Mardi Gras was well over by the time we arrived. I must say that the passengers took their disappointment very well, for which I was very grateful, and we had at least shown willing.

Leaving was a nightmare to me, for there is a very strong current running down, of course, and it is difficult to turn a ship of that size in those conditions. The ship was surrounded by small tugs but all we managed was to drift broadside down the river. There was a right-angled bend just below the berth and I remember remarking to the pilot that if the worst came to the worst, when we got to that we could go full ahead and chance it.

To my horror, at this stage another ship coming up-river rounded the bend. I fully expected her to slow down and wait to give us a chance, but she came on and it was a very near thing. The Second Officer was signalling frantically from the stern that we should go ahead, and the Chief Officer on the bow was equally insistent that we should go astern. In the end, the ship passed under our bows at such a distance, the Chief Officer swore he could have tossed the proverbial biscuit aboard her.

We just managed to get her round the corner and I came back to life... There was one bonus, though, for it provided a certain amount of excitement for the passengers watching from every vantage point. It also gave me a lot more confidence and stood me in good stead.

Capt. Geoffrey Fletcher on Andes (II), a ship he commanded during her metamorphosis from mail ship to cruise liner.

Full Time Cruise Ship

At the end of this cruise, the decision was taken to convert the ship to whole-time cruising, which in my opinion was, at least, a very courageous one. This involved wholesale changes such as enlarging the main dining room to accommodate all passengers at one sitting, considered to be an important feature and rightly so, for I think it proved to be one of the attractions of the ship.

Indeed, that and the great amount of space, particularly on deck, were the main features that enabled the ship to maintain her appeal. This included doing away with the inferior dining room which heretofore had proved such a bug-bear. In her previous life, the only accommodation which was air-conditioned had been the dining room and the adjacent bar speace, the Foyer Bar, which had always been a very popular place, especially while in the tropics...

The ship left for Flushing, as the Dutch shipyard there had secured the contract for her conversion, mainly, I suspect, because they guaranteed a completion date. The conversion was to be accomplished in two stages which must have made it a difficult job. During the first stage, various alterations were made and preparations for the second stage advanced.

The first stage completed, we returned to Southampton and set off on a cruise to Quebec and New York. This, again, was rather an ordeal for me as it was the season when trouble might be expected from ice and fog on the Banks of Newfoundland. I had had some experience, years before, as Junior Officer on a small cargo boat, but that was a different proposition where time was not of great importance as opposed to keeping a fairly tight schedule.

I decided to press on at maximum speed until we arrived at the area where ice might be expected, and thus be able to proceed with caution and at the slowest speed compatible with keeping time at Quebec. We were fortunate with the weather and did not get any fog until we arrived at the Straits of Belle Isle, when it became dense. I was able to crawl through the Straits, having time in hand, but I think this was a boring time for the passengers with the whistle sounding all the time and I think they became a little restive.

However, my reputation was saved somewhat by a sudden lifting of the fog, which revealed icebergs all round us, and they were able to take photographs before the fog came back as dense as ever...

Thereafter we returned to Flushing for the second stage... Work went on furiously, day and night, but when I returned to the ship shortly before she was to be ready, it looked impossible. Everything was chaos until the last moment, but we left in time in some sort of order. . .

Then came the great day when we set off on our first cruise proper, as you might say. This was to the Mediterranean, and very eventful it proved to be in many ways. The run-in cruise had done a certain amount of good in revealing weaknesses in the new parts of the ship but I don't think any of us had an inkling of what was to come. The main centres of trouble were the air-conditioning, the new lift to the cinema and the plumbing generally. The shipyard had sent a representative with us, a kind of guarantee man, I suppose.

Well, he and the plumber became the best-known people in the ship, for the public address system was always calling for 'Mr Schmidt' or 'the plumber'; they wondered who 'Mr Schmidt' was at first, but they soon got to know. The new and highly automatic lift gave a lot of trouble, for it was situated near the stern and the delicate controls were affected by the vibration there. It was in much use when the cinema was on.

The trouble with the air-conditioning was perpetual. It was of two types. The older, higher-priced cabins were fitted with individual units in each cabin and it had not been realised, I think, that the pipes carrying the cooling water for these would choke up so quickly with the marine growth, in the warmer water of lower latitudes, which multiplied rapidly. The other type supplied cool air generally to a number of cabins. The consequence was that it became a constant job to clear these pipes, which proved too much for the engineers assigned to the job, and at peak stages passengers had to be put on a rota for attention. This, as you can imagine, led to many complaints and needed a lot of tact... Well, we staggered on and did the best we could and although I can't say that the air-conditioning improved much, most other things did and with the – in most cases – amazing goodwill of the passengers, I think we got away with it.

The cruising having got under way, cruise after cruise came and went with little difference between them. It was pretty hard work for us all, for it was only on rare occasions that we had more than thirty-six hours between cruises. The men gradually adjusted themselves, or most did, to the changes in routine and to the new purpose of the ship. The bulk of them were accustomed to the old comfortable life when she wandered down to Buenos Aires and back with a nice time in the home port in between. On that job, everyone knew everyone else and things went along much as usual year by year. When a ship is on a regular run and carrying a certain amount of cargo, passengers tend to become regarded as a necessary evil. A ship like the Andes does not carry a great amount of cargo but the profit from it is likely to be more than that produced by the passengers, who are, of necessity, a great expense.

The ship's company is sharply divided on this issue, of course. The Purser's Department are convinced of the importance of the passengers but the other departments looked on them, I'm afraid, as of secondary importance. This, perhaps, has been one of the weaknesses of British ships as compared with their Continental rivals. One of the jobs I had, therefore, was to try and impress on us all that now the passengers were the be-all and end-all of everything, and were the source of our livelihood.

The job was not as difficult as it might have been, for the nucleus of the old crew remained with us and they were a wonderful lot of men extremely loyal to the ship. Considering the wrench it must have been to part with the old comfortable way of life, I think they were marvellous. It is easy to carp and say that they were probably better off, for the ship was usually full of passengers in place of the sparseness of the old days, but I think it is becoming more apparent every day that you cannot buy good service – it has to be given, and those men certainly gave...

Some Passengers

When we started cruising proper, the Company introduced the innovation that there was no longer a Captain's Table as such. It is well known, I think, that it has always been the custom, in British ships at least, for important people to be asked to sit at the Captain's Table during the voyage. The Company now deputed that, in future, the C-table should be left empty when the seating for the cruise was arranged. Instead, I was to invite eight people to lunch at my table, and eight for dinner.

This meant, of course, that I had to invite them beforehand to my cabin for drinks before going down to the meal. This, I suppose, was one of the biggest headaches with which the Purser and I had to contend. There were many aspects. If these meetings, for instance, were to be a success (and they wouldn't be much use if they were not) it was essential that the participants should be as compatible as possible. This was easy enough with the passengers who were well known to us, but difficult with the newcomers who must, of course, be cultivated with a view to future bookings.

I adopted one stratagem which proved useful when we were hard-pressed. It was my invariable custom to walk round the decks whenever possible from about 5 p.m. to 6 p.m. I seldom wore uniform on these occasions and there were times when some of the newcomers didn't recognise me. I would join various groups of people who appeared congenial to each other and gradually get their names, then drift off and enter as many as I could remember in a notebook. This sounds daft and undignified, perhaps, but it does illustrate to what straits we were driven at times...

Naturally I met many interesting and lovable people during my years in the Andes. One of these was the late Sir Archibald Southby RN. He was something very special for he had been incapacitated from, I think, middle age, and could only manage a few steps. The ordinary ship's companion ladder or gangway was too much for him and he could only navigate a shore gangway in his chair. If we were at anchor, therefore, the only way we could get him ashore was in what came to be known as 'Archie's Chariot'. This was, in fact, one of the ship's motor boats with boards placed over the thwarts and secured.

The boat, then, could be lowered to the level of the boat deck or lower embarking deck, the chair with 'Archie' in it be wheeled on and then the boat lowered to the water and off he went. Sir Archibald loved the sea and was never happier than when aboard the Andes, and I like to think that one of the great moments for him was when he was lowered in his chariot and away...

Hannen Swaffer was another interesting, albeit difficult, passenger; difficult in that I have never met a person so deaf. To overcome this difficulty, as I thought, I invited him and his two lady companions to a little dinner party in the small dining room, the Galleon Grill as it was known, which was reserved for just such occasions and where passengers could order a special menu selected by themselves.

The affair proved to be quite hilarious in the end for, as the only practical way of indicating what you wanted to say to Mr Swaffer was to write it down, the conversation became somewhat lop-sided and the gentleman who, in common with many deaf people, always spoke at the top of his voice – shouted, in fact – ended up by regaling the whole room with episodes from his extremely interesting past; something which, I believe, was much enjoyed by all present, the like of which would not often fall to their lot.

Summing Up

...I think her epitaph must be that she was, above all else, a gracious ship; a relic of a gracious way of living. She was spacious in everything, and that very spaciousness which had, perhaps, militated against her earning capacity in her mail-boat days, became her greatest attraction in her cruising days.

April 1971; Andes *(II) leaves Southampton for her last cruise. More than just the finale for* Andes, *this was Royal Mail's last passenger ship voyage, after almost 130 years.* (Author's photograph)

Added to that was the excellence, in general, of her crew, and their great loyalty to her. As her days lengthened and her labours increased owing to the hard drive of turn-round cruises, her troubles increased. This entailed much hard work for everybody, one way and another, but particularly for the engineers, plumbers and technical staff generally, but few were ever found wanting.

The hard core of old hands who had been with her for years were a wonderful bunch and served as a steadying influence as the more irresponsible days came along. On the bridge I was served by another wonderful lot of lads who were of the utmost comfort to me, and for whom I retain a great affection; what more could a man ask. I think it was this feeling of togetherness aboard her which contributed to the feeling of well-being as her passengers stepped aboard...

As Capt. Fletcher so clearly implied, *Andes,* in the white cruising livery which was seemingly obligatory, carved a niche for herself as Britain's premier first-class-only cruise liner. Hers was a sense of exclusiveness, though, that had more to do with comfort and service than with opulence.

Her career was not generally eventful; she came and went, with the usual range of cruise destinations and with little fuss (her career is looked at in Volume 2). Behind the scenes, though, the situation was different. After the Company's takeover by Furness, Withy in the mid-1960s, the world of *Andes* came under increasing threat. The cruising niche which Royal Mail had fostered for so long with only limited competition, now became much more competitive. That was because other companies were turning the cruise market into a bonanza at a time of growing affluence. The steady demise, world-wide, of line services, due to increasing competition from aircraft and higher costs for fuel, wages and the like, diverted many passenger liners to cruising operations.

In 1969, a year after her final refit, *Andes* reached thirty years of age. There was little hope that she could hold her place in that increasingly competitive world for much longer. Her final cruise took place in the spring of 1971. When it ended, her departure to shipbreakers didn't just represent the retirement of *Andes.* She had made the Company's last passenger voyage.

Appendix III:
The RMSP Group In 1927

Chapter 6 related the magnitude of the RMSP Group at its zenith in the late 1920s. In the annual report covering 1927 – the year in which the purchase of Oceanic SN Co by RMSP made it the largest shipping group in the world – Lord Kylsant told shareholders:

> *The Royal Mail Steam Packet Company and its associated shipping companies together own more than 500 vessels of all descriptions, aggregating over 2,700,000 gross register tons. As exemplifying the magnitude of the operations of the Royal Mail and associated shipping companies, you may be interested to know that during the year 1927 their vessels carried 1,396,000 passengers and 13,986,000 tons of cargo. They covered 19,944,000 miles, and made 75,800 entries into ports, while the average daily number of men employed on board ship was 35,500, and the shore staff numbered 22,900.*

Gigantic though those figures were, they were only part of the story. The interconnection of company shareholdings within the Group, and Kylsant's own holdings, extended RMSP's influence through many industries. On 2 May 1927 the *Daily Herald* took the unprecedented step of devoting its entire front page to a web-like graphic which detailed the links. Lord Kylsant (who had about £5 million in Group investments) was at its core, flanked by RMSP, Elder Dempster & Co. and Coast Lines. Directly and indirectly the threads then spread to other companies. This is the list of other firms which were financially enmeshed with RMSP:

Yselhaven Wharf (Rotterdam)	Oceanic SN Co.	Meat Co.
Bank of British West Africa	Geo. Thompson & Co.	Argentine SN Co.
Standard Bank of South Africa	Shaw Savill & Albion Co.	Smithfield & Argentine Meat Co.
National Provincial Bank	International Mercantile	Pacific SN Co.
Westminster Bank	Marine Co.	Harland & Wolff
Lloyd's Bank	Atlantic Transport Co.	David Colville & Sons
Midland Bank	International Nav Co.	Ocean Transport Co.
African & Eastern Trade Corp	Frdk. Leyland & Co.	Southern Railway Co.
James Dyson & Co.	Soc. Anon. de Navigation	Burns & Laird
Nigerian Dry Dock & Eng Co.	Belge Americaine	David MacBrayne & Co.
Elder Dempster (Grand Canary)	Elders Insurance	David MacIver & Co.
Elder Dempster (Tenerife)	Bullard King & Co.	Glen Line
Elders Road Transport	Durban Navigation Collieries,	Glen Line Eastern Agencies
Atlantic Coaling Co.	Dundee Coal Co.	McGregor Gow & Holland
West African Lighterage &	London & Thames Haven	Ardrossan Harbour Co.
Transport	Oil Wharves	Ardrossan Dockyard
Imperial Direct Line	London Oil Storage Co.	Moss SS Co.
Comp. Belge Maritime	King Line	James Moss & Co.
du Congo	Scottish SS Co.	Belfast SS Co.
Elder Line	British Motorship Co.	Belfast & Manchester SS Co.
Nigerian Transport Co.	Nyassa Consolidated	Rogers & Bright
African SS Co.	Nyassa Co.	Tedcastle McCormick & Co.
British & African SN Co.	Nyassa Plantations	British & Irish SP Co.
John Pickering & Sons	Lamport & Holt	City of Cork SP Co.
Thos Headley & Co.	Liverpool Brazil & RP SN Co.	Union-Castle Mail SS Co.
White Star Line Ltd	River Plate British & Continental	John Hall Jun. & Co.

MacAndrews & Co.
RMSP Meat Transports
London Maritime Investment Co.
Nelson SN Co.
H & W Nelson
Jamaica Coaling Co.
Anglo-African (Oran) Coaling Co.
Anglo-Roumanian Produce Co.
Antwerp Coal Co.
Barbados Electric Supply Corp.
Bergen Mountain Railway

Caribbean Trading Agency
Club Central (Rio de Janeiro)
Comp. Nacional de Transportes
  'Expreso Villalonga'
Cia Sansinena de Carnes
  Congeladas
Dartmouth Coaling Co.
Empreza Mar. Portugueza,
Kahan & Co. (Hostels)
Kaye Son & Co.
Mersey Insulation Co.

Moghreb Press
Mount Railway Co. of
  Madeira
Pirraca Trust, Portland &
  Weymouth Coaling Co.
Producers' & Consignors'
  Agency
Rio de Janeiro Lighterage Co.
Shirley Laundry, Swift & Co.
West India Produce Association.

That, then, was the RMSP Group at its peak. The one missing link was the involvement of Lord Kylsant's brother, Viscount St Davids, whose major investments and great influence in many of the companies culminated in a central role in the 1932 RMSP Scheme of Arrangement.

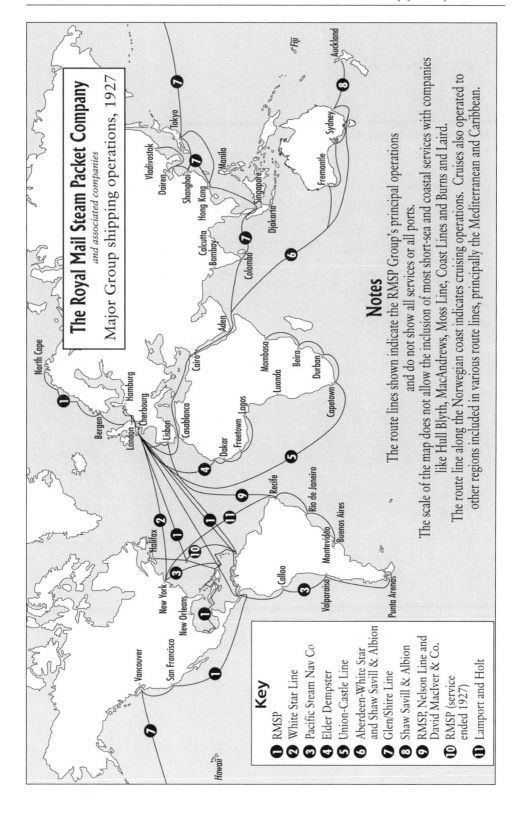

The Royal Mail Steam Packet Company
and associated companies
Major Group shipping operations, 1927

Notes

The route lines shown indicate the RMSP Group's principal operations and do not show all services or all ports.

The scale of the map does not allow the inclusion of most short-sea and coastal services with companies like Hull Blyth, MacAndrews, Moss Line, Coast Lines and Burns and Laird.

The route line along the Norwegian coast indicates cruising operations. Cruises also operated to other regions included in various route lines, principally the Mediterranean and Caribbean.

Key

1 RMSP
2 White Star Line
3 Pacific Steam Nav Co
4 Elder Dempster
5 Union-Castle Line
6 Aberdeen-White Star and Shaw Savill & Albion
7 Glen/Shire Line
8 Shaw Savill & Albion
9 RMSP, Nelson Line and David MacIver & Co.
10 RMSP (service ended 1927)
11 Lamport and Holt

Appendix IV:
Flags and Crests

The Royal Coat Of Arms
Its use on Royal Mail printed material appears to have been restricted. The earliest known use was on cabin plans for ships of the first fleet in the early 1840s. It formed the centrepiece of the Company's Corporate Seal and was carved over the doorway of its head office in Moorgate. It appears not to have been used after the late nineteenth century, except on the cover of the 1903 annual report.

Armorial Bearings
Royal Mail's armorial bearings, first used in 1929 following the Grant of Arms obtained from the College of Arms. While the origin of the armorial bearings is unclear, it is likely that Lord Kylsant initiated their creation as an appropriate reflection of the Company's stature. It was Royal Mail's graphic symbol for the remainder of the Company's existence.

RMSP Badge
This badge was used on RMSP's printed material from about 1900 until the late 1920s and was the Company's principal graphic symbol during that period.

RMSP's Corporate Seal

The Houseflag

Royal Mail's houseflag initially bore St Edward's Crown. The freedom with which the crown was adapted by various users prompted the Government to implement a change. Royal Mail's house magazine once explained:

> There is, or was, an 'Official' Crown, non-existent in fact and only a stylised design invented by the Civil Service in the early 1900s... It generally followed the form of the Imperial State Crown...

This was used for more than half a century. Queen Elizabeth II, following her accession in 1952, reinstated the use of St Edward's Crown, which Royal Mail then used for the rest of its life.

Right: *RMSP's houseflag in 1909, using the 'hybrid' crown, based on the Imperial State Crown.*

Left: *Royal Mail Lines' houseflag in the 1960s (this example is a miniature flag for ship table decorations). It uses St Edward's Crown, re-introduced in the 1950s. The crown's dipping arches make it easily identifiable from the Imperial State Crown.*

221

Appendix V: Fleet List

Column 1 – Name Name of ship in RMSP/RML ownership. Roman numerals I to IV indicate names used more than once.

Column 2 – Gross tons This list mostly uses figures from *Lloyd's Register*. Early ships did not appear in *Lloyd's Register* and are taken from the Company's centenary history or Company documents.

Column 3 – Builder The firm contracted to build the ship – machinery was sometimes sub-contracted. With the first fleet, some orders were given to the enginebuilders, who then sub-contracted the hulls – for them, details of both are given.

Column 4 – Years in RMSP/RML fleet Where a ship was built for the Company, the year is as given in *Lloyd's Register* (year of launching).

Column 5 – Hull material Self explanatory.

Note: Service details generally refer to the service for which the vessel was built or acquired. Many later traded on other routes.

Name	Gross Tons	Builder	Years in RMSP/ RML fleet	Hull Material
Clyde (I)	1,841	**Robert Duncan, Greenock**	**1841-1865**	**Wood**

Paddle steamer, side-lever engines by Caird & Co., Greenock. Sold between April and June 1865.

Tweed (I)	1,800	**Thompson & Spears, Clyde**	**1841-1847**	**Wood**

Paddle steamer, side-lever engines by Caird & Co., Greenock. Wrecked on Alecrane Reef, north of Yucatan Peninsula, Mexico 12 February 1847.

Thames (I)	1,889	**Wm Pitcher, Northfleet**	**1841-1865**	**Wood**

Paddle steamer, side-lever engines by Maudslay, Sons & Field, London. *Thames* and *Tay* inaugurated RMSP mail service, leaving Falmouth 3 January 1842. Sold at St Thomas prior to July 1865 for breaking up.

Forth	1,900	**R. Menzies, Leith**	**1841-1849**	**Wood**

Paddle steamer, side-lever engines by Edward Bury, Liverpool. Wrecked on Alecrane Reef, north of Yucatan Peninsula, Mexico 14 January 1849.

Solway	1,700	**Jas. McMillan, Greenock**	**1841-1843**	**Wood**

Paddle steamer, side-lever engines by Scott, Sinclair & Co. Lost near Coruña 1843.

Tay	1,858	**Chas. Wood, Dumbarton**	**1841-1856**	**Wood**

Paddle steamer, side lever engines by Caird & Co., Greenock. *Thames* and *Tay* inaugurated RMSP mail service, leaving Falmouth 3 January 1842. Lengthened by White of Cowes, 1853/1854. Lost near Cabo Rojo, south of Tampico, Mexico 31 August 1856.

Medina	1,800	**T. & J. White, Cowes, I of W**	**1841-1842**	**Wood**

Paddle steamer, side lever engines by Edward Bury, Liverpool. Lost May 1842, running ashore at Turk's Island, Bahamas. First loss of an RMSP ship.

Medway (I)	1,895	**Wm Pitcher, Northfleet**	**1841-1861**	**Wood**

Paddle steamer, side lever engines by Maudslay, Sons & Field, London. Sold August 1861 to Mr Marks for £3,625 (unconfirmed price) for breaking up at Vauxhall, Thames.

Dee (I)	1,849	**John Scott & Sons, Greenock**	**1841-1862**	**Wood**

Paddle steamer, side lever engines by Scott, Sinclair & Co. Sold January 1862.

Trent (I)	1,856	**Wm Pitcher, Northfleet**	**1841-1865**	**Wood**	

Paddle steamer, side lever engines by Miller, Ravenhill & Co., London. Sold between July and December 1865 for breaking up at Woolwich – last survivor of first fleet.

Teviot (I)	1,744	**Robert Duncan, Greenock**	**1841-1864**	**Wood**	

Paddle steamer, side lever engines by Caird & Co., Greenock. Laid up February 1864 and sold March 1864.

Isis	1,900	**Wm Pitcher, Northfleet**	**1841-1842**	**Wood**	

Paddle steamer, side lever engines by Miller, Ravenhill & Co., London. Grounded Puerto Rico September 1842; refloated and underwent temporary repairs. Left for England with *Medway* as escort. Abandoned in storm near Bermuda after becoming unmanageable; sank 8 October 1842.

Actaeon	650	**Clyde**	**1841-1844**	**Wood**	

Paddle steamer. Built 1837 for G. & J. Burns, for Glasgow-Liverpool service. Purchased by RMSP 1841 due to delay in completion of *Avon* and *Severn*. Wrecked on reef near Cartagena, Colombia 9 October 1844.

City of Glasgow	1,700	**Clyde**	**1841-1848**	**Wood**	

Paddle steamer. Purchased by RMSP 1841 from Thomson and McConnell due to delay in completion of *Avon* and *Severn*. Laid up Blackwall 1846 ('insufficient power' for the service); sold June 1848.

Larne (I)	300	**G. Taylor, Barking**	**1841-1851**	**Wood**	

Schooner. Built for inter-island services in West Indies. The first RMSP ship, together with *Lee*, to depart from England, sailing from the Thames 3 December 1841. Returned to England February 1851; sold July 1851 by auction (owing to poor condition).

Lee	250	**G. Taylor, Barking**	**1841-1848**	**Wood**	

Schooner. Built for inter-island services in West Indies. Together with *Larne* was the first RMSP ship to depart from England, sailing from the Thames 3 December 1841. Lost off Honduras 10 June 1848.

Liffey (I)	350	**H. Wimshurst, Limehouse**	**1841-1847**	**Wood**	

Schooner. Built for inter-island services in West Indies. Returned to England 1846; laid up; sold April 1847.

Avon (I)	1,880	**Wm Patterson, Bristol**	**1842-1862**	**Wood**	

Paddle steamer, side lever engines by Acraman, Morgan & Co., Bristol. Partially rebuilt and lengthened at Northfleet, 1852/3 (tonnage then increased to 2,069). Lost in Colon 'norther', 21 November 1862.

Severn (I)	1,886	**Wm Patterson, Bristol**	**1842-1856**	**Wood**	

Paddle steamer, side lever engines by Acraman, Morgan & Co., Bristol. Sold to Mr Marks 31 July 1856 for breaking up at Vauxhall, Thames, owing to poor condition after return from transport service in Crimea. Joint sale with *Great Western* realised £11,500.

Reindeer	600	**Liverpool**	**1845-1849**	**Wood**	

Paddle steamer. Reportedly purchased from Langtrys of Liverpool because of 1844 Admiralty stipulation that Jamaica-Santa Martha-Cartagena-Chagres-St John de Nicaragua mails be carried by steamer rather than sailing ships. Withdrawn from service 1849; engines placed in the new *Derwent*; hull broken up at Northfleet by Wm Pitcher.

Eagle	630	**?**	**1846-1861**	**Wood**	

Paddle steamer. Built 1835 for G. & J. Burns, Glasgow, for Glasgow-Liverpool service. Subsequently sold to Taylor & Scott, Dublin. Purchased by RMSP 1846 to replace *City of Glasgow* on Caribbean intercolonial services. Rebuilt and renovated 1849. Laid up Jamaica 1859; sold 1861.

Conway (I)	895	**Wm Pitcher, Northfleet**	**1846-1870**	**Wood**	

Paddle steamer. Possibly purchased during construction (RMSP report claims she was ordered by Company, but records of Capt. B.K. Berry say she was designed as a Trinity House lightship, purchased and lengthened during construction). Used for Caribbean intercolonial services and in 1852 operated experimental route Chagres-Jamaica-Nassau-Savannah. Sold June 1870.

Great Western	**1,775**	**Wm Patterson, Bristol**	**1847-1856**	**Wood**

Paddle steamer, engines by Maudslay, Sons & Field, London. Built for Great Western SS Co, Bristol; launched 19 July 1837. Purchased by RMSP 1847 as replacement for *Tweed* (lost). Sold to Mr Marks 31 July 1856 for breaking up at Vauxhall, Thames, owing to poor condition after return from transport service in Crimea – joint sale with *Severn* realised £11,500.

***Esk* (I)**	**231**	**R. Menzies, Leith**	**1849-1854**	**Wood**

Auxiliary screw-propelled schooner, to replace *Lee* (lost) in local Caribbean services. Probably purchased during or after construction. First vessel to undertake Rio de Janeiro-River Plate feeder service (1851) for new mail contract to South America. Withdrawn after a few months because of inadequate speed and accommodation. Returned to West Indies local services. Sold 1854 to Thomas Hill, Southampton; major alterations included lengthening by 34 feet. Reportedly resold 1855. Lost in Black Sea 9 April 1856 on voyage from Constantinople.

***Derwent* (I)**	**794**	**Wm Pitcher, Northfleet**	**1850-1867**	**Wood**

Paddle steamer. Used engines from *Reindeer*. Built for branch service St Thomas-Demerara. Thrown ashore during St Thomas hurricane October 1867; sold later 'as lies'.

***Amazon* (I)**	**2,256★**	**R. & H. Green, Blackwall**	**1851-1852**	**Wood**

Paddle steamer. ★ – Net tons; no gross measurement was published. Engines by Seaward & Capel, Limehouse. Built for West Indies transatlantic mail service. Lost on maiden voyage 4 January 1852

***Orinoco* (I)**	**2,901**	**Wm Pitcher, Northfleet**	**1851-1859**	**Wood**

Paddle steamer. Engines by Maudslay, Sons & Field, London. Built for West Indies transatlantic mail service. Maiden voyage 2/1852. Sold 1859 for breaking up on Thames owing to dry rot. Her engines were placed in the new *Parramatta*.

***Parana* (I)**	**2,943**	**M. Wigram, Southampton**	**1851-1876**	**Wood**

Paddle steamer. Engines by Caird & Co., Greenock. Built for West Indies transatlantic mail service. Final fitting out by RMSP establishment, Southampton owing to strike by shipyard workers. Maiden voyage April 1852. In 1860 chartered to Atlantic RM SN Co for three voyages Galway-North America. Engines removed 1868; remainder of career as Company coal hulk at St Thomas (Gregorie Channel, Water Island), replacement for hulk lost in St Thomas hurricane 1867.

***Magdalena* (I)**	**2,943**	**Wm Pitcher, Northfleet**	**1851-1865**	**Wood**

Paddle steamer. Engines by Robert Napier, Glasgow. Built for West Indies transatlantic mail service. Maiden voyage due to commence May 1852 (not confirmed). Sold second half of 1865 for breaking up on the Thames – unseaworthy owing to state of timbers.

***Demerara* (I)**	**2,318★**	**Wm Patterson, Bristol**	**see below**	**Wood**

Paddle steamer. ★ – Net tons; no gross measurement was published. Built for West Indies transatlantic mail service but stranded while leaving Bristol under tow to take in her engines (built by Caird & Co., Greenock); not accepted by RMSP. Subsequently sold and completed without engines, renamed *British Empire*, reputedly the world's largest sailing ship. Reported lost October 1867 in St Thomas hurricane. Was most likely the 2,680-ton ship (Official Number 13,775) owned in 1866 by Joshua Bros, London.

Prince	**398**	**Sunderland**	**1851-1862**	**Iron**

Paddle steamer. Purchased from Captain Andrews for £16,500 April 1851, for feeder service Rio de Janeiro-River Plate. From 1853 on local West Indies routes apart from a period in 1857 when she relieved *Camilla* on Rio-River Plate service. Sold about March 1862 at St Thomas. RMSP's first iron ship.

***La Plata* (I)**	**2,404**	**Robert Steele, Greenock**	**1852-1871**	**Wood**

Paddle steamer. Purchased on the stocks (allocated the name *Arabia* for Cunard Line) to replace *Amazon* (lost) on West Indies transatlantic mail service. Sold to Denny Bros, Dumbarton 1871 in part-payment for *Boyne*. One report states she was converted to a sailing ship at this time.

| ***Camilla*** | 539 | **Caird & Co., Greenock** | 1853-1859 | Iron |

Paddle steamer. Built 1849 for G. & J. Burns' Glasgow-Liverpool service. Bought by RMSP May 1853 for Rio de Janeiro-River Plate feeder service; name unchanged. Sold June 1859: 'purchased for national purposes' by Buenos Aires Government.

| ***Atrato* (I)** | 3,467 | **Caird & Co., Greenock** | 1853-1870 | Iron |

Paddle steamer. Built for West Indies transatlantic mail service as replacement for *Demerara* and used the engines intended for her. Sold May 1870 to J. Elder & Co., Glasgow, in part-payment for *Elbe*.

| ***Solent* (I)** | 1,804 | **T. & J. White, Cowes, I of W** | 1853-1869 | Composite |

Paddle steamer. RMSP's only composite ship. Built for West Indies intercolonial service, but occasionally made transatlantic voyages. Withdrawn August 1869, brought to England and sold December 1869.

| ***Wye*** | 819 | **Caird & Co., Greenock** | 1853-1867 | Iron |

Screw steamer. Built for West Indies intercolonial services. Final fitting out by RMSP's Southampton establishment owing to strike by shipyard workers. Lost St Thomas hurricane, October 1867.

| ***Tamar* (I)** | 1,850 | **Wm Pitcher, Northfleet** | 1854-1871 | Wood |

Paddle steamer. Last wood ship built for RMSP (though one purchased second-hand later). Built for West Indies intercolonial voyages but later traded to South America. Sold 1871.

| ***Tyne* (I)** | 1,603 | **Miller & Ravenhill, Newcastle** | 1854-1875 | Iron |

Paddle steamer. Built for West Indies intercolonial services but later traded to South America. Sold 1875, most likely for breaking up (returned to Southampton 17 February 1875 from Caribbean); *Lloyd's Register* erroneously recorded her in RMSP ownership until she left the Register in 1881.

| ***Oneida*** | 2,285 | **Scott & Co., Greenock** | 1858-1874 | Iron |

Screw steamer. Built 1855 and initially used for Crimean War service. Sold 1856 to European & Australian RM Co. Purchased by RMSP 1858 (because of E&A's financial difficulties) and re-engined. Used mostly on South America transatlantic service. Sold 1874 to H. Ellis & Sons, London. Engines removed; became ship-rigged sailing ship. Sold 1887 to H. Chaplin (Ship Oneida Ltd). Sold 1895 to Straits of Magellan Frozen Meat Co. (Spearing & Waldron, managers). In 1896 owned by Waldron & Wood. Out of Register 1897. Name unchanged throughout.

| ***Parramatta*** | 3,439 | **Thames Ironworks, Blackwall** | 1858-1859 | Iron |

Paddle steamer. Mail Contract 25 February 1858: 'Contract of 1850 extended by two years in consideration of improvements in the Brazil and West Indies Services' – *Parramatta*, *Shannon* and *Seine* built to provide those improvements. Utilised engines removed from *Orinoco*. Lost off Virgin Islands on maiden voyage.

| ***Mersey*** | 1,039 | **Thames Ironworks, Blackwall (?)** | 1859-1876 | Iron |

Paddle steamer. Builder most likely Thames Ironworks but not confirmed. Built for feeder service Rio de Janeiro-River Plate; transferred to West Indies 1865/1866. Sold in West Indies August 1876 to B Adamson, London for £1,000. Sold 1879 to W Moodie, London. In 1882 engines removed – became four-masted barque. Sold 1884 to A. Major, London. In 1887 rig reduced to 4-masted barquentine. Sold 1892 to Allen & Co., London. Sold 1893 to C. Christians, London. Sold about 1901 to Skibsaktiesel Mersey (N Jacobsen Molland), Grimstad, Norway. Name unchanged throughout. Out of Register 1903.

| ***Shannon*** | 3,609 | **R. Napier, Glasgow** | 1859-1875 | Iron |

Paddle steamer/ later screw. Mail Contract 25 February 1858: 'Contract of 1850 extended by two years in consideration of improvements in the Brazil and West Indies Services' – *Parramatta*, *Shannon* and *Seine* were built to provide those improvements. Converted to screw propulsion 1874. Lost 8 September 1875 on reef near Jamaica (since known as Shannon Shoal).

| *Tasmanian* | 2,956 | Hill, Pt Glasgow | 1859-1878 | Iron |

Screw steamer. Built 1858 for European & Australian RM Co.'s Australian service. Purchased by RMSP 1859, but RMSP effectively in control from 1858, under a mortgage agreement from E&A. 1865 underwent major overhaul including poop extention and altering passenger accommodation. Given compound engines 1872. The two upgrades raised gross tonnage from 2,253 to 2,956. Went ashore Ponce, Puerto Rico May 1878. Sold locally, 'as lies', for $2,500.

| *Seine* | 3,440 | Thames Ironworks, Blackwall | 1860-1871 | Iron |

Paddle steamer. Mail Contract 25 February 1858: 'Contract of 1850 extended by two years in consideration of improvements in the Brazil and West Indies Services' – *Parramatta*, *Shannon* and *Seine* were built to provide those improvements. Sold 1871 for breaking up.

| *Eider* (I) | 1,569 | Caird & Co., Greenock | 1864-1883 | Iron |

Paddle steamer. Maiden voyage (placement for West Indies intercolonial service) December 1864. Laid up early 1883 with intention to sell; re-used temporarily, but sold late 1883 to interests in Haiti through which she came into the ownership of Haitian revolutionaries; renamed *La Patrie*. In 1884 captured and sunk at Port au Prince, but was raised and was still afloat there in the 1920s.

| *Douro* (I) | 2,824 | Caird & Co., Greenock | 1864-1882 | Iron |

Screw steamer. *Rhone* and *Douro* built as mail steamers for South America service, but after two years transferred to West Indies route. *Douro* returned to Brazil route 1869. October 1869 inaugurated through mail service to River Plate. Lost Bay of Biscay 1 April 1882 in collision with *Yrurac Bat*.

| *Arno* (I) | 1,038 | Caird & Co., Greenock | 1865-1882 | Iron |

Paddle steamer. Built for Rio de Janeiro-River Plate feeder service; maiden voyage September 1865. Withdrawn at start of River Plate through service 1869; joined West Indies intercolonial service March 1870. Sold 1882 'at a price in excess of her book value'. Subsequently in *Lloyd's Register* under Spanish flag, but no owner, until 1885.

| *Rhone* | 2,738 | Millwall Ironworks, London | 1865-1867 | Iron |

Screw steamer. *Rhone* and *Douro* built as mail steamers for South America service, but after two years transferred to West Indies route. *Rhone* lost in St Thomas hurricane, October 1867.

| *Danube* (I) | 2,000 | Millwall Ironworks, London | 1865-1871 | Iron |

Paddle steamer. Built for West Indies services. Major delay in completion as she did not conform to contract specifications; maiden voyage September 1866. Last paddle steamer built for RMSP. Sold February 1871 to Union SS Co.; name unchanged but converted to screw propulsion. Used as mail steamer on South Africa routes. Sold 1888 and broken up shortly afterwards.

| *Corsica* | 1,134 | J. & G. Thomson, Glasgow | 1867-1877 | Iron |

Screw steamer. Built 1863; purchased by RMSP from Cunard December 1867 at Havana to replace *Wye* (lost). Previously operated New York-Havana. Sold 1877 to S. P Austin, London (gross tonnage now 1,581). Sold 1880 to Bristol General SN Co, Bristol. Name unchanged throughout. Out of Register 1882.

| *Neva* | 3,025 | Caird & Co., Greenock | 1868-1890 | Iron |

Screw steamer. Purchased by RMSP while under construction for Norddeutscher Lloyd (was to have been named *Rhein*) to replace *Rhone* (lost). According to directors' minutes, sold May 1890 by auction to Cohen & Sons, probably for breaking up.

| *Nile* (I) | 3,039 | Day, Summers, Southampton | 1869-1890 | Iron |

Screw steamer. Built for new through service Southampton-Colon in support of PNZA Co. mail service to Panama, New Zealand and Australia. Launched Northam, Southampton 7 September 1869; maiden voyage 2 February 1870. Given compound engines 1878. Sold May 1890 to Union SS Co; renamed *Roman*. Sold for breaking up 1891.

Elbe	**3,108**	**J. Elder & Co., Govan**	**1869-1902**	**Iron**

Screw steamer. First RMSP ship with compound engines. Built for new through service Southampton-Colon in support of PNZA Co. mail service to Panama, New Zealand and Australia; later transferred to Brazil and River Plate service. Given triple expansion machinery 1887. Sold to French shipbreakers (reported sold to Jules Cousin, Cherbourg December 1902 for £10,000).

Tiber	**1,591**	**Lungley, London**	**1871-1882**	**Iron**

Screw steamer. Built 1866 for Panama, New Zealand & Australia RM Co., as *Kaikoura*. Mortgaged to RMSP as part of joint venture operation; effectively came under RMSP control 1869; ownership formally transferred to RMSP 1871; renamed *Tiber*. Wrecked Porto Plata, San Domingo 10 February 1882.

Ebro (I)	**1,509**	**Randolph & Elder, Glasgow**	**1871-1881**	**Iron**

Screw steamer. Built 1866 for Panama, New Zealand & Australia RM Co., as *Rakaia*. Mortgaged to RMSP as part of joint venture operation; effectively came under RMSP control 1869; ownership formally transferred to RMSP 1871; renamed *Ebro*. Sold February 1881 to A. Cassels for £4,250, possibly as agent for Marques de Campo, Madrid, in whose ownership she appeared, name unchanged. Sold 1886 to Compania Trasatlantica, Cadiz; renamed *Baldomero Iglesias*. Sold 1898 to Bonnefoyainé, Marseilles, name unchanged. Out of register 1900/1901.

Liffey (II)	**1,504**	**Dudgeon, London**	**1871-1874**	**Iron**

Screw steamer. Built 1865 for Panama, New Zealand & Australia RM Co., as *Ruahine*. Chartered by RMSP 10 August 1865 – 25 December 1865 for West Indies intercolonial service. Mortgaged to RMSP as part of joint venture operation; effectively came under RMSP control 1869; ownership formally transferred to RMSP 1871; renamed *Liffey*. Wrecked Cape José Ignacio, near Maldonado, Uruguay 1874 – first loss of RMSP ship on South America services.

Moselle	**3,298**	**J. Elder & Co., Govan**	**1871-1891**	**Iron**

Screw steamer. Originally allocated the name *Para*; changed to *Moselle* during construction, October 1870. Built for West Indies mail service. Wrecked near Colon 30 October 1891.

Belize (I)	**1,038**	**J. & G. Thomson, Glasgow**	**1871-1888**	**Iron**

Screw steamer. Built for G. & J Burns, Glasgow, 1871 as *Bison* for Glasgow-Liverpool service. Purchased by RMSP after a few months in service for new mail contract service between Belize and Jamaica; renamed *Belize*. Sold December 1888 to Haitian Government; price quoted as £25,000 but unconfirmed. Out of Register 1890.

Tagus (I)	**3,298**	**J. Elder & Co., Govan**	**1871-1897**	**Iron**

Screw steamer. Built for West Indies mail service. Partially sunk at her berth at Colon 21 January 1876, having been struck by RMSP's *Severn*. Raised and repaired. Sold early 1897 for breaking up on Thames.

Boyne	**3,318**	**Denny Bros, Dumbarton**	**1871-1875**	**Iron**

Screw steamer. Built for Brazil and River Plate mail service. Wrecked on Brittany coast August 1875. Ship sold 'as lies' September 1875 to Kerros et fils, for 2,000 francs.

Essequibo (I)	**1,831**	**Richardson, Duck, Stockton**	**1873-1900**	**Iron**

Screw steamer. Built 1871 for Brownlow & Co., Hull as *Bladworth*. Purchased by RMSP for new service to West Indies, Spanish Main and Panama, 1873; renamed *Essequibo*. Principally cargo but limited passenger accommodation. Sold 1900, probably for breaking up in Italy.

Larne (II)	**1,670**	**C. Mitchell & Co., Newcastle**	**1873-1900**	**Iron**

Screw steamer. Built 1870 as *De Ruyter* for Engels & Co. Purchased by RMSP for new service to West Indies, Spanish Main and Panama, 1873; renamed *Larne*. Principally cargo but limited passenger accommodation. Ended RMSP career on Continental service (Southampton to Northern Europe). Sold 1900 and briefly became *Little Mary* (reportedly sold to R. de Sanna, Genoa for £4,800). In 1901 owned by Transp. Marittimi a Vapore (V Granata fu E), Bari (Italy); renamed *Mario*. Sold 1906 to Metallurgica Meridionale, Naples, probably for breaking up.

Severn (II)   **1,736**   **Oswald & Co., Sunderland**   **1873-1888**   **Iron**

Screw steamer. Not ordered by RMSP but purchased before completion for new service to West Indies, Spanish Main and Panama, May 1873, for £38,800. Principally cargo but limited passenger accommodation. Sold early 1888 to Ottoman Government and re-sold to Idarei Massousieh, Constantinople; name unchanged. Out of Register 1896.

Minho (I)   **2,540**   **Barclay Curle, Glasgow**   **1874-1888**   **Iron**

Screw steamer. Built 1872 for John Ryde, London as *Leopold II*. Purchased by RMSP 1874 (with *Mondego*) and renamed *Minho*, for Brazil and River Plate services to replace *Ebro* (transferred to West Indies) and *Liffey* (lost). Sold March 1888 to Archibald Ross, London; name unchanged. Sold 1889 to Idarei Massousieh, Constantinople, Turkey; renamed *Aslan*. Wrecked April 1901.

Mondego   **2,564**   **Tod & McGregor, Glasgow**   **1874-1888**   **Iron**

Screw steamer. Built 1872 for John Ryde, London as *Santiago*. Purchased by RMSP 1874 (with *Minho*), renamed *Mondego*, for Brazil and River Plate services to replace *Ebro* (transferred to West Indies) and *Liffey* (lost). Sold 1888. In 1889 appeared in ownership of Archibald Ross (reported sold for £9,500 in November 1888). Out of Register 1892.

Dee (II)   **1,864**   **T. Wingate & Co., Glasgow**   **1875-1901**   **Iron**

Screw steamer. Built 1872 as *Minnesota*, for State Line SS Co, Glasgow. Renamed *State of Minnesota* 1873. Bought by RMSP to support increased West Indies services February 1875; renamed *Dee*. Converted to triple expansion machinery 1887. Sold February 1901 to Niger Co. Ltd, reduced for £7,500; name unchanged. Out of Register 1911.

Guadiana   **2,504**   **London & Glasgow Co., Glasgow** **1875-1885**   **Iron**

Screw steamer. Purchased for Brazil and River Plate service. Directors' minutes indicate intention to purchase, in May 1875, *State of Florida* (presumed to be State Line SS Co) but she was not this vessel. She was not built to RMSP order (*Lloyd's Register* lists her year of build as 1874). Possibly a vessel under construction for State, or other, at the time. Wrecked Abrolhos Archipelago, Brazil 20 June 1885.

Para   **4,028**   **Cammell Laird, Birkenhead**   **1875-1903**   **Iron**

Screw steamer. Built 1873 for The Pacific Steam Navigation Co. as *Puno*. Purchased by RMSP 1875 as replacement on West Indies service for *Shannon* (lost); renamed *Para*. Converted to triple expansion machinery and extensive alterations to accommodation 1890 (the latter raising tonnage from 3,805 to 4,028). Sold for breaking up in France (reported sold to H. E Moss & Co September 1903 for £10,000).

Don   **4,028**   **Cammell Laird, Birkenhead**   **1875-1901**   **Iron**

Screw steamer. Built 1872 for The Pacific Steam Navigation Co. as *Corcovado*. Purchased by RMSP 1875 'for transatlantic services'; renamed *Don*. Replacement for *Boyne* (lost). Converted to triple expansion machinery 1889, extensive alterations to accommodation raising tonnage from 3,805 to 4,028. Sold 1901 for breaking up in France.

Medway (II)   **3,687**   **J. Elder & Co., Glasgow**   **1877-1899**   **Iron**

Screw steamer. Built 1877 – *Lloyd's Register* records first owner as J F Ure, Fairfield, Govan; RMSP not recorded as owner until 1880/1 edition. Ordered by RMSP August 1876, the agreement accompanied by a rider that 'the reduction of £1,000 to be agreed to as proposed by Messrs Elder & Co'. This related to original ownership – John Ure was a partner in Elders. Built for West Indies transatlantic mail service. Converted to triple expansion machinery 1887. Sold late 1899, probably for breaking up.

Solent (II)   **1,915**   **Oswald Mordaunt, Southampton** **1878-1909**   **Iron**

Screw steamer. Built for West Indies intercolonial services. Was RMSP's first official cruise ship, being seasonally used from 1904, but had effectively filled the role earlier. Sold June 1909 to Forth Shipbreaking Co. for £4,100.

Tamar (II)   **2,923**   **Henderson, Renfrew**   **1878-1897**   **Iron**

Screw steamer. Built 1873 as *Vancouver* for China Trans-Pacific SS Co, London. Purchased by RMSP 1878; renamed *Tamar*. Purchased for new direct service to River Plate (to overcome quarantine due to yellow fever in Brazil). Sold 1897 for breaking up in Holland.

Trent (II)   2,912   **Henderson, Renfrew**   **1878-1897**   **Iron**

Screw steamer. Built 1873 as *Vasco da Gama* for China Trans-Pacific SS Co, London. Purchased by RMSP 1878; renamed *Trent*. Purchased for new direct service to River Plate (to overcome quarantine due to yellow fever in Brazil). Sold 1897; renamed *Luigi*, broken up Italy about 1898.

Derwent (II)   2,466   **R. Thompson Jun, Sunderland**   1879-1902   **Iron**

Screw steamer. Purchased by RMSP close to completion, October 1879, for West Indies 'B' cargo service. Maiden voyage January 1880. Sold October 1902 to Extrême Orient Soc. Franc. de Nav, Dunkirk for £6,600; renamed *Lilia*. Sold to J Jenkins, Hong Kong (also her new master) 1905; reverted to name *Derwent* for rest of career. Sold 1906 to Kwok King Fat, Hong Kong (Jenkins, master). Sold 1913 to Cie Thai-Thuan (Yen Sang, manager), Hong Kong (Jenkins, master). In 1918 Jenkins ceases to be master. Sold 1925 to Yuet On SS Co; Chinese-registered (Hong Kong ownerships had been British). Sold 1926 to Lau Yue Fook, Canton. Sold 1927 to Ty Camco Sobrino, Manila (United States flag). Out of Register 1931.

Humber   2,371   **London & Glasgow Co., Glasgow**   1880-1885   **Iron**

Screw steamer. Purchased by RMSP on completion by builders, for West Indies 'B' cargo service. Maiden voyage March 1880. Vanished on voyage New York (left 15 February 1885) to UK.

Avon (II)   2,162   **J. Laing, Sunderland**   1880-1903   **Iron**

Screw steamer. Purchased by RMSP during construction as Laing's 'No. 241', for West Indies 'B' cargo service. Maiden voyage April 1880. Sold February 1903 to John Ellerman (Cedardene SS Co., Fred Swift manager); name unchanged. Out of Register 1917.

La Plata (II)   3,240   **R. & H. Green, London**   1882-1893   **Iron**

Screw steamer. Built 1879 as *Norfolk* for Australian service of M. Wigram & Sons, London. Purchased by RMSP 1882 for Brazil and River Plate service to replace *Douro* (lost); renamed *La Plata*. First RMSP voyage October 1882. Laid up Southampton Water October 1892. Sold May 1893, to a Mr Watson (probably an agent). Appeared 1894 as *Orienta*, 3,212 tons, for Orienta Steam Yachting Association (A. H. Gaze), London. Sold 1895/1896 to Norse King SS Co (R.R. Pirrie & J.J. Ballantine), Newcastle; renamed *Norse King*. Sold 1898 to Albion SS Co   (J. S. Pearson, manager); name unchanged. Sold 1900/1 to Co-operative Cruising Co. Ltd (W. H. Lunn), London; renamed *Argonaut*. Reported lost from collision with steamer *Kingswell*, 1908.

Eden (I)   2,145   **Barrow S.B. Co., Barrow**   1882-1909   **Iron**

Screw steamer. *Eden* and *Esk* built for West Indies intercolonial mail service 'with good passenger accommodation' as replacements for *Tiber* (lost) and *Eider* (sold). Stranded at Buck Island 28 November 1893; salvaged by Merritt Wrecking Co. of New York 27 February 1894. Sold 1909, probably for breaking up.

Esk (II)   2,145   **Barrow S.B. Co., Barrow**   1882-1910   **Iron**

Screw steamer. *Eden* and *Esk* built for West Indies intercolonial mail service 'with good passenger accommodation' as replacements for *Tiber* (lost) and *Eider* (sold). Maiden voyage was to South America. Sold 1910, probably for breaking up.

Dart (I)   2,641   **R. Dixon & Co., Middlesborough**   1883-1884   **Iron**

Screw steamer. Purchased during construction, for Brazil and River Plate service; she had been given the provisional name *Cavio*. Wrecked near San Sebastian, Brazil 11 September 1884 during her third voyage.

Exe   61   **Willoughby Bros, Plymouth**   1885-c1925   **Iron**

Screw steamer. Built 1885; almost certainly RMSP was original owner. Employed 1889-1905 carrying mail, passengers and produce around Grenada, for mail contract with Grenada Government. Operated by RMSP prior to this, in the Caribbean, listed under 'Plant'. July 1887 reported ashore at Barbados; also in 1887 reported operating between St Thomas and St Croix, possibly on charter to a Mr Rutter. After 1905 resumed status of 'Plant' at Barbados (1906-1910) and Trinidad (1911- c1925).

Orinoco (II)   **4,572**   **Caird & Co., Greenock**   **1886-1909**   **Steel**

Screw steamer. RMSP's first steel ship and first with triple expansion engines. Launched 13 September 1886. Built for transatlantic voyages in support of a new West Indies mail contract. Sold 1909, probably for breaking up.

Atrato (II)   **5,347**   **R. Napier, Glasgow**   **1888-1912**   **Steel**

Screw steamer. Launched September 1888. Initially on Brazil & River Plate mail service but later transferred to West Indies. Sold 1912 to The Viking Cruising Co; renamed *The Viking*. In 1914 requisitioned as armed merchant cruiser; renamed HMS *Viknor*. Went missing 1915, possibly after striking a mine.

Magdalena (II)   **5,373**   **R. Napier, Glasgow**   **1889-1921**   **Steel**

Screw steamer. Built for Brazil & River Plate mail service. Sold for breaking up at Birkenhead, and was reported still 'being broken up' in November 1923.

Waltham   **87**   **Southampton**   **1889-1903**   **Wood**

Screw steamer. Built 1881; bought by RMSP 1889 from Charles M. Browne, St George's, Grenada. Employed 1889-1903 carrying mail, passengers and produce around Grenada, for mail contract with Grenada Government. Appears to have been purchased specifically for this contract.

Thames (II)   **5,621**   **R. Napier, Glasgow**   **1889-1914**   **Steel**

Screw steamer. Maiden voyage April 1890. Built for Brazil & River Plate mail service. Sold 1914 for breaking up in Scotland; reportedly used as block ship at Scapa.

Clyde (II)   **5,618**   **R. Napier, Glasgow**   **1890-1913**   **Steel**

Screw steamer. Launched April 1890. Maiden voyage July 1890. Built for Brazil & River Plate mail service. Sold 1913 for breaking up in Scotland.

Tyne (II)   **615**   **Ramage & Ferguson, Leith**   **1891-1897**   **Steel**

Screw steamer. Built for new mail contract with Government of Leeward Islands; maiden voyage March 1891. Sold on cessation of that contract February 1897 to Cia General de Tabacos de Filipinas, Barcelona; renamed *P de Sotolongo*. About 1900 renamed *Union* – same owner but port of registry Manila, US flag. Out of Register 1911.

Taw   **180**   **J. McArthur & Co., Paisley**   **1892-1915**   **Steel**

Screw steamer sloop. Built for local West Indies services. Undergoing trials cApril 1892. Sold 1915, but remained in *Lloyd's Register* without ownership from then until 1920, when ownership given as G. H. W Bonnett, Castries, St Lucia; renamed *Vigilant*. In 1923, added to Bonnett ownership was A. Davilla, manager. Sold 1927 to André Aubery, Martinique; name unchanged. Out of Register 1937.

Tees   **180**   **J. McArthur & Co., Paisley**   **1892-1915**   **Steel**

Screw steamer sloop. Built for local West Indies services. Launched April 1892. Sold 1915 to W Hadden, Trinidad. Sold 1918 to T. H Scott, Trinidad. Sold 1919 to Vestey Bros, Trinidad. Name unchanged throughout. Out of Register 1933.

Wear   **180**   **J. McArthur & Co., Paisley**   **1892-1915**   **Steel**

Screw steamer sloop. Built for local West Indies services. Sold 1915 to W. Hadden (Venezuela flag); renamed *Condor*. Sold 1923 to Cie Générale Transatlantique and registered Fort de France (French flag); renamed *Balata*. Out of Register 1927.

Spey   **470**   **S. McKnight & Co., Ayr**   **1893-1913**   **Steel**

Screw steamer. First entry in Lloyd's Register is as *Spey* owned by RMSP, built 1892. However, was already completed when RMSP bought her, for decision to purchase was made on 22 February 1893; original name given as *Corsican*. Most likely built on speculation. Purchased for Jamaica cargo service; first voyage for RMSP May 1893. Transferred to new contract service at Tobago 1901. Sold 1913 to J Constant, London; name unchanged. Sold 1918 to V. Kibrit, London; name unchanged. Out of Register 1920.

Nile **(II)**   **5,855**   **J. & G. Thomson, Glasgow**   **1893-1911**   **Steel**

Screw steamer. Launched March 1893; maiden voyage October 1893. Built for Brazil and River Plate mail service. Sold 1911 to Pacific Mail SS Co. Later transferred to US Navy. Name unchanged throughout. Broken up 1925 by General Metal Supply Co., United States.

Danube **(II)**   **5,891**   **J. & G. Thomson, Glasgow**   **1893-1920**   **Steel**

Screw steamer. Completion delayed by labour troubles; did not undergo trials until about April 1894. Built for Brazil and River Plate mail service. RMSP's largest nineteenth century ship. Sold 1920 to Claude Langdon; renamed *Mediterranean Star*. Broken up Genoa 1922.

La Plata (III)   *3,445*   *R. Napier, Glasgow*   *1896-1900*   *Steel*

Screw steamer. Designed for Brazil and River Plate service – cargo and 3rd class passengers. Maiden voyage August 1896. Sold 1900 to Booth Line; renamed *Clement*. Sold 1915 to H. & C. Grayson, Liverpool; renamed *Freshfield*. Sold 1918 to R. Lawrence Smith, Montreal; name unchanged. Out of Register 1919 (reported torpedoed 1918).

Minho **(II)**   **3,445**   **R. Napier, Glasgow**   **1896-1903**   **Steel**

Screw steamer. Designed for Brazil and River Plate service – cargo and third class passengers. Maiden voyage 10/1896. Sold 1903 to H. F Swan (W Petersen Ltd, managers); renamed *Halifax*. (Sale of *Minho* and *Ebro* was in part payment to Armstrong Whitworth for *Caroni*, *Catalina* and *Conway*. Minutes for 11 November 1903 recorded 'Bill of Sale agreed for *Ebro* and *Minho* to be sold to Colonel Swan. This is considered by Armstrong & Co as on their account.') By 1904 renamed *Montreal* and owned by Cie Générale Transatlantique (French Line), registered Le Havre. Out of Register 1916.

Ebro **(II)**   **3,445**   **R. Napier, Glasgow**   **1896-1903**   **Steel**

Screw steamer. Designed for Brazil and River Plate service – cargo and 3rd class passengers. Launched September 1896. Sold 1903 to H. F Swan (W Petersen Ltd, managers); renamed *Quebec* (see *Minho* [II] entry). By 1904 owned by Cie Générale Transatlantique (French Line), registered Le Havre. Out of Register 1916.

Severn **(III)**   **3,760**   **R. Dixon & Co., Middlesborough**   **1898-1913**   **Steel**

Screw steamer. Built for RMSP cargo services, various routes. Initially on Brazil and River Plate routes, but thereafter mainly West Indies. In 1910 hired on long-term charter; renamed *Fernando Poo*. Sold 1913 to Cia Trasatlantica, Cadiz; name unchanged, suggesting this firm had been the charterer. Out of Register 1917.

Tagus **(II)**   **5,545**   **R. Napier, Glasgow**   **1899-1920**   **Steel**

Screw steamer. Built for West Indies transatlantic mail service. Maiden voyage late 1899. Sold 1920 to Hijos de Jose Taya S. en C, Barcelona; renamed *Principe de Viana*. Out of Register 1926.

Trent **(III)**   **5,525**   **R. Napier, Glasgow**   **1899-1922**   **Steel**

Screw steamer. Built for West Indies transatlantic mail service. Launched September 1899. Sold 1922, probably for breaking up.

Tyne **(III)**   **2,902**   **R. Napier, Glasgow**   **1900-1917**   **Steel**

Screw steamer. Launched April 1900. Built for non-contract cargo services. As HM Transport in the First World War sunk by torpedo 17 June 1917.

Eider **(II)**   **1,236**   **Campbelltown SB Co**   **1900-1927**   **Steel**

Screw steamer. Purchased as completed ship August 1900 for Continental business (initially Southampton to Bremen and Hamburg), as replacement for *Larne* (II) (sold). First voyage September 1900. Sold 1927 to Union-Castle Line (for feeder service Southampton-Continent); name unchanged. Sold 1936 to Stanhope SS Co (J.A. Billmeir & Co., managers); renamed *Stanhill*. Sold 1937 to Adriatico Tirreno Jonio Ligure Soc Anon di Nav (A Ravano, manager), Genoa; renamed *Eider* and in 1938 further renamed (under same owner) *Docilitas*. Out of Register 1948.

La Plata (IV)   4,464   **J. & G. Thomson, Glasgow**   **1901-1908**   **Steel**

Screw steamer. Built 1881 for Union SN Co (later Union SS Co) as *Moor*. Originally 3,688 gross tons; increased to 4,464 following lengthening by 55 feet in 1894. Purchased by RMSP 1901 for West Indies mail service for £35,000; renamed *La Plata*. Sold 1908 to Polytechnic Touring Association (R. Mitchell), London; renamed *The Viking*. Ownership changed to The Viking Cruising Co. (S.J. Beckett), London 1911/1912; name unchanged. Sold to Sundermann 1913 for breaking up.

Kennet   827   **J. Laing, Sunderland**   **1901-1914**   **Steel**

Screw steamer. Built 1895 for R. M. Hudson as *General Havelock*. Purchased by RMSP 1901 for new contract service for Government of Trinidad, around Trinidad and Tobago – proposed price £15,500 (unconfirmed); renamed *Kennet*. Sold 1914 to Sun Shipping Co. (W A Cox, manager), London; name shortly changed to *Sunhill*. About 1920 managers became Mitchell Cotts & Co. Out of Register 1929.

Arno (II)   745   **S. McKnight & Co., Ayr**   **1901-1917**   **Steel**

Screw steamer. Built 1894 for J. & P. Hutchison, Glasgow, as *Juno*. Purchased by RMSP 1901 for Jamaica-based service – reported price £13,650 (unconfirmed); renamed *Arno*. Sold 1917 to Roberts, Brining & Co., London; name unchanged. Renamed *Arbeeco* 1919, owners now styled SS Arbeeco Ltd (Roberts, Brining & Co., managers). Out of Register 1923.

Yare   299   **S. McKnight & Co., Ayr**   **1901-1915**   **Steel**

Screw steamer. Built 1887 for H. Reeve, Yarmouth, as *Norfolk*. Purchased 1901 by RMSP for £7,000; renamed *Yare*. Purchased for new mail contract with Government of Dominica, for coastal service, to operate from 25 December 1901. Sold 1915, probably for breaking up.

Dee (III)   1,871   **Craig, Taylor & Co., Stockton**   **1902-1918**   **Steel**

Screw steamer. Delivered April 1902. Built as cargo steamer for non-contract services, principally used on West Indies routes. Sold 1918 to John Hall Jnr & Co., Middlesborough; name unchanged. In 1920 renamed *Cid* (same owner). Sold 1921 to Limerick SS Co., Limerick; renamed *Cahiracon*. Sold 1925 to Gart Line (Whimster & Co., managers), Glasgow; renamed *Gartmore*. Sold 1935 to A. Alfino & Figli, Catania, Sicily; renamed *Anna Madre*. Sold 1937 to Società Armamento Pugliese, Bari, Italy; renamed *Peuceta*. Sold 1938 to Achille Lauro, Naples; name unchanged. Out of Register 1945.

Tamar (III)   3,207   **Craig, Taylor & Co., Stockton**   **1902-1915**   **Steel**

Screw steamer. Delivered June 1902. Built for Brazil and River Plate cargo services, but with flexibility to operate other routes. Captured by German raider *Kronprinz Wilhelm* 24 March 1915 and scuttled.

Teviot (II)   3,271   **Craig, Taylor & Co., Stockton**   **1902-1928**   **Steel**

Screw steamer. Delivered July 1902. Built for Brazil and River Plate cargo services, but with flexibility to operate other routes. Sold 1928 for breaking up at Danzig.

Parana (II)   4,515   **Workman Clark, Belfast**   **1904-1933**   **Steel**

Screw steamer. Refrigerated meat carrier, with third class passenger accommodation, for River Plate service. Sold to Hughes Bolckow Shipbreaking Co., Blyth, for £3,850, May 1933 for breaking up.

Caroni   2,628   **Armstrong, Whitworth, Ncstle**   **1904-1915**   **Steel**

Screw steamer. Built for West Indies cargo services, Armstrong Whitworth taking *Ebro* (II) and *Minho* (II) as part payment for *Caroni*, *Catalina* and *Conway*. As HM Transport in the First World War, sunk by submarine gunfire off France 7 September 1915.

Conway (II)   2,650   **Armstrong, Whitworth, Ncstle**   **1904-1930**   **Steel**

Screw steamer. Built for West Indies cargo services (see *Caroni*). Sold 1930 to Pentwyn SS Co (Lambert, Barnett & Co., managers), London; renamed *Pentusker*. Sold twice, without name change, in 1934 – to Bristol Channel & Levant Line, then to J Cashmore, Newport. Sold 1935 to Dah Loh Industrial Co., Shanghai; renamed *Dah*

Sun. Sold 1938 to G. Stanatelatos, Piraeus; renamed *Pipina*. Sold 1947 to Dah Loh Shipping Co., Shanghai; renamed *Dah Sun*. Out of Register 1958.

Pardo (I)	4,538	Harland & Wolff, Belfast	1904-1934	Steel

Screw steamer. Refrigerated meat carrier, with third class passenger accommodation, for River Plate service. Sold 5 May 1934 for breaking up.

Catalina	2,645	Armstrong, Whitworth, Ncstle	1904-1922	Steel

Screw steamer. Built for West Indies cargo services (see *Caroni*). Sold 1922 to Matsuoka Kisen KK; renamed *Nisshin Maru No. 3*, registered Shikitsu. *Lloyd's Register* entry later modified to *Nissin Maru No. 3*, owners Matuoka Kisen KK and port of registry to Hutyu. Out of Register 1948.

Potaro (I)	4,378	Harland & Wolff, Belfast	1904-1915	Steel

Screw steamer. Refrigerated meat carrier, with third class passenger accommodation, for River Plate service. Captured by raider *Kronprinz Wilhelm* 10 January 1915. Used as scout ship before being scuttled.

Aragon (I)	9,588	Harland & Wolff, Belfast	1905-1917	Steel

Twin screw steamer. Mail, passenger and refrigerated cargo ship for Brazil and River Plate service. Maiden voyage departure 14 July 1905. Sunk by torpedo near Alexandria 30 December 1917.

Oruba (I)	5,737	Naval Const. & Arm Co., Barrow	1906-1914	Steel

Screw steamer. Built 1889 for Pacific Steam Navigation Co. as *Oruba*. Entered RMSP fleet for Australian mail service in 1906 as part of its purchase of PSN's interest in Orient-Pacific Line. Sold 1914; listed 1920 owned by The Admiralty. Out of Register 1921.

Orotava	5,851	Naval Const. & Arm Co., Barrow	1906-1915	Steel

Screw steamer. Built 1889 for Pacific Steam Navigation Co. as *Orotava*. Entered RMSP fleet for Australian mail service in 1906 as part of its purchase of PSN's interest in Orient-Pacific Line. Sold 1915; in 1920 listed as owned by The Shipping Controller (RMSP, managers); name unchanged. Out of Register 1922.

Oroya	6,297	Barrow S.B. Co., Barrow	1906-1909	Steel

Screw steamer. Built 1886 for Pacific Steam Navigation Co. as *Oroya*. Entered RMSP fleet for Australian mail service in 1906 as part of its purchase of PSN's interest in Orient-Pacific Line. Sold 1909, probably for breaking up.

Ortona	7,945	Vickers & Maxim, Barrow	1906-1917	Steel

Twin screw steamer. Built 1899 for Pacific Steam Navigation Co. as *Ortona*. Entered RMSP fleet for Australian mail service in 1906 as part of its purchase of PSN's interest in Orient-Pacific Line. Converted to cruise liner, with gross tonnage raised to 8,939; renamed *Arcadian* – first cruise 1912. As HM Transport sunk by torpedo 15 April 1917.

Arcadian (I)	see *Ortona*

Marima	2,742	R. Dixon & Co., Middlesborough	1906-1911	Steel

Screw steamer. Built 1892 for British & Colonial SN Co (Bucknall Bros, managers) as *Zulu*. Purchased by RMSP 1906 for Brazil and River Plate cargo services; renamed *Marima*. Sold 1911 to George Coulouras, Andros, Greece; renamed *Marika*. Sold c1915/1916 to Hannevig Bros, Christiania, Norway; name unchanged. Foundered April 1916.

Manau	2,745	R. Dixon & Co., Middlesborough	1906-1906	Steel

Screw steamer. Built 1892 for British & Colonial SN Co. (Bucknall Bros, managers) as *Transvaal*. Purchased by RMSP 1906 for Brazil and River Plate cargo services; renamed *Manau*. Wrecked near Bahia, Brazil, 1906, on first voyage for RMSP.

Amazon (II)	10,037	Harland & Wolff, Belfast	1906-1918	Steel

Twin screw steamer. Mail, passenger and refrigerated cargo ship for Brazil and River Plate service. First RMSP ship to exceed 10,000 grt. Sunk by torpedo 15 March 1918.

***Segura* (I)**   **4,756**   **Harland & Wolff, Belfast**   **1906-1927**   **Steel**

Twin screw steamer. Built 1893 for Union SS Co as *Greek*. Purchased by RMSP 1906; renamed *Segura*. Purchased for cargo services (mostly West Indies) to reduce the amount of chartered tonnage. Within RMSP ownership renamed *Pembrokeshire* 1909 ('to meet the objections raised by members of the Eastern Conference' – indicating she was operating the traditional Jenkins routes); renamed *Chignecto* 1913 (transferred to new Canadian service and thus was given a Canadian name). Sold 1927 for breaking up in Holland.

***Pembrokeshire* (I)   see *Segura* (I)**

Chignecto   **see *Segura* (I)**

***Sabor* (I)**   **4,758**   **Harland & Wolff, Belfast**   **1906-1927**   **Steel**

Twin screw steamer. Built 1893 for Union SS Co as *Gaul*. Purchased by RMSP July 1906 for £39,500; renamed *Sabor*. Purchased principally for cargo services (mostly West Indies) to reduce amount of chartered tonnage. Within RMSP ownership renamed *Carmarthenshire* 1909 ('to meet the objections raised by members of the Eastern Conference' – indicating she was operating the traditional Jenkins routes); renamed *Chaleur* 1913 (transferred to new Canadian service and thus was given a Canadian name). Sold 1927 for breaking up.

***Carmarthenshire* (I)   see *Sabor* (I)**

Chaleur   **see *Sabor* (I)**

Araguaya   **10,537**   **Workman Clark, Belfast**   **1906-1930**   **Steel**

Twin screw steamer. Mail, passenger and refrigerated cargo ship for Brazil and River Plate service. Converted mid-1920s for full-time cruising. Sold 1930 to Jugoslavenski Lloyd, Dubrovnik; renamed *Kraljica Marija*. Sold 1940 to French State (Ministère de la Marine Marchande – managers, Cie Générale Transatlantique), Marseilles; renamed *Savoie*. Out of Register 1945 (reported sunk in convoy, 1942).

***Avon* (III)**   **11,073**   **Harland & Wolff, Belfast**   **1907-1930**   **Steel**

Twin screw steamer. Mail, passenger and refrigerated cargo ship for Brazil and River Plate service. Renamed *Avoca* during Government service in the First World War; reverted to *Avon* after war. Sold for breaking up at Briton Ferry 1930.

***Avoca*, HMS**   **see *Avon* (III)**

Monmouthshire   **5,091**   **Sunderland S.B. Co, Sndlnd**   **1907-1922**   **Steel**

Screw steamer. Built 1902 for Jenkins & Co., London. Acquired 1907 by RMSP (first part of purchase of company); name unchanged. Operated various cargo services. 1919 renamed *Tyne*. Sold 1922/3 to Tokai Kisen KK (Nisshin Kaiun Shokai, manager), Dairen, Japan; renamed *Toku Maru*. Out of Register 1935.

Tyne* (IV)**   **see *Monmouthshire

Denbighshire   **3,844**   **Sunderland S.B. Co, Sndlnd**   **1907-1922**   **Steel**

Screw steamer. Built 1899 for Jenkins & Co., London. Acquired August 1907 by RMSP for £28,500 (first part of purchase of company); name unchanged. Operated various cargo services. In 1919 renamed *Tamar*. Sold 1922 to Amelia SS Co (Logothettis & Rogers, managers), London; name unchanged. In 1924 name changed to *Joyce Nancy*, managers now Logothettis & Weston. Sold 1925 to Melissa SS Co (Antonaropulo Bros, managers), London; renamed *Sassa*. Sold 1926 to Georgios Vergottis, Argostoli, Greece; renamed *Argostoli*. Sold 1929 to N. D & J D Rossolymos & R Harrisson, Argostoli, Greece; renamed *Avgy*. Out of Register 1931.

Tamar* (IV)**   **see *Denbighshire

Flintshire   **3,815**   **Sunderland S.B. Co., Sndlnd**   **1907-1913**   **Steel**

Screw steamer. Built 1896 for Jenkins & Co., London. Acquired September 1907 by RMSP for £20,000 (first part of purchase of company); name unchanged. Operated various cargo services. Sold 1913/1914 to Ellerman Lines (Hall Line, managers); renamed *Algerian*. Out of Register 1917.

| *Asturias* (I) | 12,015 | **Harland & Wolff, Belfast** | 1907-1933 | **Steel** |

Twin screw steamer. Built for Orient-Royal Mail Line's Australia service, but expected to ultimately join Brazil and the River Plate service. Only maiden voyage and voyage 6 were to Australia. During the First World War, as hospital ship, torpedoed 20-21 March 1917; subsequently brought to Plymouth; ownership transferred to Government on basis of Constructive Total Loss. Repurchased by RMSP December 1919; repaired and converted to cruise liner, re-entering service 1923; renamed *Arcadian*. Laid up October 1930. Sold 1933 to Amakasu Gomei Kaisha, Japan, for £13,700, for breaking up.

| *Arcadian* (II) | see *Asturias* (I) |

| *Arzila* | 2,722 | **J. Laing & Sons, Sunderland** | 1908-1922 | **Steel** |

Screw steamer. Built 1907 for Mersey SS Co (Leech, Harrison & Forward, managers), Liverpool as *Arzila*. Transferred to RMSP 1908 as part of purchase of company; not renamed. Cargo plus 72 first class passengers. Withdrawn from Morocco service in the face of French competition 1919; operated then in Caribbean and on PSN service to west coast South America. Sold 1922 to Khedivial Mail SS Co (Lord E. Hamilton, manager), London; renamed *Bilbeis*. Wrecked near Jaffa, Palestine coast 5 May 1934.

| *Agadir* | 2,722 | **J. Laing & Sons, Sunderland** | 1908-1922 | **Steel** |

Screw steamer. Built 1907 for Mersey SS Co. (Leech, Harrison & Forwood, managers), Liverpool as *Agadir*. Transferred to RMSP 1908 as part of purchase of company; not renamed. RMSP operations same as *Arzila*. Sold 1922 to Khedivial Mail SS Co (Lord E. Hamilton, manager), London; renamed *Belkas*. Sold 1935 to Societe Orientale de Navigation, Beyrouth, Syria; renamed *Damas*. By 1937 Khedivial Mail SS Co. were managers. In 1939 owners and managers in voluntary liquidation. Sold 1940 to Pharaonic Mail Line SAE, Alexandria, Egypt; renamed *Sakara*. Requisitioned 1941 by Ministry of War Transport. 1946 owned Ministry of Transport. 1947 owned Khedivial Mail Line, Alexandria, Egypt. Broken up Savona 1955.

| *Berbice* (I) | 2,379 | **Harland & Wolff, Belfast** | 1909-1920 | **Steel** |

Twin screw steamer. Built for West Indies intercolonial mail services. Exceptional first class accommodation for this service was designed to improve 'yachting holidays'. Sold to The Admiralty 1920; name unchanged. Sold 1923 to Sun Sh Co. (Mitchell Cotts & Co., managers), London; renamed *Suntemple*. Sold 1924 to United Baltic Corp, London; renamed *Baltara*. Lost at Libau, Latvia, 1929.

| *Balantia* (I) | 2,379 | **Harland & Wolff, Belfast** | 1909-1922 | **Steel** |

Twin screw steamer. Built for West Indies intercolonial mail services with similar quality accommodation to *Berbice* but not used as official cruise ship. Renamed *Saint Margaret of Scotland* 1916 in recognition of Red Cross badge day in Scotland which raised money for her conversion to hospital ship. After the First World War operated UK-Madeira-Canary Islands service. Sold to Khedivial Mail SS Co, London 1922; renamed *Boulac*. Sold May 1935 to shipbreakers in Italy.

| *Saint Margaret of Scotland* | see *Balantia* (I) |

| *Deseado* (I) | 11,475 | **Harland & Wolff, Belfast** | 1911-1934 | **Steel** |

Twin screw steamer. Passenger and refrigerated cargo ship for Brazil and River Plate trade. Sold 1934 to Japanese shipbreakers.

| *Arlanza* (I) | 15,044 | **Harland & Wolff, Belfast** | 1911-1938 | **Steel** |

Triple screw steamer. Mail, passenger and refrigerated cargo ship for Brazil and River Plate service. Sold 15 July 1938 to Metal Industries Ltd for £30,000, for breaking up at Rosyth (handed over 14 September 1938).

| *Demerara* (II) | 11,484 | **Harland & Wolff, Belfast** | 1911-1933 | **Steel** |

Twin screw steamer. Passenger and refrigerated cargo ship for Brazil and River Plate trade. Sold April 1933 to Japanese shipbreakers for £12,700.

Desna 11,466 **Harland & Wolff, Belfast** 1912-1933 **Steel**

Twin screw steamer. Passenger and refrigerated cargo ship for Brazil and River Plate trade. Sold May 1933 to Japanese shipbreakers for £12,950.

Jamaica 1,138 **W. Harkess, Middlesborough** 1912-1914 **Steel**

Screw steamer. Built 1908 as *Jamaica* for Elder Dempster Shipping Ltd. Purchased by RMSP 1912 at short notice for new mail contract with Trinidad Government, for coastal service Trinidad and Tobago, pending completion of new ships *Barima* and *Belize* (II); name unchanged. Sold 1914 to Pacific Steam Navigation Co. for Central America services. Sold 1930 to Soc. Industrial del Aysen, Santiago, Chile; renamed *Coyhaique*. Out of Register 1945.

Dart (II) 1,104 **Cammell Laird, Birkenhead** 1912-1959 **Steel**

Twin screw steamer. Machinery aft. River Plate meat lighter. Sold November 1959 to Rio Frio S.A. Mar. y Comercial, Buenos Aires; renamed in 1961 *Riofrio I*. Out of Register 1964.

Alcala 10,660 **Workman Clark, Belfast** 1913-1913 **Steel**

Twin screw steamer. Built 1912 for Lamport and Holt as *Vauban*. Chartered to RMSP 1912 and briefly entered fleet 1913, renamed *Alcala*, before reverting to Lamport and Holt and original name. Sister-ship *Vandyck* also chartered but did not enter RMSP fleet. Used for Brazil and River Plate mail service pending completion of *Andes* and *Alcantara*.

Andes (I) 15,620 **Harland & Wolff, Belfast** 1913-1946 **Steel**

Triple screw steamer. Mail, passenger and refrigerated cargo ship for Brazil and River Plate service. Early ownership details are disputed; *Lloyd's Register* states initially owned by RMSP, then by Pacific Steam Navigation Co. about 1914 to 1916 before reverting to RMSP. Converted to cruise liner and renamed *Atlantis* 1930. Hospital ship during the Second World War (requisitioned 25 August 1939); after discharge sold to Ministry of Transport for service as emigrant ship, managed by RML; sold for breaking up to British Iron & Steel Corp, Faslane, arrived 27 March 1952.

Atlantis see *Andes* (I)

Doon 1,353 **Cammell Laird, Birkenhead** 1913-1919 **Steel**

Twin screw steamer. Machinery aft. River Plate meat lighter. Sold 1919 to Las Palmas Produce Co., Buenos Aires; renamed *Britanica*. Sold 1928 to Union Cold Storage Co., London (a Vestey company), as meat lighter in River Plate; name unchanged. Transferred to Blue Star Line during 1930s. Out of Register 1949.

Radnorshire (I) 4,302 **Bartram & Sons, Sunderland** 1913-1917 **Steel**

Screw steamer. Built 1913 for RMSP. Operated various cargo routes as required. Captured by German raider *Möewe* 7 January 1917 and sunk.

Caribbean 5,824 **Fairfield Co., Glasgow** 1913-1915 **Steel**

Screw steamer. Built 1890 for Donald Currie's Castle Line as *Dunottar Castle*. Purchased by RMSP for West Indies services, including intercolonial cruising, 1913; renamed *Caribbean*. Sold (reportedly to British Government) 1915; name unchanged. As a unit of 10th Cruiser Squadron in the First World War, foundered *en route* to Scapa Flow.

Merionethshire 4,308 **Bartram & Sons, Sunderland** 1913-1918 **Steel**

Screw steamer. Built 1913 for RMSP. Operated various cargo routes as required. Sunk by torpedo 27 May 1918.

Cardiganshire 9,426 **Workman Clark, Belfast** 1913-1929 **Steel**

Twin screw steamer. Built for RMSP 1913 for extension of Shire Line service from China and Japan to west coast of North America. Sold 1929 to South Georgia Co. (Chr. Salvesen & Co., managers). Converted for carriage of fuel oil and whale oil in bulk; gross tons increased to 11,909; renamed *Salvestria*. Sank after striking a mine in Firth of Forth 27 July 1940.

| *Cobequid* | 4,738 | **Harland & Wolff, Belfast** | **1913-1914** | **Steel** |

Twin screw steamer. Built 1893 for Union SS Co as *Goth*. Purchased by RMSP 1913 for new Canadian service; renamed *Cobequid*. Inaugurated the service but ran aground in Bay of Fundy and was lost 1/1914 on first voyage.

| *Caraquet* | 4,917 | **Harland & Wolff, Belfast** | **1913-1923** | **Steel** |

Twin screw steamer. Built 1894 for Union SS Co as *Guelph*. Purchased by RMSP 1913 for new Canadian service; renamed *Caraquet*. Ran aground and lost off Bermuda June 1923. Reported undergoing salvage for scrap 1952.

| *Alcantara* (I) | 15,831 | Harland & Wolff, Govan | 1913-1916 | Steel |

Triple screw steamer. Mail, passenger and refrigerated cargo ship for Brazil and River Plate service. Requisitioned as Armed Merchant Cruiser in tenth Cruiser Squadron in the First World War. Lost 29 February 1916 in battle with German raider *Greif*.

| *Carnarvonshire* | 9,406 | **Workman Clark, Belfast** | **1913-1933** | **Steel** |

Twin screw steamer. Built 1913 for RMSP for extension of Shire Line service from China and Japan to west coast of North America. Sold March 1933 to Glen Line (to whom she had been chartered for some years) – combined sale price with *Pembrokeshire* (II) £15,000; name unchanged. Reported sold October 1935 to Galbraith, Pembroke & Co and resold to Japanese buyers for breaking up.

| *Drina* (I) | 11,483 | **Harland & Wolff, Belfast** | c1914-1917 | **Steel** |

Twin screw steamer. Passenger and refrigerated cargo ship for Brazil and River Plate trade. Built 1912 under arrangement with RMSP for Elder Line (Elder Dempster & Co., managers), but operated RMSP services from the start. Taken into RMSP fleet 1914/1915. Lost 1 March 1917 – torpedoed near Milford Haven.

| *Almanzora* | 15,551 | **Harland & Wolff, Belfast** | **1914-1948** | **Steel** |

Triple screw steamer. Mail, passenger and refrigerated cargo ship for Brazil and River Plate service. In the First World War operated as Armed Merchant Cruiser (tenth Cruiser Squadron) and convoy escort, and in the Second World War as troop transport; her ship's bell was subsequently the centrepiece of Royal Mail's war memorial. Sold for breaking up at Blyth September 1948.

| *Barima* | 1,498 | **Caledon S.B. Co, Dundee** | **1914-1923** | **Steel** |

Twin screw steamer. Built for mail contract with Trinidad Government, for coastal services in Trinidad and Tobago. After the First World War chartered to Pacific Steam Navigation Co. for Central America services. Sold 1923 to Straits SS Co, Singapore (later styled Singapore Straits SS Co.); renamed *Kudat*. Out of Register 1947.

| *Towy* | 199 | **Day, Summers, Southampton** | **1914-1920** | **Steel** |

Screw steamer, machinery aft. *Towy*, *Taff* and *Teign* built for local Grenada and St Lucia services, to replace *Taw*, *Tees* and *Wear* (sold). Sold 1921 to Spillers SS Co, registered Cardiff. Sold 1929 to A. McFaul, Cardiff. Sold 1930 to Whiteabbey Shipping Co., Cardiff. Name unchanged throughout. Out of Register 1931.

| *Devon* | 1,367 | **Cammell Laird, Birkenhead** | **1914-1959** | **Steel** |

Twin screw steamer, machinery aft. River Plate meat lighter. Sold 1959 to Rio Frio SA Mar. y Comercial, Buenos Aires; renamed in 1961 *Riofrio II*. Out of Register 1986.

| *Belize* (II) | 1,498 | **Caledon SB Co, Dundee** | **1914-1923** | **Steel** |

Twin screw steamer. Built for mail contract with Trinidad Government, for coastal services in Trinidad and Tobago. Sold 1923 to Trinidad Government. Sold 1932 to Nassau-Jacksonville SS Co, Nassau. Sold 1935 to H. Johnson & Mrs G. McKinney, Nassau. Sold 1938 to Navieros Unidos SA, Vera Cruz Mexico. Name unchanged throughout. Sold 1939 to Mexican Government (operated by Transportes Maritimos, SCOP), Vera Cruz; renamed *Campeche*. Out of Register 1945.

| *Chaudiere* | 3,986 | **R. Dixon & Co., Middlesborough** | **1914-1926** | **Steel** |

Twin screw steamer. Built 1899 for Cie Belge Maritime du Congo, Antwerp, as *Philippeville*. Sold 1906 to African SS Co (Elder Dempster & Co., managers); renamed *Mandingo*. Purchased by RMSP 1914 for Canadian service to replace *Cobequid* (lost); renamed *Chaudiere*. Sold 1926 to T. W Ward for breaking up.

Taff   199   **Day, Summers, Southampton**   **1914-1920**   **Steel**

Screw steamer, machinery aft. *Towy*, *Taff* and *Teign* built for local Grenada and St Lucia services, to replace *Taw*, *Tees* and *Wear* (sold). Sold 1921 to J Little & Sons; name unchanged. Entry overprinted 'In Port Damaged, April 1921'. Out of Register 1923.

Teign   199   **Day, Summers, Southampton**   **1914-1920**   **Steel**

Screw steamer, machinery aft. *Towy*, *Taff* and *Teign* built for local Grenada and St Lucia services, to replace *Taw*, *Tees* and *Wear* (sold). Sold 1920 to Spillers SS Co, Cardiff. Out of Register 1932.

Essequibo (II)   8,489   **Workman Clark, Belfast**   **1914-1922**   **Steel**

Twin screw steamer. With *Ebro* was last ship built for West Indies transatlantic mail service. Launched 6 July 1914; maiden voyage 18 November 1914. Operated South America mail service 5 August 1915 before being requisitioned as ambulance transport, then hospital ship. After war, chartered to Pacific Steam Navigation Co; sold to PSN 1922; name unchanged. Sold 1935 to USSR, Leningrad; renamed *Neva*. Out of Register 1960.

Ebro (III)   8,480   **Workman Clark, Belfast**   **1914-1922**   **Steel**

Twin screw steamer. With *Essequibo* was last ship built for West Indies transatlantic mail service. Launched 8 September 1914; maiden voyage 28 April 1915, following which requisitioned as Armed Merchant Cruiser (10th Cruiser Squadron). After war, chartered to Pacific Steam Navigation Co; sold to PSN 1922; name unchanged. Sold 1935 to Jugoslavenski Lloyd, Dubrovnik; renamed *Princesa Olga*. Sold 1940 to Companhia Colonial de Navegacao, Lisbon; renamed *Serpa Pinto*. Out of Register 1956 (reported towed 1955 from Lisbon to Belgium for breaking up).

Carmarthenshire (II) 7,823   **Workman Clark, Belfast**   **1915-1929**   **Steel**

Screw steamer. Built for RMSP for Far East service, but the influence of the First World War saw her in other cargo trades. Sold 1929 to Chr. Salvesen & Co for conversion to whale product factory; renamed *Sourabaya*. Torpedoed and sunk 27 October 1942 *en route* New York-Clyde.

Pembrokeshire (II) 7,821   **Workman Clark, Belfast**   **1915-1933**   **Steel**

Screw steamer. Built for RMSP for Far East service, but the influence of the First World War saw her employed in other cargo trades. Sold March 1933 to Glen Line (to whom she had been chartered for some years), combined sale price with *Carnarvonshire* £15,000; name unchanged. Out of Register 1936.

Larne (III)   3,808   **R. Napier, Glasgow**   **1916-1918**   **Steel**

Screw steamer. Built 1894 for G. Thompson & Co., Aberdeen, as *Nineveh*. Sold 1907 to Eastern & Australian SS Co, London; renamed *Aldenham*. Purchased by RMSP 1916 as replacement for lost tonnage; renamed *Larne*. Sold 1918 to RMSP group company MacAndrews & Co (listed owner: Zurbaran SS Co), London; name unchanged. Sold 1923 for breaking up in Germany.

Brecknockshire   8,422   **Harland & Wolff, Belfast**   **1916-1917**   **Steel**

Screw steamer. Built for RMSP for Far East service. Maiden voyage to South America during which captured and sunk by raider *Möewe* 15 February 1917 near Rio de Janeiro. (Keel laid February 1914, completion delayed by war work).

Darro (I)   11,493   **Harland & Wolff, Belfast**   **1916-1933**   **Steel**

Twin screw steamer. Passenger and refrigerated cargo ship for Brazil and River Plate trade. Built 1912 under arrangement with RMSP for Imperial Direct Line (Elder Dempster & Co., managers), but operated RMSP services from the start. Taken into RMSP fleet 1916. Sold April 1933 to Japanese shipbreakers for £12,900.

Navasota   8,795   **S. H & Wghm R, Newcastle**   **1917-1939**   **Steel**

Twin screw steamer. Refrigerated cargo ship for River Plate service; ownership vested in RMSP subsidiary RMSP Meat Transports. Torpedoed 5 December 1939.

Sambre   5,260   **Short Bros, Sunderland**   **1919-1940**   **Steel**

Screw steamer. Built 1919; laid down as *War Swift*, completed as *Sambre* after purchase by RMSP. Cargo ship acquired to replace war losses, serving various routes as required. Lost by torpedo 27 July 1940.

Glamorganshire	8,192	Asano SB Co., Tsurumi	1919-1933	Steel

Twin screw steamer. Built 1917 for Shipping Controller as *War Armour*, managed by RMSP. Purchased by RMSP 1919; renamed *Glamorganshire*. Cargo ship to replace war losses, serving various routes as required. Sold for £4,800 to Frank Rijsdijk's Industries Ltd for breaking up at Rotterdam, February 1933.

Nagara	8,803	S H & Wghm R, Newcastle	1919-1943	Steel

Twin screw steamer. Refrigerated cargo ship for River Plate service; ownership vested in RMSP subsidiary RMSP Meat Transports. Torpedoed 29 March 1943; sank 5 April 1943.

Segura (II)	5,295	Richardson, Duck, Ncstle	1919-1921	Steel

Screw steamer. Completed 1919 for Shipping Controller as *War Pansy*. Purchased on completion by RMSP; renamed *Segura*. Cargo ship acquired to replace war losses, serving various routes as required. Sold 1921 to Buenos Aires Great Southern Railway Co. Ltd (A. Holland & Co., managers), London; name unchanged. Sold 1935 to Houlder Bros & Co., London; renamed *Langton Grange* (Houlders purchase specifically 'to carry out a particular contract'). Sold 1936 to J. A. Coulouthros & N N Embiricos, Andros; renamed *Nicolaos M. Embiricos*. Reported to be a war loss in 1939.

Somme	5,265	Short Bros, Sunderland	1919-1942	Steel

Screw steamer. Laid down for Shipping Controller as *War Toucan*. Purchased by RMSP before completion; renamed *Somme*. Cargo ship acquired to replace war losses, serving various routes as required. Lost by torpedo 16 February 1942.

Severn (IV)	5,246	Short Bros, Sunderland	1919-1932	Steel

Screw steamer. Laid down for Shipping Controller as *War Pelican*. Purchased by RMSP before completion; renamed *Severn*. Cargo ship acquired to replace war losses, serving various routes as required. Sold 1932 to A. Vestarhis, Piraeus; renamed *Leonidas II*. Out of Register 1935.

Radnorshire (II)	6,723	J. L Thompson, Sunderland	1919-1930	Steel

Screw steamer. Laid down for Shipping Controller as *War Diamond*. Purchased by RMSP before completion; renamed *Radnorshire*. Cargo ship acquired to replace war losses, serving various routes as required. Sold 1930 to H. Thompson; renamed *Sithonia*. Lost 13 July 1942 by torpedo.

Silarus	5,101	C. Connell, Glasgow	1919-1931	Steel

Screw steamer. Laid down for Shipping Controller. Purchased by RMSP before name allocated. Cargo ship acquired to replace war losses, serving various routes. Sold 1931 to G.N. Stathatos, Ithaca; renamed *Nemea*. Out of Register 1941.

Siris	5,242	Harland & Wolff, Glasgow	1919-1942	Steel

Screw steamer. Laid down for Shipping Controller. Purchased by RMSP before name allocated; named *Siris*. Cargo ship acquired to replace war losses, serving various routes as required. Lost by torpedo and gunfire 12 July 1942.

Narenta	8,266	Workman Clark, Belfast	1919-1939	Steel

Screw steamer. Laid down for Shipping Controller as standard replacement refrigerated carrier *Neganti*. Purchased by RMSP for River Plate meat trade before completion; renamed *Narenta*. Sold 1939 – *Fairplay* recorded sale to Mitsubishi Syozi Kabusiki Kaisya of Tokyo for about £68,000, for whaling purposes in South Pacific; RML records state sold to Japanese buyers Nippon Suisan K.K. 7 February 1939 for £64,125 – more than double what was received for the almost identical *Nictheroy* two years earlier; renamed *Kosei Maru*. Torpedoed by US submarine 1943.

Arno (III)	344	Gebrs Bodewes, Martenshoek	1920-1933	Steel

Auxiliary screw motorship schooner (paraffin motor). Built 1916 for Nösteds Rederi Akties (Pehrson & Wessel, managers), Drammen, Norway; named *Nösted III*. Purchased by RMSP 1920 for local West Indies services; renamed *Arno*. Stranded and lost on Jamaica coast 10/1933 during hurricane.

Nictheroy	8,265	Workman Clark, Belfast	1920-1937	Steel

Screw steamer. Laid down for Shipping Controller as standard replacement refrigerated carrier. Purchased by RMSP for River Plate meat trade before name allocated; named *Nictheroy*. Sold 17 February 1937 to Achille Lauro, Naples for £29,000; renamed *Cuma*. Out of Register 1945.

| *Orcana* | 7,814 | A. Stephen, Glasgow | 1920-1922 | Steel |

Twin screw steamer. Built 1903 for G. Thompson & Co., Aberdeen, as *Miltiades*. Originally 6,765 gross tons; increased 1912 when ship lengthened by 50 feet (second funnel added). Purchased by RMSP 1920; renamed *Orcana*. Though owned by RMSP, operated PSN services, to whom sold 1922; name unchanged. Sold 1924 to Frank Rijsdijk Shipbreaking Co., Holland.

| *Oruba* (II) | 7,848 | A. Stephen, Glasgow | 1920-1923 | Steel |

Twin screw steamer. Built 1903 for G. Thompson & Co., Aberdeen, as *Marathon*. Originally 6,765 gross tons; increased 1912 when ship lengthened by 50 feet (second funnel added). Purchased by RMSP 1920; renamed *Oruba*. Operated PSN services under RMSP ownership. Sold 1923 for breaking up.

| *Natia* | 8,723 | A. Stephen, Glasgow | 1920-1940 | Steel |

Twin screw steamer. Refrigerated cargo ship for River Plate service; ownership vested in RMSP subsidiary RMSP Meat Transports. Lost by torpedo and gunfire 8 October 1940.

| *Nariva* | 8,723 | A. Stephen, Glasgow | 1920-1943 | Steel |

Twin screw steamer. Refrigerated cargo ship for River Plate service; ownership vested in RMSP subsidiary RMSP Meat Transports. Lost by torpedo 17 March 1943.

| *Nebraska* | 8,261 | Workman Clark, Belfast | 1920-1944 | Steel |

Screw steamer. Purchased during construction and completed for River Plate meat trade. Lost by torpedo 8 April 1944.

| *Sarthe* | 5,271 | Wm Gray, W. Hartlepool | 1920-1942 | Steel |

Screw steamer. Laid down for Shipping Controller. Purchased by RMSP before completion; named *Sarthe*. Cargo ship acquired to replace war losses, serving various routes as required. Lost by torpedo 9 October 1942.

| *Sabor* (II) | 5,212 | Earles Co., Hull | 1920-1943 | Steel |

Screw steamer. Laid down for Shipping Controller. Purchased by RMSP before completion; named *Sabor*. Cargo ship acquired to replace war losses, serving various routes as required. Lost by torpedo 7 March 1943.

| *Montgomeryshire* | 6,650 | Armstrong, Whitworth, Ncstle | 1921-1931 | Steel |

Screw steamer. Built for RMSP for general cargo services. Sold 1931 to Soc Commerciale di Nav, Genoa; renamed *Riv*. Out of Register 1945. *Lloyd's Register* initially showed year of build as 1920, but later this was changed to 1921 (she had not entered service in June 1921).

| *Lochkatrine* | 9,419 | John Brown & Co., Clydebank | 1921-1942 | Steel |

Twin screw motorship – RMSP's first diesel-powered ship (engines by Harland and Wolff, Glasgow). Built for new joint service with Holland-America Line to Pacific coast of North America. Launched 5 August 1921; inaugural North Pacific voyage 22 January 1922. Lost by torpedo 3 August 1942.

| *Lochgoil* | 9,462 | Harland & Wolff, Govan | 1922-1939 | Steel |

Twin screw motorship. Built for new joint service with Holland-America Line to Pacific coast of North America. Launched 24 August 1922. Struck mine 6 October 1939, approx 10 miles from Mumbles Head. Beached Swansea Bay and salvaged but declared Constructive Total Loss. Subsequently repaired, owned by Government, managed by RML; renamed *Empire Rowan*. Lost by aircraft torpedo 27 March 1943.

| *Culebra* | 3,044 | Irvine's SB&DD Co., W. Hrtpl | 1923-1942 | Steel |

Screw steamer. Laid down for Shipping Controller as *War Mirage*; completed 1919 as *Riposto* for Atlantic & Eastern SS Co (John Glynn & Son), Liverpool. Purchased by RMSP for West Indies cargo services 1923; renamed *Culebra*. Lost by torpedo and gunfire 17 January 1942 – no survivors.

| *Orca* | 16,063 | Harland & Wolff, Belfast | 1923-1927 | Steel |

Triple screw steamer. Built for Pacific Steam Navigation Co. 1918. Purchased by RMSP for New York service and cruising, 1923; name unchanged. Sold 1927 to White Star Line; renamed *Calgaric*. Sold for breaking up in Scotland 1935.

Orduña (I)   **15,499**   **Harland & Wolff, Belfast**   **1923-1926**   **Steel**

Triple screw steamer. Built for Pacific Steam Navigation Co. 1914. Purchased by RMSP for New York service 1923; name unchanged. Re-sold to PSN 1926; broken up 1951.

Orbita (I)   **15,486**   **Harland & Wolff, Belfast**   **1923-1926**   **Steel**

Triple screw steamer. Built for Pacific Steam Navigation Co. 1915. Operated RMSP's River Plate service briefly after the First World War. Purchased by RMSP 1923 for New York service and cruising; name unchanged. Re-sold to PSN 1926; broken up 1950.

Ohio   **18,940**   **A.G. Weser, Bremen**   **1923-1927**   **Steel**

Twin screw steamer. Laid down before the First World War as *München* for Norddeutscher Lloyd; completion delayed until after war, when she was taken as reparations and purchased by RMSP for New York service 1923; renamed *Ohio*. Sold 1927 to White Star Line; renamed *Albertic*. Sold 1934 for breaking up.

Lochmonar   **9,412**   **Harland & Wolff, Belfast**   **1923-1949**   **Steel**

Twin screw motorship. Built for new joint service with Holland-America Line to Pacific coast of North America. Launched 8 December 1923. November 1927 grounded River Mersey and broke her back. Stern portion intact; new fore section built and attached and vessel resumed service. September 1948 grounded on reef in Cayman Islands during a hurricane. Salvaged and temporarily repaired; returned to London, but declared a Constructive Total Loss.

Asturias (II)   **22,048**   **Harland & Wolff, Belfast**   **1925-1945**   **Steel**

Twin screw motorship, later steamer; re-engining, lengthening and internal changes May-Oct 1934. Built for mail, passenger and refrigerated cargo service to Brazil and River Plate. Owned by RMSP Meat Transports. Requisitioned 26 August 1939 as Armed Merchant Cruiser. Torpedoed 24 July 1943; towed to Freetown. Reduced to Care & Maintenance April 1944. Towed to Gibraltar for temporary repairs 2/1945. Towed to Belfast May/June 1945 for permanent repairs. Declared Constructive Total Loss; repaired and re-entered service under Ministry of Transport ownership, managed by RML (sold about 27 December 1945 to Minister of War Transport). Sold to shipbreakers at Faslane September 1957.

Alcantara (II)   **22,209**   **Harland & Wolff, Belfast**   **1926-1958**   **Steel**

Twin screw motorship, later steamer; re-engining, lengthening and internal changes Nov 1934-April 1935. Built for mail, passenger and refrigerated cargo service to Brazil and River Plate. Owned by RMSP Meat Transports. Requisitioned 20-21 September 1939 as Armed Merchant Cruiser. Resumed mail service 1948. Sold 1958 for breaking up (first British ship sold to Japan since before the Second World War); renamed *Kaisho Maru* for voyage to Japan.

Arun   **384**   **Svendborg Skibsvaerft, Svendborg**   **1928-1952**   **Steel**

Screw motorship, machinery aft. Built Denmark 1925 for A/S Ove Steen & Jespersen (C N Jespersen, manager), Copenhagen as *Polonia*. Ownership transferred to builders 1926/1927 – A/S Svendborg Skibsvaerft & Mask.bygeri (T C Christensen, manager); name unchanged (suggesting vessel repossessed by builders pending re-sale). Purchased by RMSP for local West Indies trades 1928; renamed *Arun*. Sold 1952 to American Coast Line Inc, Puerto Cortes, Honduras; renamed *Carib*. Sold 1953 to Rogelio (or Rogello) Jhones, Puerto Cortes; name unchanged. In the mid-1980s described as general cargo ship and appeared to still have her original Danish diesel engine. Out of Register 1998/1999.

Nasina   **7,206**   **Russell & Co., Pt Glasgow**   **1932-1935**   **Steel**

Twin screw steamer. Built 1915 as *Meissonier* for Liverpool Brazil and River Plate SN Co (Lamport and Holt). Sold to Nelson Line 1930; name unchanged. Entered RML fleet 1932 under Scheme of Arrangement; renamed *Nasina* about August 1933. Used on various routes, mostly River Plate or North Pacific. Sold 16 June 1935 to Soc Anon Co-operativa di Nav Garibaldi, Genoa; renamed *Asmara* (RML listed sale as to Italian Ministry of

Marine for £30,000). Recorded 1938 in ownership of Italian Navy, operated by Garibaldi. No subsequent reference in *Lloyd's Register* (reported torpedoed 1943).

Nela	7,206	**Russell & Co., Pt Glasgow**	**1932-1945**	**Steel**

Twin screw steamer. Built 1915 as *Molière* for Lamport and Holt. Sold to Nelson Line 1930; name unchanged. Entered RML fleet 1932 under Scheme of Arrangement; renamed *Nela* about August 1933. Used on various routes, mostly River Plate or North Pacific. Sold 1945, probably for breaking up.

Nalon	7,206	**Russell & Co., Pt Glasgow**	**1932-1940**	**Steel**

Twin screw steamer. Built 1915 as *Murillo* for Lamport and Holt. Sold to Nelson Line 1930; name unchanged. Entered RML fleet 1932 under Scheme of Arrangement; renamed *Nalon* about July 1933. Used on various routes, mostly River Plate or North Pacific. Lost by bombing 6 November 1940.

Nogoya	8,442	**Barclay, Curle, Glasgow**	**1932-1936**	**Steel**

Screw steamer. Laid down for Shipping Controller as standard replacement refrigerated carrier. Purchased by Nelson Line before completion, 1920; named *Highland Warrior*. Entered RML fleet 1932 under Scheme of Arrangement; renamed *Nogoya*. Employed as cargo offered, including South Africa; laid up at times. Sold 9 October 1936 for £19,500 to Kaye, Son & Co., London; renamed *Marlene*. Lost by torpedo off West African coast 4 April 1941.

Sicily	3,457	**Richardson, Duck, Stockton**	**1932-1933**	**Steel**

Screw steamer. Built 1914 for David MacIver & Co., as *Sicily*. Entered RML fleet 1932 under Scheme of Arrangement; name unchanged. Used briefly in West Indies trade. Sold 27 July 1933 to Maris A Embiricos, Andros for £5,200 including bunkers; renamed *Pagasitikos*. Sold 1937 to Soc Commerciale d'Affrêtements et de Commission, Paris; renamed *Francois*. Captured during Spanish Civil War and under Spanish ownership had successive names *Vigo* (1937) and *Castillo Andrade* (1939). (Lloyd's Register entry as *Castillo de Andrade* appears to have been an error.) First Spanish owner was Cia Trasmediterrania, Cadiz; in 1944 listed as Spanish Government, with former owners as managers. Ownership transferred 1947 to Government-owned Empresa Nacional 'Elcano' SA. Abandoned and sunk, on fire, 1944; later raised and laid-up. Renamed *Antartico* about 1948 and rebuilt as motorship; owners unchanged. Wrecked Santander 1959.

Thessaly (I)	3,135	**Richardson, Duck, Stockton**	**1932-1933**	**Steel**

Screw steamer. Built 1909 for David MacIver & Co., as *Thessaly*. Entered RML fleet 1932 under Scheme of Arrangement; name unchanged. Attempted sale December 1932 to former Group company Cia Argentina de Navigacion Mihanovich fell through; sold March 1933 to T.W. Ward for £2,625; broken up Briton Ferry.

Lombardy (I)	3,379	**Richardson, Duck, Stockton**	**1932-1956**	**Steel**

Screw steamer. Built 1921 for David MacIver & Co., as *Lombardy*. Entered RML fleet 1932 under Scheme of Arrangement; name unchanged. Placed initially on West Indies service. Sold 1956 to Far East Metal Industries & Shipping Co., Hong Kong; renamed *Metal Trader*. Broken up Hong Kong 1957.

Brittany (I)	4,772	**A. McMillan & Son, Dmbrtn**	**1932-1942**	**Steel**

Screw motorship. Built 1928 for David MacIver & Co., as *Brittany*. Entered RML fleet 1932 under Scheme of Arrangement; name unchanged. Placed initially on Brazil and River Plate service. Lost by torpedo 29 October 1942.

Gascony	4,716	**A. McMillan & Son, Dmbrtn**	**1932-1958**	**Steel**

Screw motorship. Built 1925 for David MacIver & Co., as *Gascony*. Entered RML fleet 1932 under Scheme of Arrangement; name unchanged. Placed initially on Brazil and River Plate service. Sold 1958 for breaking up Hamburg.

Araby (I)	4,936	**A. McMillan & Son, Dmbrtn**	**1932-1940**	**Steel**

Screw motorship. Built 1923 for David MacIver & Co., as *Araby*. Entered RML fleet 1932 under Scheme of Arrangement; name unchanged. Operated Brazil and River Plate and West Indies services. Mined and sunk near Nore Light Vessel 27 December 1940.

Highland Brigade **14,135**   **Harland & Wolff, Belfast**   **1932-1959**   **Steel**

Twin screw motorship. Built 1929 for Nelson Line. Entered RML fleet 1932 under Scheme of Arrangement; name unchanged. Operated passenger and refrigerated cargo service to Brazil and River Plate. Sold 1959 to John S. Latsis; renamed *Henrietta*, then shortly renamed *Marianna* (same owner). Sold to Taiwanese shipbreakers 1965.

Highland Chieftain **14,135**   **Harland & Wolff, Belfast**   **1932-1959**   **Steel**

Twin screw motorship. Built 1929 for Nelson Line. Entered RML fleet 1932 under Scheme of Arrangement; name unchanged. Operated passenger and refrigerated cargo service to Brazil and River Plate. Sold 1959 to Calpe Shipping Co., Gibraltar; renamed *Calpean Star*, to operate as whaling store ship. Foundered off Montevideo 1960.

Highland Monarch **14,139**   **Harland & Wolff, Belfast**   **1932-1960**   **Steel**

Twin screw motorship. Built 1928 for Nelson Line. Entered RML fleet 1932 under Scheme of Arrangement; name unchanged. Operated passenger and refrigerated cargo service to Brazil and River Plate. Sold April 1960 to British Iron & Steel Corp. for breaking up on the Clyde.

Highland Patriot **14,172**   **Harland & Wolff, Belfast**   **1932-1940**   **Steel**

Twin screw motorship. Laid down for Nelson Line as replacement for *Highland Hope* (lost), but entered RML fleet prior to completion, during 1932, under Scheme of Arrangement; name unchanged. Operated passenger and refrigerated cargo service to Brazil and River Plate. Lost by torpedo 1 October 1940.

Highland Princess **14,100**   **Harland & Wolff, Belfast**   **1932-1959**   **Steel**

Twin screw motorship. Built 1930 for Nelson Line. Entered RML fleet 1932 under Scheme of Arrangement; name unchanged. Operated passenger and refrigerated cargo service to Brazil and River Plate. Sold 1959 to John S. Latsis; renamed *Marianna*. Sold 1960 to Czechoslovak Ocean Shipping; renamed *Slapy*. Sold about 1962 to People's Republic of China (later China Ocean Shipping Co); renamed *Guang Hua*. Out of Register 1987.

Highland Rover **7,490**   **Russell & Co., Pt Glasgow**   **1932-1932**   **Steel**

Screw steamer. Built 1910 for Nelson Line. Briefly owned by RML, entering the fleet under RMSP Scheme of Arrangement in August 1932; name unchanged. Sold for breaking up in the same month that she entered the fleet.

Lochavon **9,205**   **Harland & Wolff, Govan**   **1938-1939**   **Steel**

Twin screw motorship. Built for North Pacific joint service with Holland-America Line. Lost by torpedo 14 October 1939.

Andes (II) **25,895**   **Harland & Wolff, Belfast**   **1939-1971**   **Steel**

Twin screw steamer. Built for mail, passenger and refrigerated cargo service to Brazil and River Plate but used as troopship in the the Second World War immediately on completion. First commercial voyage 1/1948. Converted to full-time cruise liner 1960. Sold for breaking up at Ghent, Belgium, for £325,000; handed over 7 May 1971.

Pampas (I) **5,415**   **Harland & Wolff, Belfast**   **1940-1942**   **Steel**

Screw motorship. Entered war duties straight from builders. Lost by bombing, Valetta Harbour, Malta 26 March 1942.

Pardo (II) **5,400**   **Harland & Wolff, Belfast**   **1940-1965**   **Steel**

Screw motorship. General freighter suitable for various trades but often used to South America. Sold 1965 to Fortunegate Cia Nav SA (M. A. Karageorgis), Panama; renamed *Aristarchos*. Out of Register 1968.

Potaro (II) **5,410**   **Harland & Wolff, Belfast**   **1940-1965**   **Steel**

Screw motorship. General freighter built principally for Brazil and River Plate services. Sold 1965 to Ioannitsa Cia Nav SA (M. A. Karageorgis), Panama; renamed *Aristipos*. Flag changed to Greek 1968. Out of Register 1971.

Palma **5,419**   **Harland & Wolff, Belfast**   **1941-1944**   **Steel**

Screw motorship. Initially entered South America trade but subsequently taken over for war duties. Lost by torpedo between Colombo and Madras 29 February 1944.

Deseado (II)	9,641	**Harland & Wolff, Belfast**	**1942-1968**	**Steel**

Twin screw motorship. Built for Brazil and River Plate refrigerated trade. Laid up River Fal 1966. Early 1967 chartered for storeship voyage to Saigon, Viet Nam. On return, July 1967, laid up Belfast. Sold for breaking up to Eisen und Metall, Hamburg 2/1968, for £11 February - per light ton.

Darro (II)	9,732	**Harland & Wolff, Belfast**	**1942-1967**	**Steel**

Twin screw motorship. Built for Brazil and River Plate refrigerated trade. Sold 1967 to Embajada Cia Nav SA, Panama; renamed *Surrey* for resale to Taiwanese shipbreakers November 1967.

Pampas (II)	5,576	**Harland & Wolff, Belfast**	**1943-1965**	**Steel**

Screw motorship. Initially completed as Infantry Landing Ship; refitted late 1944 for Far East campaign and emerged as HMS *Persimmon*. After de-commissioning and refitting at Belfast, entered RML service as *Pampas*. General freighter built principally for Brazil and River Plate services. Sold 1965 to Amigos Cia Nav SA (M A Karageorgis), Panama; renamed *Aristodimos*. Out of Register 1968. [NB: She was reportedly launched as *Pampas*, in memory of her namesake lost at Malta. However, *Lloyd's Register* records she was launched as *Parramatta*, so the tribute to *Pampas* (I) must have been decided between launching and completion.]

Parima	5,595	**Harland & Wolff, Govan**	**1944-1962**	**Steel**

Screw motorship. General freighter built principally for Brazil and River Plate services. Sold 31 October 1962 to Mary Shipping Co., Panama; renamed *Michalios X*. Sold 1966 to Ionia Shipping Co. SA, Panama; renamed *Fortune Dragon*. Out of Register 1968.

Paraguay	5,560	**Harland & Wolff, Belfast**	**1944-1965**	**Steel**

Screw motorship. General freighter built principally for Brazil and River Plate services. Sold 1965 to Mountpleasant Cia Nav SA, Panama; renamed *Elire* (Greek flag from 1968). Out of Register 1970.

Drina (II)	9,785	**Harland & Wolff, Belfast**	**1944-1965**	**Steel**

Twin screw motorship. Built for Brazil and River Plate refrigerated trade. Sold 1965 to Shaw Savill Line; renamed *Romanic*. Sold to Taiwanese shipbreakers July 1968.

Durango	9,801	**Harland & Wolff, Belfast**	**1944-1966**	**Steel**

Twin screw motorship. Built for Brazil and River Plate refrigerated trade. Sold 1966 to Shaw Savill Line; renamed *Ruthenic*. Sold 1967 to Embajada Cia Nav SA, Panama; renamed *Sussex* for resale to Taiwanese shipbreakers.

Pilcomayo	5,567	**Harland & Wolff, Glasgow**	**1945-1965**	**Steel**

Screw motorship. General freighter built principally for Brazil and River Plate services. Sold 1965 to Varkiza Cia Nav SA (M A Karageorgis), Panama; renamed *Aristagelos*. Out of Register 1968.

Loch Ryan	9,904	**Furness, Haverton Hill**	**1946-1960**	**Steel**

Screw steamer. Built 1943 as *Empire Chieftain*, owned Ministry of War Transport, managed by RML. Purchased by RML 1946 for Pacific coast of North America joint service with Holland-America Line; renamed *Loch Ryan*. Sold 18 January 1960 to Argonaut Shipping & Trading Co., London for breaking up Far East; renamed *Fair Ryan* for the voyage to breakers.

Teviot (III)	7,056	**Shipbuilding Corp, Nwcstle**	**1946-1960**	**Steel**

Screw steamer. Built 1944 as *Empire Abbey*. Purchased by RML from Government May 1946; renamed *Teviot*. General freighter used in various trades. Sold 1960 to Mullion & Co., Hong Kong; renamed *Ardellis*. Sold 1963 to Hai An Shipping Co., Hong Kong; renamed *Tung An*. Out of Register 1967.

Tweed (II)	7,056	**Shipbuilding Corp, Nwcstle**	**1946-1959**	**Steel**

Screw steamer. Built 1944 as *Empire Lady*. Purchased by RML from Government May 1946; renamed *Tweed*. General freighter used in various trades. Sold 21 August 1959 to British Iron & Steel Corp. for breaking up.

Brittany (II)	5,089	**W. Pickersgill & Sons, Sndlnd**	**1946-1962**	**Steel**

Screw motorship. General freighter in various trades, often Spanish Main routes. Sold 2/1962 to Armar Shipping Co., Piraeus; renamed *Armar*. Sold 1970 to Armar Shipping Co., Famagusta, Cyprus; name unchanged. Out of Register 1972.

Barranca   7,252   **Oregon SB Corp, Portland**   1947-1956   **Steel**

Screw steamer. Completed 1943 as *Samthar* (see also Ships Managed list). Purchased by RML 1947; renamed *Barranca*. General freighter used in various trades. Sold 1956 to Corrado Società di Nav, Genoa; renamed *Cesco Corrado*. Broken up Spezia 1967.

Berbice (II)   7,294   **New England SB Corp, Maine**   1947-1958   **Steel**

Screw steamer. Completed 1943 as *Samphill* (see also Ships Managed list). Purchased by RML 1947; renamed *Berbice*. General freighter used in various trades. Sold 1958 to Mareante Cia Nav SA, Monrovia, Liberia; renamed *Nikolas S*. Sold 1961 to Compania Naviera Aisnicolas SA, Beirut, Lebanon; name unchanged. Broken up Taiwan 1967.

Beresina   7,298   **New England SB Corp, Maine**   1947-1956   **Steel**

Screw steamer. Completed 1943 as *Samspring* (see also Ships Managed list). Purchased by RML 1947; renamed *Beresina*. General freighter used in various trades. Sold 1956 to West Africa Nav Co., Monrovia, Liberia; renamed *African Monarch*. Sold 1959 to General Nav Co., Monrovia; name unchanged. Broken up Split 1969/1970.

Balantia (II)   7,235   **Bethlehem/Fairfield, Baltimore**   1947-1958   **Steel**

Screw steamer. Completed 1944 as *Samfaithful* (see also Ships Managed list). Purchased by RML 1947; renamed *Balantia*. General freighter used in various trades. Sold 1958 to Cia Nav Betacruz SA, Monrovia, Liberia; renamed *Betamar*. Sold 1965 to Acme Shipping Co., Famagusta, Cyprus; renamed *Acme*. Broken up Shanghai 1969.

Araby (II)   5,039   **Lithgows Ltd, Pt Glasgow**   1947-1961   **Steel**

Screw motorship. General freighter used in various trades, often Spanish Main routes. Sold 1961 to Shamrock Shipping Co. (C .S. Brown, manager), Belfast; renamed *Glynn*. Sold 1962 to Aris Compania Nav SA (Pateras Bros, managers), Piraeus, Greece; renamed *Aris*. Sold 1968 to Astrovalido Cia Nav SA, Mogadishu, Somalia; renamed *Aria*. Sold 1971 to Aria Shipping Co., Famagusta, Cyprus; name unchanged. Broken up Spain 1971.

Loch Avon   8,617   **Harland & Wolff, Belfast**   1947-1967   **Steel**

Screw steamer. Built for Pacific coast of North America joint service with Holland-America Line. Sold 1967 to International Export Lines, Nassau; renamed *Hongkong Observer*. Sold 1968 to Singapore Malaysia Overseas Line, Singapore; name unchanged. Reportedly broken up Taiwan 1971, though did not leave *Lloyd's Register* until 1974.

Loch Garth   8,617   **Harland & Wolff, Belfast**   1947-1968   **Steel**

Screw steamer. Built for Pacific coast of North America joint service with Holland-America Line. Sold 1968 for breaking up in Belgium.

Magdalena (III)   17,547   **Harland & Wolff, Belfast**   1948-1949   **Steel**

Twin screw steamer. Built for passenger and refrigerated cargo service to Brazil and River Plate. Wrecked off Rio de Janeiro on maiden voyage April 1949.

Ebro (IV)   7,785   **Harland & Wolff, Glasgow**   1952-1969   **Steel**

Screw motorship. General freighter used in various trades but most often West Indies, Spanish Main and southern US ports. Sold 1969 to Fortunewind Maritime Ltd (Continental Navigation & Enterprises Ltd, managers), London; renamed *Fortune Victory*. Sold 1970 to Union of Burma Five Star Line Corp, Rangoon; renamed *Kalemyo*. Out of Register 1980.

Essequibo (III)   7,785   **Harland & Wolff, Glasgow**   1952-1968   **Steel**

Screw motorship. General freighter used in various trades but most often West Indies, Spanish Main and southern US ports. Sold 1968 to China Navigation Co. (John Swire & Sons), London; renamed *Ningpo*. Sold 1970 to Union of Burma Five Star Line Corp, Rangoon; renamed *Kalewa*. Out of Register 1977.

Loch Gowan   9,718   **Harland & Wolff, Belfast**   1954-1970   **Steel**

Screw steamer. Built for Pacific coast of North America joint service with Holland-America Line. Sold 1970 for breaking up in Taiwan.

| *Escalante* | 7,791 | **Harland & Wolff, Glasgow** | **1955-1970** | **Steel** |

Screw motorship. General freighter used in various trades but most often West Indies, Spanish Main and southern US ports. Sold 1/1970 to Maresencia Cia Nav SA, Piraeus; renamed *Manes P.* Within a month or two ran aground in storm at Negrotown Point, Saint John West, New Brunswick. Subsequently re-sold for breaking up.

| *Eden* (II) | 7,791 | **Harland & Wolff, Belfast** | **1956-1969** | **Steel** |

Screw motorship. General freighter used in various trades but most often West Indies, Spanish Main and southern US ports. Sold September 1969 to Neptune Orient Lines, Singapore; renamed *Neptune Garnet.* Out of Register 1980.

| *Tuscany* | 7,455 | **Harland & Wolff, Glasgow** | **1956-1970** | **Steel** |

Screw motorship. General freighter used in various trades but most often Spanish Main. Sold 1970 to Random Ltd (J. & J. Denholm [Management] Ltd), Montreal; renamed *Federal Hudson.* Sold 1972 to Cornwallis Shipping Ltd, Montreal; name unchanged. Sold 1973 to Goldtopps Nav Co. SA, Panama; renamed *Golden King.* Sold 1975 to Carnation Shipping (Liberia) Co. (Char Hwa Marine Co., managers), Panama; renamed *Char Hsiung.* In 1979 owners were Chaffinch Shipping Co. SA (Good Harvest Marine Co), Panama; name unchanged. Out of Register 1981.

| *Thessaly* (II) | 7,299 | **Harland & Wolff, Glasgow** | **1957-1971** | **Steel** |

Screw motorship. General freighter used in various trades but most often Spanish Main. Sold May 1971 to Union SS Co, Monrovia, Liberia; renamed *Japan.* Sold 1976 to Li-Ta Shipping Co. (Pte), Singapore; renamed *Liho.* Out of Register 1981.

| *Picardy* | 7,306 | **Harland & Wolff, Belfast** | **1957-1971** | **Steel** |

Screw motorship. General freighter used in various trades but most often Spanish Main. Sold May 1971 to Union SS Co, Monrovia, Liberia; renamed *Europe.* Sold 1976 to Lira Shipping Co. (Pte), Singapore; renamed *Lira.* Out of Register 1978.

| *Albany* | 7,299 | **Harland & Wolff, Glasgow** | **1957-1971** | **Steel** |

Screw motorship. General freighter used in various trades but most often Spanish Main. Sold May 1971 to Union SS Co, Monrovia, Liberia; renamed *Taiwan.* Sold 1975 to Li-Ta Shipping Co. (Pte), Singapore; renamed *Lido.* Out of Register 1981.

| *Loch Loyal* | 11,035 | **Harland & Wolff, Belfast** | **1957-1971** | **Steel** |

Screw motorship. Built for Pacific coast of North America joint service with Holland-America Line. Sold March 1971 to Aeakos Compania Naviera SA, Piraeus; renamed *Aegis Loyal.* Sold 1972 to Althamas Shipping Co., Famagusta, Cyprus; name unchanged. Broken up 1974.

| *Amazon* (III) | 20,368 | **Harland & Wolff, Belfast** | **1959-1968** | **Steel** |

Twin screw motorship. Built for mail, passenger and refrigerated cargo service to Brazil and River Plate. Transferred 1966 to subsidiary Welldeck Shipping Co; name unchanged. Transferred 1968 to Shaw Savill Line; renamed *Akaroa* (tons now 18,565). Sold 1971 to A/S Uglands Rederi, Grimstad, Norway; renamed *Akarita*; converted to side-door vehicle carrier (tons now 11,081). Sold 1977 to Sagitta (Liberia) Ltd, Monrovia; renamed *Hual Akarita*; 1981 renamed *Akarita* (same ownership). Out of register 1983 (broken up Taiwan).

| *Yacaré* | 1,022 | **Van der Werf, Deest** | **1959-1974** | **Steel** |

Screw engines-aft motorship. River Plate meat lighter. From late 1960s ownership vested in La Mala Real Argentina SA. Sold about 1974 to Comercial e Inmobiliaria Paraguayo Argentina SA, Buenos Aires; name unchanged. Out of Register 1986.

| *Yaguarete* | 1,022 | **Van der Werf, Deest** | **1959-1974** | **Steel** |

Screw engines-aft motorship. River Plate meat lighter. From late 1960s ownership vested in La Mala Real Argentina SA. Sold about 1974 to Comercial e Inmobiliaria Paraguayo Argentina SA, Buenos Aires; name unchanged. Out of Register 1986.

| *Aragon* (II) | 20,362 | **Harland & Wolff, Belfast** | **1959-1969** | **Steel** |

Twin screw motorship. Built for mail, passenger and refrigerated cargo service to Brazil and River Plate. Transferred 1969 to Shaw Savill Line; renamed *Aranda* (tons now 18,575). Sold 1971 to Leif Höegh & Co A/S, Oslo, Norway; renamed

Höegh Traveller and converted at Rijeka to side-door vehicle carrier (tons now 10,665). Sold 1977 to Ace Navigation Co., Monrovia; renamed *Hual Traveller*; 1981 renamed *Traveller* (same ownership). Out of register 1983 (broken up Taiwan).

Arlanza (II)   20,362   **Harland & Wolff, Belfast**   **1960-1969**   **Steel**

Twin screw motorship. Built for mail, passenger and refrigerated cargo service to Brazil and River Plate. Transferred 1969 to Shaw Savill Line; renamed *Arawa* (tons now 18,595). Sold 1971 to Leif Höegh & Co A/S, Oslo, Norway; renamed *Höegh Transit* and converted at Rijeka to side-door vehicle carrier (tons now 10,658); 1972 renamed *Höegh Trotter* (same ownership). Sold 1977 to Ace Transportation Co., Monrovia; renamed *Hual Trotter*; 1981 renamed *Trotter* (same ownership). Out of Register 1983 (broken up Taiwan).

Special notes – tonnage

Tonnages of *Amazon* (I), *Orinoco* (I), *Magdalena* (I), *Parana* (I), *Demerara* (I)

These ships were essentially built to the same design, but the tonnages given for *Amazon* and *Demerara* are more than 25% lower than for the others. Tonnages given for *Magdalena*, *Orinoco* and *Parana* are gross tons quoted in October 1852 RMSP report, when they were in operation. Those for *Demerara* and *Amazon* are 'builder's measurement' (i.e. net) given in RMSP report for April 1851 while they were being built. They did not remain long enough for completed gross tonnages to be published. The two sets of figures were as follows:

Date of report	Amazon	Demerara	Magdalena	Orinoco	Parana
10 April 1851 [net]	2,256	2,318	2,250	2,245	2,252
14 October 1852 [gross]	-	-	2,943	2,901	2,943★

★ From April 1855, while tonnages for *Magdalena* and *Orinoco* remained unchanged, that for the *Parana* became 3,070.

'P' ship (1940s) tonnages

The eight 'P' ships built 1940-1945 recorded major tonnage changes. The following list shows gross tonnages recorded in *Lloyd's Register*, the increases caused by changed shelter deck status. Some reverted to about 5,500 tons after sale by RML.

Ship	1942	1946	1950	1957	1958	1961
Palma	5,419	-	-	-	-	-
Pampas (I)	5,415	-	-	-	-	-
Pampas (II)	-	8,244	5,576	5,576	5,576	7,589
Paraguay	-	5,560	5,554	5,554	7,555	7,555
Pardo (II)	5,400	5,400	5,405	7,480	7,480	7,480
Parima	-	5,595	5,596	7,543	7,543	7,543
Pilcomayo	-	5,567	5,574	5,574	7,540	7,540
Potaro (II)	5,410	5,410	5,416	5,416	7,433	7,433

Furness Withy Group

Arlanza was the last ship to enter Royal Mail Lines' fleet as an independent company. Following its takeover by Furness, Withy & Co Ltd in 1965, Royal Mail's fleet list became less meaningful. In the 1971/2 *Lloyd's Register*, for instance, RML owned 13 ships, about half having formerly been owned by The Pacific Steam Navigation Co., one by Manchester Liners and another by Prince Line. A year later it owned three. These entries are restricted to brief summaries.

Duquesa	9,726	Hawthorn, Leslie, Newcastle	1968-1973		Steel

Screw steamer. Previously owned by Furness-Houlder Argentine Lines, built 1949.

Stolt Abadesa	13,398	S. H & Wghm Rchdsn, Ncstle	1968-1971		Steel

Screw motorship. Tanker. Built 1962 as *Abadesa* for Furness-Houlder Argentine Lines. Transferred to RML 1968. Renamed *Stolt Abadesa* 1969 in support of long term charter to Norwegian operators J Stolt Nielsen, when she was converted from crude oil carrier to product carrier (fats, bulk chemicals and general bulk cargoes).

Douro (II)	10,785	Hawthorn, Leslie, Newcastle	1969-1971		Steel

Twin screw motorship. Built 1946 as *Hornby Grange* for Houlder Bros. Purchased by RML 1969; renamed *Douro*. Transferred 1971 to Prince Line.

Manchester Freighter	8,105	Burntisland SB Co., Bntslnd	1969-1971		Steel

Screw motorship. Built 1958 as *Cairnforth* for Cairn Line. Renamed *Manchester Freighter* 1965. Renamed *Lombardy* 1969. Sold August 1971 to Premier Shipping Corp, Monrovia; renamed *Pacific Reliance*.

Lombardy (II)	see *Manchester Freighter*				
Derwent (III)	13,593	Cammell Laird, Birkenhead	1969-1971		Steel

Twin screw steamer. Built 1949 as *Persic* for Shaw Savill Line. Sold to RML 1969; renamed *Derwent*. Transferred 1971 to Prince Line.

Pacific Envoy	9,439	Vickers Armstrong, Nwcstle	1970-1971		Steel

Screw steamer. Built 1958 for Furness, Withy & Co as *Pacific Envoy*. Renamed *Loch Ryan* 1967; owner unchanged. Transferred 1971 to Royal Mail Lines; renamed *Pacific Envoy*. Sold April 1971 to Chelsea Compania Naviera SA, Panama City; renamed *Aegis Strength*.

Pacific Stronghold	9,337	Vickers Armstrong, Nwcstle	1970-1971		Steel

Screw steamer. Built 1958 for Furness, Withy & Co. Transferred 1970 to Royal Mail Lines. Sold March 1971 to Arditos Compania Naviera SA, Panama City; renamed *Aegis Honor*.

Southern Prince	5,443	Harland & Wolff, Glasgow	1971-1971		Steel

Screw motorship. ex-*Medic* 1960; ex-*Southern Prince* 1958. Built 1956. Sold July 1971 to Eastern Glory Enterprising Co., Hong Kong; renamed *Argosy*.

Chandeleur	3,447	Hall, Russell & Co., Aberdeen	1971-1972		Steel

Screw motorship. ex-*Cienfuegos*, 1968. Built 1959 for Pacific Steam Navigation Co.

Cotopaxi	8,559	Denny Bros, Dumbarton	1971-1973		Steel

Screw steamer. Built 1954 for Pacific Steam Navigation Co.

Eleuthera	3,447	Hall, Russell & Co., Aberdeen	1971-1972		Steel

Screw motorship. Built 1959 for Pacific Steam Navigation Co.

Kenuta	8,494	Greenock Dockyard Co., Grnck	1971-1972		Steel

Screw steamer. Built 1950 for Pacific Steam Navigation Co.

Pizarro	8,564	Greenock Dockyard Co., Grnck	1971-1973		Steel

Screw steamer. Built 1955 for Pacific Steam Navigation Co.

Somers Isle	3,552	Harland & Wolff, Belfast	1971-1972		Steel

Screw motorship. Built 1959 for Pacific Steam Navigation Co.

Orbita (II)	8,396	Cammell Laird & Co., B'head	1972-1980		Steel

Screw motorship, engines aft. Built 1972.

Orduña (II)	8,396	Cammell Laird & Co., B'head	1973-1984		Steel

Screw motorship. Built 1973. Renamed *Beacon Grange* 1982.

Beacon Grange	see *Orduña* (II)				

Ortega	8,396	**Cammell Laird & Co., B'head**	**1973-1982**	**Steel**

Screw motorship. Built 1973. Renamed *Andes* 1980

Andes (III)	**see *Ortega***	

Kayeson	28,132	**Hawthorn, Leslie, Newcastle**	**1974-1977**	**Steel**

Screw steamer. Built 1961 for 'K' SS Co, London (Kaye Tanker Management Ltd).

From 1985/1986 there was no listing for Royal Mail Lines in *Lloyd's Register*. Despite the continuing technical existence of the Company under the ownership of C. Y Tung, and then, from 1990, of Hamburg-Süd, this can be regarded as the effective closure of the Company.

Ships Managed By RMSP and RML

Russian Volunteer Fleet

Russia established the Russian Volunteer Fleet Association (RVFA) in the 1870s. Ships were acquired and run from community subscriptions, operated by the Government as trading ships, and intended as warships when necessary. Their names were mostly towns and cities whose people had paid for them. After the Russian Revolution, ships in British waters were seized by the British Government, which opposed the communist regime. Various shipping companies were asked to manage the ships on behalf of the Government. Some were eventually returned to the Soviet Union and others sold to new owners. These twelve ships were managed by RMSP from 1918/1919.

Name	Gross Tons	Builder	Years in RMSP management (Approx)	Hull Material
Ekaterinoslav	6,581	**J.C. Tecklenborg, Geestemunde**	**1918-1924**	**Steel**

Screw steamer. Built 1898 as *Assyria* for Hamburg-Amerika Line. In 1906 reportedly sold to Russia and renamed *Sveaborg*; became *Ekaterinoslav*, owned by RVFA, registered Libau, also 1906. Owned by The Shipping Controller from 1918/1919, managed by RMSP. Probably broken up 1924/1925.

Irtysh	4,970	**Sir J. Laing, Sunderland**	**1919-1923**	**Steel**

Screw steamer. Did not appear in *Lloyd's Register* under RMSP management but is listed in internal Company documents. Built 1901 as *Dortmund* for Hamburg-Amerika Line. Sold 1916 to RVFA; renamed *Irtysh*. British Government ownership and RMSP management c1919-1923. Sold 1923 to Arcos Ltd (Russo-Norwegian Nav Co., managers); British flag; name unchanged. Out of register 1925.

Kamenetz-Podolsk	5,071	**Bartram & Sons, Sunderland**	**1918-1923**	**Steel**

Screw steamer. Built 1915 for RVFA, registered Archangel. Owned by The Shipping Controller from 1918/1919, managed by RMSP. Sold about 1923 to Anglo-Russian Volunteer Fleet Ltd, London; name unchanged. 1924 now with managers Arcos SS Co. 1927 owned Arcos SS Co. Sold 1928 to Sovtorgflot, Leningrad; name unchanged. Out of Register 1945.

Koursk	6,254	**S.H. & Wghm Rchdsn, Ncstle**	**1919-1923**	**Steel**

Screw steamer. Built 1911 for RVFA, registered Odessa. Owned by The Shipping Controller from about 1919, managed by RMSP. Sold 1923/1924 to Anglo-Russian Volunteer Fleet Ltd, London; name unchanged. 1924/1925 now with managers Arcos SS Co. 1927 owned Arcos SS Co. Sold 1928 to Sovtorgflot, Leningrad; name unchanged. Out of Register 1934.

Krasnoiarsk	5,812	**Nrthmblnd SB Co, Nwcstle**	**1918-1922**	**Steel**

Screw steamer. Built 1915 for RVFA, registered Archangel. Owned by The Shipping Controller from 1918/1919, managed by RMSP. Sold about 1923 to St Mary SS Co. (Williams Bros [Cardiff], managers), Cardiff; renamed *Eastway*. Out of Register 1927.

| *Mogileff* | 6,377 | **Armstrong Whitworth, Nwcstle** | **1918-1922** | **Steel** |

Screw steamer. Built 1911 for RVFA, registered Odessa. Owned by The Shipping Controller from 1918/1919, managed by RMSP. Sold about 1923 to Limerick SS Co, Limerick (S J K Roycroft, manager); renamed *Kilcredane*. Sold 1931 to Rederi A/S 'Vikar' (G P Knudsen, manager), Bergen; renamed *Bonus*. Out of Register 1933.

| *Novgorod* | 5,285 | **J. Laing & Co., Sunderland** | **1918-1923** | **Steel** |

Screw steamer. Built 1913 for RVFA, registered Odessa. Owned by The Shipping Controller from 1918/1919, managed by RMSP. Sold about 1923 to Wm Thomas Shipping Co. (R J Thomas & Co., managers), London; renamed *Cambrian Duchess*. Sold 1932 to A/S Skjold (V Skogland, manager), Haugesund, Norway; renamed *Valhall*. Sold 1933 to N.E. A. Moller, British flag but registered Shanghai; renamed *Lilian Moller*. Out of Register 1940.

| *Omsk* | 7,464 | **C. Connell & Co., Glasgow** | **1919-1922** | **Steel** |

Four-masted screw steamer. Built 1898 as *Knight Errant* for Greenshields Cowie & Co., Liverpool. Sold 1914 to European & Brazilian Shipping Co. (Petersen & Co., managers), London; renamed *Rio Tiete*; 1915 owners styled London-American Trading Co. Sold 1916 to RVFA, registered Petrograd; renamed *Omsk*. Owned by The Shipping Controller from about 1919, managed by RMSP. Sold 1922 to London SS & Trading Corp (W J M Bell, manager), London; renamed *Calanda*. Sold 1923 to D. L Flack & Son, London; renamed *Flackwell*. Sold 1925 to Hvaefanger A/S Globus (Melsom & Melsom, managers), Larvik, Norway; renamed *Lancing* – converted for bulk whale and fuel oil. Out of Register 1945.

| *Tambov* | 4,441 | **Denny Bros, Dumbarton** | **1918-1923** | **Steel** |

Twin screw steamer. Built 1893 for RVFA, registered St Petersburg (later Odessa). Owned by The Shipping Controller from 1918/1919, managed by RMSP. Probably sold for breaking up 1923.

| *Vologda* | 4,784 | **J.L. Thompson & Sons, Sndlnd** | **1918-1923** | **Steel** |

Screw steamer. Built 1913 as *Mottisfont* for Century Shipping Co. (Harris & Dixon, managers), London. Sold 1916 to RVFA; renamed *Vologda*, registered Petrograd. 1918 owned by The Shipping Controller, managed by RMSP. Sold 1923 to St Mary SS Co (Williams Bros, managers), Cardiff; renamed *Tideway*. Sold 1933 to I. Margaronis (Rethymnis & Kulukundis Ltd, managers), Panama; renamed *Nellie*. 1938 ownership vested in Oceanos Maritime SS Co (I, A & G. Margaronis), Piraeus. Out of Register 1943.

| *Voronej* | 5,616 | **Denny Bros, Dumbarton** | **1918-1923** | **Steel** |

Twin screw steamer. Built 1896 for RVFA, registered Odessa. Owned by The Shipping Controller from 1918/1919, managed by RMSP. Approx. 1923-1926 listed without owner, registered in Germany; out of Register 1927.

| *Yaroslavl* | 4,495 | **Denny Bros, Dumbarton** | **1918-1923** | **Steel** |

Twin screw steamer. Built 1892 for RVFA, registered Odessa. Owned by The Shipping Controller from 1918/1919, managed by RMSP. Approx. 1923-1926 listed without owner, registered in Germany; out of Register 1927. There is a report that she was returned to Russia but was lost on Dutch coast during return voyage.

War-related management

Name	Gross Tons	Builder	Years in RM management (Approx)	Hull Material
War Armour	8,192	**Asano SB Co., Tsurumi**	**1917-1919**	**Steel**

Owned by The Shipping Controller, managed by RMSP 1917-1919. (See main fleet list under *Glamorganshire*.)

| *War Lance* | 8,182 | Asano SB Co., Tsurumi | 1918-1919 | Steel |

Twin screw steamer. Owned by The Shipping Controller, managed by RMSP 1918-1919. November 1919 sold to British India SN Co; renamed *Hatipara*.

| *Meteor* | 3,617 | **Blohm & Voss, Hamburg** | 1919-1921 | **Steel** |

Screw steamer. Built 1904 for Hamburg-Amerika Line. Presumed seized as reparations 1918. Listed post-war owned by The Shipping Controller (RMSP, managers). Sold 1921 to H. J Jewell, London. Sold 1923 to Bergen Line. Used as cruise ship by Bergen Line. Out of Register 1946. Name unchanged throughout.

| *Orotava* | 5,851 | **Naval Const. & Arm. Co., Barrow** 1920-1922 | | **Steel** |

Owned by The Shipping Controller (RMSP, managers) 1920-1922. Out of Register 1922. (See main fleet list.)

| *Prosper* | 759 | **Schömer & Jensen, Tönning** | see below | **Steel** |

Screw steamer; machinery aft. Built 1904 for Hanseatischer Lloyd, Lubeck. About 1911/1912 sold to Danziger Rhederei Akt Ges, Danzig. 1915 in Admiralty ownership – now 1,075grt, British. Sold 1918 to J. Cory & Sons, London. Name unchanged throughout. Not previously shown with Royal Mail connections, but is listed in Company documents; probably managed and/or operated by RMSP for a period during the First World War.

| *Western Australia* | 2,937 | **Stabilmento Tecnico, Trieste** | see below | **Steel** |

Twin screw steamer. Built 1901 as *Mongolia* for Chinese Eastern Railway Co. (Russian, reg. Vladivostok). By 1909 owned by Russian East Asiatic SS Co, Vladivostok. Sold 1913 to Western Australian Government, Fremantle; renamed *Western Australia*. Sold 1920 to Åugf A/B Thule (H Metcalfe, manager), Gothenburg; renamed *Patricia*. Not previously shown with Royal Mail connections, but is listed in Company documents; probably managed and/or operated by the Company for a period during the First World War on behalf of the owners.

| *Empire Rowan* | 9,544 | **Harland & Wolff, Govan** | 1940-1943 | **Steel** |

(See main fleet list, under *Lochgoil*).

| *Empire Confidence* | 5,023 | **Bremer Vulkan, Vegesack** | 1940-1946 | **Steel** |

Screw motorship. Built 1935 for Norddeutscher Lloyd as *Düsseldorf*. Left Valparaiso 13 December 1939 for Hamburg, but captured by HMS *Despatch* off Chilean coast. Taken to Bermuda; renamed *Poland*. On arrival London renamed *Empire Confidence*. During RML's management was owned by the Ministry of War Transport.

| *Empire Widgeon* | 6,737 | **Bethlehem Steel Co., Quincy** | 1941-1942 | **Steel** |

Screw steamer. Built 1940 as *Exemplar*, probably owned by US Maritime Commission. Renamed *Empire Widgeon* 1941; owned Ministry of War Transport.

| *Empire Egret* | 7,248 | **Newport News SB & DD Co** | 1941-1942 | **Steel** |

Screw steamer. Built 1939 as *Nightingale*; owned by US Maritime Commission. Renamed *Empire Egret* 1941; owned Ministry of War Transport.

| *Empire Bittern* | 8,546 | **Harland & Wolff, Belfast** | 1941-1944 | **Steel** |

Screw steamer. Built 1902 as *Iowa* for White Diamond Line (G Warren & Co., managers). Sold 1912 to Hamburg Amerika Line; renamed *Bohemia*. Seized 1917 by US Government; renamed *Artemis*. In 1941 renamed *Empire Bittern*; owned by Ministry of War Transport.

| *Empire Peacock* | 6,098 | **Federal SB Co., Kearny, NJ** | 1941-1946 | **Steel** |

Screw steamer. Built 1919 for US Shipping Board (later US Maritime Commission) as *Bellhaven*. Ownership acquired 1941 by Ministry of War Transport; renamed *Empire Peacock*. Out of Register 1947.

| *Empire Tide* | 6,978 | **Lithgows Ltd, Pt Glasgow** | 1941-1943 | **Steel** |

Screw motorship. Entered Ministry of War Transport ownership from builders. 1943 management transferred to Sir R. Ropner & Co.

| *Empire Geraint* | 6,991 | **C. Connell & Co., Glasgow** | 1942-1944 | **Steel** |

Screw steamer. Entered Ministry of War Transport ownership from builders. 1944 management transferred to Lamport and Holt. Lost by torpedo off Milford Haven 6 March 1945.

| *René Paul* | 545 | **Beliard, Crichton, Ostend** | **1942-1945** | **Steel** |

Screw motorship. Machinery aft. Built 1937 for Armament René Geurts, Antwerp. Owned Ministry of War Transport from 1942. Returned to Belgium 1945, ownership vested in Belgian State. 1947 returned to original owners.

| *Empire Chieftain* | 9,904 | **Furness, Haverton Hill** | **1943-1946** | **Steel** |

(See main fleet list, under *Loch Ryan*).

| *Samthar* | 7,252 | **Oregon SB Corp, Portland** | **1943-1947** | **Steel** |

Screw steamer. Built 1943 as *Charles A. Broadwater*. Under Ministry of War Transport renamed *Samthar*. (See main fleet list, under *Barranca*).

| *Samphill* | 7,294 | **New England SB Corp, Maine** | **1943-1947** | **Steel** |

Screw steamer. Built 1943 as *Barrett Wendell*. Under Ministry of War Transport renamed *Samphill*. (See main fleet list, under *Berbice* (II)).

| *Samspring* | 7,298 | **New England SB Corp, Maine** | **1943-1947** | **Steel** |

Screw steamer. Built 1943 as *Charles A. Young*. Under Ministry of War Transport renamed *Samspring*. (See main fleet list, under *Beresina*).

| *Samzona* | 7,200 | **Oregon SB Corp, Portland** | **1943-1948** | **Steel** |

Screw steamer. Built as *Victor C. Vaughan*. Under Ministry of War Transport renamed *Samzona*. Returned to US Maritime Commission 1948.

| *Samakron* | 7,200 | **New England SB Corp** | **1943-1947** | **Steel** |

Screw steamer. Built as *Jeremiah L. Chaplin*. Under Ministry of War Transport renamed *Samakron*. Returned to US Maritime Commission 1947; renamed *Jeremiah L. Chaplin*.

| *Samfaithful* | 7,235 | **Bethlehem/Fairfield, Baltimore** | **1944-1947** | **Steel** |

(See main fleet list, under *Balantia* (II)).

| *Samtyne* | 7,200 | **New England SB Corp** | **1944-1947** | **Steel** |

Screw steamer. Acquired 1947 by Houlder Bros and renamed *Argentine Transport*.

| *Empire Spearhead* | 7,177 | **Consolidated Steel Corp, Wilm. Cal** | **1944-1947** | **Steel** |

Screw steamer. Built 1944; launched as *Cape Girardeau* but completed as *Empire Spearhead*. Immediately entered service of Ministry of War Transport on bareboat charter from owners WSA.

| *Empire Ken* | 9,523 | **Blohm & Voss, Hamburg** | **1945-1957** | **Steel** |

Screw steamer. Built 1928 for Deutsche Ost-Afrika Line (German East Africa Line) as *Ubena*. Surrendered by Germany after the Second World War and entered ownership of Ministry of Transport; renamed *Empire Ken*. Operated as troopship. Sold for breaking up Dalmuir 1957.

| *Asturias* (II) | 22,048 | **Harland & Wolff, Belfast** | **1945-1957** | **Steel** |

Repaired after the Second World War and re-entered service under Ministry of Transport ownership, managed by RML. (See main fleet list.)

| *Atlantis* | 15,620 | **Harland & Wolff, Belfast** | **1946-1952** | **Steel** |

After discharge from the Second World War service, sold to Ministry of Transport for emigrant service, managed by RML. (See main fleet list.)

Bibliography

Books

Anderson, R. ....White Star

Bonsor, N.R.P. ....North Atlantic Seaway

Brooks, J. (Ed) ....South American Handbook (1974 edition)

Bushell, T. A. ....Royal Mail 1839-1939

Bushell, T. A. ....Eight Bells

Cable, B. ....History of the P&O

Cameron, S. .... Caribbean Islands Handbook (2001)

Cornewall-Jones, R.J. ....The British Merchant Service

Davies, P.N. ....The Trade Makers (Elder Dempster 1852-1972)

Dowden, P.&G.F. Campbell.............Ships of the Royal Mail Lines

Lee, S. (Ed) ....Dictionary of National Biography, 1893

Legg, L.G.W. (Ed)...........Dictionary of National Biography 1931-1940

Leslie, H.W. ....The Royal Mail War Book

Murray, M. ....Union-Castle Chronicle 1853-1953

Napier, J. ....The Life of Robert Napier

Nicol, S. ....Borda Landfall *(unpublished)*

Nijinsky, R. ....Nijinsky

Parker, Capt W.H. ....Leaves from an Unwritten Log-Book

Pearse, A.W. ....Windward Ho

Sawyer, L.A. & W.H. Mitchell ....The Liberty Ships

Sawyer, L.A. & W.H. Mitchell ....British Standard Ships of World War I

Shields, J. ....Clyde Built

Stevens, E.F. ....One Hundred Years of Houlders

Talbot-Booth, E.C. ....Merchant Ships (1943)

Wardle, A.C. ....Steam Conquers the Pacific (PSN, 1840-1940)

Warwick, W.C. ....Random Recollections

Woolward, R. .... Nigh on Sixty Years at Sea

-...................................HMS Almanzora (record of WW1 service)

- ....British merchant vessels lost or damaged by enemy action during Second World War (Admiralty)

-......................The City of London - 6th edition

- ....Link of Empire (RMSP 1839-1909)

- ....Lloyd's Register (various issues)

- ....Port of London Guide 1959-60

Other sources

Atlantic & Pacific Breezes (RML/PSN house magazine), 1959-1966

Log, The (Furness Withy Group house magazine), 1966-1971

Royal Mail News (newsletter of the Royal Mail Association), 1990-2000.

Macqueen, J. – A General plan for a mail communication by steam between Great Britain and the eastern and western parts of the world; also Canton and Sydney NSW, westward by the Pacific.

Macqueen, J. – A Letter to Francis Baring Esq, MP, Secretary to the Treasury, August 1838.

Macqueen, J – Private letters.

Blackwood's Edinburgh Magazine – various issues, 1820s.

RMSP Royal Charters 1839, 1851, 1882, 1904, 1912, 1920.

RMSP/RML annual reports and half-year reports, 1843-1936

RMSP/RML directors' minute books 1839-1909, 1932-1940

Bushell, T.A. – *Royal Mail 1839-1939*: author's files

Bushell, T.A. – *Eight Bells*: author's files

Chambers' Edinburgh Journal, April 1845. Description of RMSP West Indies services.

Officers Book: extracts of biographical and internal reports on captains and officers (principally 1841-1860s).

Agreement between RMSP and Orient Line regarding purchase of PSN interest in Orient-Pacific Line, 1906.

Rex v Lord Kylsant and Rex v Harold John Morland, July 1931 – trial transcript.

The Shipbuilder & Marine Engine-builder, May 1949 [re *Magdalena* (III)].

Magdalena (III) - Proceedings of court of enquiry.

Aragon (II), Captain's Voyage Report, Voyage 1-Voyage 48

Arlanza (II), Captain's Voyage Report Voyage 1-Voyage 45

Media statement 11 May 1965, detailing purchase of share capital in RML by Furness, Withy & Co.

Furness Withy Group staff memorandum 13 November 1970, detailing ships to be withdrawn from service.

Index

Listed entries in Appendix III and Appendix V are not included
References in brackets () are image numbers on colour pages

General

Ships